A Concise History of the Qing Dynasty

A Concise History of the Qing Dynasty

Volume 3

Dai Yi

SILKROAD PRESS

Published by

Enrich Professional Publishing (S) Private Limited
16L, Enterprise Road,
Singapore 627660
Website: www.enrichprofessional.com
A Member of Enrich Culture Group Limited

Hong Kong Head Office:
2/F., Rays Industrial Building, 71 Hung To Road, Kwun Tong, Kowloon, Hong Kong, China

Beijing Office:
Rm 1108A, Culture Plaza, No. 59 Zhongguancun St., Haidian District, Beijing, China

Translated by Lan Fangfang, Liu Bingxin and Liu Hui

ISBN (Hardback) 978-981-4332-20-0
ISBN (ebook) 978-981-4332-67-5 (pdf)
978-981-4332-68-2 (epub)

Contents

Preface vii

Chapter 8
Class Structure in the Qing Dynasty and the Class Struggle in the Early 18th Century 1

Chapter 9
Russia's Early Aggression against China and the Anti-Aggression Struggles of Various Nationalities of China 83

Chapter 10
Unification of Ethnic Minority Areas on the Frontier and the Consolidation and Development of a Multiethnic Country 137

Chapter 11
Cultural Policy and the Development of Sinology in the Qing Dynasty 225

Notes 277

Glossary 303

References 309

Index 319

Preface

The Qing Dynasty was a feudal institution with the Manchu, a minority in China, as the upper class and was the last feudal monarchical dynasty in the long feudal history of China. The Qing Dynasty ruled China, a vast country, for two hundred and sixty eight years. China was an independent feudal state in the stage of late feudal society when the Qing rulers broke through the border in the year 1664 to usurp the achievements of the Peasants' War in the late Ming Dynasty and establish its rule over the whole country. After more than one hundred years of development, the Qing Dynasty reached its peak in the mid-eighteenth century. Within the vast territory the unity of all ethnic groups in China was further enhanced, and the feudal politics, economy and culture were developed to their peak. Following this, due to the growth of internal contradictions in the feudal society and the bud of capitalism in China, the crisis of feudal rule occurred. In the late eighteenth century, peasant uprisings broke out all over the country. As a result, the Qing Dynasty began to decline. At this time the Western European countries had already completed their bourgeois revolutions and moved into a capitalist society, plundering their colonies all over the world. Finally, feudal China became one of their important targets of predation. With the outbreak of the Opium War in 1840, the armed capitalist invaders opened the door to China. From then on China gradually stepped into a semi-colonial and semi-feudal society and onto the stage of modern history. At the same time as imperialism colluded with feudalism in China to force China to beome a semi-colonial and semi-feudal society, the Chinese people never gave up their fight against the imperialists and their lackeys. In the Opium War, the Taiping Revolution, the Sino-French War, the Sino-Japanese War, the Hundred Days Reform and the Boxer Rebellion, the Chinese people demonstrated their indomitable courage and fighting spirit. In the Revolution of 1911 the bourgeoisie overthrew the Qing Government, which had become the lackey of imperialism, ending the autocratic monarchy of more than 2,000 years in China and establishing a democratic republic.

The "long river" of the history was surging forward. These two hundred and sixty years witnessed the rise, prosperity, decline and downfall of the Aisin Giorro dynasty, but more importantly it witnessed the development, creativity and struggle of the great people of all nationalities in China. During this long and arduous period, the Chinese people suffered enormous hardship and frustration, created beautiful ideas and hopes and undertook continuous exploration and combat. In the most difficult years of hardship the Chinese people still left an extremely rich and valuable heritage. In this two hundred and sixty eight years we can find innumerable passionate and epic battle stories; strong, brave, diligent and wise figures; brilliant economic and cultural achievements; and vivid and rich experience and lessons. The Qing Dynasty is an important chapter in China's long history, a great turning point between the past and future and a ladder used by the Chinese people to wage arduous struggles, grope in the dark, get through the "fog" and go forward to the future. Since the history of Qing Dynasty is close to us and closely associated with practical struggle, it is worth serious study and research.

This book describes the history from the rise of the Manchu to the Opium War which broke out in 1840, after which China walked into its modern era in which the natures of society and revolution began to change dramatically and were fundamentally different from the early and mid Qing Dynasty. Various works of detailed modern Chinese history have been published, with which the basic content of this book can link up.

This book is written by the Institute of Qing History of Renmin University of China and edited by Dai Yi assisted by Ma Ruheng. Chapter 1 of Volume 1 was written by Li Hongbin, Chapter 2 by Lin Tiejun, Chapter 3 by Du Wenkai, Chapter 4 by Zhang Jinfan, Chapter 5 by Ma Ruheng, Zhang Jinfan and Ma Jinke, Chapters 6 and 7 by Li Hua. At first, part of Volume 2 of this book was drafted by Ma Xin, Ma Ruheng, Ma Jinke, Li Hua, Zhang Jinfan, Hu Mingyang and Qin Baoqi et al. Later, due to the structural changes in the book and personnel changes, the writing work was re-organized. Finally, Chapter 8 was written by Luo Ming, Wang Sizhi and Lin Tiejun, Chapter 10 by Mu Ruheng, Chapter 12 by Lu Yingfan, Wang Daocheng and Chen Yalan, Chapter 13 by Li Hua, Chapter 14 by Lin Tiejun and Ma Ruheng, and Chapter 15 by Wang Junyi. Dai Yi wrote the other chapters and revised the whole book. Illustrations were collected by Li Hua and Li Hongbin. We would like to express thanks to institutions such as the Chinese History Museum and the First Historical Archives of China which provided great assistance in the collection of illustrations.

We sincerely look forward to any suggestions on the shortcomings of this book.

Dai Yi

8

Chapter

Class Structure in the Qing Dynasty and the Class Struggle in the Early 18th Century

Classes and Grades

In a class society people belong to different classes and social strata. The class structure and mutual relationship and struggles between the various classes determine social outlook and historical trends. Therefore historical materialism holds that the method of class analysis must be used to analyze the status, interests and characteristics of the various classes in order to study the relationship, balance of power and the rise and fall between them. Only in this way can the history of various periods in class societies be properly understood so that we are not likely to be puzzled by all kinds of chaotic and multifarious historical phenomena. Lenin said: "Marxism has given us a guiding clue, enabling us to find regularity in such a state of chaos and vagueness. This clue is the theory of class struggle."[1]

Different status and different ownership relationships of the means of production of people are the main symbols by which to distinguish classes because they determine the status and mutual relationships of various social groups and the distribution of social wealth. The class with ruling status in economics is also that with ruling status in politics. It can occupy and plunder the fruits of the labor of the ruled classes by using its economic and political advantages, making the society split into the opposition between the two camps i.e. the exploiting class and the exploited class. The different class status of people determines their different political stances and world outlook.

In feudal society there was opposition between the two classes of landowners and peasants. The history of feudal society developed around this basic axis. However there were different strata within the landowner class, which had different interests and desires. They either collaborated with each other or contended against each other. Among the peasants there were differences between yeomen, tenant peasants and farm hands as well as wealthy peasants and poor peasants. In addition to the two classes of landowners and peasants, there were businessmen, master handicraftsmen, artisans, homeless people, the lowest class people, slaves and so on.

In ancient times, many classes and strata formed a n intricate and manifold gradation of ruling and being ruled from top to bottom in a hierarchical way. The differences between of classes and strata were often expressed as a complicated hierarchy. As is said in the *Communist Manifesto*, "In the earlier epochs of history, we find almost everywhere a complicated arrangement of society into various orders, a manifold gradation of social rank...and in almost every class there are a variety of unique, etc."[2] Lenin also said: "In the slave society and feudal society, class differences are also fixed by rank division of the residents, and also establish a special legal status in the country for each class. Therefore the classes in slave and feudal societies (and serfdom society) also contain some special ranks... The arrangement of society into classes is the common phenomenon of the slave society, feudal society and bourgeois society, but in the first two societies there are classes with orders, and in the latter society there are non-order classes."[3]

The so-called "order" is a social group with certain rights and obligations, which is permitted and acknowledged by the state in the form of rescript, imperial edict and law. The economic and political status of these social groups is very different, and even within the same class each order is not equal. An autocratic emperor is at the top of the manifold order pagoda. He has supreme status and power, wields absolute power over the people, and "no one can do harm to him". Under him the highest order in the Qing Dynasty was the imperial family, aristocrats and bureaucrats; the Manchurian and Mongolian aristocrats were the most eminent. In the imperial family of the Qing Dynasty all the direct descendants of Takeshi, father of Nurhachi (honored as Xianzu in the Qing Dynasty), were members of the imperial clan, who wore a golden yellow ribbon as their symbol and were known as the "yellow ribbon"; the collateral descendants of Takeshi's uncles and brothers were all Jueluo, who used a red ribbon as their symbol and were known as the "red ribbon". A titular rank could be conferred on a member of the imperial clan who made contributions. Such titular ranks were Heshuo Prince, Duoluo Prefecture Prince, Duoluo Beile, Gushan Beizi, Fengen Zhenguo Gong, Fengen Fuguo Duke, Burubafen Zhenguo Duke, Buru Bafen Fuguo Duke, Zhenguo General, Fuguo General and Fengen General in order. Those without a titular rank were known as the idle imperial clan. In the Qing Dynasty there were 12 families with a princely title "which was inherited without replacement", namely the Li Prince (Daishan), Rui Prince (Duoergun), Zheng Prince (Jierhalang), Yu Prince (Duoduo), Su Prince (Haoge), Cheng Prince (Shuosai), Shuncheng Prefecture Prince (Lekedehun) and Keqin Prefecture Prince (Yuetuo) in the early period after the founding of the Qing Dynasty. Later Yunxiang, a son of Emperor Kangxi, was granted the title of Yi Prince; Yixin, a son of Emperor Daoguang, was granted the title of Gong Prince; Yihuan was granted the title of Chun Prince; Yonglin, a son of Emperor Qianlong, was granted the title of Qin Prince; and his grandson, Yikuang was granted the title of prince with "inheritance without replacement". These 12 families inherited the title of prince generation after generation because of their special contributions and for other reasons. The ranks of other princes and prefecture princes were relegated to the next lowest rank from generation to generation.

Those conferred as prince, duke and other senior titular ranks included some Manchurian and Mongolian aristocrats because of relationship by marriage or meritorious service. Since the rebellion of the three seigniors there had been no prince from the Han Chinese, and the titular rank conferred on the Han Chinese was duke, marquis, count, viscount or baron. This group of nobility obtained benefits and largesse from the court and owned great wealth and a large amount of land, slaves and maids. They were rulers and parasites of society. However it should be pointed out that the titular rank of descendants and collateral branches of the Jueluo of the imperial clan and meritorious ministers among aristocrats were degraded and declined day by day. Although they still retained the status of the yellow ribbon and the red ribbon and were nominally privileged, most of them had no way to make a living, used up their resources in idleness and were penniless and frustrated, and so were in the same situation as ordinary bannermen.

There were a number of incumbent officials and retired officials with high positions who were rich and powerful. When they were officials they sought private gains and bent the law for the benefit of relatives or friends, and they oppressed the common people. These people constituted the bureaucracy. Like the nobility with titular ranks, they belonged to orders in a prominent position and enjoyed privileges in varying degrees. In the law and ritual system their status was higher than that of the civilian population. There were also gentry in different places, who were not officials, but their ancestors had been officials, or they obtained a nominal title by contributing money or grain, or they passed the imperial examination at the county level and became a *Xiucai* (秀才) and were a successful candidate in the imperial examination at the provincial level (*Juren* 舉人). They also had some privileges in litigation and tax paying. Generally speaking the aristocracy, bureaucracy and gentry typically had more land and relied on their political power to rob by force or trickery. Moreover the higher an official's post, the more wealth he had.

Basically, the Qing government represented the interests of the landowner class. It was identical in politics with landowners and bureaucracy with privileges. Under the protection of the feudal regime, aristocrats, officials and gentry landowners could do as they pleased in villages, and bully and oppress kind and good people. Moreover the Qing government saw this group of privileged landowners as the basis of their rule and needed to win their endorsement and support. However privileged landowners were cruel, not benevolent, and insatiably avaricious and did evil things, so that they often aroused the opposition of the people and disrupted local public order. Sometimes, when their power expanded, the central ruling of the Qing government would be weakened and the tax revenues of the government would be influenced and reduced. Therefore the Qing government also had some contradictions with them. In the Qing Dynasty aristocrats, officials and gentry were allowed to have legal rights, but the Qing government also adopted some suppression policies to limit their extra-legal rights, such as prohibiting gentry from obtaining land by violence; stipulating that only the taxation of an official or *Xiucai* or student of the imperial college himself could be exempted, limiting the scope of their priority in exemption from taxes and corvée, punishing gentry landowners who were in arrears with money and grain, prohibiting country gentlemen from forcing tenants to be slaves and common people to be the lowest class; prohibiting private acquisition of a board or rod and arbitrary punishment of tenants etc. As a result the rights and powers of aristocratic bureaucratic landowners and gentry landowners were much weaker than in the Ming Dynasty. Of course, the restrictions in the Qing Dynasty were not very strict. There were endless examples of rich and influential gentry families bullying and oppressing common landowners. Peasants were "harshly dealt with, defrauded and prosecuted by rich and influential families and were like meat on a chopping board."[4] When collecting land tax, local governments often "used floating collection from small households to offset the shortage from big households."[5]

What co-existed with the aristocratic, bureaucratic and gentry landowners were a large number of common landowners without privileges. After the peasant uprising in the late Ming Dynasty, together with the policy that the Qing government encouraged and rewarded land reclamation, such common landowners had some development. In the early Qing Dynasty some affluent rural yeomen or tenants emerged and their economic status improved from the violent looting, taxes and corvée imposed by privileged landowners in the late Ming Dynasty. At first they sporadically accumulated wealth, purchased land and developed from poor to rich and from small to big owing to harder and harder work, or well-managed farming, or by virtue of superior natural conditions. When the land they possessed was too much for them to work on their own, they hired farm laborers or rented out the land. Quantitative change finally caused qualitative change. Their class status also changed from self-sufficient farmer to a landowner who exploited others. In the literature of the Qing Dynasty, there were records of "building up a family fortune by industrious farming". The so-called "industrious farming" often depended on not just on their own labors. As the landowner class, they always needed to exploit the surplus labor of tenants and hired laborers in the process of getting rich. However these landowners had been poor peasants at first, and many of them were displaced from other places to a strange land to reclaim the land and make a living. They did not have political privileges, but they could work hard and farm industriously, save on food and clothing and accumulate surplus money and rice to gradually improve their economic conditions and build up their family fortunes. Of course, only a very small number of peasants could rise to become landowners, and most peasants became poorer in the polarization. Since there was a vast territory with a sparse population and much unreclaimed land in the early Qing Dynasty, a peasant family with strong labor capability could easily expand the cultivated area and so common landowners increased considerably. In the contract documents, land records, editorial volumes and family division instruments there were a large number of small and medium landowners possessing land of a hundred *mu* (畝) or so. They mainly relied on economic power to buy land. Due to financial constraints, the quantity of land purchased each time was not large and the speed of land accumulation was slow. It usually took several decades or a century to accumulate a large amount of land and wealth. They had distinct differences from the aristocratic, bureaucratic and gentry landowners who relied on political privileges to annex land and rapidly built up family fortunes. Such common landowners, together with businessmen, yeomen, tenants, artisans, soldiers and others were called "ordinary people", or "civilians" or "common people". It was the order with the most population and very complicated connotations, and was also the main taxpayers, providers of service and objects of governance in the Qing Dynasty. "Ordinary people" included not only exploiters such as common landowners but also a large number of working people. The rights and obligations of all "ordinary people" were equal in law, and they did not have an affiliation relationship with each other. The exploiters among the "ordinary people" did not enjoy privileges from the State, and in theory the exploited people among the "ordinary people" enjoyed personal freedom from the legal perspective and had the right to take part in imperial examinations and take official positions, but in fact the economic conditions of various members of the "ordinary people" were very different. The landowners and rich businessmen politically sang the same tune as the aristocrats, bureaucrats and gentry. The Qing government implemented a subscription system, so landowners and rich businessmen could buy an official post to join the ranks of the gentry.

In the Qing Dynasty, the tenancy system increasingly developed. Tenants were a large number of basic laborers. Under the landowner economic system, laborers were not closely attached to the land. In the Qing Dynasty, tenants generally could leave the land and moved freely. There was no law to prohibit refugees to industriously farm to feed themselves. Although the landowner class had ownership of the land, it could not control the agricultural laborers who rented the land at will. The personal affiliation between tenant and landowner was looser than in previous dynasties. Economically, tenants were attached to landowners, but they belonged to "ordinary people" in politics and law as did common landowners. The relationship between them was a contractual relationship between rent collector and rent payer. The Qing law stipulated: when they "sit and eat together on ordinary days, a tenant and a landowner shall address each other as equals and a tenant shall not be ordered about and serve the landowner", and they "shall not have the name of master and servant". Of course, as tenants were economically poor and weak, their social status was inevitably low. In real life landowners had different levels of super-economic privileges, and bullying, oppression and insulting of tenants by landowners were very common.

In 1727 (the 5th year of the Yongzheng period), considering the fact that gentry landowners deemed tenants as slaves, illegally punished tenants and raped their women, the tenants swallowed their hatred, local officials practiced favoritism and turned a blind eye to maltreatment, and the harm went very deep, Tian Wenjing, the governor of Henan, requested the court to legislate against such acts. Later, after discussion, the Ministry of Personnel and the Ministry of Justice decided the ordinance restricting landowners' maltreatment of tenants. While agreeing this restriction, Emperor Yongzheng proposed preventing tenants from being in arrears with land rents and treating landowners with little respect. Finally, the Ministry of Personnel and the Ministry of Justice established the ordinance text as follows (in part): "Where lawless gentry privately acquire a board or rod and arbitrarily punishes a tenant, they shall be convicted and treated in accordance with violation of imperial edicts and law.[6] The officials in charge of supervising gentry shall prosecute wrongful acquisition by gentry of a private board or rod. A local official who neglects his supervisory duty shall be dealt with by the Ministry. Those who seize women as slaves or concubines shall be jailed and hanged. A local official who neglects his supervisory duty, practicing favoritism and conniving, and the superior of this official, who does not disclose and impeach such acts, shall also be dealt with by the Ministry. A stubborn tenant in arrears with rents or bullying and slighting the landowner shall be given 80 strokes of the cane; the owed rent shall be paid to the landowner according to the correct amount."[7] This is the criterion of the relationship between landowner and tenant as clearly defined in the feudal code of the Qing Dynasty. It prohibits gentry from punishing tenants, and raping and seizing women by relying on the authorities to protect the inviolable freedom of the person of a tenant and weakens super-economic coercion by the landowner class, making the personal dependence relationship between landowner and tenant looser; it also safeguards the interests and dignity of the landowner class, and uses the political power to press for payment of land rent in arrears to safeguard the legal exploitation right of landowners and to protect feudal private land ownership.

In the laws of the Qing Dynasty, those below the "ordinary people" included "hired laborers" and "untouchables". "Hired laborers" were not free people and they had some personal relationship of dependence with their employer. In law, the relationship between an employer and a hired laborer was just like the relationship between the head of a family and his descendants and inferiors. Hired laborers should obey their employer's orders and should not violate "decrees", and their labor has a certain degree of compulsory nature. In the Qing Dynasty, with economic development, employment relationships became increasingly common and statutes on"hired laborers" were constantly amended, so that the scope of application of such statutes was gradually narrowed and a large number of agricultural laborers got rid of the legal status of "hired laborers" and were sentenced as "ordinary people", and became free hired laborers.[8]

In the Qing Dynasty those at the lowest level of society were"untouchables" or "the lowest class people". Peasants, soldiers, businessmen and salt makers were known as the "four common people", under which there were the lowest class people. "The four common people are common people; servants, entertainers, prostitutes and Yamen runners are the lowest class people". Distinguishing common people and the lowest class people was an important order boundary and a principle for getting along with people and dealing with matters.

Among the "the lowest class people", slaves and maids were at the very bottom of society. Although society in the Qing Dynasty already developed into the late feudal society, the remnants of slavery were still very strong and the habit of keeping slaves and maids was very popular. "In an official's family, servants are as many as a forest."[9] The status of slaves and maids was the lowest. They did not have personal freedom and could only let their master use and mistreat as if they were animals. The "untouchable slave and maid are the same as livestock." The slaves and maids in the Qing Dynasty mainly came from the following sources: first, captives taken in the wars before entering the Pass; second, Han Chinese who went and sought refuge with powerful people and worked as servants; third, criminals who were sentenced to be servants; fourth, poor people who were sold as servants. In the early Qing Dynasty, the first two accounted for a larger number, and later mortgaged or sold persons became the main source of slaves and maids. For example, Qingwen, Yiren, Yuanyang, Fangguan and Lingguan in *Dream of the Red Chamber* are all slave girl and actresses. At that time, in order to supply the demand of official families for slaves and maids, professionals and markets specializing in human trafficking appeared. For example, "there are speculators in the Su Prefecture who see the daughters of poor families and try to buy them, and support them at home, and then sell them to a remote province as concubines or maids in order to make more money. They break up families and harm people for all their lives. No harm is greater than this."[10] In some places, every market day, "all kinds of goods ranging from big ones such as horses, sheep, slaves and maids and small ones such as a *dou* (斗) of rice and a *chi* (尺) of cloth are sold in the market from various places. All the goods are gathered in the market on the market day."[11] There were also some places where poor families had to sell their children because of droughts and famines. For example, in the 20th year of the Kangxi period, "Datong, Xuanfu and other places suffered famine for years, so poor people had to sell their children. A small child cost only several hundred *wen* (文), and an adult was only one or two taels of silver. Those who heard about this were sad at such news... Big carts and small carts came in an endless stream, and goods passed through many hands to sell."[12] In some places the slave trade was rampant. Human traffickers formed groups and colluded with officials and soldiers to openly and unscrupulously do whatever they wanted through abduction, kidnapping and looting. For example, in Sichuan, "There was a kind of ruffian, known as a local leopard, who gathered dozens of people to steal women. They stuffed the mouths of women with cotton, put them into bags and then carried them to open brothels. The women were sold to Hubei along the Chuan River by boat. When passing a customs post, officials and bailiffs privately let them pass after being bribed. Passers-by witnessed this but dare not intervene. Prefecture and county governments knew, but they turned a blind eye."[13]

Slaves, maids and hired laborers were also oppressed people established under the patriarchal clan system, and the status of slaves and maids was the lowest. There was a strict "bond of master and servant" between patriarch and slave and maid. Not only the patriarch himself but also all members of his family and his relatives were masters of the slaves and maids. The relationship between master and servant was not only lifelong, but also extended to future generations. A maid could become the concubine of her master or be presented to other people as a concubine, but a slave or maid could not get married with common people. There was an insurmountable barrier between common people and the lowest class people. A slave could only get married with a maid, and their children were "inborn servants" who were still slaves and maids of the master. In order to facilitate control of slaves and maids, the rulers produced a set of distorted truths on the master and servant relationship. Emperor Yongzheng said: "The bond of master and servant is to identify high and low and define inferiority and superiority. It is right and proper, and indulgence cannot be allowed... Once the bond of master and servant is defined, such a bond cannot be changed for all their lives. A servant and his wife and children rely on the master for food and clothing and depend on the master to support them, so they must not think of betrayal. Their descendants shall serve for a long time, and shall not dare to think of indulgence and impudence."[14] Advocating such fallacies and distorting facts to justify oppression was meant to make the vast numbers of slaves and maids obey their masters forever.

In the early Qing Dynasty, most of the slaves were "able-bodied men" in imperial demesnes and the manors of aristocrats. They were strictly tied to the land to engage in extremely heavy agricultural labor. They were mistreated and had no personal freedom. Their status was that of slave or serf. "Able-bodied men" could not bear the oppression and a great number of them resisted and fled. Although the Qing court legislated to prohibit this, it could not stop the practice of fleeing. Later, due to economic development and constant fleeing and resistance by slaves and maids, the slavery relationship became hard to maintain and gradually tended to decline. Let us take Jifu imperial demesne in 1745 (the 10th year of the Qianlong period) as an example. Among 518 grange heads, according to the reports of more than 460 grange heads, there were a total of more than 16,800 able-bodied men under their jurisdiction. Most of them did not engage in productive labor and only something over 290 able-bodied men could be driven by grange heads to "do useful farming for long time", accounting for less than 2% of the total number of able-bodied men. It can be seen that the imperial demesne dominated by serfdom was already been near the end and could not be maintained. The officials of the Imperial Household Department were forced to admit that "too many able-bodied men under a grange head are actually useless". The Qing court had to allow the transfer of able-bodied men in imperial demesnes in various places to local officials to "register them in the common people census register and allow them to make a living according to their will."[15] This was liberation of the serfs. As a result it was reported to the Accounting Division of the Imperial Household Department by more than 460 grange heads that a total of 16,000 able-bodied men had left and become common people, and only something over 290 people kept the status of serf. After that, imperial decrees on "leaving a banner organization and becoming common people" were issued time and again. A large number of able-bodied men were successively released to be common people from manors under the Imperial Household Department. Furthermore they were allowed to "buy commoners' land by contract and to reclaim land", and "engage in an occupation."[16] Thus many "able-bodied men" with the status of serfs and slaves obtained the status of "common people". Some of them had their own land. Some of them still farmed in the imperial demesnes, but they only paid rent to grange heads so this had already turned into a feudal tenancy relationship. The manors of other princes, dukes and aristocrats, due to the large number of runaway able-bodied men, had to recruit tenants and collect rents. In the middle of the 18th century there were already very few "able-bodied men" farming in manors.

Fig. 8.1. The Qing government's orders to demote the Yu family to be the domestic slaves of Landowner Cheng

There were a number of slaves, mainly servants and maids used within a family, who "redeemed themselves to become common people" through paying their masters a certain amount of money. In the early Qing Dynasty there was a strict restriction on "redeeming". Even if a slave or maid had saved enough money, they could not redeem themselves at will. However, later, restrictions on redeeming were gradually relaxed and there were "red deeds" and "white deeds" in slave and maid trading. "Red deed" refers to a body trading deed which was registered and paid tax to the government. "White deed" refers to a tax certification which was proved by common people and did not go through government formalities. Both of them were equally effective in law, but the legal status of a red deed slave or maid was lower and they were generally not allowed to be redeemed. However, a white deed slave or maid was generally allowed to redeem themselves after a certain number of years. It was stipulated in the Qing statutes that "after the first year of the Yongzheng period, a single person and a person with wife and children sold by a white deed shall be allowed to be redeemed. If the buyer has married him to a wife, he shall not be allowed to be redeemed. A red deed person is a servant and a white deed person is a hired laborer."[17] In the Qianlong period of the Qing Dynasty the number of red deed servants was significantly reduced and the number of white deed slaves and maids significantly increased. Cases of selling people and redeeming people were more and more common. According to the files of the mid-Qianlong period, "in recent years there have been vagrants without household registration who are sold as servants by white deeds. As soon as they accumulate some money they are reluctant to be servants any longer and try their best to redeem themselves."[18] In the trend of economic development of the whole society, commodity-money relations permeated all aspects, bringing a change to the system of slavery. By redeeming themselves slaves and maids could buy their personal freedom, which meant a weakening of the power of slave owners and increasing relaxation of the personal dependence relationship.

There were a number of the lowest class people and servants who gained personal freedom through the intervention of political power. This was because development of the economy impacted on political restrictions and made the slave system become increasingly unprofitable, and also because the lowest class people and slaves carried out continuous struggle. In order to stabilize the political order, the Qing government had to conform to historical developments and ordered various places to "abolish the lowest class people registration and promote them to ordinary people", such as the *Lehu* (樂戶, musician families) in Shanxi and Shaanxi, *Duomin* (惰民, lazy people) in Shaoying of Zhejiang, *Bandang* (伴當, companion) and *Shipu* (世僕 , servants for generations) in south of Anhui, *Gaihu* (丐戶, beggar) in Changshu and Zhaowen of Jiangsu, and *Danhu* (疍戶) in Guangdong. Because of their political and economic status, they were listed in the the lowest class people registration from generation to generation. Their social status was very low and was not equal with ordinary people, and they were deeply discriminated against and oppressed. According to records, as for *Duomin* in Zhejiang, "Men can only be allowed to engage in catching frogs, selling tin and driving out ghosts; women study to be a matchmaker, or comb hair, or make jewelry for the brides of ordinary people. They often go to street, lanes and markets in groups...If they go to other places, people all look down upon them."[19] Bandang from Huizhou was servants of Ningguo Mansion. "They are called *Ximin* (細民) by local people, their social status is almost similar to *Lehu* and *Duomin*. Moreover two families may have the same number of people and come from the same village, but one family is the other family's servants for generations. If the master family holds a wedding ceremony or funeral, the servant family should go to provide service. If a member from the master family is not satisfied, he can beat a member from the servant family."[20] *Danhu* in Guangdong "live on boats and engage in fishing. On every river throughout the whole province there are boats of *Danhu*. They have a large population. Cantonese regard *Danhu* as a mean and low people, and do not allow them to land. *Danhu* also dare not contend with ordinary people. They always fear ordinary people, bear things patiently, live on boats, and cannot get a piece of land all their lives."[21]

Fig. 8.2. The edict of abolition of seven issues in the 13th year of the Yongzheng period

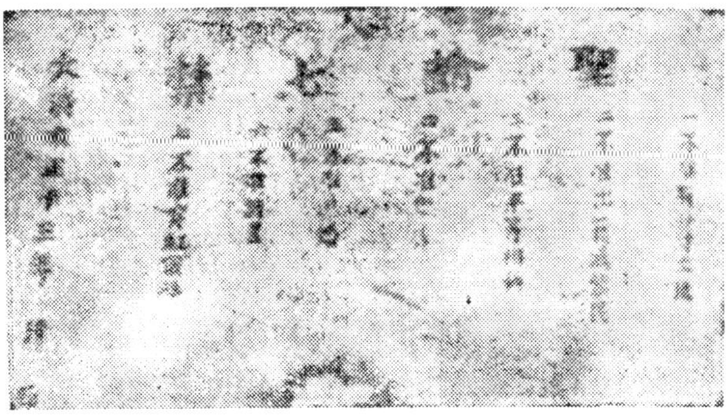

In the 3rd month of the first year of the Yongzheng period, Emperor Yongzheng issued a decree as follows: "abolish Jiaofang Yueji in Shanxi and Shaanxi, and change them to ordinary people."[22] In the 9th month he issued a decree, "abolish *Danmin* and *Gaihu* of Shaoxing, Zhejiang"; in the 4th month of the 5th year of the Yongzheng period, Emperor Yongzheng issued a decree for all *Bandang* and *Shipu*, "for a long period of time the deeds have not existed, servants are not supported by the master family, and no one can call them

Shipu."[23] In the 7th year, Emperor Yongzheng issued a decree allowing *Danhu* from Guangdong to land on the bank and "live in a village near the water, and list them as ordinary people for the convenience of inspection. Powerful people and villains shall not bully them."[24] In the 5th month of the 8th year of the Yongzheng period, original *Gaihu* were "abolished, and listed as *Mang* (氓, ordinary people) in accordance with the examples of *Leji* and *Duomin*."[25] This series of imperial decrees abolished the "the lowest class people register" of quite a lot of people and listed them in four ordinary people category, and acknowledged they had the same status with the general population. Although when these decrees were implemented, different places were very different. In some places they were overtly agreed, but covertly opposed. Until the 20th century, a small number of "the lowest class people" continued. However the "making the lowest class people to be ordinary people" was a weakening of and blow to the survival of slavery and played a positive role in productivity and social development.

China is a country with a vast territory and many ethnic groups. The social and economic development of different ethnic groups was very uneven. Some ethnic groups were at the stage of feudal serfdom, some were in the stage of slavery state, and some were still in the primitive stage. Their social and class structure had their own historical and national characteristics, their situations were extremely complex and were very different from in the Han areas. For example, Mongolia was in the stage of feudal serfdom. Their feudal lords owned large tracts of land, a large number of herds, and some subordinates called "*Suiding*" (隨丁) who were under the direct control of the lord and could be freely used as servants by the lord. Feudal lords were sheltered by the Qing government and most of them were given the titles of prince, duke and Zhasake. Except for the *Suiding* most other working people were called "*Jianding*" (箭丁), who were in fact husbandry slaves in servitude to the state who had to pay tax and be on active service duty for the Qing government. With economic development, rich or poor farm households and herdsmen were differentiated from the *Jianding*. Another example is that Tibet was also in the stage of feudal serfdom. There were many manors of feudal lords. Serfs were tied to the manors and they were personally attached to the serf-owners. They used heavy labor and tax to exchange for a small piece of land. Their status was very low. Serf-owners and serfs had very strict class differentiation, which was reflected in dress and personal adornment. In Tibet, serf-owners and Lamaism monasteries had a very close relationship and had the distinct features of unification of monk and common people and that of the state and the religion.

In addition the Yi people living in the Liangshan Region between Sichuan and Yunnan were in the stage of slavery. The class composition included *Heiyi* (Black Yi), *Qunuo, Aja, Xiaxi*, etc. The *Heiyi* were rich slave owners, *Aja* and *Jiaxi* were slaves, and *Qunuo* were farmers with a subordinate relationship. In the Qing Dynasty some ethnic groups were still in the stage of primitive society. There was no obvious class distinction, only clans and tribes, such as the *Elunchun* and *Ewenke* in the Northeast and some ethnic groups in Yunnan.

The Clan System

The clan leaders, clan rules, ancestral temples, and clan fields

The remnants of the patriarchal relationship in ancient China were strengthened after the Song and Ming Dynasties, and gradually formed a strict patriarchal clan system with the power of the clan head as the core of authority, and genealogy, clan rules, ancestral temples and clan fields as the means. In the Qing Dynasty such clan organization with consanguinity as a link existed across the country and became an organic part of the feudal social structure. Descendants of one surname often inhabited a place for generations and combined into a large clan group. In the early Qianlong period, Jiangxi Governor Chen Hongmou said, "Among the provinces, only people in Fujian, Jiangxi and Hunan live with the clan and each clan has its ancestral temple."[26] In places under the jurisdiction of Suzhou, "even after brothers divide up family property and live apart, they also do not go to live in other places. Their houses and ancestral graves are always together. Therefore, in a village, dozens to hundreds of households have the same surname."[27] Zhang Haishan also said: "There are a lot of strong clans and big surnames. In Shandong, Jiangsu, Jiangxi, Fujian and Guangdong, their customs pays special attention to the inhabitation of a region. A big clan includes more than ten thousand households, and a small clan has several hundred households."[28] Many of the big clans with descendants in thousands of households were aristocratic families with a long history. For example, the Zhang family in Changshu were the descendants of Zhang Jun, a famous general in the Northern Song Dynasty. In Wuxi and Jinkui there were descendants of Lu Zhi of the Tang Dynasty, and Zhou Dunyi, Fan Zhongyan, Qin Guan and Hu Yuan of the Song Dynasty. In Tongcheng there were distinguished families with the surname of Fang, Zhang and Yao. In Fujian, Lin, Zheng, Chen, Wang and other surnames all had a big clan and a big population. They all had deep roots and numerous leaves. In some regions, "the living place of a clan covers hundreds of miles.

Even in the city, each clan occupies a district and no people with another surname live among them."[29] Confucius' descendants were a prominent large clan, and were divided into north clan and south clan. The north clan lived in Qufu, conferred with the title of Duke Yansheng and the south clan lived in Quzhou, Zhejiang, with the hereditary title of Five Classics Boshi. In the early Ming Dynasty the Kong (Confucius) family had 60 households, that is to say it was divided into 60 branches of the Kong clan. In the Qianlong period, when the genealogy was amended, there were already no less than 20,000 people in the genealogy.[30] In the Xianfeng period, 60 households had developed into a population of 40,000.[31]

Patriarchal clan organizations, especially in some weak clans, also played a role in solidarity and mutual assistance, and had the functions of providing relief and social security in supporting the old and the poor in the feudal society dominated by the peasant economy. "Gather a lot of grain to help the poor, the old, the disabled, children and widows in the clan. Gather the remaining grain and some money to assist girls who cannot get married, widowers who cannot get married, those learning without support, and those who have passed away but cannot be buried."[32] But it should be pointed out that a more important function of the clan system was as a tool by which the landowner class ruled and oppressed the vast majority of people, and it colluded with government institutions and each other to effectively maintain the feudal system of exploitation.

The patriarchal clan system was organized based on the principle of the patriarchal system of the father's right. The patriarch was the master of the clan and head of the whole clan. He was respected and had high prestige, was very powerful, and was the embodiment of "clan rights". Within the patriarchy it was divided into numerous branches according to affinity and relationship. Under a branch there were "houses", and each house had its head. Some big clans also had executors such as Zuzheng, Zongzhi and Hutou to assist the patriarch in dealing with various matters. The patriarch was usually selected according to seniority in the family, age, virtue, prestige and official post. For example the Tu family from Yunyang, Sichuan stipulated: "In the patriarchal clan, one patriarch and two Zuzheng are established to manage the clan affairs. They are chosen by the whole clan from honest, clean, just and prestigious persons."[33] In fact high official position and salary were the most important conditions to be patriarch because the higher the position, the greater the appeal within the clan and he had enough power over asylum clansman outside the clan as well. Gu Dongao said: "if the patriarch has no salary, how can he make others obey him; if he has no official position, how can he rule the clansmen?"[34] Some clans expressly stipulated that clan affairs should be managed by a "person with scholarly honor in the clan."[35] The right of the patriarch was based on "rites" and "law". From the perspective of rites, according to a set of rites system in clan law, three main-stays and five constant virtues, and feudal ethical code, the patriarch was in a position of "respect". "For people with respected name and position, a pedestrian should humbly retreat, and cannot affront him."[36] In addition the patriarch could implement "family law" just as official's implemented "national law". "A family with a head was like a country with an official. If anyone dared abuse the respected elder, and did not act according to the rites, the whole clan had the right to punish him together in accordance with the seriousness of the offense."[37]

The "Regulations of the Clan" (also referred to as the "clan agreement", "family regulations", and "family instructions") were rules of conduct that the whole family must abide by. It was the backbone of the patriarchal clan system and was also tool through which the patriarch "manages and controls" clansmen. The Regulations of the Clan were almost similar to national law, and both of them were mandatory. "A king administers the country by himself, so there is law; a gentleman teaches family members by himself, so there are family instructions". Without law, the whole country is unjust; without law, the world is not stable .Without family instructions, the family is not in good order. In a family there were differences between old and young, inside and outside, public and private, close relation and distant relation, virtuous people and stupid people, and stubborn people and outstanding people. Without instruction, no one can consciously do everything properly."[38] It can be seen that the "Regulations of the Clan" and "family instructions" were very important to constrain clan members. The ideological basis of the regulations of the clan was the feudal cardinal guides and constants. Within the clan, ancestors and the father's generation were the most dignified. Their orders and will must be obeyed. "Where a descendant is blamed by his superior, he must accept this and cannot defend himself, regardless of right and wrong. A daughter-in-law waiting on her parents-in-law shall abide by the same principle."[39] "They are superior to me, so I should obey them in everything. Even if I feel wronged, I should find an opportunity to tell them calmly. If I answer with some angry words, I shall surely offend them."[40] It was stipulated in Qing Code: Where a father commits a crime except for treason and heresy, his son shall "cover up and conceal" for him; if he appeals to the local authority, the son has violated the "encroachment" law; even if he told the truth to the authority, punishment of father can be mitigated or annulled, but the son shall be sentenced. Within the clan, one must absolutely obey his parents and elders. Out of the clan, one was required to shift filial piety to being loyal, which is the so-called "seeking an official loyal to the sovereign out of the door of a dutiful son". It regarded the country as an enlarged clan, and the spirit of patriarchal ethics permeated political relations. In general people deemed taking an examination and becoming an official and getting promoted as a great undertaking that brought honor to their ancestors. Therefore, under the patriarchal system, it was most suitable to cultivate officials and obedient people loyal to the autocratic emperor.

Another basic thought in the "Regulations of the Clan" and "family instructions" was to advocate "abiding by the law", "family harmony" and "submitting to the will of heaven", and attempting to cover up sharp class confrontation with sentimental patriarchal relations. With social and economic development and intensified land acquisition, popularization between the rich and poor inevitably occurred within a clan. A small number of clansmen became rich landowners, and most people became the exploited. Within a clan "an older brother may be rich but a younger brother is poor, or perhaps lineal descendants are flourishing but non-lineal descendants are poor". In a big clan like the Kong family in Qufu, the big patriarch was the hereditary Duke Yansheng and was naturally wealthy and powerful. However the vast majority of descendants of Confucius were poor farmers. The "descendants of Confucius have numerous branches. Most of them are too poor to make a living, and even sell themselves to become tenants, temple families, etc."[41] It was just because of rapid differentiation within the clan that "Regulations of the Clan" and "family instructions" repeatedly warned clansmen that no matter whether they were poor or rich, gentry or common people, clansmen were the descendants of a common ancestor. "In my eyes they are thousands of people, but in the ancestor's eyes they are one person."[42] It used the doctrines of the theory of reconciliation and the theory of predestination to require clansmen to admit "no matter whether poor or rich, noble or common, it is destined". It required that "members of the same clan shall be harmony", "sincerely observe ethics" and the poor should not have presumptuous desires and or actions. "Root and branch come from same vein, and must have vicissitudes. If it is cut down by oneself, it will do harm to branches and leaves and the root is really pulled first."[43] In this way, it aroused clansmen's thinking of their origins, and stopped the wakening of their class consciousness.

Although in the "Regulations of the Clan" there were regulations that the rich should not bully the poor, the noble should not oppress the common people, and the strong should not insult the weak, and it was required that the rich "have pity for" the poor and "have compassion for" the clansmen, not many people could really do so. An important part of the patriarchal clan system was the ancestral temple. Zhang Lixiang said, "Now, if one wants to gather the hearts of men, nothing is bigger than attaching importance to the fundamental and uniting the clan, and nothing is more urgent than building the ancestral temple."[44] The ancestral temple was the symbol of the patriarchal clan, in which the tablets of ancestors were housed, and a place for the whole clan to assemble and handle affairs. The ancestral temple of a huge clan was grand, magnificent and costly in scale, shape and structure. "An ancestral temple built in a village pays great importance to the choice of every material. Its founder is sure to require that the ancestral temple is magnificent to show filial piety and to make its appearance solemn."[45] In a big ancestral temple, "the niche hall is built on the upper side to place the altar and list the ancestors in order, the meeting hall is established in the middle for all descendants to show filial piety and worship on bended knees, verandas at the left and right are used for juniors to study poetry and literature."[46] The ancestral hall was also called the "family hall". When the ancestor ritual was held in spring and autumn, the ceremony was grand and the atmosphere was solemn. It was generally officiated over by the patriarch. "In the morning, all members of the clan gather in the place of offering sacrifice and pay homage to the ancestors. "The superiors are in front and the juniors are at the back. Everyone must be uniform and as serious as if ancestors were present. There are no joking, laughing, talking or other irregularities."[47] Those with official ranking and titular honors must dress in official robes, and other people must dress neatly and seriously. "Those who wear short clothes and are barefoot shall not kowtow in the line."[48] In fact, to worship the ancestors was to promote the status of the living patriarch and head of the family, and to increase their control over clansmen and family members. It was also to inspire admiration of members of clan for their ancestors and give them a sense of honor and closeness so as to enhance ties within the clan and the dependency of clansmen on the patriarch and head of the family.

The ancestral hall was also a place to entertain guests and friends, educate the younger people, handle affairs in the clan and implement family law. In some "regulations of the ancestral temple" it was stated that "where there is a public affair in the clan, the patriarch convenes the clansmen in the family temple. It should be handled in a just and peaceful way and talked over and discussed."[49] In many "Regulations of the Clan" it was stipulated that in the case of a dispute between clansmen, it should be mediated and solved in the ancestral temple of the clan, and should not be appealed to local authority first. For example, the regulations of the Tu family in Yunyang, Sichuan stipulated: "disputes about land, tombs, debt and other issues or quarrels, and minor dislikes between clansmen, must be dealt with by the patriarch and heads of house in the ancestral temple and shall not be arbitrarily filed as a lawsuit."[50] It was stipulated in the regulations of the Dongting Yan family that "a dispute about land or debt between branches shall not be filed as a lawsuit. It shall be reported to the patriarch and branch head first and reasoned out together in the ancestral temple. No discrimination in favor of one party shall be made. If settlement is not agreed, it can then be filed as a lawsuit."[51] In some clan regulations it was directly stipulated that "anyone who does not tell the head of branch and directly appeals to the local authority shall be called to the ancestral temple to be seriously punished."[52] Mediation settlement within the clan and the family was very binding. Generally speaking, clansmen must obey."Disputes for any reason in the clan shall be reported to the head of the clan according to the facts. The patriarch shall determine a date to inquire into the details and mediate together with respectful men and virtuous men and other men. Where there is unfavorable criticism behind the back and someone dares to file a lawsuit, the patriarch shall investigate and punish them, and the penalty shall be determined publicly."[53]

When he acted contrary to the rites and law, a clan member should not go through the government and "the patriarch shall inform the whole clan through handbills to assemble in the ancestral temple and tell the ancestors. His name shall be removed from the genealogy, and he is not allowed to take part in offering sacrifice to the ancestors. In addition, anyone who was at fault shall be punished according to seriousness of fault."[54] Family law was executed in the ancestral temple, just as national law was executed by the government.

Ancestral temple and clan fields were consistent with each other. Where there was a clan, there were clan fields. Both were necessary. Someone said: "the ancestral temple is a place to worship ancestors. The clan field is used to unite clan members. The souls of ancestors rely on spirit tablets, and spirit tablets rely on the ancestral temple. Without an ancestral temple, there is no place to install the dead. The lives of descendants rely on food, and food comes from fields. Without clan fields there is no way to maintain life. Therefore the ancestral temple and clan fields shall be given equal attention, and neither can be neglected."[55] Clan fields were also an important part of the patriarchal clan system and the material basis of clan power.

Clan fields were all donated by the rich and the noble among the clansmen, that is, a part of exploited income given by landowners, bureaucrats and rich businessmen to benefit members of the clan. The Qing government vigorously advocated the magnanimous act of "donating fields to support clansmen." Such an act should be "prepared into an account book of facts and sent to the Ministry of Rites." The Ministry of Rites should present it to emperor to honor, and a person who donated fields with a value of more than 1,000 taels of silver should be built a memorial archway by the local government. Under the encouragement of the Qing government, the clan fields of big clans were easily calculated by 1,000 *mu*. According to the regulations, rental income from clan fields was used to give emergency help to widowers, widows, orphans and childless couples, and disabled and poor clansmen. "If their marriages miss the season, they are helped with money; if they feel cold, clothes are made for them; if they are ill, medicines are bought for them, and if they die, they are dressed and laid in a coffin and buried."[56] Some people also established clan schools to educate descendants of the clan, and used charity to reduce flood and drought famines, and the money was also used to praise filial sons and virtuous women and reward enrollment in school and passing imperial examination. In the name of encouraging the clan, ensuring family harmony and respecting relatives and the old, clan fields provided limited economic assistance to strengthen the patriarchal clan concept of clansmen and to ease the class contradictions within the clan.

Clan fields were a special form of feudal land ownership, and their management right was in the hand of officials and gentry. Farmers who cultivated the clan fields were members of the clan or poor farmers from outside the clan, and both had to pay very heavy rent and were under feudal exploitation. Income from clan fields was often embezzled by the patriarch and keepers. Sometimes they quarreled and were involved in a lawsuit over the division of the spoils. "Brothers had wars fighting for the produce of the ancestral temple. This happened in most of the huge clans in modern times. It is much far removed from the original meaning of respect."[57] Some local tyrants and bullies and unworthy descendants even stole by selling clan fields and the produce of the clan. For example Liu Hongao, a Hubei water conservancy official, wrote the *Establishing the Tablet for Putting an End to Stealing Money from Ancestral Temples* and established a tablet to make clear to all that it was prohibited to steal clan fields to sell, and to protect the clan system. On the tablet it said: "In the 6th year of the Daoguang period, I was assigned here. Just as I arrived there was a case of Dongting Xishan Shen stealing clan fields to sell. I immediately punished him and recovered the original articles and gave them to Liangshan ancestral hall. After several months, Dongshan Yan Guotao and other people accused Yan Zhaoyu of embezzling more than 700 fields of the clan."[58] In a short period of time there was continuous occurrence of cases of embezzling the products of ancestral temples, and it can be seen that such incidents were many.

The combination of the patriarchal clan system and the feudal regime

The patriarchal clan system, and clan power with the patriarch and head of house as the representatives, played a very important role in maintaining the feudal system of exploitation and consolidating the feudal autocratic rule. Chairman Mao deemed clan power, husband power, political power and divine power as "ideology and systems which represented all feudal clan law and four very big ropes used to bind up the Chinese people, especially farmers."[59]

In the feudal society of ancient China, family and clan were the cell and grass-roots structure of society. The stability of society depended on whether the family and clan could effectively control its members. An old Chinese saying was: one must first "regulate the family", and then one can "rule the country and give peace to the world". China had a large population and a vast territory, and many nationalities lived in the vast spread of land. The autocratic emperor situated high above; bureaucratic institutions were corrupt and incompetent. Their efficiency was very low and it was difficult to study the situation carefully, visit everywhere, and carry out tight control of the people. Therefore the clan system throughout the urban and rural areas must be used to supplement the inadequacy of official rule. Through the relationship of families in the same clan and the friendly feelings of father, brother and the elders, members of clan were educated, influenced and supervised and their words and deeds were made to observe the feudal rites and law to "quell a rebellion before it sprouted". Someone said "human relationships under heaven have never been stable without a way of maintaining them, and the way must start from those close to it... Establishing the head of a clan (i.e. patriarch) to maintain a clan is having near influence and easily understood from feelings."[60] Therefore, "Nothing is more important than clan law" in collecting and gathering hearts of people, controlling people, and consolidating the rule. Someone even thought that the reason why the Qing Dynasty could have a heyday of more than 100 years was the result of the Qing government advocating the patriarchal clan system." "Our country is ruled through filial piety. All aristocratic families and huge clans are influenced by such a policy and have same the ideas, and respect the ancestors...None of them does not preach the imperial edict, and say affection from the father and filial piety from the son...For more than 100 years, the country has been peaceful." In the view of the rulers, the patriarchal clan system and the feudal regime supported each other, and they were two in one; when it was promoted, the patriarchal ethical relationship was loyalty to the court so the patriarchal clan system was emphasized and could "transfer filial piety into loyalty" and consolidate the feudal rule. Moreover, the pervasiveness of the patriarchal clan system was attributed to the advocacy and support of the government, and "it was cultivation by the dynasty that made it so."[61]

The Qing rulers attached great importance to the role of the patriarchal clan system, and some of them even wanted to use it to replace the Bao-jia system. In the early Yongzheng period, when rectifying the Bao-jia system, officials of Zhaoqing, Guangdong "proposed to choose persons with virtuous conduct in the clans and make them head of clan to investigate unworthy clan members, and those who practice favoritism shall be punished, when they discussed huge castles and big villages in the prefecture and counties."[62] In the early Qianlong period, considering that Jiangxi had a numerous population and "members of the same clan lived together and each clan had an ancestral temple", Jiangxi Governor Chen Hongmou determined that the government formally entitled the patriarch or head of clan to manage and control clansmen. He hereby issued the *Agreement on Electing the Head of Clan*, ordered affiliated prefectures and counties to prepare an account book of the number of ancestral halls and name of patriarchs, and report it to the higher authorities. The government should issue them with an official license and grant them powers. He said: "the head of clan holds official law to examine the descendants in the clan. The name and identity are certain, and they are bound by a certain relationship, so it is easier to detect and control than Bao-jia from other family with different surnames."[63] Granting official power to patriarchs meant political power was directly combined with the power of the clan, and of course it would obtain more results in constraining descendants and ruling people. Thus a governing net with "Baojia as the warp and the clan as the weft" reached far into poor regions and became a handy ruling tool for the Qing government. Later Wei Yuan said: "There are hundreds of clans in each county and kingdom under each province. They are irregularly scattered in counties, and the court uses the big patriarchal clan system to connect them. They educate and guard themselves; widowers, widows, orphans and childless couples, the disabled and the ill, have something to support them; there is something to rely on in flood and drought famine: customs can be investigated, and other small surname clans attach themselves to a big clan. The human heart is maintained and is as solid as rock, and robbery does not arise. If there was no such a measure, there would be almost no effect on future generations after three generations!"[64]

The patriarchal clan system also played a role in guaranteeing taxes. In many clan regulations clansmen were warned to "pay tax first", "complete paying the grain according to the limit" and "do not be in arrears". Some clan regulations also focused on explaining the relationship of standing together through thick and thin between government and clansmen (landowners), and urged the clansmen to pay taxes and grain. "The court does not collect grain to turn it into the private property of the emperor. Salaries of civil and military officials come from this, soldiers are supported with this, and the costs for driving away enemies come from this. It is taken from the people and shall return to the people. Therefore people can be calm, safe and happy when farming and enjoy their safety and security. It is not necessary for the government to urge payment and officers to chase payment! Those who are in arrears in paying grain and taxes and hope to be forgiven, and embezzle and cheat to line their pockets, shall not be tolerated by heaven, earth and the gods. All my family members shall pay grain on time when crops are harvested in summer and autumn. Do not get involved in a legal action. It is really one side of loyalty and is a way to protect the family."[65]

When the class struggle was fierce and there were successive peasant uprisings, the huge clans and big families in various places often organized armed forces to fight against the peasant uprisings. They were stationed in castles and walled villages to massacre peasants and became the accomplices of the feudal government. For example, at the turn from the Ming Dynasty to the Qing Dynasty, the whole country was in great turmoil. In the 4th year of the Shunzhi period, Qiu Minzi from Ninghua, Fujian led peasants in an uprising. They ordered landowners and gentry to return stolen goods and forced them to pay salary for the soldiers, which greatly upset the local feudal order. Li Shixiong, leader of a big clan in Ninghua, gathered his clansmen in the ancestral temple and claimed that "hot blood is spilled on the ground, eyes are sad when they are opened, swear on the altar and build defense work at strategic positions and feel proud."[66] He said: "Since the year of Jiashen of the Chongzhen period, thieves have been everywhere. They attacked cities and looted towns. It is clear that staying in a city is not as safe as in a castle."[67] Therefore he led his clansmen to build a castle. This castle was 160 *zhang* (丈) in circumference, 1.6 *zhang* high and 1 *zhang* thick. Around the castle there was a moat. The gate of castle was connected with blunderbuss city and there were portholes on the three walls. Inside the castle there was an ancestral temple, houses and a well to prepare for being besieged. There were seven streets in the castle. All the houses faced the street. There were 138 buildings for farmers to live. The buildings had three storeys and were of equal height with the city wall."Roads in the city are to the back gate of the city. Where there is an alarm, one can go to a small gate."[68] His clansmen and attached small surname clans and farmers lived in the castle and a method for providing service and levying military salary was established. When the rebels attacked the castle, the clansmen and farmers beat drums, erected flags, and took up knives and blunderbuss to fight. This armed force was maintained by the clan relationship, had the castle as shelter, and usually were trained, so it had strong fighting strength. Later, in the White Lotus Rebellion, Taiping Rebellion and Nian Rebellion, such rural soldiers and castles with clans as the core were very active and became strong opponents of the rebels.

The power of clans was developed under the advocacy of state political power, and only with the support of the power of the clans could state political power be consolidated. Both of them were closely combined with each other and shone more brilliantly in the other's company. However the power of the clan and state political power also came into conflict. A strong clan meant expansion of local forces, so that the state political power lost control. These strong clans had a large population, considerable strength and a long history, so they were in a pivotal position in the local area. "They love fashion and dress in luxury, and are enough to the establish hope of all people."[69] Within the clan there was strong cohesion because of the blood relationship. In particular the patriarch's and heads' words and acts and the things they paid attention to often had a resonance in many clansmen. They were linked through genealogy, had a wide base, made arbitrary decisions in the villages, and even undertook legal cases, gambled and prostitute trafficking. The feudal government found it hard to cope with them. Therefore despite it being stipulated in the clan regulations that they should "be loyal to the court" and be "law-abiding", Emperor Qianlong said: "there are few heads of clan who abide by the law". The Qing government hoped that development of a clan would be restricted to the local area of their village and town, and that they would strictly observe the regulations of the cardinal guides and constant virtues.

Another manifestation of the indulgence and peremptoriness of big clans was mutual fighting with weapons. It was stipulated in the clan regulations if a clansman was bullied by people with another surname, their clansmen should come forward to help. Thus because of quarrels, minor dislikes and money, clans gathered people to fight against each other, resulting in tragic cases of killing people and causing long-term vendettas. This practice was especially prevalent in the Guangdong, Fujian and Jiangxi areas. Landowners and gentry manipulated and deceived their clansmen to provoke and make use of fighting with weapons for their own personal gain. In large-scale fights it was mostly lower-class farmers who were injured or killed. They were the victims of the feudal patriarchal thought.

Class Struggles from the Mid-Kangxi Period to the Mid-Qianlong Period

The case of the 3rd Prince of Zhu

In the early Kangxi period, after putting down the rebellion of the three seigniors including Wu Sangui and recovering Taiwan, the ruling order of the Qing Dynasty gradually stabilized and large-scale anti-Qing wars faded away. Except for in border areas and other ethnic minority areas, the Qing Dynasty had not used military forces for a long time. It had recovered and developed economically and had gained relative stability and peace politically from the late 17th century to the latter half of the 18th century (from the mid-Kangxi period to the mid-Qianlong period). Of course, even in such a relatively peaceful situation, social contradictions and class conflicts did not stop. All kinds of class struggles still existed all over the country. Beneath the quiet long river of history, many whirlpools and undercurrents were swirling and stirring.

The rule of the Ming Dynasty had finished. Corruption and internal strife among several small courts of the Southern Ming Dynasty meant that the Han landowners failed in the struggle for national sovereignty. However, in the hearts of many Han Chinese, they still hated the new Manchu regime and were sentimentally attached to the former rule of the Ming Dynasty. Therefore restoring the Ming Dynasty was still a banner for many anti-Qing patriots. In the Kangxi period, the case of the 3rd Prince of Zhu was the last radiance of the setting sun of this old time. As early as in the Shunzhi period, when the anti-Qing wars were spreading like wildfire, there were many people who claimed to be the son of Emperor Chongzhen and fled from Beijing to organize anti-Qing activities. For example, in 1655 (the 12th year of the Shunzhi period), Zhu Zhou, who was captured in Yangzhuo, was called the 3rd Prince of Zhu and organized anti-Qing activities in the north of Jiangsu. The following year Zhu Ci, captured at Pingshan, Zhili, called himself the son of Chongzhen and plotted to stage an uprising in Zhengding. In 1673 (the 12th year of the Kangxi period), Yang Qilong in Beijing claimed to be the 3rd prince of Zhu and was preparing to stage an uprising in capital to respond to Wu Sangui's anti-Qing rebellion. Since it was revealed this uprising was quickly suppressed by the Qing government and Yang Qilong escaped from Beijing. Later, cases of the 3rd prince of Zhu often occurred throughout the country and the Qing rulers sensed danger everywhere and suffered from false alarms. In 1679 (the 18th year of the Kangxi period) Yuele, a prince, presented a memorial to the throne that he had seized Zhu Cican, crown prince of Emperor Chongzhen. Emperor Kangxi did not recognize that was the true crown prince. In his imperial edict he said: "I have asked the old eunuch about this. He said that at that time Zhu Cican was very little, and surely could not flee out. Then how can he survive today? It is probably false."[70] The following year it was reported from Sichuan that Yang Qilong who claimed to be the 3rd prince of Zhu had been seized. The result of trial was that the man was not only not the crown prince, but also he was not Yang Qilong. "On his face there were scars of tattoo characters. He was obviously an escaped person from the banner. He joined Yang Qilong's uprising and knew his reasons, so he initiated a rebellion in Shanxi in the name of Yang Qilong."[71] In 1708 (the 17th year of the Kangxi period), Zhang Nianyi (Monk Nianyi) who staged a rebellion against the Qing in Dalanshan, Zhejiang, confessed he had connections with the 3rd prince of Zhu and that he was hidden in Shandong. The Qing government captured the 3rd prince of Zhu. According to Kangxi, "Zhusan is an imperial member of the Ming Dynasty. He is 76 years old. He and his son traveled to teach and depended on others for a living." Although this 76 year-old man had concealed his name, made a living by teaching, and had committed no criminal acts made the Qing rulers restless and uneasy when hearing his name and life history. Therefore this innocent old man was put to death by dismemberment and his whole family, young and old, were all killed. At that time, anti-Qing activities using the name of descendants of the imperial family of the Ming Dynasty were numerous. Emperor Yongzheng said that "in the Kangxi period, wicked and crafty people in various places secretly launched rebellions and frequently used the name of the 3rd prince of Zhu, such as Monk Nianyi and Zhu Yigui. They were numerous. Recently a Shandong person called Zhang Yu claimed that his surname was Zhu and that he was a descendant of the imperial family of the Ming Dynasty and was reckoned to have a fate of emperor by a physiogynomist. He hoped to use this to attract foolish people. Now he has been seized, investigated and questioned by the Yamen of the Commander-General of the Metropolitan Infantry."[72]

Among numerous 3rd princes of Zhu in the Shunzhi and Kangxi period, which one was real? Due to the inadequacy of documents it is very hard to prove the authenticity of the 3rd prince of Zhu. There were numerous events and figures like this which are not easy to clarify. What was important was not the 3rd prince of Zhu himself, but was that this name aroused many people's emotions and their fondness for the former dynasty and hatred for the new regime. He was the symbol of the struggle against the Qing Dynasty. The war between the Ming and Qing Dynasties had ended, but its repercussions rippled on and could not be calmed down for a long time. A long-lasting intense domestic national struggle made a deep mark in history for many generations in the future. Many struggles against oppression and exploitation used the banner of the Ming Dynasty of Zhu. It should be noted that the anti-Qing rebellions in the name of the 3rd prince of Zhu all remained clandestine activities and were not developed into large-scale open movements, although they could attract attention. It can be seen that they were only "name" and "banner", and could not cause the upsurge of class struggle. Large-scale mass struggle needs profound content and the necessary conditions. At that time, the main contradiction in society was no longer the contradiction between Manchu and Han but the class contradiction between landowners and farmers. This historical content determined the form of class struggle.

The anti-rent struggle

One form of manifestation of class struggle between landowners and farmers was decentralized, small but sharp and frequent anti-rent struggles. Marx said: "No matter what the origin of rent, as long as it exists, it is an object of heated dispute between land manager and land owner."[73] In the Qing Dynasty, in the relatively developed areas of the tenancy relationship and especially in many provinces in the south, anti-rent struggles rolled on with full force. In the periods of Kangxi, Yongzheng and Qianlong when the class struggle was at low ebb and the Qing government's rule was relatively consolidated, anti-rent struggles were also very frequent and widespread. For example, in Jiangxi, "stubborn tenants who had failed in their plans often occupied fields and resisted paying rent. Ninety percent of tenants made things difficult for landowners."[74] In Fujian, "landowners and tenants were not in harmony. They hated each other. The tenants regarded the anti-rent struggle as a good thing;"[75] in Hubei, "recently there are a few good tenants, but many cunning and stubborn tenants;"[76] in Jiangsu, "anti-rent struggles by tenants in the middle part of Jiangsu has become an obstinate habit;"[77] in Hunan, "there are many problems with occupying land but refusing to pay rent;"[78] in Guangdong, "stubborn tenants deem rent due as inherent, and bullied the landowners as they wish."[79] Even in some minority group areas there were often anti-rent struggles. For example, "the Yao people mix with ordinary people. They exchange tenant fields for goods. They forcibly occupy land to farm, but do not pay rent. Sometimes, they are overbearing."[80] The Dong people in Guangdong and Guangxi also "rented to farm waste lands, and gather a lot people and force out the landowner to occupy the village."[81] The tenancy relationship in the north was not as developed as in the south. The relationship between owner and tenant was different, and there were relatively fewer anti-rent struggles. However in the banner lands of banner of Zhili, the tenancy relationship was also formed under special conditions. In the early Qing Dynasty large tracts of lands were given to Manchu people, but many Manchu people were not good at farming so the land had to be cultivated by the original farmers. Therefore many banner lands "were still farmed by the original farmers themselves, ordinary people did farming and banner people waited to collect rents."[82] For a long time, cases of owing rent and anti-rent struggles were frequent. In 1782 (the 47th year of the Qianlong period), Zhili Governor Yinglian said: "in Zhili there are 77 counties which have banner lands rented out, and in 42 counties people owe rent. The accumulated rent owed has been owed for as long as 20 years and amounts to more than 240,000 tael of silver."[83] Especially in the case of some supplementary appropriated land, landowners all live in other villages and remote places, completely apart from production, and they even do not know where their land is situated. Therefore farmers often owed rent, and anti-rent often happened. Sometimes it also happened that "more than 100 tenants gathered by ringing bells and beating drums"[84] for anti-rent fight on a larger scale.

The causes of the anti-rent struggles were diverse. Some were because of flood and drought famines, and farmers were unable to pay the rent. For example, in the middle of the Kangxi period, "Songjiang had a famine... Some of the lands were completely waste, and there on half of the land the grain harvested on one *mu* was only one or two *dou*. Cunning tenants even resisted in gangs using the excuse of famine and no harvest."[85] There was also the problem that the Qing Government exempted the taxes of the landowner, so the tenants also required the rent be reduced accordingly. For example, in 1746 (the 11th year of the Qianlong period), in Shanghang, Fujian, Luo Riguang and Luo Rizhao organized people to resist against rent. The reason was that the Qing Dynasty "exempted the tax and grain, so the villages wanted to divide the rent which had paid to the landowners in the proportion of 4 : 6."[86] It caused conflicts between landowner and tenants. The government intervened, which finally led to a case of refusing to be arrested and resisting officials. Emperor Qianlong was biased towards the landowner and was very angry. He said: "I exempt taxation by my favor. It cannot be determined by ordinary people. As to whether the rent shall be reduced, the tenants should listen to the landowner. Even with edicts it is hard to order the landowners to do so. This is no reason that the amount of rent can be reduced by tenants themselves and are refused to pay."[87] Some conflicts between landowner and tenant were because the tenant wanted to keep the right of renting the land for

Fig. 8.3. A ticket showing that Confucius' mansion arrested tenants from Yuncheng in the 51st year of the Qianlong period

a long time, objected to the land being rented to other people, and strove for rights in perpetuity.

Most anti-rent struggles were due to the heavy exploitation and violent means used by the landowner class. Those greedy wealthy people were heartless. When collecting rent they used a big *dou* to measure and collect excess rent; or freely plundered and evicted farmers from land leased to them by increasing rents; or even set up an illegal court and illegally punished tenants. For example, in the Yongzheng period Shi Dashou, a local tyrant in Chongming, added charges for sedan chairs, meals, and miscellaneous money for his family, He colluded with officials and established a clan relationship with Garrison Commander Shi who had the same surname. He "sent beautiful girls, money and cloth to Garrison Commander Shi. The two families communicated with each other and he relied on power to charge more rent."[88] Farmers rose to resist the local tyrants and officials. Another example was that anti-rent struggles in Fujian were often caused by the "correcting drum". The "correcting drum" meant that tenants were required to use the correct rice drum for rent being collected. "Landowners wanted to get more than the normal amount and use some trick to collect more, so they made a big *dou* to collect rent. Four or five extra sheng were collected. Of course, the tenants did not obey. Accordingly, some local villains took the opportunity to collude with each other and cunning tenants privately established *dou*. Such action was joined by hundreds of people to resist the landowners. This trend was inevitable and it survives today. Its damage is not shallow."[89] One person who was an official in Taizhou saw that landowners bullied tenants and felt it very unfair. He said: "Most Taiwan residents were heartless and intent on nothing but profit. It was heard that after sealing documents at the end of a year, fierce and tough servants were sent to separately ask for rents. They took everything in the tenants' house, and even took tiles, picked up the door, tied up his wife and children, and escorted the tenant himself with chains and locks to be hit in every possible way. Do not such unreasonable actions break the law? It really hurts moral principles!"[90] In the Kangxi period, the Changsha county magistrate also talked about harsh exploitation and humiliation of tenants when listing local advantages and disadvantages. He said that "hired laborers and tenants are always the people who provide labor service. They are not same as slaves. Recently I have found that the feelings of Hunan people are shallow and they bully the weak...Common people have to bear suffering and dare not argue. They are really to be pitied. They also arbitrarily make tenants into slaves and willfully use them, asking too much in rent. They exploit compound interest, and even ask the women of tenants to serve in their home. The tenants have to obey. Moreover when some tenant dies the landowner sells or marries off his wife and children because the tenant has no clansman, and collects the tenant's property."[91] Some landowners "indulge their servants to be cruel like tigers and wolves, to go out in a crowd and act as they please. As soon as they get to the home of a tenant, they would first ask for wine and food. After eating and drinking, they start to urge for money. If the tenant does not present money or the amount of money is not enough, he will take everything in the house, regardless whether cloth, rice, chickens or geese. All the things in the house are looted. They even tie up the tenant with rope or chains and beat the tenant, and insult his parents, wife and children."[92] In short, the landowner class carried out terrible exploitation. They were as ruthless as wolves, as poisonous as snakes and scorpions. Farmers had to swallow their hatred if they wanted to survive, but it was not easy. In order to protect themselves, they had to take risks and carry out resistance.

The primary forms of anti-rent struggle were disputes, quarrels, fighting, death or injury between individual tenants and individual landowners because of rent due, asking for rent, and conflict over rent. Such civil and criminal litigation cases occurred frequently. In the *Memorials of the Criminal Department* in the files of the Qing court, such cases were everywhere. In these individual conflicts the landowner class used their economic and political advantages and tenants often got the worse of it and were bullied.

When trying such cases, officials were always biased towards landowners. Slowly, tenants contacted each other on the basis of common interests. They used acting, events, drinking blood wine and becoming promised brothers to unite and fight against landowners in an organized way. For example, in the late Kangxi period, nearly all the "tenants in villages" in Suzhou raised funds to act in a play, drink bloody wine and made promises to resist against landowners."[93] Sometimes the tenants were united and could get some victories in a particular struggle, forcing the landowner to reduce the amount of rent. Such a victory would encourage the struggles of the masses and promote further development of the anti-rent struggle and make it more organized and have more the nature of mass struggle. In some places, there were the Tiechi Society, Wulong Society, Changguan Society etc., which became the organizations of tenants for implementing anti-rent struggles. For example, in 1748, (the 13th year of the Qianlong period) Censor Lu Zhi presented a memorial to the throne. He said: "in Tingzhou, Xinghua and other places in Fujian, the custom is sly and fierce. Ninghua County has the so-called Tiechi Society, and Shisan Taibao as well. The Tiechi Society is in Ninghua, Shanghang, Qingliu and other counties under Tingzhi. It acts blindly and violently, bullies ordinary people, and despises national law."[94] In 1753 (the 18th year of the Qianlong period), tenant Du Zhengqi and other persons from Shaowu, Fujian "colluded with several dozens of people and repeatedly made trouble with landowners, relying on their powerful boxing, they went to market tyrannically. Gradually, their number became more and more. Then they privately plotted and gave each one an iron ruler, and their party was called the Tiechi Society (Iron Ruler Society)."[95] In some places clubs were established and a head of tenants was elected. They even established armed forces to openly confront with the landowner class. For example in Xingguo, Jiangxi, the tenants "established a club and it promoted far and near. Every autumn, it advocated the difference between eight harvests and seven harvests. Any landowner who collected rent according to the original amount should be punished. They called on many people, damaged the landowner's houses, and seized the rents collected by the landowner for the club."[96] The Xingguo tenant club maintained its struggle although besieged by the landowner class and the government. It lasted for 14 years from the 52nd year of the Kangxi period when it was established to the 4th year of the Yongzheng period when it was banned. The tenants in Yuedu Jiangxi elected a "head of tenants" as their leader. Most of them were fair-minded, chivalrous and could maintain the interests of poor tenants. They "called on fellows, and if someone had trouble with the landowner the head of tenants raised funds to help him. They even openly resisted physically. For a small case, they would resist rent and end the litigation, and for a big case, they would gather people together and seize property."[97] The tenants in various counties of Fujian and Jiangxi also organized "tenant soldiers" and took up weapons to fight with the landowners. The earliest case was in 1646 (the 3rd year of the Shunzhi period), when Huang Tong from Ninghua, Fujian assembled farmers and requested the "correcting drum". At that time, when collecting rents, landowners used a big drum. Twenty *sheng* (升) was a big drum which was called the "rent drum". However, when selling grain, the landowners used a small drum. Sixteen *sheng* was a small drum, known as the "*Ya* drum". "Notify all the villages. Paying rents shall be based on the 16-*sheng* drum. All removing farming, winter beasts, bean grains and sending them to the warehouse (note: they were all items established by landowners to exploit farmers)" and other issues shall be based on the same criterion. The villagers cheered loudly and scrambled."[98] Huang Tong organized tenant soldiers, gave himself the title of company commander, and seized political power in some townships. "Lawsuit began not to have anything to do with officials. They were all determined by ...Therefore rich and influential families in the town and the tenants hated each other."[99] Huang Tong led the tenant forces to break through Ninghua and severely punish unlawful landowners. Meanwhile Qingliu, Fujian, Shicheng, Ruijin and Ningdu, Jiangxi, also organized tenant soldiers. The tenant soldiers organized by He Zhiyuan from Ruijin had "all flags written with 'dividing land equally in eight townships'". Equally means to divide the landowner's land into three parts, and one part shall be the root of farming of tenant people. Although the land they do cultivation change surname, tenants would never be changed. Such land shall be tenure land. Any household with tenure land in his home dare to have disagreement, his houses shall be burned down immediately, and he shall be killed. Therefore, fierce ones walked first and coward ones followed them. They entered the city like gathering ants and forced county magistrate to print kind posts in ten thousands."[100] Here we can see that the farmers then were eager to get the land, but also showed their bold actions and might. Afterwards, in this area, there were still activities by land soldiers. For example, in 1670 (the 9th year of the Kangxi period) in the Shicheng, Wu Bashi and other people "raised land troops and carried a tablet to erect at the gate of the county in the name of tenant". He "led his troops to surround the city for 3 days."[101] In 1688 (the 27th year of the Kangxi period) in Ningdu, "Li Ai, Li Man, Wang Huanying and other people gathered tenants to resist against rent. They occupied fortresses to loot and were called tenant soldiers."[102] In Rui'an, Huang Xiaowu "called on hungry people to rise in rebellion to respond", and called himself "Junqing King".[103] They organized armed forces, killed landowners, resisted offices and officials, and besieged prefectures and counties. The anti-rent struggles began to move from anti-rent struggle to armed uprising.

The Qing Dynasty was the regime of the landowner class and of course it would protect the interests of the landowner. When the anti-rent struggle had developed to a certain scale, it would certainly come out to intervene and repress. In the Yongzheng period it was stipulated that a tenant who did not pay rent on time and bullied a landowner should be given 80 strokes of the cane. The rent due should be paid to the landowner. Therefore governments in various places helped landowners to ask for payment of rent. They often arrested a lot of farmers, beat them and put a heavy instrument of torture around their necks, showing their power and prestige. For example, in Suzhou, "if a tenant does not pay rent due, and the owner chases and shouts but the tenant does not answer, the owner often appeals to the local authority and escorts and hands over the tenant to the local authority. Usually there are dozens or hundreds of tenants escorted."[104] In front of the country office of Yuanhe County, "No less than hundreds of tenants did not pay rent or did not pay on time and are tied with iron chains."[105] In Kunshan County, "The people who resisted rents and wore heavy yokes as examples were everywhere on the road inside and outside of the area around the city gate."[106] In Shanyang County, Jiangsu, regulations were made and tablets were established to prohibit anti-rent activities. The tenants were condemned as "evil tenant", "cunning tenant", "stubborn tenant", "robbery tenant" and "sly tenant". Emperor Qianlong also issued edicts repeatedly and required anti-rent farmers be severely punished. He said "the practiced of starting disputes for reducing rent and illegally acting violently shall not be encouraged. I order that they be punished severely to warn the sly and stubborn ones."[107] "The principal criminal shall not be indulged. He shall be severely punished to warn against sly practices."[108]

From it nature, the anti-rent struggle is an economic struggle. Farmers put for forward the economic requirement of decreasing rent. Their targets are individual landowners, or landowners in a certain region. Generally speaking such struggle does not have a definite plan and organization in advance. Although there are similar economic interests among tenants they do not have common political beliefs. The struggles have strongly local and spontaneous natures, which makes it difficult to call on people in a wide range and roll out a huge revolutionary storm, so they suddenly rise and suddenly fall, and are easily put down by landowners and the government.

Fig. 8.4. A tablet of strictly prohibiting tenants from anti-rent activities in Shanyang County, Jiangsu in the 7th year of the Daoguang period

However, the anti-rent struggle had profound social roots. It arose from the feudal tenancy exploitation relationship and was produced by the basic contradiction between landowners and peasants. As long as this system of exploitation existed it would continue to produce contradictions and create antagonism. Although anti-rent struggles are easily suppressed and are difficult to directly develop into a large-scale uprising, they are more difficult to prevent and eradicate. If it is put down this year, next year it will re-start; it is quiet here, but struggle begins over there. It forms an endless situation with regularity and extensiveness.

The anti-Rent struggle and peasant uprisings all occurred on because of basic contradictions in feudal society. They were interconnected. When certain political beliefs of secret societies spread among farmers, the anti-rent struggle would become an open armed uprising, and economic struggle would walk toward political struggle. It can be said that the anti-rent struggle was the preparation and rehearsal for the peasant uprising, and the peasant uprising was the continuation of the anti-rent struggle.

The struggles of urban artisans

With social and economic development in the late feudal society, urban handicraft and commerce showed some growth. Therefore in addition to anti-rent, robbing rice and peasant uprisings in the vast rural areas, urban people's struggles also occurred frequently and became a part of whole anti-feudal class struggle.

Among urban people's struggles the most notable was that of the *Chuai Jiang* (踹匠, labor working on the last process of cotton cloth) and *Ji Jiang* (機匠, labor working in silk or cotton). Suzhou was a center of the cotton and silk industry. In the dying process, it needed a large number of craftsmen to tread stones to press the dyed cloth smooth and clean. Most of *Chuai Jiang* were strong young people. They were poor and had no other skills. They had solidarity with each other and were full of fighting spirit. "This artisan must be young and strong. They were all from north of the Yangtze River or south of the Yangtze River. They were introduced to work in the workshops one by one. Most of them were single, and did not remain in their proper sphere. Because they often gathered together and combined their strength together, they were both common people and scoundrels."[109] In the Qing Dynasty, the resistance struggles of the *Chuai Jiang* in Suzhou were continuous. In 1670 (the 9th year of the Kangxi period), *Chuai Jiang* leader Dou Guifu "said that the rice price in this famine year is expensive. He used leaflets to agree with the *Chuai Jiang* to stop working and ask for increased wages."[110] The mercery asked the government to suppress this. Dou Guifu was sentenced to be caned and driven out of Suzhou. In 1692 (the 31st year of the Kangxi period) Luo Gui, Zhang Erhui and other people "stirred up the whole industry to demand increased wages and even formed gangs, looted and damaged official notices". They "gathered people to levy them, advocated increased wage, acted violently, fought and cheated."[111] The Qing government intervened. The *Chuai Jiang* were shackled and Luo Gui and another 15 people escaped. After the case was ended, 76 merceries engraved the government's order on

Fig. 8.5. A list of examples of artisan strikes in some areas in the early Qing Dynasty

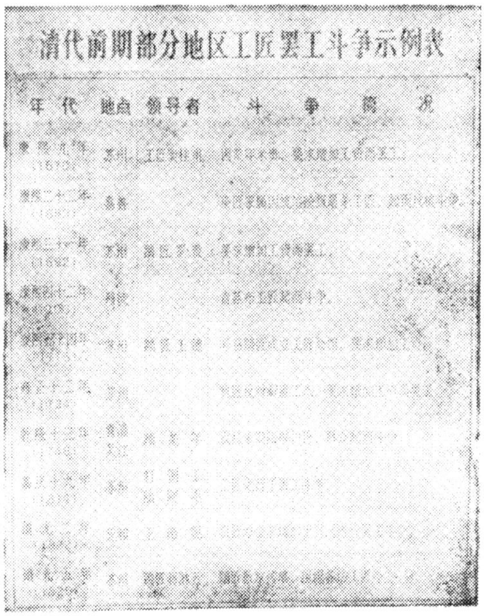
清代前期部分地区工匠罢工斗争示例表

年代	地点	领导者	斗争情况

a stone tablet, and salry for a *Chuai Jiang* was still 1.1 *fen* (分) for a piece of cloth. "Observe the established rules, and do not increase or decrease." "An unlawful villain who knowingly follows the example of a wrongdoer shall never be forgiven."[112] In 1700 (the 39th year of the Kangxi period), a struggle was initiated by the *Chuai Jiang*. The cause was that the foreman (owner of *Chuai* cloth) deducted salary, and finally it led to a huge wave. "As soon as the villain's order was issued, thousands of *Chuai Jiang* followed him. They mobbed and fought for consecutive days so that the foreman was scared and the shop owners had no way out. No one dared start operation and begin to *chuai*. The riot was worse than previous years. Businessmen and common peoples suffered for almost one year."[113] The Qing government was left with a deep impression by this struggle. In order to prevent others in advance, *Chuai Jiang* were strictly managed. "*Chuai Jiang* in Suzhou shall be constrained by two *Dianshi* of Changzhou and Wu County together with the city defending commissioner as well as the foremen. On ordinary days, regulations shall be declared to them and their expressions observed. Do not allow them to make trouble at night, drink, gamble and assemble to talk randomly". The foreman was responsible for checking the background of *Chuai Jiang* and establishing a circulating book. "The place of birth, recommendation, time of entering the shop and going out of the shop of a *Chuai Jiang* shall be entered in the book. Every 15th day, the book shall be submitted to the workshop owner, and be entered into the bond, and a new circulating book issued. Make sure to inspect mutually, and interrogate and examine the history. Where anyone dares to take in bandits and brings disaster to the local area, if one workshop has trouble, nine workshops shall be implicated in the charge."[114] The administration of the government was very strict, but the struggles of the *Chuai Jiang* were still very active. In the late Kangxi period, they still often made trouble. "After a long time, the law is implemented loosely, cunning craftsman can do what they want... together with a group of villains, who lived in temples and appeared occasionally in *Chuai* workshops...stirred up the *Chuai Jiang* to increase the salary of the whole industry, sued on their behalf, levied legal costs, re-charged remunerations. The villains were greedy, they ceaselessly caused trouble."[115] In 1723 (the 1st year of the Yongzheng period), *Chuai Jiang* Luan Jingong and other people planned to "set a fire and plunder the warehouse", and rose in rebellion against the Qing, However the plan was disclosed did not get succeed. In 1729 (the 9th year of the Yongzheng period) Luan Erji, nephew of Luan Jingong, and other people "kowtowed to become promise brothers, formed an alliance, paid homage to god and drank wine". They struggled with foreman Qian Yu who supported artisans but were suppressed. At that time there were 20,000 *Chuai Jiang*. The Qing government decided they were places of hiding for bad people. In order to prevent the *Chuai Jiang* from making trouble, they were rectified again. In 1731 (the 9th year of the Yongzheng period), *Baojia* were established in the *Chuai Jiang*. Li Wei, Zhejiang Governor who administered the region south of Yangtze River, presented to the throne that "most of such *Chuai Jiang* are single and bad. Please refer to the method of *Baojia* and establish a head of *Jia* to try to mutual check and examine with the original established head of the workshop."[116] In the Qianlong period, prices rose gradually and the *Chuai Jiang* repeatedly asked for an increase in wages. In the 44th year of the Qianlong period it was agreed that "wage shall be issued as per each piece of cloth. The total wage including timber, vegetables and rice shall be silver of one *fen* and three *li* (里) in total for a piece of cloth."[117] The Suzhou *Chuai Jiang* waged a long-term struggle and only achieved such a small and specific result. *Ji Jiang* in the silk industry in Suzhou also gathered many times to "ask for a break". "Most of loom owners in Suzhou city hired people to weave, and loom owners invested and managed themselves. The wage of a *Ji Jiang* shall be calculated according to his work. They originally had a mutual need and had no objections. There were some unlawful people who were dismissed by the loom owner because they were not familiar with the work. They were jealous, so in the name of help they advocated to blackmail silver and made the loom owner stop weaving and the *Ji Jiang* stop working". The Qing government intervened upon the request of the silk loom owners and said "in the future, if there are any unlawful people who dare to make the workers stop and hope to make a profit from it, loom owners and their neighbors can seize him and turn him in to the local authority to be tried. He shall be sentenced in accordance with controlling industry and market law and yoked for one month to show warning."[118] Under the high pressure policy of the Qing government, the activities of *Chuai Jiang* and *Ji Jiang* did not develop further. Their struggles often failed, but the struggles always continued. In the early Daoguang period, in the silk industry in Suzhou, "every time a bandit craftsman tried to force an increase in wage, if he was not satisfied he would threaten by stopping working to erode profit. He even privately pledged the threads on the loom and sold them for money to use. If he was reasoned, he would ask others to stop working and go to work for another loom owner."[119] In the *Chuai* cloth industry there was also a *Chuai Jiang* named Jiang Linyun. He "distributed leaflets and ordered *Chuai Jiang* to stop working and to damage goods."[120]

In addition to Suzhou's *Chuai Jiang* and weavers, Beijing's mint workers also carried out many struggles. In the mint factories affiliated to the Baoquan Bueau and Baoyuan Bureau of the Ministry of Revenue and Ministry of Works, foremen always deducted wages, and abused and ill-treated workers. They"set up instruments of torture, boards, exhibitions in the stocks, Zazi and whips. Where oven workers and other people bent the law for relatives or friends, they would be punished accordingly."[121] The workers could not bear the abuse and turned to resistance. In 1741 (the 6th year of the Qianlong period) more than 2,000 workers from four factories affiliated to the Baoquan Bureau stopped the ovens and went on strike to oppose the deduction of wages by the foremen. The Yamen of the Commander-General of the Metropolitan Infantry Brigade sent troops to suppress them. All the workers "climbed the mounds in the plant, threw bricks and shouted." The infantry actually shot at unarmed people. Later, Emperor Qianlong did not think the suppression was effective. He remarked in red with a brush: "You are too cowardly! There is no harm in killing one or two of such trouble-making people." "Such an evil practice is really disgusting... Order Shuhede and other people to strictly investigate the principal man, who must be punished severely to give a warning to others."[122] In 1816 (the 21st year of the Jiaqing period), a strike was caused because oven foreman pocketed all the additional material silver without sharing with anyone else. "Craftsmen and workers of the Bureau of the Ministry of

Fig. 8.6. A tablet of prohibiting *Ji Jiang* from strike in Yuanhe County in the 2nd year of the Daoguang period

Revenue (refers to the Baoquan Bureau) surrounded and threatened the oven foreman, and made a commotion in front of the Ambassador Hall; craftsmen and workers of the Bureau of the Ministry of Works (refers to the Baoyuan Bureau) openly guarded and closed the gates of the plant, detained the officer, and disregarded all laws and regulations."[123] In other industries the struggle of artisans also frequently occurred. For example, the ruling class said porcelain workers at Jingdezhen "fight over the smallest trifle and seek revenge for even an angry look. If there are very small flaws in the quality of silver, food and so on, they would inform people of the same trade to go on strike, and even gang upto fight with others."[124] "Each kiln needs dozens of people. Once there is something that they do not feel satisfied with, they immediately stop working."[125] Another example was when in 1756 (21st year of the Qianlong period) Zhang Shengming and other paper-making workers from Suzhou "wanted to increase their wage. On the excuse that the workshop owner discounted the quality, they incited workers to stop working."[126] In 1826 (6th year of the Daoguang period) Suzhou candle-making worker Shao Xianzhao and others "ganged up with workers to water candles, collectively stopped work, and collected money and acted violently to shops."[127] In the Jiaqing and Daoguang period there were 6 firework workshops. "Their 400 workers liked fighting. They were always trouble for those who defended the region."[128] The opponents of artisans' struggles were not only workshop owners and businessmen, but also the powerful feudal government standing behind the workshop owners and businessmen. There was a great disparity in the balance of power. The feudal government used the most brutal and ruthless means to deal with artisans who conducted resistance. The workers had no other means of struggle, but only relied on the unity of their team. However the feudal government workshop owners and businessmen always did everything possible to undermine and obstruct the unity of the workforce. The artisans realized the importance of establishing an organization. In 1715 (the 54th year of the Kangxi period), in Suzhou, Wang De and other *Chuai Jiang* (labor working on the last process of cotton cloth) advocated establishing the *Chuai Jiang Huiguan*. Officials of the Qing government strongly opposed this. They accused Wang De and other people "of deluding craftsmen, and taking on filing a lawsuit to wantonly levy for increasing the price of work". "Once this *Huiguan* (會館) is established people without artisan registration will flock in, and its harm will be unpredictable."[129] As a result Wang De and other five persons were caned and driven back to their hometown. In the Yongzheng period, Suzhou weavers "advocated making everyone have a break in the name of *Banghang*(幫行)." Such *Banghang* and *Huiguan* were just organizations that artisans wanted to establish, but the feudal rulers did not allow the appearance of artisans' organizations. After the Qianlong period, until the Tongzhi and Guangxu periods, there were people called "*Xiaojia*" (小甲) and "*Hangtou*" (行頭) in many handicraft industries and transport, quite similar to the leaders of artisans. It was said that "in Suzhou, if there was a business industry, there was a person called "*Xiaojia*". They make trouble and extort. Their actions were really disgusting." "*Xiaojia* in the wood industry has a long history...they are head of the raft artisans."[130] The Qing government did not allow the existence of *Xiaojia* and *Hangtou*. It "strictly orders the abolition, and engraves inscriptions to prohibit this forever". However artisans' organizations could not be completely prohibited. Therefore there were still *Xiaojia* and *Hangtou* in various industries in Suzhou. There were also organizations of artisans in other places. For example, "capital bricklayers and carpenters are mostly from Jizhou, further beyond the eastern suburb of Beijing. Their regulations are quite strict. All apprentice workers have *Huiguan*."[131] Such *Huiguan* were like an association of people from the same place, but their members were apprentice workers and they had the color of industrial workers' organizations. In addition, weavers in Guangzhou organized *"Xijiahang"* (西家行) to oppose the *"Dongjiahang"* (東家行) organized by loom owners. After that artisans continued to ask for increased wages and improved benefits, but to establish *Huiguan* and *"Gongsuo"* (公所) and elect *Hangtou* and *Xiaojia* increasingly became their urgent demand and the goal in their struggle, which was extended after the Opium War and had a more pronounced effect.

Due to their own interests, artisans began by aiming their struggle at workshop owners and businessmen who directly exploited and oppressed them, but development of the struggle was bound to endanger the stability of the feudal order. Therefore the government would always would step forward and actively intervene on the side of workshop owners and businessmen, making the struggles of workers almost always end in failure. Although workshop owners and businessmen as business owners also had contradictions with the feudal government, and opposed government corruption and non-compliance with laws and taxing the people to the bone, workshop owners and businessmen were inextricably linked with the feudal forces. To a great extent they had to rely on the government to survive. At that time, without the government's permission and shelter, there was no room for individual industry and commerce to conduct activities. Workshop owners and businessmen would rather suffer the extortion of the government than make concessions to the demands of the workers. When they were threatened with strikes by the artisans they had no hesitation in asking the Qing Government assistance and protection. In the history of the Qing Dynasty before the Opium War it was very rare that urban industrialists and businessmen associated with artisans to oppose the oppression of the feudal government together, as was seen in the history of Western Europe. The level and characteristics of China's social and economic development determined the degree of weakness and dependence of the urban middle class, which was unable to form a force to counteract the feudal regime. Although urban artisans launched a number of struggles, they were not supported by the middle class. On the contrary there was mutual hostility, and thus the anti-feudal forces were weakened. Therefore the struggles in the cities never developed into a large-scale armed uprising and the main source of strength against the feudal rule was still in the broad rural areas and the vast numbers of farmers.

The anti-Qing uprisings

The earliest large-scale peasant uprising in the 18th century was the Taiwan Zhu Yigui Uprising in 1721 (the 60th year of the Kangxi period). This was a class struggle which occurred in the period when the rule of the Qing Dynasty was stable and its economy was rising. It showed that irreconcilable social contradictions were breeding behind the prosperity of the feudal society.

Zhu Yigui was from a poor family in Changtai County, Zhangzhou, Fujian. In 1713 (the 52nd year of the Kangxi period), he crossed the straits to Taiwan and made a living by raising ducks. He was a knight-errant and made friends with all parties. The official administration of the Qing Dynasty was corrupt. The Taiwan Prefecture Magistrate Wang Zhen "collected tax severely and violently. He arrested 200 people who privately cut wood in the mountains and punished them."[132] In order to object to the persecution by corrupt officials, Zhu Yigui and other people rose in rebellion at Luohanmen on May 14, 1721 (the 19th day of the 4th month of the 60th year of the Kangxi period). In the south, Du Junying and other people "assembled the farmhands from the eastern part of Guangdong at Danshui and Binglanglin"[133] in response. Zhou Yinglong, brigade commander of the Qing Dynasty, led an army to arrest them. The Qing troops killed villagers and burned and plundered villages, thus arousing more anger among the masses. "Therefore many villages successively echoed and erected the flag of rebellion."[134] On May 23, the rebels inflicted a major defeat on the Qing troop at Chi Mountain, and Zhou Yinglong fled in utter confusion. Regional Commander Ouyang Kai led 1,500 soldiers and camped at Chunniupu. The army was frightened at night, and the Qing troop collapsed without fighting. On May 26, the rebels captured Taiwanfu city. Big and small officials of the Qing goverments strove to cross the strait to flee. Zhu Yigui occupied Taiwan Fu, and captured Zhuluo County and Fengshan County. "In seven days, the whole of Taiwan was captured."[135] Zhu Yigui professed himself "Zhongxing King", established title of his reign as Yonghe, conferred titles of duke, general, minister etc. upon his subordinates, and issued a call to arms against Qing. He professed they would: "cross the sea, join forces for a Northern expedition, and water their horses at the Great Wall. Attack his court, kill their ugly class."[136] However, just after the rebels took control of the whole of Taiwan, there was dispute within the rebels. Du Junying wanted to establish his son Du Huisan as King. He did not obey the orders of Zhu Yigui, and his discipline was very bad. "He was arrogant, and looted seven women to keep in his camp."[137] Zhu Yigui and other people stopped his adultery and looting behavior. Du Junying sent troops to fight against Zhu Yigui. The Qing government had lived a peaceful life for a long time. Their generals were proud and the soldiers were lazy. When they encountered a sudden change, they did not know what to do. They organized to launch an attack ten days after the uprising started. Admiral Shi Shibiao and Regional Commander Lan Tingzhen led 12,000 soldiers, and 6,000 sailors to cross the sea to Taiwan in over 600 vessels. There was a dispute within the rebels, and a powerful enemy outside. Moreover the armed forces of the landowners in Taiwan had been active. The rebels were defeated by the Qing troops. At the end of July, Zhu Yigui retreated to Gouweizhang and his subordinates fled away. The armed forces of the landowner cheated him by claiming to "kill cattle to treat them, and allow him to call on strong men from 6 villages to help him."[138] At night, the troops in ambush came out and Zhu Yigui was captured. Although Zhu Yigui failed, he refused to yield. At the trial, "Yigui was still exalted and great. He wanted to meet the admiral as equals, and stood proudly. When he arrived, Tingzhen scolded him to kneel down. Yigui still called himself king and his words were very insolent."[139] He was sent to Beijing and was put to death by dismemberment. After being defeated, Du Junying hid in mountains. In November he accepted the conditions offered by the Qing troop and surrendered,. He was beheaded by the Qing government.

Zhu Yigui's uprising occurred in the late Kangxi period. Although it was still the heyday of the Qing Dynasty, sporadic resistance and struggles rose here and subsided there, and were increasingly frequent. In 1724 (the 2nd year of the Yongzheng period) the magistrate of Wanquan County, Shanxi privately apportioned oppressive tax and thousands of of people went to the town and burned the government office. The magistrate fled by climbing over the wall. In Linfen, because the magistrate cruelly treated the people, the people rushed into the government office, "took off clothes of his dependent, tied him around a pillar and made the magistrate kneel at the hall to be watched...Recently I heard Shandong had a mint consumption charge, eight *qian* (錢) was added on a tael. The people have no means of livelihood. Henan is the same". Various places were not peaceful. Therefore, someone said: "the matter of besieging a city is often seen."[140] During the reign of Emperor Yongzheng, a larger struggle was the uprising of Xie Luzheng from Yuanzhou, Hunan which started in the late Kangxi period. The Qing troops crusaded and arrested people for a long time, but the uprising was not suppressed. Xie Luzheng kept fighting. He "fought for eight years by relying on using dangerous terrain". In the 4th year of the Yongzheng period, a Qing troop of 1,300 soldiers fought against Xie Luzheng. They intercepted, pursued and captured, but did not seize Xie Luzheng because of incapability of the leader. Emperor Yongzheng was very angry. His remarks in red were: "ridiculous. Good Governor-General. Good provincial commander-in-chief. You are so-called experts in judging people's worth and in knowing how to employ them to the best advantage. You can be said to arrange and operate methodically."[141] In 1729 (the 7th year of the Yongzheng period), the masses' anti-Qing uprising led by Li Mei occurred in Guangdong and Guangxi. They threatened to attack Enping County seat. The Qing army dispatched 1,000 people, and searched out 50 criminals and the seal, flag and other things, but Li Mei fled without a trace. After 20 years, in 1741 (the 6th year of Qianlong), Li Mei's brother Li Cai and Li Mei's son Li Kaihua gathered several hundreds of people, and "took weapons, and carried several flags with the Chinese characters of 'heaven and moral conduct'. They all wore a yellow kerchief. The leader wears yellow clothes and takes a sedan chair. I heard that they came to attack Qianjiang County seat."[142] After that Li Mei and Li Kaihua's name were frequently found in anti-Qing movements, and became symbol of anti-Qing struggle. According to the report of officials in the early years of Qianlong period, "after Guangdong rebel Li Mei fled to a western pronvince, there were rumors about him digging a pit and taking out silver. The more absurd, the more people would believe. Even in Hunan, Yunnan and Guizhou, such things really exist". "In Xiangyang, Hubei, someone "uses Li Mei's name to write a rebellion notice."[143] Li Kaihua's name was frequently seen in uprisings in many places. The White Lotus Society, the Heaven and Earth Society and other secret groups often used his name as a call.

In the Yongzheng period there were quite a few anti-Qing struggles in arious forms. In 1729 (the 7th year of the Yongzheng period) the Wuxi magistrate was "cruel and disregarded human life", "villagers were pressed to pay rent and do compulsory labor service, and several hundred of people gathered in Mountain Hudai and almost caused turmoil."[144] The following year an anti-rent incident happened in Chongming, It developed to the level where "shop owners closed their shops", resisted officials and refused to be arrested, and assaulted patrols. In the same year, because the people objected to clearly measuring land and apportion and extortion, mass struggles happened in Zhongzhou, Sichuan. These struggles were not large in scale and the Qing government could control the situation and suppress them, but theft and anti-government activities in various places were very frequent. Around the country, a spark of class struggle often flared up. The official documents of the time disclosed that in Jingsu and Jiangxi, "the number of robbery cases filed in one month was actually 109."[145] "Not only the region south of the Yangtse River generally has many thieves and robbers, I heard that on the roads in Henan, Hunan and Hubei some officials passing by have been robbed. Prefecture and county magistrates bribe the victims to conceal the case together."[146] "Robbery cases in Zhili are usually more than other provinces."[147] "Robbery cases in Guangdong are numerous, and its folk customs are tough and intrepid. An official in charge of rectifying customs should be established."[148] "Hunan and Hubei...People are cunning and savage... Hubei people always do not recognize the law. They regard mobbing and closing businesses as trifling matter."[149] Jiangxi's "custom is savage. There are often cases of resisting officials and refusing to be arrested."[150] The Yongzheng period was known as a period with strict rule of law and stable order. In fact it was not really a peaceful paradise.The Qing government worried about such a situation. Yongzheng repeatedly stressed severely suppressing resistance activities in various places. He said that to clear away robbers was the first task to settle the people down"[151] and took a series of measures. In 1725 (the 3rd year of the Yongzheng period), an inspection official specializing in arresting robbers was set up in each province. In 1726 it was stipulated that cross-border pursuit of robbers did not have to be notified in advance. The government could secretly pursue robbers while sending a notification document, so as to catch robbers quickly."[152] In 1727, penalties for robbers were increased. The imperial edict said that: the capital city and its environs are an important place, and should be safe. Recently, robbery cases are more than in other provinces... Emperor Shengzu showed leniency to robbers ... he only beheaded principal robbers who preplan and hurt people, the remainder were dismissed with an abatement penalty...Since the 1st day of the 5th year of the Yongzheng period, robbery cases in Zhili shall observe the old rules. Both principal criminals and accessory criminals shall be beheaded."[153] In the same year it was stipulated that tenants shall not pay rent in arrear and "bully and slight" landowners. It also prohibited teaching and exercising martial arts so as to prevent mob rebellion. The ruling class racked its brains, took carefully precautions and adopted harsh punishments and strict laws, but it still could not curb the development of resistance and struggle.

In the early Qianlong period, the struggles developed further and were more frequent and intense than in the Yongzheng period. For example, officials in Sichuan said: "throughout Sichuan, in the Kangxi period, there were only more than 10 cases being reheard in autumn; in the Yongzheng period, such cases increased to more than 100 and more than 200 cases. In this year i.e. the 7th year, cases being reheard in autumn were actually as many as 413."[154] Resistance activities of the masses secretly grew, and numerous trickles were bound to converge into a vast river and became a tremendous power to impact on feudal rule. Although in the early Qianlong period the rule of the Qing Dynasty was shining like the sun at noon, some persons of insight felt the hidden crisis. In 1743 (the 8th year of the Qianlong period) Zhao Xianming from Korea was on a diplomatic mission in China. After returning to Korea he talked about the situation of the Qing Dynasty as follows: "It looks peaceful outside, but its inside is actually addled. In my opinion, within several decades, there must be big turmoil."[155] As things turned out, three decades after he said these words, the Wang Lun uprising broke out in Shandong and became a prelude to social upheaval; five decades later the White Lotus Rebellion broke out in Sichuan and Hubei, and the rule of the Qing Dynasty began to decline.

In the early Qianlong period, the larger mass struggles were concentrated in 1743 (the 8th year of the Qianlong period) and 1752 (17th year of the Qianlong period). During the 7th year and the 8th year of the Qianlong period, the region south of the Yangtze River suffered floods for successive years, famine refugees gathered, and cases of looting rice rose in swarms. For example in Jiangxi, "There were more than 160 cases of robbery in the 2nd and 3rd months in the Quanzhou area. The places under Nan, Ji, Fu and Rao followed suit after hearing the news. After the government catches people, it would quieten down. But when one place is put down, robbery in other places rises. The robbery cases are numerous."[156] "In winter of the 7th year and spring of the 8th year of the Qianlong period, Hunan, Hubei, Jiangxi, Jiangnan and other places all had cases of grain robbery. In Jiangxi grain robbery cases were particularly serious. In one county there were actually more than 100 such cases."[157] In this year the situation in Fujian was also very serious. "Scoundrels clustered in hundreds or dozens. They wore white cloths as sign, or held flags and carried weapons, blew conch shells, tied on head cloths, and recklessly robbed and looted."[158] In particular, in the Zhangpu and Zhaoan areas, organizations such as the "Zilong Society" and "Knife Society" appeared. The Zhangpu magistrate went to arrest people who had joined the society but he was killed, causing turmoil of killing officials and besieging the town. In Gutian and Minqing, Luo Huineng etc. gathered many people, forcibly occupied mountain fastnesses, looted rich people, and made a contract out of damask silk with the characters of "Lanlong Emperor Li Kaihua". In Taiwan, because the landowner outrageously locked and completely banned access to the water course and they could not irrigate, Guo Xing and other tenants resisted angrily. They set up flags, called on the masses, and seized camps. The 7th year of the Qianlong period was also an eventful year in Jiangsu. "Chongming, Jingjiang, Dantu and Baoying fabricated disaster to obtain relief, refused to pay rent, and closed businesses to resist officials."[159] The next year Gaoyou, Baoying, Shanyang and other counties "gathered a crowd to close businesses, carried a statue of god to harass the law court and government office, and extorted to relieve victims."[160] In this year Hubei also suffered floods. In the Jingkou and Jiangling area, "flood victims became bandits using the flood as an excuse. They named themselves the

Luokang Society, and gathered women and men to extort rice and grain in the name of borrowing". "Anlu, Jingmen and Jingzhou bordered with each other, and ignorant stupid villagers followed their example after hearing the news."[161] In Liling, Baling, Leiyang, Xingning and Hengshan in Hunan there occurred a wave of rice robbery by the poor because well-off families raised food prices. In Guizhou "villagers in Bijie County extorted to borrow rice and grain and street people closed businesses."[162] In Sichuan there was "Guolu" activity. According to official documents in the 8th year of the Qianlong period, "idlers from Hunan, Hubei, Jiangxi, Shaanxi, Guangdong and other provinces studied martial arts and can use talismanic water to control penalties. They seduced unworthy villains in Sichuan, wore broad swords, and acted recklessly in small groups called "Guoluzi".[163] From the above various records it can be seen that in the 7th and 8th year of the Qianlong period, in the region south of the Yangtze River, incidents occurred repeatedly and contradictions were very acute.

The scale of the frequent stirring up of trouble about relief, robbery of rice, forming gangs and resisting officials then was small, and most of them were out of economic requirements and were largely spontaneous. Ten years later i.e. in 1752 (the 17th year of the Qianlong period), resistance activities reached a new peak after a relative downturn. At that time the features were: the spearheard of the struggle was directed at the Qing government, and the political color was more intense. In this year the anti-Qing case of Ma Chaozhu was unearthed. Ma Chaozhu carried out activities in Luotian, Hubei and Huoshan, Anhui for many years. He fabricated miracles, contacted the masses, professed to have a book on the art of war, a precious sword, a mythical flag, etc., organized anti-Qing activities and acted in the name of Zhu Hongjing, a descendant of the Imperial Family of the Ming Dynasty and Li Kaihua. Most of his followers were "poor farmers who dug hills and made charcoal". His adherents were spread throughout Anhui, Hubei, Hunan, Henan, Sichuan, Jiangxi and other places. The Qing government uncovered this case. Ma Chaozhu led people to guard the Tiantang Stronghold but was defeated by Qing troops. More than 200 people were arrested, but Ma Chaozhu fled. The Qing court searched for him but was unable to catch him. Seven years later (the 24th year of the Qianlong period), Jesuit Missionary Loo almost turned pale at the mention of searching for Ma Chaozhu. "In order to arrest a well-known traitor ... a lot of innocent people were arrested, tried and imprisoned ...because of a little bit of suspicion... In rumor, if Ma Chaozhu's name was mentioned, not only were people uneasy when they heard it but also a kind of terror was disseminated... I have been arrested two or three times as I was regarded as his fellow. My fellow travelers were very astonished. Fortunately,

I was set free soon."[164] In the same year He Yasi from Shangrao, Jiangxi, who "made a living by farming and making charcoal", dug 370 tael of hidden silver out of a piece of land. Physiognomist Li Dexian said that he had great fortune in his fate and abetted him to provide the funds for casting a seal, making banners and making broad swords and canes. He said there would be secret assistance from heavenly soldiers who would kill people with flying knives. He also used the names of Li Kaihua and Zhu Hongzhu, and gathered local villagers to fight with the Qing troops. At the same time, scholar Cai Rongzu and Taoist priest Feng Heng from Zhangzhou, Fujian formed an alliance and worshiped heaven. They recruited the masses, made military weapons and gunpowder, and plotted together to raise troops and established the "State of Great Ning". Because their secret was revealed, the case was discovered. In addition, in Dongguan, Panyu, Boluo, Zengcheng and other places in Guangdong, Mo Xinfeng etc. gathered many people to form an alliance, bound soldiers and seized prisoners and engraved seals. They also rose in rebellion in the names of Li Kaihua and Zhu Hongzu. There were many other struggles in the early and middle Qianlong period. In addition to the climax of struggles in the 7th, 8th and 17th years of the Qianlong period, in 1739 (the 4th year of the Qianlong period) Liang Chaofeng preached "heresy" and set up a banner and rose in rebellion in Yiyang, Henan. He and female religious leader Cai became sworn sister and brother. Cai had the nickname of "a branch of flowers". There was folk rumor as follows: "a branch of flowers is 17 or 18 years old, and can hold off a large number of mounted and foot soldiers". "People worship her, and call her female Comander-General. Quite a lot of people echo her incitement. Some people call her yulan magnolia mother, some people call her god. They are all sorcerers. The evil gods worshiped by them are Three-religion Grandmother, Twelve Old Mothers and Nine Dragon Mother. On the 1st day and 15th day of the lunar month they lure villagers to burn incense and seduce them into joining the religion." [165] In 1746 (11th year of the Qianlong period) the Qing government unearthed the Mahayana religion. The religious leader Zhang Baotai lived in the Jizu Montains, Dali, Yunnan. Zhang Baotai opened a hall to preach and professed to be the 49th Shouyuan Zushi. As early as in the 10th year of the Yongzheng period, Zhang Baojiu was captured by the government and died in prison. However the Mahayana religion spread very widely. Its adherents were all over Yunnan, Guizhou, Sichuan, Hunan, Hubei, Jiangxi, Jiangsu and Zhili. In the 11th year of the Qianlong period a major raid was carried out. Many people were implicated. In 1748 (the 13th year of the Qianlong period) the Fujian Ouning Laoguanzhai religion (i.e. Luo Religion) assembled over 1,000 people to set up flags and held sorcerers' dances. They worshiped "Wuji Shengzu" and planned to loot rice and break into a jail and rescue prisoners. They shouted out the banner slogan of "act for god" and "persuade the rich and aid the poor". In 1768 (the 33rd year of the Qianlong period) Xiao Ran and other people "making a living by making charcoal" from Gutian and Pingnan, Fujian became sworn brothers and rose in rebellion. They prepared banners and seals, established "Huguo General", "Governor-Marshal" and other official titles, and plotted to attack Gutian county seat and seized a warehouse by force. In the same year Huangjiao in Gangshan, Taiwan resisted arrest by the government. They gathered people to rise in rebellion, burned camp houses, and fought with Qing troops for half a year. In 1771 (the 36th year of the Qianlong period) Yan Shilong, He Shirong and other people from Jingshan, Hubei gathered many people to become sworn brothers. They privately made clothes and hats, established official titles, and plotted to seize warehouses. They had a seal engraved with "Saving the Central Plains" and used "Tianyun" as a reign title. These resistance struggles were not large in scale and many times they were unearthed and suppressed by the Qing government before they openly rose in rebellion. However the clear trend was that they had developed from pure economic requirements to have some political aims. They made use of religion, miracles, burning incense and becoming sworn brothers to enhance the call and unity, and established official titles, put forward simple political views, recruited soldiers and made weapons, and consciously planned to prepare for armed struggle. Compared with resisting payment of rent and grain, claiming relief and looting rice, these resistance activities were more organized and more persistent, and more threatening to the feudal regime. The people's resistance and fighting spirit were increasingly strong. Finally in 1774 (the 39th year of the Qianlong period) the Qingshui Religion uprising led by Wang Lun from Linqing, Shandong broke out. This uprising opened the prelude to peasant uprisings in the mid-Qing Dynasty. After that civil religions and societies such as the White Lotus Society and the Heaven and Earth Society spread like a rising wind and scudding clouds, anti-Qing struggles were continuous and their scale was bigger and bigger, forming a new situation of blazing class struggles at the end of the 18th century.

Civil Religion and Secret Organizations

The spread of the White Lotus Society

In the Qing Dynasty, civil religion and secret societies were prevalent. Many large-scale peasant uprising made use of religion and societies, for example the White Lotus Rebellion, the uprising of the Heaven and Earth Society, the Taiping Rebellion and the Chinese Boxer Movement, and even the 1911 Revolution led by the bourgeoisie was closely related to a society. This historical phenomenon gave the false impression that the spread of civil religion and secret societies produced uprising and revolution. In fact this was certainly not the case. Religion and societies themselves were not the reasons for struggle. On the contrary, they were the product of struggle. It was the intensification of mass struggle that made civil private organizations aimed at worshiping Buddha, doing good deeds and forming an alliance to help each other revolutionary, and they became a tool for the people to start an uprising. Of course civil religion and secret societies played a very important role in promoting anti-feudal struggle. Before an uprising started they were an effective means for the revolutionary party to hide and accumulate forces and publicize revolutionary opinions. After the uprising started, they were an organizational form of commanding the masses in carrying out armed struggles. When social contradictions became increasingly sharpen, the long-term smoldering of resistance among the masses was bound to break forth and blaze. The Qing rulers carefully prevented resistance activities by the people and suppressed them very severely. The revolutionaries urgently needed a means to promote and organize the masses to adapt to the development of the situation, avoid the attention of the Qing Dynasty and quickly attract the masses to the revolutionary side. If they could not do so, revolution and uprising could not be launched. However this means must be adapted to the level of consciousness of the farmers. It had not only to defend the interests of farmers but also be understandable and acceptable by the masses. In feudal society, farmers were generally lacking in culture and uneducated. They believed in gods, miracles and supernatural powers and hoped they could be blessed by the god in the struggle against the landowner class. Civil religion and secret societies provided organization means and spiritual strength for the lower classes. The doctrines and myths looked to be absurd on the surface but they could lead people to reject the reality and turn to resistance, and could inspire their joy in struggle and confidence of victory. Engels said: "These uprisings are like mass movements in the Middle Ages, always wearing the cloak of religion ... but behind the religious fanaticism, a real secular interest is hidden every time."[166]

The most important civil religion and secret society in the Qing Dynasty had two systems: one was the White Lotus Society and the other one was the Heaven and Earth Society.

The White Lotus Society was a civil religion which was very widespread and launched large-scale uprisings many times. It had a long history which could be dated back to the Eastern Jin Dynasty. It originated from the Pure Land Sect of Buddhism and deemed the ideal of the white lotus pond in the Western pure land as the final destination. At the early stage it was just a general religious organization and was spread among the lower class masses. After experiencing all kinds of evolutions it turned into an organization opposed to the feudal rule. In the late Yuan Dynasty, Han Shantong spread the White Lotus Society, burned incense and gathered people, which developed into a peasant uprising in the late Yuan Dynasty. Under the rule of the Ming Dynasty the White Lotus Society continued its activities and organized a number of uprisings. In the late Ming Dynasty, 'White Lotus societies were throughout the country. Wherever a founder or leader of religion was, people gathered around him."[167] In 1622 (the 2nd year of the Tianqi period of the Ming Dynasty), the White Lotus rebellion led by Xu Hongru broke out and shocked the rule of the Ming Dynasty. In the early Qing Dynasty, the White Lotus Society was still active. In 1645 (the 2nd year of the Shunzhi period), in the Xuanhua and Shuozhou area, the Huangtian Qingjing Shanyou Society organized the masses to resist against the Qing troops. They were powerful and dynamic. "Enemy soldiers, armed with spears, broad swords, bows and arrows, filled the fields."[168] Another example was Wang Fengxie, Dong Baixian etc. from Daocheng and Wuji, Zhili, who spread the White Lotus Society. They "professed as if they were drunk and crazy, they actually dared start an uprising."[169] This group once besieged Zhendingfu City. From very beginning, the Qing Dynasty strictly prohibited the activities of civil religions. It issued orders repeatedly to ban folk religions and took all kinds of repressive measures. "Since establishing the capital, our dynasty only administers the country in accordance with Yao and Shun's political letters and martial arts from generation to generation. Therefore strict laws are made against heresies. Penalties including being cangued, being caned, imprisonment, banishment, being hanged, being beheaded and being put to death by dismemberment, and their seriousness shall be determined in accordance with the level of the crime committed."[170] In the 3rd year of the Shunzhi period, "order the Court of Censors, Five City Censor, police Yamen, provincial governors and other officials to strictly arrest immediately and punish as felonies if they encounter various religious sects."[171] Due to the harsh repression by the Qing rulers, and decentralization and the loose organization of folk religious organizations, religion heads in different places secretly set up branches, and independently developed their strength.

As a result, in the White Lotus Society, there were numerous branches under various names. Among them the more famous were Wenxiang, Dacheng, Longhua, Hunyuan, Wuji, Wuwei, Xiantian, Shouyuan, Bagua, Tianli, Qingshui, Yuanjiao, Sanyang, Changsheng, Qinglian, Luozu, Hongyang, Huangtian, Shanyou, Jiumen, Shimen, Randeng, Xilai, Qingchamen etc. Among so many sects, some did not belong to the same system as the White Lotus Society but their doctrines and classics were basically the same. Some of them changed their names to avoid being tracked down by the Qing government; their names were different, but they had the same content. They all derived from the White Lotus Society. These sects were scattered throughout the country, relied principally on the lower classes, secretly carried out activities and spread widely, so no powerful force and harsh criminal law could destroy them all. Once the conditions were ripe civil religion, just like kindling buried among the masses, would flare up and finally cause a prairie fire.

In the process of spreading among the people, the secret religions created and published a number of scriptures. "For every society that is established, a scripture shall be published."[172] The doctrine of each sect had its own characteristics but they also have common content, generally containing the following three aspects:

The genesis doctrine

This is the fundamental doctrine of the White Lotus Society and other sects. It believed that the world was originally chaos Qi, and later it turned into a goddess named Eternal Mother (no birth mother). It was said that "Eternal Mother emerged earlier than heaven". Then, "Eternal Mother gave birth to a female and a male."[173] They got married, and multiplied to produce 9.6 billion imperial sons and daughters. These children fell to the red dust world in the east, and thus the world appeared. Due to this genesis doctrine they thought that all the ordinary people in the world were the "children of no birth parents, and were born in the heavenly palace, so the heavenly palace was their hometown,"[174] which was called the "pure (vacuum) land". The "pure land" was the place of birth of ordinary people and also their final destination. Eternal Mother sent Maitreya Buddha to descend to the world to save the masses of mankind. As long as one joined the religion and conducted religion practices, one could be saved from falling into hell and be raised up to "bliss country", called "returning Yuan to the hometown". "Come to the east, lost in the red dust world. Send you a letter from home and tell you to meet at Longhua", "Eternal Mother saves the masses of mankind to ascend the heaven together."[175] Accordingly, the so-called "Eternal Mother" became "creator" and "savior". The "eight character real words" worshiped and chanted by the White Lotus Society and other sects, the so-called "pure land and Eternal Mother" sum up the fundamental doctrine of this "Genesis Doctrine".

At first glance, this genesis doctrine was only a non-scientific concept about the universe and the formation of the world, did not touch on the ideological content of feudal rule at all, and was even not a program for peasants' struggle. It just looked forward to a "blissful" life in the "pure land" and getting eternal life from the "Eternal Mother". Therefore even the rulers of that time thought that "religious bandits use the 8 characters of 'pure land and Eternal Mother' to fool people. This expression is unreasonable and perverse."[176]

Why did the "eight character real words", which appeared to be meaningless and absurd, become a powerful slogan mobilizing the peasants to revolt? It was because the White Lotus society and other religious sects had characteristics that general religions did not have. Its doctrines were closely linked with real life, and the "eight character real words" can be explained with changes in social contradictions. It led people to aspire to and pursue the "pure land", "heavenly palace" and "paradise country" and was also a direct rejection of the real world and showed dissatisfaction with the "red dust world". In the Ming Dynasty they claimed that "the throne of the Ming Dynasty cannot remain stable"; in the Qing Dynasty it was proposed to "defend and assist the Ming Dynasty" and that "sun and moon are combined to restore the Great Ming."[177] With the deepening of feudal exploitation, social contradictions became increasingly intensified and the vast majority of farmers were in dire straits. The doctrines of religion reflected the requirements of the poor farmers to a certai n extent, who yearned for "Eternal Mother" to lead them to change the real world and walk to the "pure land" as to end their sufferings in reality. These opinions were already the highest ideal for small producers and individual farmers.

The "eight character real words" publicized the bliss state, which was fundamentally opposite to the real social system. The so-called "pure land" showed dissatisfaction with the real world. Of course it was deemed as"heresy" by the rulers of the Qing Dynasty, and the White Lotus Society was also described as "heresy" and was severely suppressed.

The doctrine of three periods of time

In order to adapt to the poor people's discontent with the present situation and desire to pursue an ideal future, the White Lotus Society

Fig. 8.7 Spell handbill of the White Lotus Society

and other sects thought occurrence and development of the world experienced three stages or three periods of time of past, present and future, and called them the "doctrine of three periods of time". The theory of three periods of time is actually is hodgepodge of some viewpoints of Buddhism, Taoism and Ming Confucianism. It holds that the "past" is called Wuji, the cyan sun is in power, and Dipamkara is in charge of it; the "present" is called Taiji, the red sun is in power, and Buddha Shakyamuni is in charge of it; the "future" is called Huangji, the white sun is in power, and Maitreya is in charge of it. The core of the doctrine of three periods of time is to preach development and change in the world. The sufferings in the past will be ended, and coming of a good world in the future can be expected and struggled for. Now is the time that the red sun and the white sun are in an alternating position. Such alternation is the so-called "*jiebian*" (劫變, disaster change), when the "disaster of the red sun ends, and the white sun rises". "*Jie*" is a concept in Buddhism. Its original meaning is continuation of time, and it is extended to mean disaster. Buddhism preaches that the experiences of the whole universe and of human beings are full of small or big disasters. The universe is a big sea of disaster. After experiencing numerous disaster changes, the world will become empty. Buddhism uses negation of the material real world to lead people to look forward to and seek the non-material other side of the world. However, in certain conditions, the disaster change doctrine of secret civil religion contained rejection of the current feudal rule. The real red sun world brings endless disaster, people are going to suffer, and the world will have a great change. As long as people convert to Eternal Mother and are under the charge of Maitreya, the white sun will be in power and they will enter into a heaven of joy where "heaven and earth have no differences and people have no difference between being young or old, life and death, and also have no female appearance."[178] The "doctrine of three periods of time" and "doctrine of disaster change" put forward a forthcoming good world in opposition to the real world. Once the people firmly believed that heavy suffering could be got rid of and a happy new era would come, they would not hesitate to fight and make sacrifices for it. Therefore the ruling class said that such religious thought "tempts the idiotic and stupid by seek benefit and escape disaster."[179] They "stealthily plot the future, and it is really a reason for plotting rebellion."[180] "Those who join its religion will go to heaven; those who don't join its religion will fall into hell. Those who join its religion can avoid disaster and ascend to heaven, and those who do not join its religion will have a big disaster and fall into a sea of suffering."[181] The White Lotus Society and other religions achieved the power of mobilizing the masses and encouraging the masses through these false and absurd religious doctrines.

The concept of equality of "same wealth and same variety"

The so-called "same wealth" stipulated that "when joining the religion, it does not matter how much subscription money based on wealth are paid, and the amount of Shengdan silver paid quarterly can vary."[182] "After joining the religion, all properties obtained in the religion are equally shared."[183] "People learning the religion do not take money and food, and share clothes and food when joining other groups."[184] They also advocated "helping those that need help, and traveling around in the world without taking any money."[185] The so-called "same variety" advocated eliminating distinction between various varieties, including eliminating distinctions between young and old, men and women etc., thus eliminating all desires. In their scriptures there were expressions such as "men and women originally have no difference; they all rely on the natural *Qi* (氣) of Eternal Mother,"[186] and "order that men and women throughout society do not need to distinguish between each other."[187] This concept of equality of dividing property equally and eliminating differences had a great attraction for the long-suffering lower class masses.

The scriptures of various religious sects had a strong folk color. Most of them were written with popular tunes at that time. Some them used Qingjiangyin, Zhuyunfei, Huangyinger, white lotus tune and other tunes in Kun Opera, and some of them used the talking and singing lyrics of Wujingdiao, Dashizhixian, Dalianhualuo and Bangziqiang. The doctrines of religions were preached in the forms loved by people. Such preaching was easy to understand, easy to chant, and easily accepted by the lower classes. In addition they also "served as doctor or physiognomist or did business to go to villages and teach religions in person."[188] Through practicing medicine and treating diseases for the poor, teaching martial arts, relieving victims of natural calamity and other means, their influence increased and they were welcomed by the vast number of farmers, small handicraftsmen and vagrants. Of course, these folk sects took individual small producers as their mass base and had their ideological limitations. They had spread in feudal society for a long time, so were inevitably influenced by feudal orthodox thinking and hierarchy concept. Therefore, in the doctrines of the religions, there was a lot of superstitious, backward and conservative thinking. They not also absorbed the doctrines of Buddhism and Taoism, but also adopted Confucianist thought; not only worshipped the Eternal Mother and Maitreya, but also dragged in the Jade Emperor, Confucius and various figures in myths and legends to be worshipped. Many scriptures were full of hackneyed talk of doing good deeds and cultivating moral character, and the concepts of being loyal, righteous and filial, the three cardinal guides and five constant virtues, observing fate and being law-abiding, and incarnation and retribution. In normal times many sects were monopolized by a small number of hereditary missionary families and became tools for them to grab money and get rich. Religious leaders had privileges and gradually became fat wealthy men. There were also an order of superiority and inferiority, clear duties, and a strict hierarchy within religious sects. In an period of intensified class struggle a large number of bankrupt and unemployed lower classes flooded into secret religious organizations. Accordingly, revolutionary factors were greatly enhanced, the sects became active, and the direction of activity and scope of these sects changed so they emerged from the latent state and met and called for the arrival of revolutionary storms with a thriving, high-spirited, robust and brave posture.

The Founding of the Heaven and Earth Society

The White Lotus Society was a folk secret religion with a long history, but the Heaven and Earth Society was a lower-class secret society that only began to appear in the Qing Dynasty.

There are different opinions about specific the age and founder of the Heaven and Earth Society. During the 1911 Revolution in China, revolutionary Tao Chengzhang engaged in the work of mobilizing the society. He explored its history and purpose, studied many instances within the society, and wrote a book entitled *Origin of the Church*. He thought the Heaven and Earth Society was an anti-Qing organization established by adherents of the Ming Dynasty. "The first advocator was Zheng Chenggong. Chen Jinnan followed, improved and maintained it". According to this opinion, Zheng Chenggong died in the 1st year of the Kangxi period, but the time of advocating the Heaven and Earth Society cannot be later than this. The second opinion was based on "the 25th day of the 3rd month of the year of Jiayin in the Kangxi period of the Qing Dynasty was the date when the Hong Gang became sworn brothers or sisters."[189] The year of Jiayin of the Kangxi period was 1674 (the 13th year of the Kangxi period), so some think that, "the founding year of the Heaven and Earth Society, passed down by the Hong Gang, was Jiayin, the 13th year of the Kangxi period of the Qing Dynasty."[190] The third opinion holds that "Jiayin" should be Jiayin of the Yongzheng period, not Jiayin of the Kangxi period. This opinion is based on a statement in the *Chronicle of Xilu* in *Historical Materials of Modern Secret Societies* compiled by Xiao Yishan, which specifies that the Heaven and Earth Society was founded on "the period from one to three a.m. of the 12th month of the Yongzheng period". Thus the founding of the Heaven and Earth Society was 60 years later, delayed to 1734 i.e. Jiayin of the 12th year of the Yongzheng period.[191] The fourth opinion holds that the Heaven and Earth Society was founded in 1761 (the 26th year of the Qianlong period).[192] It is mainly based on the memorial to the throne by Fujian Governor Wang Zhiyi in the 4th year of the Jiaqing period. He said that "I follow the order to investigate bandits of the Heaven and Earth Society, originated in the 26th year of the Qianlong period. Bandits in Zhangzhou and Quanzhou hatched a sinister plot, secretly colluded with each other and spread to Taiwan."[193] Another memorial to the throne by Wang Zhiyi said: "It is found that the Heaven and Earth Society in Fujian Province started in the 26th year of the Qianlong period. It was first advocated by Monk Tiyi from Zhangpu County."[194] There is a fifth opinion which thinks that the Heaven and Earth Society was founded in 1767 (the 23rd year of the Qianlong period). It is mainly based on the memorial of Sun Shiyi, Governor of Guangdong and Guangxi, to the throne in the 52nd year of the Qianlong period attached with the confession of Xu Axie, a member of the Heaven and Earth Society. Xu Axie explained an argot of the Heaven and Earth, which was "*Mu Li Dou Shi Zhi Tian Xia*" (木立斗世知天下). "*Mu* refers to the 18th year of the Shunzhi period; *li* refers to the 61st year of the Kangxi period; *dou* refers to the 13th year of the Yongzheng period; *shi* refers to fact that the Heaven and Earth Society was founded in the 32nd year of the Qianlong period, so it is hidden by using character *shi*."[195] Because the Heaven and Earth Society was a secret association, it only started to be known after Lin Shuangwen from Taiwan led the Heaven and Earth uprising in the 51st year of the Qianlong period. Prior to this the Qing government had not found any activities of the Heaven and Earth Society. Accordingly, there was no record of the Heaven and Earth Society in government files and private records, and the Society itself did not leave any documents or data. Therefore, at present, it is still hard to determine the exact time of its founding. However from the data seen so far the opinion that the Heaven and Earth Society was founded in the middle Qianlong period seems more credible. This is because: first, the first three opinions which say that the Society was founded in the period of Kangxi, Yongzheng or earlier are mainly based on documents of the Society itself.[196] The *Preface of Xilu* is really a fairy tale which was created later to add interest to the Heaven and Earth Society. It is not a real history, so it cannot be used to assert the founding time of the Heaven and Earth Society. Members of the Heaven and Earth Society at an earlier stage did not know the story in the *Preface of Xilu* because after the Lin Shuangwen uprising, the Qing court made great efforts to find out about the origin of this Society from members that had been Earth captured and confessions of many members did not mention this story. Secondly, in the Kangxi and Yongzheng period, not many secret organizations were unearthed by the Qing court. In the Qianlong period the number of discovered secret organizations greatly increased and the names of secret organizations numbered as many as several hundred. Before the 51st year of the Qianlong period, there was no name of Heaven and Earth Society. If the Heaven and Earth Society was founded very early, the Qing Government could not know anything about it during its long-term expansion and activities. Thirdly, when Qing officials vigorously investigated the founder and year of founding of the Heaven and Earth Society, there was no view that it was founded in the Kangxi and Yongzheng periods. Sun Shiyi said it was founded in the 32nd year of the Qianlong period, and Wang Zhiyi said it was founded in the 26th year of the Qianlong period. Regarding these two views, Sun Shiyi said when his was put forward it was still at the early stage of the investigation, and investigation work was still being conducted (early 52nd year of the Qianlong period), and Wang Zhiyi said that his view was put forward after the end of the investigation (the 4th year of the Jiaqing period). Wang Zhiyi's view is the final conclusion of the investigation, and should be more credible.

Like the White Lotus Society, the emergence of the Heaven and Earth Society was also a product of gradually intensified class contradictions after the Qianlong period. In the archives of the Qing Dynasty there were a total of 215 secret society cases. Among them, 199 cases were unearthed after the 20th year of the Qianlong period, and there were only six cases before then. The emergence of the Heaven and Earth Society was connected with intensified class struggle.

Fig. 8.8. **Notebook of the Heaven and Earth Society hidden by Yao Dagao, leader of the Heaven and Earth Society in Donglanzhou, Guangxi (the 7th day of the 5th month of the 16th year of the Jiaqing period)**

According to existing information, the Heaven and Earth Society first appeared along the water and land transport lines in Fujian and Guangdong regions, neither in the rural areas nor in cities with concentrated handicraft industry. During the Yongzheng and Qianlong periods of the Qing Dynasty, due to intensive land acquisition, many farmers were thrown off the land. On the other hand, development of the commodity economy needed a large labor force engaging in goods transportation, and many farmers who left the land and lost their means of livelihood engaged in such transport work which did not require much technology but was very heavy labor. Their lives were unstable, as they had no fixed employers or fixed positions. If there was work to do, they were employed workers; if there was no work to be done, they became unemployed vagrants. This was a group of people who followed rivers and lakes to seek for adequate food and clothing. They left their familiar environment and work where they had grown up, came to an unfamiliar place with complete strangers, engaged in unfamiliar work, and lived a life with certainty of food. They were alone, wandered everywhere, had no one to turn to for help, and were unable to resist the blows of all kinds of disasters and the oppression of underworld forces. The weak suffering the same fate required organization and mutual assistance to protect their right to survive. In order to maintain life, the lower class masses mutually connected and organized to become a powerful social force, which was the source of the Heaven and Earth Society. As the Qing officials said: "All items of the Heaven and Earth Society originated from inland, and were privately handed down. There is a kind of loafer bandits who make trouble and disturb people, called Luohanjiao. As the Heaven and Earth Society represents safety in numbers, they all obey and join the Heaven and Earth Society. If one does not belong to the Heaven and Earth Society, he will be robbed. Therefore those who have a little property and vendors had to obey them for fear of being robbed, and members of the Heaven and Earth Society along the two south-north routes are increasing."[197] "When anything crops up they help each other. In the Society there are also local people, but 80% to 90% of them are people from other places."[198] Most of the early members of the Heaven and Earth Society were poor laborers including transport workers, small vendors, artisans, vagrants and farmers. From the confessions of captives from the Lin Shuangwen uprising collected by the archives, it can be seen that the occupational situation was as follows (excluding participants after the outbreak of the uprising):

Occupation	Number of people
Small vendor	11
Hired worker	9
Farmer	6
Runner	1

In the Jiajing and Daoguang periods the Heaven and Earth Society developed considerably. Some poor lower-class intellectuals participated and some rich people also joined the Society, but in general small vendors and hired laborers accounted for the majority. According to 226 leaders and backbone members in 28 cases of the Heaven and Earth Society in the Jiaqing and Daoguang periods kept in China No.1 History Archives, their occupations were as follows:

The occupation distribution of members of the Society as reflected by the above two incomplete statistics have two characteristics. One is that they were poor. In the Qianlong period, no one from a well-off family joined the Heaven and Earth Society. In the periods of Jiaqing and Daoguang, only 1% members came from a well-off family. The second is occupational mobility. The first characteristic shows that at first, the Heaven and Earth Society was mainly a voluntary organization of poor laborers and was an instinctive struggle for survival by the helpless. It lacks historical basis to say that the Heaven and Earth Society was an anti-Manchu organization manipulated by the landowner class with the purpose of overthrowing the Qing and restoring the Ming. The second characteristic meant that this secret organization had its own characteristics. It was neither similar to historical secret organizations of the people nor similar to secret organizations which existed simultaneously

Occupation	Number of people
Small vendor	32
Farmer and vendor	58
Hired laborer and trader	36
Hired laborer	9
Farmer	9
Artisans (including part-farming persons)	8
Poor intellectual	18
Monk	4
People from well-off family	2
Runner	6
Unknown persons[199]	44

such as the White Lotus Society. It had a strong ethic of equality but lacked of authoritative ideology. Its organization developed rapidly, but lacked uniform leadership. It fought bravely, but lacked discipline. These characteristics became increasingly obvious with its rapid development. Although for a long period of time in the future it developed rapidly, had many members, and was powerful and dynamic, it never formed a very powerful force in the struggle against the feudal government. At its early period it did not organize and initiate a big uprising like that of the White Lotus Society, which covered five provinces and continued to for ten years. In its later period it could not achieve military successes like the Society of God-worshippers. Until the demise of the Qing Dynasty it had been an auxiliary force instead of the main force in various great struggles.

When it was first appeared, the Heaven and Earth Society could not be said to be political. It had a strong self-defense and mutual aid nature. Yan Yan, who was arrested in the 53rd year of the Qianlong period and was the first to spread the Heaven and Earth Society in Taiwan said in his confession as follows: "The reason to join this society was originally because it can subsidize money for marriages and funerals; it can assist in fighting with others; if a robber is encountered they will not rob as soon as the password of the same society is heard; if one spreads the doctrine of the society to others, one can get remuneration. Therefore a lot people are willing to join this society."[200] Confessions of members of the Heaven and Earth Society from Guangdong and Fujian, who were arrested before this, were generally similar. In general members of the Heaven and Earth Society did not join for an obvious political purpose and their daily activities were not of an anti-government nature. However the government could neither protect the people nor allow the people to protect themselves. China's feudal regimes in various dynasties uniformly strictly prohibited assembly and association of the people because feudal autocratic governments most hated social organizations. The country was the only social organization. When the people could only deal with national authority as loose sand-like individuals, the national authority was at its most solid. Therefore any association was prohibited or controlled. In the view of the government, an association was perhaps cover for a rebel organization. In the 51st year of the Qianlong period, after the activities of the Heaven and Earth Society in Taiwan was exposed, officials severely suppressed it, investigated endlessly, and implicated the innocent, which so members of the Heaven and Earth Society were in a situation where regardless of rebellion or no rebellion, death was the only prospect. Finally the Lin Shuangwen Uprising broke out. In the existing over 20 documents of the Lin Shuangwen Uprising, the slogans are still about being oppressed by officials and sweeping away corrupt and evil officials. After the Li Shuangwen Uprising the Qing Government prohibited the Heaven and Earth Society very strictly, and included it in the Great Qing Code. The spearhead of the Heaven and Earth Society was directly turned against the Qing government, and it put forward the slogan of "overthrow the Qing and restore the Ming". In the dissemination process, many works publicizing "overthrow the Qing and restore the Ming" were compiled by many unknown small intellectuals. Among them, the most famous one was the *Preface of Xilu*. It was a political declaration of the Heaven and Earth Society and contained neither religious preaching nor obscure language. Through a tragic story it exposed the fact that the Qing rulers returned kindness with ingratitude, persecuted good people, and were unconscionable, fatuous and self-indulgent rulers. Only by overthrowing them and re-establishing the country of the Han people could "clarifying the Yellow River" be realized, and people live a peaceful life. The Heaven and Earth Society developed from a self-defense and mutual assistance organization into a political organization with a clear political objective. This change was closely related to the intensification of social class contradictions at that time and the bad administration of officials of the Qing Government.

The Heaven and Earth Society was spread to Taiwan by immigrants from Fujian to Taiwan in the Qianlong period. After the Jiaqing period, the Society was successively spread to Jiangxi, Guangxi, Hunan, Hubei, Zhejiang, Guizhou and other provinces and to Southeast Asia through overseas Chinese, and gradually became an important secret anti-Qing organization in the region south of the Yangtze River. The spread of the Heaven and Earth Society was carried out under strict prohibition by the Qing government. In order to avoid official eyes and ears, the Heaven and Earth Society used different names such as Tianti Society (founded by Su Ye and Chen Sulao from Tongan, Quanzhou, Fujian in the 57th year of the Qianlong period), Knife Society (in the 59th year of the Qianlong period, Zheng Guangcai and other people from Zhanghua, Taiwan formed a society which was so named because all the people who joined the society carried a knife), Heyi Society, Sandian Soceity, Honglian Society, Shuangdao Society, Baizi Society, Jianghuchuanzi Society, Reyisanxian Society, Parents Society, Carriers' Society (which was spread to Hunan in the late Jiaqing period. Most people who joined the society were carriers, so it was named Carriers' Society), Equal Head Society (it appeared in the 25th year of the Jiaqing period. Because "members of the society were addressed as equals", it was named Equal Head Society), Sanhe Society (it was first founded in the 11th year of the Daoguang period), Protect Home Society etc.[201] There may be many names which have not been found yet. Regardless of the names of these organizations in different regions at different times, their purposes, forms and ways of activities all maintained the appearance of the Heaven and Earth Society. Before the Opium War, the Heaven and Earth Society was the most powerful anti-Qing organization in the southern provinces.

Internal Struggles of the Ruling Class during the Kangxi and Yongzheng Periods

Two removals of the crown prince

Historically, in addition to struggles between rulers and the ruled, and exploiters and exploited, internal struggles in the ruling class have also varied in intensity from time to time. Power struggles, mutual suspicion and deception, and subversion and exclusion, were the normal state of internal relationships in the ruling class in feudal society. In order to scramble for power and profit, conflicts happened between father and son, between brothers, and between husband and wife, to the level of life and death. Usurping, robbery, murder and seizing by force were very common in history. This completely abandoned the warmth of natural bonds and ethical relationships between family members, tore aside the thin veil of virtue and filial piety, and nakedly exposed the ferocious and bloodthirsty nature of the ruling class. The Qing Dynasty, as a feudal dynasty, also had power struggles within the ruling class. However the focus and forms of expression of the power struggles were different from previous dynasties. The feudal autocratic right of the Qing Dynasty was the most centralized, and imperial power overwhelmed other powers. In view of the lessons learned from previous dynasties, the Qing rulers took a series of preventive measures against various forces that might infringe on or usurp imperial power. The powers and scope of activities of the empress dowager, relatives of the emperor on the side of his mother and wife, eunuchs, cliques and influential officials and border ministries were strictly suppressed and controlled. Therefore, in the three hundred years of the Qing Dynasty, except when Empress Dowager Cixi in the late Qing Dynasty intervened in political affairs, there were no serious disasters caused by the interference of such people as had occurred in the Han, Tang, Song and Ming Dynasties. The emperors in the early and mid-Qing Dynasty generally handled state affairs in person. They arrogated all authority to themselves and firmly grasped the central power. There was neither an open threat of usurping and murdering the sovereign from other forces, nor a situation where power fell into other hands, influential officials usurped political power, and the emperor was manipulated. The internal struggles of the ruling class of the Qing Dynasty were mainly over the succession of imperial power. After an old emperor passed away, intense contending around which prince would succeed to the throne usually took place. The ascent to the throne of Huangtaiji and Shunzhi had set off a political storm, and the transfer of imperial power from Emperor Kangxi to Emperor Yongzheng experienced long-term intense contention and led to turmoil in the political order.

Kangxi had 35 sons and 20 daughters in total. Among them, 20 sons and 8 daughters grew to adulthood. Kangxi's first empress was Empress Xiaocheng, granddaughter of Suoni. She and Kangxi had profound conjugal love. In 1674 (the 13th year of the Kangxi period), Empress Xiaocheng gave birth to Yinreng (the second prince), but died of dystocia. The next year, Kangxi established Yinreng as crown prince. This crown establishment method complied with the rites of inheritance by the oldest son of the wife of the Han imperial family of the previous dynasty, but it did not conform to Manchu tradition. The oldest son of the wife inheritance method was used in order to clearly determine the successor early on to put an end to coveting and prevent contending. However establishing the crown prince too early would also make ministers toady to the crown prince for future high official positions and riches and gang together for clandestine and illegal activities, and thus virtually formed a second center of power and even caused intense conflict between emperor and crown prince, such as with Emperor Wu of Han and Crown Prince Li, and Taizong of Tang and Crown Prince Chengqian. It was at this point that Kangxi repeated the mistakes of history.

Yinreng was clever and well versed in both polite letters and martial arts. Emperor Kangxi loved him very much. He said Yinreng's "riding, shooting, language and literature were not inferior to others". French Missionary Joachim Bouvet, who worked in the court then, praised that "the crown prince is well-read and has high attainments in Chinese", "His handsome appearance is the most perfect in the imperial clan of the Beijing court of the same age. He is a perfect crown prince, so everyone in the court praises him.[202] Kangxi employed the most famous scholars Zhang Ying, Li Guangdi, Xiong Cili, Tang Bin and Geng Ji as his teachers to teach him to read. Kangxi often took him and other princes to go hunting or on inspections. Sometimes, when he went on an expedition, Kangxi ordered Yinreng to stay in Beijing and handle state affairs to provide experience for him. Important matters could be determined by the crown prince.

The long-term position of crown prince made a group of forces attached to and supporting him gather around Yingreng. These forces were led by Suoetu. Suoetu was the son of Suoni and uncle of Empress Xiaocheng, Yinreng's own mother. In the early years of the Kangxi period, Suoetu was trusted with important positions and many meritorious ministers and influential officials came from his family. Suoetu's power was very great and overriding. He and Mingzhu, another influential official conflicted with each other. "Suoetu was high-born, arrogant and presumptuous. He discarded those who did not attach themselves to him, and only had a good relationship with Li Guangdi. Mingzhu was humble, regarded money lightly, and liked to give in charity to attract new peoples. He used conspiracies to trap aliens, and took up with Xu Qianxue and others. Suoetu treated the crown prince well. However Mingzhu stealthily worked against those ministers serving the crown prince. He recommended Tang Bin as teacher of the crown prince for the purpose of subverting Tang Bin."[203] The Mingzhu group was impeached by Censor Guo Xiu in the 27th year of the Kangxi period. Mingzhu was dismissed from the position of grand secretary, made grand minister of the imperial household department, and was not trusted with an important position any longer. Afterwards, when the crown prince grew up, his influence gradually developed and he began to have contradictions with Kangxi himself. In the Wulanbutong battle in 1690 (the 29th year of the Kangxi period) Kangxi went on expedition himself. On the way Kangxi was ill, and he called Yinreng and the third prince Yinzhi to him. Yinreng and other people rode quickly to the temporary dwelling place to pay their respects. He "did not look distressed at all, which was shown in by words and expressions. The emperor thought Yinreng was not patriotic and loyal to his imperial father. He was very unpleasant, and ordered him to go back to the capital first."[204] The ruling class carefully avoided mentioning any struggle for the central power, and did not leave written records. Therefore, today, we know very little of what happened at that time. We can only see that the relationship between the Emperor and Crown Prince was deteriorating from some clues. In 1694 (the 33rd year of Kangxi period) the Ministry of Rites worked out the rites of sacrifice and put the crown prince's kneeling mat inside the threshold of the Hall of Ancestral Worship. Kangxi ordered it moved outside the threshold. Shamua, minister of the Ministry of Rites, feared that the crown prince would him blame in the future and requested the imperial instruction be written on file, which showed the fear of the minister of the crown prince's clique. Kangxi was so unhappy that he dismissed Shamua from his position. In 1697 (the 36th year of the Kangxi period), Kangxi executed Huala from the imperial kitchen and other people who privately worked for the crown prince. It can be seen that there was a major rift between Kangxi and his son. Kangxi had to weaken and cut off the forces of the Crown Prince. The next year, Kangxi conferred titles upon his sons. The first son Yinti was conferred Zhi Prefecture Prince, the third son Yinzhi was conferred Cheng Prefecture Prince, and the fourth son Yinzhen, the fifth son Yinqi, the seventh son Yinyou and the eighth son Yinsi were conferred Beile. His sons had titles and were also cultivating their own trusted followers. They coveted the position of crown prince and were ready to make trouble, making the situation more complicated. Accordingly, members of the crown prince's clique were more anxious and fearful.

In 1701 (the 40th year of the Kangxi period), Suoetu retired because of old age. The following year Emperor Kangxi took the crown prince to implement an inspection tour of the south. When arriving at Dezhou, Emperor Kangxi suddenly announced a halt to the southern inspection and a return to Beijing. The reason was that the crown prince was ill, and he was left in Dezhou for recuperation. Strangely it was the retired Suoetu who was ordered to Dezhou to serve the crown prince. It is possible that a plot of the crown prince's clique had been discovered and Suoetu was called in to interrogate him. The inspection tour of the south was postponed for two months. In the following year (the 42th year of the Kangxi period), after the inspection tour of south had just ended, Suoetu was immediately imprisoned for "complaining and discussing state affairs seriously at the Emperor's back." Suoetu and his people lost trust of Kangxi, and felt the position of the crown prince had been threatened, so they complained, hated Kangxi, avidly mustered adherents was and had an axe to grind. Kangxi blamed Suoetu that "your complaints at the back can't be publicized", and said "I point out one corner of conducts, you can be executed here", and "If I don't anticipate, you will anticipate", and "you show your power and threaten. Could it be said that the people in the whole country fear you?"[205] Soon, Kangxi put Suoetu to death. After many years, Kangxi still had a deep-seated hatred of Suoetu. He said: "Suoetu is really the worst sinner in this dynasty."[206]

This sudden storm was the outbreak of long-term accumulated conflicts. Moreover once the two power centers openly confronted each other there was no room for compromise and reconciliation. Although all was kept quiet for five years after Suoetu was punished, and there was nothing disclosed in the files, struggles were carried out by undercover means. The relationships between Kangxi, the crown prince and the princes were very tense. Yinreng was still at a disadvantage since he was suspected by Kangxi above and was trapped by the princes below. Another and larger blow was bound to fall on him. In October 1708 (the 8th month of the 47th year of the Kangxi period), Emperor Kangxi issued an imperial instruction accusing princes of whipping and insulting ministers. "You want to divide my authority and let you wantonly act. You do not know it is impossible to divert even a little power to others." At that time his eighteenth son Yinjie was seriously ill. Emperor Kangxi seemed to have some important problem and wanted to go back to Beijing urgently, so he hastily departed and returned to Beijing. Halfway there he announced the removal of the crown prince. He "convened officials, and instructed with tears: 'I see that Yinreng does not follow the example of the virtuous deeds of the ancestors and does not obey my instructions, only wantonly does evil things and mistreats people. He is ruthless, tyrannical and sexually promiscuous. I have tolerated him for 20 years. He does evil things rampantly, insults princes, Beiles, ministers and officials in the court, grabs all the power, gathers adherents, pries into my living and all my actions... More astonishingly, he approaches cracks of my tent and peeks inside every night. In the past, Suoetu helped him secretly plan for great events. I knew everything so I put Suoetu into death. Now Yinreng wants revenge for Suoetu, he gathers adherents, making me not know whether I will be poisoned today or will be killed tomorrow. I have to be vigilant, prudent and restless day and night. How can I trust the great course of the ancestors to such a person?' After giving his instructions the emperor fell to the ground with a great cry."[207] It can be seen that the power struggle had made the relationship between father and son deteriorate to the point of life and death. Kangxi was not timid and incompetent. In face of the threat from the crown prince's clique, Kangxi had to remove the crown prince and imprisoned him.

Emperor Kangxi's other sons were also drawn into the conflict. All of them were very talented. A foreign missionary said: Among the fourteen older princes, "ten princes are handsome and talented."[208] Many of them were opposed to Yinreng and did not play a helpful role in the relationship between Emperor Kangxi and Yinreng. Once Yinreng was removed and the position of crown prince was vacant, they would all come out to contend in a mad rush to be the first. The first prince Yinshi was also liked by Kangxi. He was often ordered to go on an expedition or handle political affairs. He was older than the crown prince, but he was not established as crown prince because he was the son of a concubine. After Yinreng was removed he hoped that according to the rule of "establishing the oldest", the crown would fall on his head. He brazenly encouraged Kangxi to kill Yinreng. He said to Kangxi: "Now, if you want to kill Yinreng, it is not necessary that it be done by imperial father", showing he would kill Yinreng. Kangxi was very angry. He denounced Yinti as a "rebel and traitor, who is not allowed to exist by heavenly principles and national law". The third prince disclosed that Yiti once asked a Lama to curse Yinreng by wizardry, making Yinreng insane. Kangxi believed that the absurd conduct of the crown prince was the result of Yinti's curse, so he deprived Yinti of the title of prince and had him imprisoned for life.

Yinsi, the eighth son of Emperor Kangxi had great energy. He was talented and good at currying favor with people. He had a lot of folloers and was ambitious. He also had deep contradictions with Yinreng, and attempted to murder Yinreng. A physiognomist named Zhang Mingde "once practiced physiognomy on Yinsi and said that Yinsi must be have noblility in the future". After these plots were exposed, Yinsi was scolded severely by Emperor Kangxi: "The eighth prince tries to win an inflated reputation everywhere. He contributes all the forgiveness and bounty I did to him, so he is praised by everyone. What can I do? You are another crown prince! If one praises you, I will immediately kill him. How can I agree to give this power to others?" "Yinsi is apparently gentle, but inside he is treacherous. He is ambitious for the throne. I know it very well. His followers gang together. He plotted the murder of Yinreng. He has been exposed. Catch Yinsi with a lock and deliver him to the Deliberative Council to deal with."[209]

Those who were imprisoned included the third prince Yinzhi, the fourth prince Yinzhen (i.e., Emperor Yongzheng) and the fifth prince Yinqi. According to the *Outline of General Annals of the Imperial Family of Qing* by Hongwang (son of Yinsi), on the 11th month of the 47th year of the Kangxi period, "the emperor did not feel well. The third prince, Emperor Shizu (Yongzheng), the fifth prince, the eighth prince and crown prince was set free". It can be seen that when the crown prince was removed the first time, at least six princes were imprisoned. The first prince Yinti was not set free because his crime was too big. The princes imprisoned included Yinzhen, who ascended to the throne later. However details of how Yinzhen contested for the position of crown prince and of his imprisonment cannot be found in official books and files. Probably, these files were destroyed. Later, when Yongzheng was emperor, he made a self-confession which reflected the contradictions between him and Yinreng. He said: "someone suspects that I did not get along well with the second prince. When the second prince was crown prince, he was the future emperor. Before the second prince committed an offence I only performed my duties of being younger brother and minister. I was respectful and cautious in everything. Because our late imperial father showed me favor and gave me deep affection, the second prince was afraid that I would hinder him. Therefore he did something not good for me. Nevertheless, I only performed my own duty and revered and obeyed him. All this is well known."[210] These words of Yongzheng showed he wanted to dress himself up as law-abiding and honest without ambition, but the remaining fragments of historical data and his own words show that in the contest for throne, he was also one of those who contested very energetically.

An old feudal autocratic ruler who is at the peak of power for a long time often worries about power falling into the hands of others and is afraid that there is a center of power beyond his control. Therefore he is suspicious and fickle, always on guard and handles affairs erratically and indecisively. In his later years it seems that Emperor Kangxi was in such a situation. Two months after Yinreng was removed i.e. in the 11th month of the 47th year, Emperor Kangxi ordered courtiers to discuss and establish a crown prince. Emperor Kangxi had not expected that the courtiers would unanimously recommend the eighth prince Yinsi. Among the courtiers were Tong Guowei (brother of Kangxi's wife), Maqi, grand academician of the Wuying Hall, Alinga (son of Ebilong and brother of Kangxi's concubine), commander of the imperial guards, Eluntai (son of Tongguogang), Kuixu (son of Mingzhu), Wang Hongxu, the Han Minister etc. There were also members of the imperial clan such as Yu Prince Baotai (Kangxi's nephew), sons and grandson of An Prince Maerhun, Wuerzhan and Sehengtu, Beizi Sunu. Moreover the ninth prince Yintang, the tenth prince Yine and the fourteenth prince Yinzhen (later renamed Yinti) were on friendly term with Yinsi. Yinsi enjoyed great popularity, which not only did not please the old emperor but led to suspicion. Kangxi chided Tong Guowei and Ma Qi. In the third month of the 48th year, Kangxi made an unexpected move. He re-established Yinreng as crown prince. The reason was that due to being cursed by wizardry Yinreng had suffered from madness, so his behavior was abnormal. Now that his madness was cured he was re-established as crown prince. The measure caused chaos and panic among ministers. Because Kangxi had solicited opinions on establishing the crown prince, ministers had stated their views publicly and supported Yinsi. However the result was that Kangxi blamed them for ganging up for clandestine and illegal activities, and re-established Yinreng as crown prince. Ministers did not know what to do and sighed "there is a death in two places." Even the Korean envoy commented that Kangxi's action was inappropriate, "he had just removed the crown prince, and then restored his position. He hit Ma Qi, but still let his son be an official. His way of handling affairs is very disordered." "The first prince has been imprisoned for four years, but the emperor still does not set him free... Other princes often do things undesirable, so the emperor feels troubled often acts abnormally. Big and small ministers feel as if they are sitting on a bed of nails."[211]

In this struggle for political power the relationship between Kangxi and Yinreng had already broken down and was hard to make up and compound. The facts showed that Emperor Kangxi's removal and re-establishment of the crown prince were all hasty decisions taken without careful consideration and rehabilitative measures. Moreover Yinreng's arrogant and willful character had been cultivated for a long time and his ambition to seize power remained. It was recorded by a Korean that: "The crown prince is cruel in nature. It is openly said among the people that he is disloyal and unfilial, and secretly commits adultery with his sisters. No other princes are crueler than the crown prince". "The crown prince is Scottish, voluptuous and impenitent. He sent people to rich places in three provinces to seek a bride, ordering them to buy beautiful girls. If his wish is even slightly not met he will conduct bring false charges... Ministers close to him from the cabinet to ministries ask him to help, and he surely practices favoritism and commits irregularities". It was also said: "it is heard that crown prince has revolted. He often said: has there been a 40-year crown prince under heaven from the ancient ancients to nowadays? From his words, we can know his nature and conduct."[212] After Yinreng was re-established as crown prince, a group of followers very quickly gathered around him. Emperor Kangxi warily watched their activities. Commander-in-chief of infantry Tuoqisu, Minister Genge, Qi Shiwu and other people who attached themselves to the crown prince were put to death by Kangxi immediately. In the end of the ninth month of the 51st year of the Kangxi period, Kangxi removed the crown prince again. In the imperial instructions, it said: "Yinreng's madness has not been cured. He loses the support of the people. The great course of the ancestors can never be trusted to this person." "Yinreng is cruel in nature, and forms a gang with bad villains. Because I am his father, Yinreng had no disloyalty, but the villains fear that they will be killed in the future. If they do mischief to me it connects with my reputation throughout my life."[213] The removal of the crown prince this time seemed to also have some connection with other princes. Matteo Ripa, an Italian missionary who worked in the Qing court and returned to Beijing with the emperor from Rehe, witnessed the scene when the crown prince was removed again. He recorded: "when we arrived at the Changchun Garden, we saw with horror that in the garden there were eight to ten officials and two eunuchs kneeling, bareheaded and their hands tied back. Not far away, princes were standing in a row, bareheaded and their hands tied at their chests. Soon the Emperor was shouldered from the room to in front of the princes by sedan chair. He shouted out his anger like a tiger's roaring, blamed the crown prince, shut him in the palace and publicly announced removal of this unfortunate prince."[214]

Long-term disputes around establishing a crown prince made Emperor Kangxi resentful, depressed and mentally and physically exhausted. Thereafter Emperor Kangxi did not establish a crown prince again until he passed away. Moreover this issue also became a secret anguish in his heart. He did not allow people to discuss it. Those who suggested establishing a crown prince were either killed (Zhu Tianbao) or demoted (Wang, Tao Yi etc.). The princes still secretly carried out activities, took up with followers, cultivated trusted followers and spied out opportunities. The so-called "princes respectively establish private gangs. If Kangxi passes away, state affairs can be known."[215] After two removals and establishments, the opportunities and strength of the princes contesting the position of crown prince had some changes. Former crown prince Yinreng and the first prince Yinlu suffered failure. They were imprisoned for life. Although they were still active and hoped for revival, in fact they already had no hope of inheriting the throne. Another prince who suffered serious failure was the eighth prince Yinsi. He was talented, had many adherents and seemed a quite possible selection, but he was too powerful and too active. He provoked Kangxi's doubts and abhorrence, and was severely rebuked. In the imperial instructions in the 53rd year of the Kangxi period, it said: "Yinsi was brought into the world by a low-born woman of Xinzheku. He has been insidious since he was a little boy. He listened to the words of physiognomist Zhang Mingde, so he greatly violated the principles and duties of being a minister. He hired people to murder the second prince, which was known by the whole nation... He formed a gang with rebels and traitors etc. and secretly implemented malicious things. He said that I was already 70 years old and did not have much time to left, and when I died who would dare to dispute as he had been recommended by ministers, so he said he cannot fail under any circumstances. I fully understand his unfilial and unjust position...

The relationship of father and son between I and Yinsi must stop. I am afraid that there will be a prince in line with dogs and pigs, who will start a war and cause disaster to force me to abdicate and make Yinsi emperor by relying on his bounty. If so, I can only smile and die...Because he was not established as crown prince, Yinsi hated me to the core and all his followers hate me to the core. The second prince often lost the support of the people. Yinsi often ties up the will of the people. This person is 100 times more dangerous than the second prince."[216] Kangxi's words were this unsympathetic. The relationship between him and Yinsi was as incompatible as water and fire. Yinsi also could not legally inherit the throne. He and the ninth prince Yintang, the tenth prince Yine and other people turned to support Yinti.

At this time, the most promising heir to the crown seemed to be the fourteenth prince Yinti. Yinti's original name was *Yinzhen* (胤禎), who was born to the mother of the fourth prince *Yinzhen* (胤禛) (i.e. Emperor Yongzheng in the future). Emperor Kangxi had praised him as "really a good general" and "having the ability to lead troops, so the emperor ordered him to be in charge of important tasks of life and death."[217] Yintang said that he was "extremely clever" and "has talents and virtue, other brothers are inferior to him."[218] Yinti was younger and was not deeply involved in the contention for the position of crown prince in the early period, but he was on friendly terms with Yinsi. When Emperor Kangxi removed the crown prince for the first time in the 47th year of the Kangxi period and arrested and imprisoned Yinsi, Yintang and Yinsi begged for forgiveness for Yinsi. In 1718 (the 57th year of the Kangxi period), when the Junggar troops entered Tibet and invaded Hami, the western line was tense. Yinti was appointed as Fuyuan General to be in charge of the western military affairs. It was a major appointment, concerning the safety of Qinghai, Tibet and the Northwest region and the stability of the Qing dynasty. The power of the general was very great and the level of rites was very high. At that time Yinti was only a Beizi, but he could use the plain yellow banner feather decoration and prince system and was called general prince. This appointment gave some people the impression that the old emperor had fixed his mind on him. Therefore when Yiti went out to war, Yintang said that "Lord No. 14 goes out to war and the emperor attaches great importance to him, so he must be crown prince in the future."[219] Yinti was stationed in Qinghai and Gansu for four years. He defeated the Junggar, and achieved military renown. Because military affairs were not completed he did not withdraw troops from the front. At that time Emperor Kangxi died. Yinti, who had once seemed to have the possibility to succeed to the throne, was far away on the western border. He was too far away to be able to help and his dream of achieving the crown came to nothing.

Yongzheng's succession to the throne

The death of Emperor Kangxi and succession of Yongzheng to the throne was over 260 years ago. So far no adequate and reliable documents have been found regarding this historical mystery, and its truth and details are difficult ascertain. According to official records, what happened was as follows:

Fig. 8.9. Portrait of Yongzheng

In the eighth month of 1722 (the 61st year of the Kangxi period), Emperor Kangxi hunted for a month in Rehe. After returning to Beijing, he went to hunt in Nanyuan. It seemed that his physical condition was normal. On the seventh day of the eleventh lunar month, he went back to the Changchun Garden and said he "occasionally caught a cold." It seemed that it was not a serious illness and it improved day by day. At that time he ordered the fourth prince Yinzhen to go out and live in a fasting place so as to carry out the great sacrifice on the emperor's behalf on the winter solstice in the southern suburbs. In the early morning of the 13th day, Kangxi's condition suddenly deteriorated, so he called the princes to speak to them. Between three and five o'clock in the morning, the third prince Yinzhi, the seventh prince Yinyou, the eighth prince Yinsi, the ninth prince Yintang, the tenth prince Yine, the twelfth prince Yintao, the thirteenth prince Yinxiang and Longkeduo, commander-in-chief of the infantry and minister of the Ministry of Tribal Affairs went to the imperial bed, and were given the imperial edict as follows:

"The character of the fourth prince Yinzhen is good, and he is very similar to me. He certainly can inherit the position of emperor. I order him to succeed me to ascend the throne and be the emperor."

When this edict was issued, Yinzhen was not present. When he reached the Changchun Garden it was already between nine and eleven o'clock. He went to see and ask after Kangxi three times. At that time Kangxi could still speak and he "told me the reason why his condition was increasingly worse." When Kangxi passed away between seven and nine o'clock in the morning, the imperial edict of Kangxi before his death was announced and stated to Yinzhen by Longkeduo. It was said that Yinzhen was not mentally prepared to be emperor, "I was shocked and grieved, and fell in a faint after hearing it". Yinzhi and other people kowtowed to him, so he ascended the throne and changed the designation of the imperial reign to Yongzheng.

On the subject of this official record there have always been two opinions. One thinks that the official record is basically credible. Yongzheng's succession was lawful and was based on the last decree of Emperor Kangxi before his death. The other does not believe the official record and thinks that Yongzheng usurped the throne on the pretext of an imperial edict. When Emperor Kangxi was at his last gasp, Yongzheng and Longkeduo controlled the situation. They could deliver a false imperial edict and seize the throne. Even the death of Emperor Kangxi was very suspicious. Both of these views have some basis, but the basis is also inadequate. The *Real Record* of the Kangxi period recorded Kangxi's death in detail, but the record was compiled and corrected during the reign of Emperor Yongzheng and what it says is naturally favorable to Yongzheng. Existing files have also been compiled and corrected or destroyed by Yongzheng, and no obvious evidence of usurping was left. If we completely believe these materials and compile history according to them, we will inevitably recognize the legitimacy of Yongzheng's succession. It is not fair only to believe one side of the story and not to listen to the appeal of the other party in a trial. However in the harsh environment at the time, the other party could not lodge and leave a sufficient and powerful appeal. We can only see some rumors recorded in the *Dayi juemi lu,* which say that the Yongzheng's plots to usurp the throne were devious and clever, and the situation was very different from the record in the official books. "Emperor Shengzu originally bequeathed the throne to '*shisi a ge*' (十四阿哥, the fourteenth prince) and the new emperor changed *shi* (十, meaning "ten") into *yu* (于, meaning "to"). It was also said when Emperor Shengzu was seriously ill in the Changchun Garden, the new emperor presented a bowl of ginseng soup. Somehow, Emperor Shengzu passed away, and the new emperor ascended to the throne. Then he called Yunti back to imprison him. The empress dowager wanted to meet Yunti. The emperor was very angry and the empress dowager killed herself by crashing herself on an iron column, and the emperor also left his concubine and other imperial concubines in the palace". We need to assume that these rumors came from Yongzheng's political enemies. How many of them are credible? The historical mystery is difficult to solve through the ages. Today it is difficult to put forward sufficient and certain bases to judge whether Yongzheng usurped the throne on the pretext of an imperial edict.

After making a comprehensive survey of a variety of materials, we can see that there are some doubts and flaws in the account of Emperor Yongzheng's succession to the throne. The time of granting and receiving was not clear, and statements of defense had contradictions. We can only raise the problems with the attitude of remaining neutrals.

The plot of Kangxi's bequeathing the crown to Yongzheng before his death had obvious flaws. According to the *Dayi juemi lu*, when Emperor Kangxi was in critical condition, the testamentary edict on the inheritance of the crown was given to eight persons (Yinzhi, Yinyou, Yinsi, Yintang, Yinge, Yintao, Yinxiang and Longkeduo) before Yongzheng arrived at the Changchun Garden. Moreover Yinlu, Yinli, Yinyang and Yinwei "were all waiting respectfully out of the sleeping palace." This was the most powerful proof of Yongzheng's legal succession. However, after studying all kinds of materials, we have reason for suspicion. Eight people were instructed with the testamentary edict at the same time because Yongzheng arrived at the Changchun Garden within one *shichen* (two hours) and was called to meet Emperor Kangxi within ten hours after the "eight people were instructed with the testamentary edict". At that time Emperor Kangxi could still speak and he "told me the reason why his condition was increasingly worse", but he did not say a word about the fact that he had instructed the eight people on bequeathing the crown to Yongzheng in person. Did Emperor Kangxi forget it? Did he want to keep it a secret from Yongzheng? Thise does not seem reasonable. Moreover these eight persons did not mention this event of paramount importance to Yongzheng until Emperor Kangxi died and Longkeduo conveyed the will of Kangxi. Later Emperor Yongzheng said that "I never had any desire for the throne. I really thought it was a miserable thing. On the 13th day of the eleventh month last year, my late imperial father began to issue an imperial edict. I actually did not know about it. If I knew, I would have had my plan. After my late imperial father passed away, the imperial edict was announced to me."[220] Moreover, when hearing the imperial decree, Yongzheng was "shocked and grieved, and fell in a faint after hearing it". The process was too bizarre to be believed. A reasonable explanation is there was no event of "eight people being instructed with the imperial edict". This was a scene fabricated by Yongzheng to prove his legal succession because the *Dayi juemi lu* was produced in the ninth month of the 7th year of the Yongzheng period, and there was no record of "eight people being instructed with the imperial edict" in preceding documents. In the eighth month of the 1st year of the Yongzheng period, the emperor instructed: "Shengzu...ordered me to succeed to the throne. On the 13th day of the eleventh month last year, the major program was determined in a word hastily."[221] Here too there was no mention of "eight people being instructed with the imperial edict". In the tenth month of the 5th year of the Yongzheng period, the record of princes being instructed with the imperial edict appeared, but the princes were not named. The imperial edict said: "before he passed away, my late imperial father called my brothers and Longkeduo for an audience. He instructed the imperial edict in person, and delivered the throne to me. Among the ministers, only Longkeduo received the imperial edict."[222] The *Dayi juemi lu* named seven princes and Longkeduo as witnesses to Yongzheng's legal succession. However among these eight people, Yinsi and Yintang had been murdered, Longkeduo died in prison, and Yine was still in prison. None of them could come out to deny this issue. Yinzhi and Yintao committed offences, one was stripped of the title of prince and the other of the title of prefecture prince, and Yinyou was too frightened and only sought to survive. Yongzheng praised him as "abiding, obedient and careful". How could the three men dare to come out and make trouble? Yinxiang was a confidant of Yongzheng. Yongzheng praised him as "a virtuous prince, and no one has been more loyal and considerate to the country than him since ancient times". In the usurpation on the pretext of imperial edict, he probably made contribution. The scene of "eight people being instructed with the imperial edict" was revealed by Yongzheng seven years after Emperor Kangxi died, and of course no one could come out to deny it. Furthermore, some words said by Yongzheng himself were also contradictory with "eight people being instructed with the imperial edict". Yongzheng said that both Yinsi and Yintang received the imperial edict from Kangxi in person, so they "are willing to be obedient, say nothing and acknowledge allegiance to me". However Yongzheng also said that "on the day when my late imperial father passed away and I was in sorrow, Saiqihei (Yintang) suddenly came in front of me and sat face to face with me with his legs stretched out. He was arrogant and impolite, and his intention could not be estimated. If it was not that I was calm and tolerant, it would inevitably have caused trouble."[223] "When Emperor Shengzu Ren passed away, Aqina (Yisi) was not sad. He stood alone and meditated, leaning against a column out in the courtyard. When he was asked to handle affairs, he took no notice and did not answer. His disagreement and anger were obvious."[224] Yinsi and Yintang's behavior did not look as if they already knew the imperial edict 16 hours previously but were indignant when hearing the news that Yongzheng was to ascend to the throne. Furthermore the scene of "eight people being instructed the imperial edict" had Yinli, the seventeenth prince, and other people waiting outside the imperial sleeping palace but Longkeduo said that "on the day when Emperor Shengzu passed away, I returned to the capital first. Guo Prince (i.e., Yinyou) was on duty in the palace. When he heard the great event, he went out of the palace and met me at Xizhimen Street. I told him that the emperor would ascend to the throne. Guo Prince looked wild and unreasonable, similar to mad. I heard that he ran back to his mansion and did not receive anyone and waited for the emperor in the palace."[225] It seems that Yinli did not wait outside the imperial sleeping palace at all, and he did not know the imperial edict on bequeathing the throne to Yongzheng when he was on duty in the palace in the city. When he heard the news of Kangxi's death, he left for the Changchun Garden and met Longkeduo at Xizhimen Street. Only at that time did he discover that Yongzheng was to ascend to the throne. He was astonished and so he fled home. However Yinli could trim his sails to the wind. Later he attached himself to Yongzheng, impeached Yinsi and was granted the title of Guo Prince. After Yongzheng passed away, he was ordered to assist in handling state affairs in the imperial edict left by Yongzheng before his death. A stranger thing is the offence of Longkeduo. In the imperial edict in the 5th year of the Yongzheng period, it said: "On the day when Emperor Shengzu Ren passed away, Longkeduo was not in the presence of the emperor, and did not send our attendant either. He falsely alleged that he took a dagger to prepare for any contingency."[226] Longkeduo was a key figure in the succession case in the period between Kangxi and Yongzheng. When Emperor Kangxi died, he must be beside Kangxi. However in order to fabricate crimes, Yongzheng talk recklessly and even denied the presence of Longkeduo. It can be seen that the reality of "eight people being instructed with the imperial edict" is extremely doubtful.

Of course, folk rumors cannot be completely believed. For example, it was said that Kangxi's testamentary edict "bequeath the fourteenth prince the crown" (位十四皇子) was changed into "bequeath the crown to the fourth prince" (位于四皇子). This view has been denied by experts because according to writing patterns in the Qing Dynasty, Yinti was written as "the fourteenth prince" (皇十四子) and Yinzhen was written as "the fourth prince" (皇四子). The first character *"huang"* (皇) could not be omitted. Therefore it was impossible to change *"shi"* (十) to *"yu"* (于). However to deny this folk rumor does not exclude Yongzheng's usurping on the pretext of an imperial edict. Emperor Kangxi's intention might have been to bequeath the crown to Yinti, and it also could be that the emperor did not have time to designate his successor before he died. His sudden death created an opportunity for Yongzheng. Matteo Ripa, a missionary who was in Beijing at that time, said that "after ascending to the throne, Yongzheng issue an order shocking the whole country. Zhao was arrested and put to death. His property was confiscated and his children became slaves."[227] Zhao refers to Zhao Chang. Although his status was not high, he was an attendant of Kangxi in his later years and often conveyed Kangxi's orders. Why did Yongzheng want to kill him as soon as he ascended the throne? Why did the death of this person shock the whole country? A reasonable explanation is that Zhao Chang knew too much and was not willing to follow Yongzheng, so Yongzheng had to get rid of him immediately. Moreover on the eighth day after he ascended to the throne i.e. on the 27th day of the 12th month of the 61st year of the Kangxi period, Yongzheng issued an order and required ministers to turn in Kangxi's decrees with remarks written in red with a brush. "All the decrees with remarks written in red with a brush of my late imperial father shall be presented after being sealed. Anyone who is found in the future to have copied, kept, concealed, burnt or discarded them in the future shall never be forgiven and shall surely be severely punished". Was it because he was worried there were some evidence unfavorable to his succession to the throne that he took back the former emperor's own handwritten comments in such a hurry? Then Yongzheng turned the spearhead on his brothers. First he recalled Yinti, who had the military power and was most likely to inherit the throne, to Beijing. Yinti felt angry and ill-used when he found the throne was seized. Yongzheng rebuked him as "ignorant, unfilial, arrogant and proud". As soon as he came back to Beijing, Yinti was put under house arrest. He was sent to guard the tombs. At the same time, other princes were segregated, pushed out and attacked. Yine was sent to Zhangjiakou and soon was imprisoned for life. Yintang was first sent to Xining. Later he was called to Baoding and was killed. Yinsi was left in Beijing. He was both talented and powerful. At first he was conferred with the title of Prince of Lian and exercised general supervision over state affairs. This was Yongzheng lulling him into a sense of false security. Yinsi knew this. He privately said: "the emperor grants grace today. How do you know whether it means not being killed tomorrow? All his favors given at present are unreliable."[228] As expected, Yinsi was constantly accused and attacked. His supporters were killed or exiled. Finally Yinsi was also murdered during imprisonment for no apparent reason. In addition, Yinzhi was stripped of his title and imprisoned because he "formed a gang with Aqina, Saiqihei and Yinti. Hongsheng, his son, is fierce, unrestrained, wanton, wild and hard to control, and helps his father do evil."[229] Yintao was also dismissed of his title for something. Yongzheng hated Yinsi and Yintang most. Yinsi was renamed Aqina (dog), and Yintang was renamed Saisihei (pig). On one hand there was certainly animosity and a profound accumulated rancor between them in the later years of Kangxi; on the other hand, because they were unwilling to fawn on and echo new emperor, and exposed situation of his usurping, which greatly damaged Yongzheng's political reputation.

When problem of the princes was gradually resolved, Yongzheng turned on Nian Gengyao and Longkeduo who helped him become an emperor. Nian Gengyao was originally an old friend of Yongzheng. His younger sister was Yongzheng's concubine. He served as governor-general of Shaanxi, handled logistics for the west expedition army, and was in a favorable position to monitor Yinti. Longkeduo was the son of Tong Guowei. Their family originally belonged to Yinsi's party, but Longkeduo himself turned to support Yongzheng at a critical time. He was both the only minister who got an imperial posthumous edict and brother of the empress. He worked as commander-in-chief of the infantry and held the military power of guarding Beijing and the Changchun Garden. Without his help, Yongzheng could not have seized the throne. In the early years after Yongzheng ascended to the throne, he was grateful to these two ministers who had made great contributions, and tried his best to win them over. Their relationship was not constrained by the form of monarch and minister. For example, he said to Nian Gengyao that"regarding Uncle Longkeduo, in the past, you and I not only did not know him very well, but also we really made a big mistake. He is really a loyal minister of my late imperial father, my meritorious minister, a good minister of the state and No.1 outstanding rare minister in the present age". Another example is that he approved Nian Gengyao's memorial in the 2nd year of the Yongzheng period as follows: "There are always monarch and minister who can get along together and have a good personal friendship. However this may not be as good as ours. It is needless say that if you rejoice; my joy is also unparalleled. In short, let you and I be an example of monarch and minister where monarch appreciate the minister's ability through the ages. Let future generations admire us. I am really carefree and joyous. Thank heaven, earth and the gods for so much blessing."[230] Such sweet words sound nauseating and it is rare that such words come from an emperor. Unexpectedly, he spoke the sweetest words but did the most diabolic things. He covered the dagger with a smile. He was honey-mouthed and dagger-hearted. One year later, it seemed that the sweet words were still ringing in the ears but Nian Gengyao was dismissed because "he showed disrespect for his accomplishment". At the end of the 3rd year of the Yongzheng period, Yongzheng framed him of 92 crimes and ordered Nian Gengyao to commit suicide. Meanwhile, Longkeduo also was stripped of the titles of Taibao and duke. In the 5th year of the Yongzhen period, Longkeduo was confined until he died because of hiding a jade plate for his own. If there were hidden secrets about Yongzheng's succession to the throne, Yongzheng may have worried about Nian Gengyao and Longkeduo apart from the princes who had been cut off. They knew the private secrets of Yongzheng, which might be the reason that they suddenly lost favor and suffered a fatal disaster.

If he usurped on the pretext of imperial edict and used cruel means to punish his brothers, Emperor Yongzheng had to be condemned. Later, Emperor Qianlong said: Yinsi and Yintang "coveted and attempted to steal throne, which was unavoidable. When my late imperial father ascended to the throne they complained and slandered, which was human nature. They did not show obvious disloyalty. In his later years, my late imperial father repeatedly talked about this with me. He was not happy and seemed to have regrets."[231] Did this disclose shame and uneasiness in the heart of Emperor Yongzheng? His behavior was also abnormal. He always said he was a filial son who was most admired by Emperor Kangxi. After ascending to the throne, it seemed that he was afraid and avoided the soul of Emperor Kangxi. Kangxi lived in the Changchun Garden, which was the largest and most magnificent imperial garden. Emperor Yongzheng abandoned it and did not use it. He built a new residence and spent money to expand Yuanmingyuan Garden as his temporary dwelling place. Emperor Kangxi often went to Rehe Mountain Resort and carried out activities there for nearly four or five months each year. He hunted, trained troops, exercised in martial arts, and received Mongol princes and dukes. In the past Yongzheng often accompanied his father to live in Rehe, but in 13 years after ascending to the throne he had not been to the mountain resort once. The tombs of Emperors Shunzhi and Kangxi are in Malanyu, Zunhua, east of Beijing, where the situation is high, steep and magnificent there is wide ground. However Yongzheng changed the place of his tomb. He built the west tombs in Yi County, southwest of Beijing. It seemed that he deliberately avoided Kangxi. Are these all meaningless coincidences? We should know that Yongzheng was ingenious and very knowledgeable, but strongly superstitious. He said: "things of ghosts and gods are principles of heaven and earth, they cannot be ignored. Small hills and big rivers and mountains all have gods, so we should respect and believe."[232] "I deeply believe in the correspondence between heaven and man, and know it very well."[233] If a person, who believes in god's will, ghosts and gods did something bad to his father and brothers, he would feel guilty. His living, entertainment and tomb would be far away from his father. Although this cannot be taken as direct evidence of usurping, it can be good circumstantial evidence if there is other evidence.

There are many doubts over Yongzheng's succession to the throne. We say this not to deny the historical role of Emperor Yongzheng. It should be said that mutual killing among the ruling class often happens, and a very wise ruler also often needs to use conspiracies and brutal struggles to open up the road for him. Yongzheng was no exception. However, as a supreme ruler, he had outstanding ruling ability. He was diligent in government affairs, knew the ways of the world clearly, worked conscientiously, managed subordinates strictly, corrected the drawbacks of slack administration of officials and open corruption and graft in the later years of Kangxi in a vigorous and effective manner, and ended the long-term contention among members of the imperial family. He used military forces in the northwest and implemented "changing tribal authorities to regular officials", ensuring peace in Khalkha Mongolia, Tibet, Qinghai, Yunnan, Guizhou and Sichuan, and consolidating national unity. He consolidated finance, checked money and grain, and implemented "tax based on land", "returning fees to the public coffers" and other policies. All these measures were conducive to economic development and political stability. Emperor Yongzheng reigned for 13 years. It was not a very long time, but was an important period for Qing Dynasty rule. He inherited and carried forward the political achievements of Emperor Kangxi and promoted economy, politics and culture in the late feudal society, laying a foundation for the future Qianlong "heyday".

9

Chapter

Russia's Early Aggression against China and the Anti-Aggression Struggles of Various Nationalities of China

Russia's Armed Invasion of Northeast China

The Boyakefu and Khabarovsk invasion of northeastern China

In the 17th century the Manchu rose in the northeast, established the Qing Dynasty, and entered the Pass and seized sovereignty of the whole country. This was the period in which early colonial forces were running rampant and expanding rapidly, and many countries and nations were cruelly plundered and enslaved. Portugal, Spain, Netherlands, Britain and France came to the southeast coast of China one after another. Russia also scurried over the north and northeastern borders of China. The early colonial powers clamped China from south and north like a pair of pliers. Since its establishment of sovereignty over the whole country, the Qing Dynasty had met complicated and intractable contradictions with the Western countries and was faced with difficult international situations which had never been experienced by preceding dynasties. In particularly, Russia's armed invasion of Northeast China and long-term looting and harassment in the Heilong River basin infringed China's territorial integrity, undermined the peaceful lives of people of various nationalities on the border of China, and also threatened the rule of the government of the Qing Dynasty. The Chinese people of different nationalities and the Qing government had to strengthen defense and implement self-defense counterattack against the Russian aggressive forces.

Russia is a European country. Its original boundary was far in the west to the Ural Mountains, was thousands of miles away from China and did not border on China. In the late 15th century and early 16th century, based on the Duchy of Moscow, Russia formed a unified country and gradually expanded outwards. In 1552 (the 31st year of the Jiajing period of the Ming Dynasty), Russia first annexed the Kazan Khanate. In 1556 (the 35th year of the Jiajing period of the Ming Dynasty) Russia conquered the Astrakhan Khanate, and occupied the entire Volga River basin. In the late 16th century a Cossack team led by adventurer Yermake crossed over the Ural Mountains and invaded the Sybil Khanat with the support of the Tsarist government and the wealthy Site luo Romanov family. In the early 17th century the Russian army advanced from the Ob River to the Yenisey River. In 1619 (the 47th year of the Wanli period of the Ming Dynasty, the 4th year of the Tianming period of the Later Jin Dynasty), the Russian army established Yenisei Trask. Then it advanced towards the Lena River. The author of the *General History of the Soviet Union* wrote: "Groups of people who wanted to get rich rushed to the Lena River from the Yenisei Trask and Manjiajieyar almost at the same time. They attacked the Yakutsk people living on the banks of the Lena River, plundered their leather goods and livestock, and captured women and children. Military service personnel in Yenisei Trask and Manjiajieya not only looted inhabitants one after another, but also fought with each other for plunder."[1]

Fig. 9.1. Map of Russia invading northeastern China and northern border, and anti-Russia struggles of the people of various nationalities of China

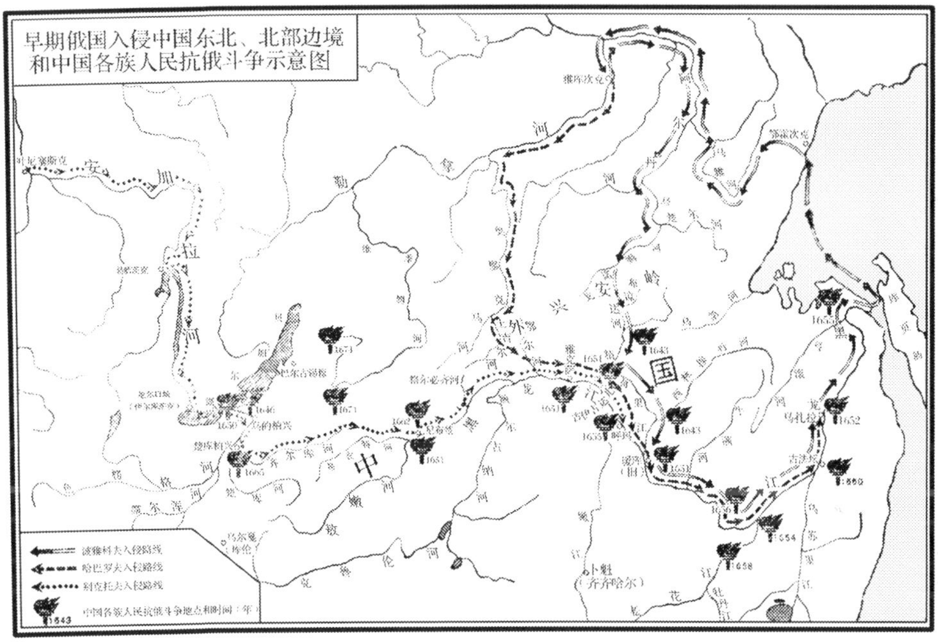

Russia's eastward expansion was very rapid. After crossing over the Ural Mountains in the second half of the 16th century, it took only a few decades for Russia to reach the Sea of Okhotsk and successively build scattered aggressive strongholds in the vast land of Siberia. In the 1630s it approached the northeast border of China. In 1636 (the 9th year of the Chongzhen period of the Ming Dynasty, the 1st year of the Chongde period of the Qing Dynaty), a team of Russian Cossacks building strongholds at the Aldan River heard about the Heilong River for the first time. In 1643 (the 16th year of the Chongzhen period of the Ming Dynasty, the 8th year of the Chongde period of the Qing Dynasty) Golovin, military governor of Yakutsk, sent an expeditionary force led by Vasily Boyakefu, the clerical officer. This expeditionary force had a total of 133 people and carried firearms and ammunition to the Heilong River. In winter of that year they crossed over the Stanovoy Range and invaded Chinese territory. Because they were short of food and walking in the snow, they were in a difficult situation. When they reached the mouth of the Wumuliekan River, they found a Chinese Daur village. The local inhabitants received these unexpected guests with hospitality, gave them food and introduced the local situation. They said that people here paid taxes to the Chinese emperor, and the emperor was a "great man",[2] had a large population under his jurisdiction and sent soldiers to patrol two or three times a year.

Although they knew clearly that they were already deep in the territory of China and the local inhabitants treated them kindly, these aggressors sent a unit to loot when they found out that a Daur village at the mouth of the Xilimudi River stored grain. They caught the people coming to receive them to use as hostages, and attempted to rush into the village. In order to defend the motherland's territory and their homes, the Daur people used simple weapons to fight with the aggressors, killing ten soldiers of the aggressor.

Throughout the winter of 1643 (the 16th year of the Chongzhun period of the Ming Dynasty, the 8th year of the Chongde period of the Qing Dynasty), Daur people at the Jingqili River had fought bravely with the Russian aggressors. Russian robbers wantonly massacred and plundered the Daur people, and they even gave full play to their animal dispositions to eat human flesh. According to the report written by Boyakefu's companion after he returned to Russia: "Boyakefu drove them (the Russian Cossacks) out of the stronghold and ordered them to eat the remains of the local inhabitants who had been killed."[3] In line with his order, a total of 50 people were eaten in this winter. In the spring of 1644 Boyakefu scurried to the lower reaches of the Heilong River. He burned, plundered and did many evil things along the way. In 1646 he returned to Yakutsk via the Sea of Okhotsk. Boyakefu and other people harassed the Heilong River for three years. Under the attack of people of various nationalities of China, among the 133 people of the whole force only 53 people returned to Russia alive.

Boyakefu wrote the first chapter of the history of Russia's aggression against China with his atrocities. A foreign scholar wrote that: "Boyakefu's action left such a profound and terrible impression that the inhabitants of the Amur River would have a picture of torture, kidnapping, death and barbarian uncivilized people in their minds as long as the 'Cossacks are coming' is said", and "no matter how big the problems China's tax collectors had caused, they had never committed inhuman crimes against local inhabitants as the Russians did. If the inhabitants of the Heilong River are allowed to freely choose which country's subjects they are willing to be, they will choose to remain loyal to China without hesitation."[4]

In 1649 (6th year of the Shunzhi period), Russia launched a second armed invasion into the northeast region of China. The aggressive activity was organized and commanded by Yerofei Khabarovsk. In January 1650 (the 7th year of the Shunzhi period), Khabarovsk led 70 Cossacks to cross over the Stanovoy Range, invade the territory of China and scurry west to Yakesa. This area was under jurisdiction of Chinese Daur Leader Lafukai. When learning that Russian robbers were coming the local residents had strengthened the defenses, cleared the fields and evacuated. Khabarovsk rushed into an empty place. He searched three villages, but no one was found. When they searched in the village, Lafukai came to find out what was happening in person and met with Khabarovsk. Khabarovsk tried all means of deception and threats. On the one hand, he said he came to do business; on the other hand, he absurdly asked the Daur people to pay taxes to the Tsar and accept the Tsar's protection. Lafukai categorically rejected such aggressive requirements. He said to Khabarovsk: "Who are you cheating? We know you Cossacks well ... You wanted to kill all of us, loot our beasts, and kidnap our wives and children."[5] Lafukai also said that the Daur people "have already paid taxes to Bogdo Khan (i.e. emperor of the Qing Dynasty) and do not have mink at hand."[6] With these words, Lafukai led his followers away. On arriving at the fourth village, Khabarovsk caught an old Daur woman. Khabarovsk asked her to tell him the whereabouts of the Daur people by torturing her with beating and baking her with fire. The old woman said that the Daur people were in front and not far away. They would fight against aggressors, and behind the Daur people there was the extremely powerful Bogdo Khan.

Khabarovsk saw that the Chinese people had made preparations and his strength was weak, so he decided to return to Yakutsk for help. He plundered grain, set fire to villages, rushed back to Yakutsk, and made a report to the Yakutsk governor. Khabarovsk recruited a troop of 117 people, and Yakutsk governor allocated 20 Cossack musketeers. Before Khabarovsk set out again, Military Governor Falancibokev gave him an instruction as follows:

> Ask Bogdo Khan (refers to the emperor of the Qing Dynasty) to lead his clan, tribe and all the people to accept the rule of the Tsar of Russia Grand Duke Alexis Mihajlovic and be slaves for ever... Bogdo Khan himself and his kin shall pay the Tsar tributes of gold, silver, precious stones and embroidered fabrics ...
>
> If Bogdo Khan and his clan, tribe and all the people do not obey the Tsar, do not pay tax in kind to the Tsar and hand over hostages, Yerofei (i.e., Khabarovsk) shall lead soldiers and hunters to secretly suppress them by war ... to kill and destroy them all, fight to the end, and their

wives and children as prisoners.[7]

Khabarovsk rushed to the Heilong River basin with this instruction once again in early 1651 (the 8th year of the Shunzhi period). He first attacked Yakesa and invaded and seized this strategically important place. In June of the same year, Khabarovsk moved quickly towards the middle and lower reaches of the Heilong River. He carried out an appalling massacre in Guyigudaer village.

Guyigudaer had "about 1,000 people, including women, children and some Manchu people." "In that whole night of summer, Russians used artillery to bombard the soil walls of villages. Large gaps were blasted open. The bombardment scared the women and children who had never seen artillery and guns before. In the morning, the soil walls of two villages had been turned into ruins. Frightened residents crowded inside the walls of a third village, which was also the soil wall of the last village. However the wall was bombarded down very soon. The weak resistance of the residents had already stopped. They wanted to flee, but it was too late and the enemy was in front of them. All-night fighting stirred the bloodthirsty brutish nature of the Cossacks. Their yells for killing were covered by the cries of children and women. Children and women were killed or seized by Cossacks' hands covered in the blood of their fathers, husbands and brothers. Listen to Khabarovsk's song of 'victory': 'by God's blessing, by the right of the Tsar, we beheaded all Daur people that we captured. In fierce fighting 427 Daur adults and children were killed. All the Daur people were assembled and all the Daur people participating in the attack and fighting were killed. A total of 661 adults and children were killed...By the right of the Tsar, we seized this village. There were livestock and prisoners. Captured female prisoners including old women, young women and little girls were 243 in total, and captured children were 118. We took 237 small or big horses and 113 cattle and sheep from the Daur people.'"[8]

The next target of Khabarovsk was Duolunchan village at the mouth of the Jingliqi River. It was the richest village in this area. The village head was Duolunchan and his two brothers, Tuoyinqi and Wumuqi. Duolunchan was a relative of Baerdaqi, son-in-law of the emperor of the Qing Dynasty. In order to prevent Chinese residents from evacuating, Khabarovsk adopted the method of starting the raid from a distance. On one night of August 1651 (the 8th year of the Shunzhi period) the Russian robbers suddenly rushed into the village. A fight with disparity in strength began. Duolunchan led the villagers to resist without weapons. Many villagers were killed, and Duolunchan and Tuoyinqi were captured because of exhaustion. The Russian aggressors seized 270 Chinese. Khabarovsk required them to submit to Tsar and extorted mink furs from them. Russia aggressive army confined villagers in the village, and imprisoned Duolunchan and Tuoyinqi as hostages.

The Chinese people were not willing to be coolies and slaves. Before dawn on September 13, 1651 (the 8th year of the Shunzhi period), when the Cossacks were still sleeping, the people of the whole village collectively escaped from the village. Khabarovsk cruelly tortured Duolunchan and other people and closely questioned them on the whereabouts of the villagers. Duolunchan and the others showed dauntless heroism. They answered that "Now that we have fallen into your hands, we would rather let us die than let our people die,"[9] "cut off our heads! We are not afraid of death!"[10] Finally, Duolunchan was taken by the aggressors and Tuoyinqi killed himself with a knife. They suffered all kinds of tortures for the motherland and the people, and sacrificed their lives.

Khabarovsk continued to hurry down along the Heilong River. In October 1651 he reached Wuzhala village (over 600 *li*) to the east, now the mouth of the Hongjiali River in Russia), and rested and reorganized and spent the winter there. This area was a place where the Hoche people (also known as the Aqiang people, or Nateke people) of China lived. On the one hand, Hoche people resisted the Russian aggressors with simple weapons; on the other hand, they sent people to report the danger to the Qing troop stationed in Ningguta. At that time the main forces of the Qing army had entered the Pass, and there were only a few of troops stationed in the northeast. However such a serious aggressive event could not be ignored. After receiving orders from the Shengjing party, troops in Ningguta immediately set out. However the leaders of the troops in Ningguta greatly underestimated the seriousness of the Russian invasion. They thought it was just the misconduct of a small number of bandits. Underestimation of the enemy's situation brought losses in the initial fighting.

Haise, Zhangjing of Ningguta, led 600 soldiers to Wuzhala village. The people of various nationalities along the Heilong River basin, who came to assist in fighting, included "500 Daur people, 420 people from Manjingzhan and 105 Duqier people from the Songhua River."[11] At dawn on April 3, 1652 (the 9th year of the Shunzhi period), when the aggressors were still sleeping, Chinese soldiers and civilians approached Wuzhala village. However Haise did not suddenly pounce but fired guns from a distance, and the enemies were awakened. After the fighting began, the Qing soldiers and people of various nationalities fought the enemy bravely, broke through the enemy's castle walls, rushed into the camp and encircled 200 Russian aggressors tightly. Just at this critical point when the enemy could be annihilated very soon Haise issued an absurd order, which was that Russian aggressors could only be captured and could not be killed. This order tied the hands and feet of the

Qing soldiers, who could not freely kill the enemy. The result turned victory into defeat. The Qing army lost the battle and retreated from Wuzhala village. Although the first battle was lost, the soldiers' blood did not flow in vain. A joint counterattack by Chinese soldiers and civilians made the Russian aggressors tremble with fright. Khabarovsk did not dare to go any further and quickly retreated to the upper reaches of the Heilong River. During the retreat the aggressor troops were attacked by the Qing army and people of all nationalities along the river. The Russian aggressors were restless with anxiety, suffered several surprises overnight, their internal morale was low, and mutinies also occurred in the troops, making the aggressors fall into a dilemma. In the report to the military governor of Nerchinsk written by Khabarovsk in August 1652, Khabarovsk bemoaned: "We do not know how to spend the winter. We dare not stay on the land of Dawoliya at the mouth of the Jiya River (mouth of the Jingjili River) or the mouth of the Songhua River...We cannot conquer the local people. There are so many people here, and they have weapons. However without the order of the monarch we dare not leave the Amur River either."[12]

When Khabarovsk was hard-pressed the Tsar sent him reinforcements and transferred Khabarovsk back to Moscow to report success and receive rewards. In recognition of his contribution in aggression and expansion, the Tsar granted Khabarovsk huge tracts of land and a title of nobility. After that this vanguard of invasion of China was touted as the hero of "developing new land" by the hack writers of the Tsar.

The complete collapse of Stepanov's aggressive army

After Khabarovsk returned to his country, his aggressor troops were still left at the Heilong River and their command was taken over by Stepanov.

Stepanov led hundreds of Cossacks to harass and run amuck in China. They did all evil things. The Chinese army and people of all nationalities of China defended their homeland and launched a bloody battle with the Russian aggressor army. In 1653 (the 10th year of the Shunzhi period), the Qing government set up Angbangzhangjing of Ningguta, and appointed Sharhuda the first Angbangzhangjing to fight against the Russian aggression and defend the peace of the border.

In 1654, Sharhuda led 300 Manchu soldiers and Hurha led 300 soldiers and 100 Korean soldiers who came to assist in fighting at the mouth of the Songhua River. They encountered 370 Russian aggressor soldiers. The Russian troop relied on big ships and greater firepower to defiantly challenge the Qing and Korean troops. The Qing and Korean troops made use of the terrain and set an ambush to lure the Russian troops to land, and fought back fiercely. The Russian troops were defeated. They were depressed and fled in utter confusion. Stepanov himself said, "Many military service personnel (ie Russian soldiers) were injured, they already could not fight with the Chinese."[13]

In early 1655 the Qing government "ordered Gushanezhen Mingandali to lead officers and soldiers to go on a punitive expedition against the Russians at Heilong River."[14] Stepanov's troops hid themselves in Humaer city, and made use of strong fortifications and good and sharp-edged weapons to stubbornly resist. The Qing troops attacked the city for ten days, but they were unable to capture Humaer. Because the Qing troops used large forces to fight, and had marched a long way, and food they brought was not sufficient, so they could not fight for long time and had to retreat. It was recorded in historical books: "In the 12th year (of the Shunzhi period), Minister and Commander-in-chief Mingandali went to crusade against the Russians from the Capital. They arrived at Humaer and attacked the city. They killed a lot of Russian soldiers. Before long they withdrew the troops from the frontier owing to lack of food."[15]

In addition to Stepanov's regular forces there were many Russian bandits who scurried into our territory and burned and looted everywhere. They also encountered resistance and attack from the Chinese people. The aggressors headed by three Sorokin brothers had 300 people in total. In 1655 (the 12th year of the Shunzhi period), they entered Chinese territory and had a battle with the Hurha people of China, and all invading robbers were killed. According to the Russian historian Slovtsov,"during 10 years, no less than 1,500 Russians went to the Amur River (i.e. Heilong River), but all of them died over there."[16]

On July 10, 1658 (the 15th year of the Shunzhi period), Stepanov led 500 Cossacks to the Songhua River. Sharhuda led the Qing troop to stand ready in battle array by taking 47 boats at the confluence of the Songhua River and the Mudan River, and 260 Korean soldiers came to assist in the fighting. The Russian aggressors were encircled and fell into chaos. 180 aggressors broke away from the big group and fled to the back road. Stepanov and more than 300 aggressors were unable to get away. After a fierce battle, over 270 aggressors were killed or captured, 47 slipped through the net. Stepanov, leader of the aggressors, was killed and 3,080 pieces of booty marten fur in the boats were captured. It was written down in Chinese historical records: "Sharhuda, Angbangzhangjing guarding Ningguta and other people reported: they defeated the Russian soldiers, and captured Russian people, weapons and other articles. The Ministry of War was ordered to review and reward officers and soldiers who made contributions with the things captured by them."[17] In 1659 (the 16th year of the Shunzhi period), Sharhuda died and his son Bahai succeeded him in the post of Angbangzhangjing of Ningguta. In 1660 (the 17th year of the Shunzhi period), Bahai led the Qing troops to mop up at the Heilong River. They eradicated the remaining Russian aggressors at the middle and lower reaches of the Heilong River.

Nicholas's diplomatic mission to China and Russia's further aggression and expansion

Stepanov's invading army was wiped out, but the struggle did not end. Russia's invading army did not completely withdraw from Chinese territory. They still occupied Nerchinsk city at the upper reaches of the Heilong River (Shileka River), waited for reinforcements, spied out opportunities, and moved busily in preparation for action. In 1665 (the 4th year of the Kangxi period), a group of Russian invaders re-took Yakesa. The Russian troops built forts, set up work, extorted taxes, kidnapped people as hostages, established colonial farms, enslaved and suppressed local residents of all nationalities of China in Nerchinsk and Yakesa, and continuously harassed and expanded toward the middle and lower reaches of the Heilong River.

In order to coordinate with activities of armed aggression at the Heilong River, the Russian government had repeatedly sent envoys to China to collect intelligence, put forward all kinds of unreasonable requirements to the Qing government, and conduct intimidation and blackmail. In 1656 (the 13th year of the Shunzhi period) the Bayikov mission came to Beijing. At that time Stepanov's group was running amuck at the Heilong River. An official of the Qing government said to Bayikov "you come here as an envoy, but the Cossacks are fighting with us."[18] Bayikov had no answer. In 1670 (the 9th year of the Kangxi period), Russia sent Milovanov and other people to Beijing, and absurdly asked Emperor Kangxi to pay tribute and submit to the old Tsar. In the document that it gave to the Qing government, it said: "The Imperial might of His Majesty Russian Tsar Oleksandr Mikhailovich reaches far away. There are already monarchs of many countries submitting to the supreme rule of His Majesty... Your Chinese emperor should also try your best to obtain the grace of His Majesty the Tsar... His Majesty Oleksandr Mikhailovich will surely cherish the Chinese emperor under his infinite royal grace, and protect him from enemies' encroachment. Your Chinese emperor can uniquely convert to His Majesty, and be under the supreme rule of His Majesty the Russian Tsar permanently, and pay tributes to the great monarch."[19] This document fully exposed the old Tsar's ambition of attempting to merge with China.

In 1676 (the 15th year of the Kangxi period), the Russian government sent Nicholas's mission to Beijing. The Qing government ceremoniously received the Russian mission. Emperor Kangxi interviewed the mission twice, and hoped to settle border disputes between China and Russia with the Russian mission through negotiation. However Nicholas considered he was the imperial envoy of a superior country, so his attitude was arrogant and aggressive. The officials of the Qing Dynasty required the Russian troops to stop invading China. "In the future, do not harass border area. If you do so, the two countries can foster cordial relations and send envoys and trade."[20] However, Nicholas pretended to be deaf and dumb, made excuses and refused to admit anything. He pretended to have no knowledge of Russian troops' invasion activities in China, refused to negotiate on the border issue, boasted of the power of Russia, and tried to intimidate the Qing government. He said that "the Tsar is the sun in the sky, which illuminates the moon and all the stars. The Tsar's grace not only shelters Russia's subjects, but also sovereigns of all countries are sheltered by Tsar, as stars are shone on by the sun."[21] He unreasonably required the Qing government to send 20,000kg silver and a great number of silks and precious things to Russia every year. He also colluded with Jesuit missionaries in Beijing to steal a lot of information.

Nicholas' insolence, lying and cheating caused the Qing government's doubts and mistrust. After negotiating with Nicholas, officials of the Qing Dynasty thought that "although there is expression of fostering cordial relations between two countries in what the envoy said and letter of the Tsar, it is incredible. The suspect places are quite obvious" and "All words said by Nicholas are incredible."[22] Later, Emperor Kangxi also said that "In the past, the behavior of Nicholas from your country were perverse and brutal when he was in China."[23] Despite this, the Qing government still hoped that Nicholas could forward to the Tsar the requirement to stop Russian troops' invasion of China and maintain border peace.

In fact, the Qing government's desire completely drew a blank. Nicholas' mission was not to seek peace with China. On the contrary, it was just to coordinate with armed aggression and pry into China's actual situation so as to deploy further aggressive activities. At that time China was experiencing the rebellion of the "three seigniors" launched by Wu Sangui etc. The Qing government fought the rebel army with all its strength. Nicholas reported the unrest in China's domestic situation to the Tsar. He said that "if there are 2,000 regular forces of your majesty in Dawuliya region (refers to east of Lake Baikal, including the whole Heilong River basin), not only Dawuliya but also all the lands outside of the Great Wall of China can acknowledge allegiance to the rule of Your Majesty."[24] On his way to Russia, Nicholas passed by the Nen River and Hulunbeier. He coveted China's vast fertile land, so he ordered Russian troops at Nerchinsk to "build a fort at the Argun River or the Hailar River, and all residents living between Nerchinsk and the Nen River can acknowledge allegiance to Russia."[25]

Just when Nicholas was sent on the diplomatic mission to China, Russia's aggressive activities at the Heilong River basin intensified. The Russian government dispatched many Cossacks, allocated a large number of guns, artillery, goods and materials to Nerchinsk and Yakesa to strengthen the forces of aggression. Moreover the Russian government also ordered Russian troops to nibble away at and expand towards inland China along several different routes. As a Russian historian said: "1676 was the start of implementing an active policy in East Siberia."[26]

From 1676 to 1682 (the 15th year to the 21st year of the Kangxi period), Russian troops advanced along different routes. They arrived at various tributaries of the Heilong River, built forts, established strongholds, pressed for payment of taxes and persecuted of people of various ethnic groups of China. In 1676 they established aggressive strongholds at the Gelou River (i.e. the Guli River. In the Ming Dynasty, the Guli River Garrison was established); in 1678 they established Jieyasike fort at the upper reaches of the Jingqili River; in 1679 they established Xilinmubinsike at the Xilinmubinsike River; they established Duolunchan (it was called as Duolunsk by Russians) at the mouth of Jingqili River; in 1681 they built Argun fort at the Argun River, kidnapped Alihan and Bajiiuhan, leaders of local Chinese residents, as hostages, forced payment of taxes and explored and mined silver ore; in 1682 the Yakesa Russian military authorities dispatched a large number of Cossacks to harass the lower reaches of the Heilong River. "They met nearly 300 Natuoji people and Jilike people (i.e. China's Hoche people and Feiyaka people), they defeated those people and looted all their things."[27] Russian troops built Dujigensike, Wudisike, Tuguersike, Niemilunsike and other aggressive strongholds on the lower reaches of the Heilong River and in the coastal areas. The aggressive talons of Russsian troops stretched farther and farther. As mentioned in Chinese historical records, they "occupy Yakesa city as a nest... repeatedly harass the Suolun, Hezhen, Feiyaka and Qileer people, plunder the population, and cause unrest to local people," "go deep into inland, wantonly plundering civilian children, and cause disturbances ceaselessly,"[28] "Suolun people are often killed by them, and their children, ginseng and mink are plundered nearly clean."[29] Qing officials repeatedly required that the Russian troops stop the aggression. In 1681, Emperor Kangxi specially sent Mingai, minister of the Court of Judicial Review, to Bukui (now Qiqihar) to negotiate with the Yakesa Russian military authority. He required that the Russian troops demolish the forts they had built. Qing officials warned the Russian side that "Duolunchan was originally our place. You built houses and let people live there. It is quite improper. You should move your people. If you do not move there will be a border dispute and we must drive you to move with strength of the masses. By that time, it will be too late for regrets."[30]

However constant negotiation, persuasion and repeated warnings and protests were useless. The Russian troops not only turned a deaf ear, but also their aggression activities were intensified. The Qing government could not stand it any longer. In order to defend the country's territorial integrity and the safety of the lives and property of the people, the Qing Government had to make preparations for self-defense and a war against the aggression was already inevitable.

The Yakesa War and the *Sino-Russian Treaty of Nerchinsk*

The first Yakesa War

Russia's invasion of the northeastern border infringed China's territory and sovereignty and threatened the safety of the Chinese people and the rule of the Qing Dynasty. Moreover the Heilong River basin was the home of the Manchu and the birthplace of the Qing Dynasty. Naturally, the Qing Dynasty could not tolerate that this place was invaded and seized by Russian troops. To expel the Russian troops and regain lost ground was the strong desire of the rulers of the Qing Dynasty. Emperor Kangxi said: "since I started to handle state affairs in person at the age of 13 (it was 1667 i.e. the 6th year of the Kangxi period that Emperor Kangxi began handling state affairs in person), I have paid attention to this issue (refers to the Russian invasion and occupation of the Heilong River basin) and carefully investigated the terrain, road distance and people's temperaments."[31] It can be seen that Emperor Kangxi realized the invasion forces from Russia should not be underestimated. After ascending to the throne, he immediately paid close attention to frontier defense in the Northeast. His determination to resist aggression was unshakable. However, for quite a long period of time after entering the Pass, the Qing government concentrated its entire strength on achieving rule over the whole country. It was impossible to use a lot of power to take into account the defense of Heilongjiang. When the rebellion of the three seigniors was put down in 1681 (the 2nd year of the Kangxi period), the Qing government concentrated on the Northeast and prepared for to expel the aggressors with armed forces.

The principle followed by the Qing government was simultaneous implementation of military struggle, diplomatic negotiation and improving frontier defense. In the process of long-term negotiations with Russia, the Qing government gradually understood that it was impossible to persuade the Russians to give up aggression and withdraw from Chinese territory without powerful armed forces, strong frontier defense and fierce fighting. Meanwhile, the Qing government also understood that both China and Russia were big feudal countries. It was impossible for one of them to conquer the other by military force and there could only be stability on the border and long-term peace through determining a boundary line that both countries could accept by peace negotiations. Therefore the result of military struggles was to have negotiation, the purpose of fighting was for self-defense and seeking a relatively just peace. As an American historian said, "Emperor Kangxi did not want to conquer Russia, but wanted to show Russia that: he had the power to resolve the problem with Russia by negotiation."[32]

Emperor Kangxi summarized Chinese soldiers' and civilians' experiences in fighting with the Russian aggressors for more than 30 years, made a careful plan and carried out detailed preparatory work. In 1682 (the 21st year of the Kangxi period) i.e. the year after putting down the rebellion of the three seigniors, after paying homage at his ancestral mausoleum in Shengjing (Shenyang) in April, Emperor Kangxi went out of Liutiaobian via Fushun, Xingjing and Hadacheng (now Xifeng). In May he arrived at Chuangchang (or Jilinwula, now Jilin City), sailed on the Songhua River and inspected the frontier defense institutions in person. In September of the same year Emperor Kangxi sent vice Commander-in-chief Langtan and Duke Pengchun to lead several hundred people to investigate the geographical situation and water and land traffic near Yakesa in the name of hunting deer. In January of 1683 Langtan returned to Beijing and reported as follows: "it is easy to attack and seize the Russians. It is enough to dispatch 3,000 soldiers."[33] They also suggested that the government immediately take action. Emperor Kangxi did not agree with this opinion which purely considered the military perspective. He thought that the government must do more sufficient preparations, first build forts and station armies in Heilongjiang (i.e. Aihui) and Humaer, store grain, build ships, plan to open up wasteland and grow food grain, and open up post roads to achieve the purpose of winning in battle and defending the city after winning.

In summer of 1683 (the 22nd year of the Kangxi period) the first batch of

1,000 Wulaningguta officers and soldiers led by Sabusu, vice commander-in-chief, arrived at Aihui. In autumn of 1684, 1,000 Wulaningguta officers and soldiers and additional Duhanr officers and soldiers with their family members went to Heilongjiang to open up wasteland and grow food grain. These two batches of troops had 2,000 people in total. They were the main force for defending the border and fighting against the Russians. In winter of 1683, in order to fight in coordination, 500 to 600 soldiers were dispatched from Beijing to Heilongjiang. In early 1865, in order to deal with the Russians' firelocks, 420 Fujian rattan shield soldiers stationed in Shandong, Shanxi and Henan were mustered to the front line. These two batches of troops had 1,000 people in total. After they participated in the fighting, they were immediately withdrawn to their original stations.

After arriving at Aihui, the Qing troops immediately built a castle on the ruins of the ancient city on the east bank of the Heilong River. The castle was named Heilongjiang and was commanded by a general, and Sabuqi served as the first general of Heilongjiang. Moreover Qing troops opened up wasteland and grew food grain there. "In the 24th year of the Kangxi period, officers and soldiers in Shengjing were sent to open up wastelands of more than 1,500 *shang* (晌)."[34] Qing troops also sent people to teach the Daur and Suolun people who did not engage in farming. These people obtained achievements in farming methods, and a good harvest of crops."[35] In order to ensure the food supply for soldiers stationed in Heilongjiang, 12,000 *dan* (擔) of grain were requisitioned from ten banners of Horqin, Xibe and Wula official stocks to prepare grain needed for three years. The Qing troops also sent people to buy cattle and sheep from regions where the Suolun people lived.

It needed a large number of warships and transport ships to march for Yakesa. The Qing government actively prepared wood, assembled artisans and set up a factory in Jilin to build ships on a large scale. Yisanga, minister of the Ministery of Revenue, was specially sent to supervise. Various types of vessels were built and soldiers, servants and exiled criminals were called up as sailors. Moreover segmented transport was organized and implemented from Shengjing (Shenyang) to Heilongjiang (Aihui). This transportation route was as long as 5,000 *li* and passed by the Liaohe River, Songhua River and Heilong River. Along this transportation route, defense soldiers were positioned, corvees were recruited, rivers were dredged, barns were established, and people were sent to survey distance of route and water depth so as to determine sizes and carrying capacities of the ships built. Furthermore ships loaded with rice were sent for a pilot voyage from Tongzhou to Yingtai. In addition, a 1,340-*li* new post road was opened up from Wula to Aihui.

Along this post road there were 9 post stations to deliver official documents and military information.

Qing troops were stationed in Heilongjiang and they first started to clear away aggressive strongholds set up by Russian troops on the lower reaches of the Heilong River. In July 1683 (the 22nd year of the Kangxi period), when they marched to the mouth of the Jingqili River, a vanguard troop led by Boke, an officer from the Suolun ethnic group and subordinate of Sabusu, encountered 66 Russian aggressors scurrying from Yakesa. Melnik led this group of aggressors and prepared to intrude on and attack the lower reaches of the Heilong River. With the help of local people, the Qing troop encircled the Russian aggressors. Except for a few people who fled for their lives, Melnik led most of people to lay down their arms and surrender. When getting the news of the setting out of Qing troops, the Russian troops stationed in the Duolunchan and Xilimubinsike strongholds withdrew and escaped. The Russian troops in the Xinzesike stronghold at the upper reaches of the Jingqili River did not get the news of the setting out of the Qing troops, were encircled by the Qing troops, and surrendered very soon.

The Chinese people of various nationalities in the Northeast also successively took up arms to fight and fiercely strike at the Russian aggressors. Xinuganu and other people from the Qileer ethnic group at the Numan River area killed more than ten Russian soldiers, Zhuerkengke and other people from the Oroqen ethnic group at the Jingqili River area killed many aggressors. The Feiyaka and Qileer ethnic groups at the lower reaches of the Heilong River carried out fierce fighting with Russian troops, and "killed a great many Russians."[36] Russian troops came to reinforce, and the Feiyaka people asked for help from the Qing troops. General Eluoshun of Qing led 300 soldiers and braved ice, snow and cold to support them. They fought with the Russian troops at the mouth of the Hengun River. The Russian troops were defeated. Some of them threw down their weapons to surrender and some of them escaped towards the Sea of Okhotsk. With the cooperation of local people, Qing troops removed a lot of strongholds of aggression and regained a vast piece of territory of China.

The Qing government did not simply take military means. For each battle, the Qing government tried peaceful means before resorting to force, sent people to carry out political persuasion, and said that as long as the Russian army stopped aggression the Qing Dynasty was willing to maintain peace with Russia. Moreover the Qing government provided Russian officers and soldiers captured with preferential treatment, and required that "officials in charge pay attention to supporting them. Do not let them lack food, so as to show the meaning of deep mindfulness and compassion."[37] In 1684 the Qing government asked Russian prisoners of war to take the official document of the Chinese government to Yakesa. The official document included Emperor Kangxi's decree, and still hoped that the Russian troops would withdraw from the territory of China to avoid fighting. It said that "now if Russians in Yakesa and Nerchinsk correct their former mistakes and hurry back to their native place, both parties shall be at peace with each other. This is very beneficial to them. If they adhere obstinately to their error and stay in our border, they will inevitably be punished by heaven and cannot avoid being killed and punished at that time."[38] However repeated persuasion and warnings had no effect, and the unilateral peace intention did not make the aggressors lay down the butcher's knife. The Qing government had no other choice but to expel the aggressors with armed force.

In January 1685 (the 24th year of the Kangxi period), Kangxi sent Commander-in-chief Gongwashan and other people to Heilongjiang to meet and discuss with Sabusu and others. He determined to dispatch an army to regain Yakesa after it got warm in spring. Emperor Kangxi issued a decree: "fighting is not a good thing. It is used if there is no other way. In the past, Russians invaded our border without reason and received our escaped criminals. Later, they gradually crossed the border, invaded and harmed Suolun, Hezhe, Feiyake, Qileer and other places, and people were unable to settle down. Russians looted and caught people, plundered villages, stole marten furs and wantonly did all kinds of evil. Therefore we repeatedly sent people to announce orders, and additionally issued official documents to their envoys. The Russians did not report on completion of the mission. On the contrary, they went deep into the Hezhe and Feiyake area and the harm caused by their intrusion became more serious. When we dispatched an army to Heilongjiang and took control of their communication route, the Russians continued as usual and did not send back the escaped criminals. Therefore, they should be immediately wiped out". At the same time, he expressed China's wish for peace once again: "if you us want to live in peace with each other, you can quickly go back to Yaku. With Yaku as the boundary, you can catch mink and collect tax, and stop causing disturbances inland any more. You send back our escaped criminals, and we will also send back escaped criminals from Russia. If so, trade can be done at the boundary. Both parties settle down and have no fighting against each other."[39] Before the army marched for Yakesa, the Qing Government made another effort for peace. Emperor Kangxi directly wrote to the Tsar and hoped the Tsar would "quickly withdraw the Russians in Yakesa, and the people in our two countries live with Yaku and other places as the boundary line. If this happens I will immediately order the army going on a punitive expedition to stop marching. In this way the border areas can get peace and need not worry about intrusion. Both countries can mutually trade and send envoys and live in harmony."[40] This letter was sent to Russia with six Russian prisoners of war via Khalkha Mongolia.

Although the Qing government made great efforts for a peaceful settlement of the border disputes, the Russian side did not give up its ambition. The Russian government made a thorough adjustment of the military command structure of colonial occupation in the Heilongjiang region. Vlasov and Tolbuzin, who were familiar with situation and were well-known for being capable, vigorous and brave, were respectively appointed to act as military governors of Nerchinsk and Yakesa. They increased deployment of reinforcements, stored food and materials, constructed fortifications, strengthened city defenses and were ready to be entrenched there for a long time. In addition, the Russian government appointed and dispatched a Prussian officer named Biden to recruit Cossacks at Tobolsk and to form military troops to march to fight with China.

In June 1685 the Qing troops arrived at Yakesa. They first sent Feiyaoduoli and other Russian prisoners of war to enter Yakesa with two official documents. One document was a letter from Emperor Kangxi to the Tsar, and the other document was an official communication written by Peng Chun, commander of the Qing troops, to the Russian troops in Yakesa which required Russian troops to withdraw from China, and issued a final warning to the aggressors. On June 23 the headquarters of the Qing troops was moved under Yakesa city and had a dialogue with the Russian side. "The Russians spoke insolently."[41] On June 24 the Qing army arrayed its troops and surrounded Yakesa. On June 25 a team of Russian troops sailed downstream along the Heilong River and attempted to rush into Yakesa, but they were intercepted by the Qing troops. A fierce battle was carried out on the river. Finally, more than 40 Russian soldiers were killed and wounded. Then the Qing troops set up artillery to violently bombard Yakesa. Everywhere around the city caught fire and the Russian troops suffered serious casualties. They were terror-stricken and helpless. The Qing troops repeatedly shot letters persuading them to surrender into the city. The surrender conditions were very generous. As long as the Russian troops withdrew from Yakesa and guaranteed not to come again, they could keep their lives and were allowed to take their weapons and property away. Tolbuzin, leader of the Russian troops, put up a flag of surrender. The Qing troops allowed more than 700 Russians to withdraw from

Yakesa and sent them to the mouth of the Argun River. There were 45 Russian soldiers such as Bashli who were not willing to go back to their country and asked to stay in China, and went back to Aihui with the Qing troops. There were also more than 160 Chinese Suolun people and Arbahu people had who had been seized by the Russian troops as hostages. All of them were set free. The first Yakesa war ended with the Russian troops' defeat, surrender and withdrawal from Yakesa.

The second Yakesa War

Tolbuzin led the Russian troops to retreat from Yakesa to Nerchinsk, but his aggressive ambition did not die and he still wanted to return. At that time, 600 reinforcements led by Biden arrived at Nerchinsk. The strength of the Russian troops was increased. At the same time they heard that after winning the war, all the Qing troops had withdrawn to Aihui and had not left soldiers stationed in Yakesa. Therefore Tolbuzin and Biden immediately led troops to re-occupy Yakesa and fully build the castle fortifications to attempt a desperate struggle. Since Russian troops had re-captured Yagesa, the Qing government had to dispatch troops. In March 1686 (the 25th year of the Kangxi period) Emperor Kangxi ordered: "Now the Russians have returned to Yakesa and are constructing fortifications for settlement. If we do not quickly exterminate them, they will accumulate grain to stand fast at the city. It will then be difficult for us to capture the city. I order General Sabutai and other people... quickly repair the warships and lead officers and soldiers at Wula and Ningguta to hurry to Heilongjiang City (Aihui). Then leave Shengjing soldiers to guard the city, and only take 2,000 troops to attack and seize Yakesa."[42] In July Sabusu led more than 2,000 Qing soldiers to Yakesa. He first set free Russian prisoner of war Ekesuobuguo and asked him to take a letter into the city. He once again warned the Russian troops: "You stealthily returned to the city, rebuilt the castle and are entrenched in it. You also bully our fishermen, hunters ...Now our troops are at the city gate. We shall never give up. You know this very clearly. You will be driven out and have no strength to come back. The outcome is just like this."[43]

There were a total of over 800 Russian aggression forces in the stronghold of Yakesa. The Russian troops had more firearms, plenty of ammunition, food and forage, and solid city defense fortifications. They frequently attacked from Yakesa and did not allow the emplacements and siege equipment of the Qing troops to approach the walls. Except for some artillery, the Qing troops only had 50 firelocks and all the soldiers fought with bows, arrows, swords and spears. Such weapons were less lethal and were not conducive to assaulting a strong defensive installation. Therefore the Qing troops were not able to quickly seize Yakesa. However the high morale of the Qing troops together with assistance from local residents of all ethnic groups in the fighting meant that the Qing troops repeatedly defeated the Russian troops who came out of city to challenge them. Within several days of the war starting the Qing troops had killed more than 100 aggressors and Tolbuzin, leader of the Russian troops, was also killed by artillery.

The Qing army and Russian army were locked in a stalemate at Yakesa. The cold season on the Heilong River was approaching. Due to their lack of firearms, in order to avoid too much sacrifice, the Qing army stopped storming the city, and built fortifactions and dug trenches around Yakesa to besiege Yakesa. After long-term fighting and siege, most of Russian forces were killed in war or died of disease. Of more than 800 Russian troops finally only 66 people were left, and food and ammunition were exhausted. Moreover the troops in Nerchinsk were unable to dispatch reinforcements. Therefore the aggression army hemmed in in Yakesa had no other way but to wait for death.

Although the Qing government's military operation achieved great success, in order to obtain a stable peace on the border, the Qing government still tried to negotiate with Russia. In September 1686 the Qing government commissioned Netherlands Envoy Binxianbazhi who was going back to the Netherlands to take a letter to the Russian Tsar. In the letter the Qing government suggested that the two countries cease fire and have a negotiation. We "hope the Tsar will withdraw his subordinates. Let us take some place of Yaku as the boundary line. Chinese and Russians can hunt within their boundary and live in harmony with each other."[44] The Qing government also delivered a letter with the same content to Portuguese missionary Domingo Fernandez Navarrete to take to Europe and try to forward to the Tsar. In short, the Qing government tried every way to strive for settlement of the border conflicts by negotiation. A French historian commented that "sending these letters was enough to show China has the intention to reach an entente."[45]

In November 1686, when the besieged Yakesa city could be seized overnight, a group of Russian couriers led by Wenniukefu and Fawoluofu, started from Moscow and arrived in Beijing at full speed. They spent one year on the way. It turned out that the Russian government had already known news of the Yakesa war, and several letters of Emperor Kangxi had been successively brought to Moscow. The Russian government knew that China's counterattack in self-defense would turn its results of years of aggression into nothing, so Russia was very anxious. However at that time Princess Sofia, sister of Peter I, held the reins of government, aristocrats struggled for power and interests, and the rule was very unstable. Moreover Russia had fought in the west year after year, its soldiers were tired and finance was exhausted. It was impossible for Russia to dispatch a large number of troops to China, and the Russian troops barricaded in Yakesa could be wiped out. In order to ease the emergency situation in the Far East, the Russian government determined to accept the suggestion of the Qing government to hold a border negotiation and sent a negotiation mission headed by Golovin. Wenjiukefu and Fawoluofu were ordered by the Russian government to go to Beijing in advance to deliver letters from the Tsar to Emperor Kangxi, requesting the Qing government stop attacking Yakesa and hold a negotiation when the Golovin Mission arrived.

The Qing government showed great sincerity for peace, and received the Russian messengers with rites. In the situation where Yakesa was easy to obtain, the Qing government agreed with Russia's request, stopped fighting, lifted the siege and realized unilateral withdrawal of army. Emperor Kangxi sent people to announce the order:"Sabusu and other people should withdraw the army in Yakesa, gather in a place, set up camp near the warships, and explicitly tell the Russians in the city that they are allowed to freely go in and out. Do not randomly take action to seize them. After the Russian mission arrives, have a negotiation with them."[46] Yakesa city was besieged for 5 months, nearly all the Russian troops died, the city lacked food and wood. The Qing troops sent food to the city and also prepared to send doctors to treat the Russian troops in the city. In 1687 the Qing troops unilaterally withdrew from Yakesa and returned to Aihui to wait for the coming of the Russian mission.

As the Chinese side proposed peace negotiations and ceasefire and withdrawal of the army, the Second Yakesa War was able to end. After that the history of Sino-Russian relations entered into the negotiation stage.

China and Russia sent their negotiation missions and their principles of the negotiation

Considering the situation and its own strength at that time, the Russian government weighed the pluses and minuses and had to accept the negotiation proposal of the Qing government. It sent a negotiation mission headed by Golovin. However sending a negotiation mission neither meant it would give up aggression, nor meant it would stop using force. For Russia, this was only an adjustment of strategies and means. Because Russia's wanton armed aggression was strongly counterattacked by China, the Russians had to change deployment and alternate use military invasion and diplomatic negotiation to achieve their expansion goal. Both the composition and mission of Golovin's mission reflected the characteristics that Russia combined war with negotiation.

Golovin's mission had more than 1,900 officials and soldiers, including artillery, hackbuteers, dragoons etc. The Russia government granted Golovin broad rights. He not only could negotiate with China to sign a treaty, but also could move troops in Siberia to fight with China when he thought it was favorable. The Russian government stipulated the tasks and negotiation plans of the mission. The highest requirement in the negotiation plan was to demarcate using the Heilong River, that is, to occupy the whole north bank of the Heilong River; if this requirement could not be met, it required to demarcate using the Bisitela River (i.e. the Niuman River) or the Jieya River (i.e. the Jingqili River), and occupy the north bank of the middle reaches of the Heilong River; if this requirement also could not be met again, it required to demarcate using Yakesa but to keep fishing and hunting grounds shared by China and Russia at the Niuman River and Jingqi River area. The Russian government also instructed Golovin that "If the Chinese insist on their original ideas, make no concessions and are not willing to conclude a treaty under above-mentioned conditions, the envoy must follow the command of His Majesty the Tsar and the military orders of the Siberian department to take action (action about fighting)."[47] It can be seen that although the Tsarist government sent a negotiating mission, it did not give up achieving the purpose of aggression by means of war.

In February 1686 (the 25th year of the Kangxi period), Golovin started from Moscow. In September 1687 he arrived at the east bank of Lake Baikal. At that time Russia's domestic and international situations had changed. In spring of 1687 the war between Russia and Turkey broke out. The Russian troops were defeated in the Crimea, and the Tsarist government could not afford another war with China in the Far East, so Russia had to slightly reduce its expansionist activities in the Far East and correspondingly changed its position in the negotiation with China. In June 1687 the Tsarist government issued instructions to Golovin that Golovin could accept the idea of Russian withdrawal from Yakesa, but required that both China and Russia could station troops and build military fortifications in Yakesa.[48] After that, according to the instructions of the Russian government, Golovin prepared specific negotiation plans, in which one plan was that in addition to withdrawal of Russian troops from Yakesa, Russia also prepared to make some other concessions. In short, in the face of the difficult domestic and international situation, Russia dared not start a war with China rashly. Therefore Russia had to consider spitting out a little fruit of aggression to reach a compromise with China.

Golovin's mission had reached the east bank of Lake Baikal and stayed there for two years. At that time the Qing troops had kept their promise of ceasing fire and withdrawal from Yakesa, so Golovin was not eager to have a negotiation with China. On the one hand, he spied on the actual situation of China and the intentions of the Qing government; on the other hand, he threatened and induced various tribes of Khalkha Mongolia and attempted to make the Mongolian tribes break away from China and acknowledge allegiance to Russia. This dirty trick was seen through by Mongolian leaders Tuxietuhan and Zhebuzundanba, and was firmly rejected. Golovin had brought a letter of credence from the Tsar to Tuxietuhan, which required Tuxietuhan to help Russian troops and lead the army to attack China. At this time Golovin did not dare to deliver this letter. "Why did he not give this letter of credence to the Mongolian envoy, or send some capable aristocrat in military service to take it to Mongolia? The reason why Golovin did not do so was because in his impression, Tuxietuhan and Wendugegen (i.e. Zhebuzundanba) had a close relationship with Manchu Emperor Kangxi (later, when military action had been developed and the political power layout was very clear, this view was fully confirmed). However in the letter of credence from the Tsar to Tuxietuhan the Tsar suggested that the Mongolian Khan "provide assistance when necessary" and jointly oppose Kangxi. Golovin thought to deliver this letter of would not achieve the desired effect. This was based on fact that'Mongolian lords and the Chinese have a good impression of each other'."[49] It can be seen that Mongolia's leaders had patriotic enthusiasm, they were closely united around the central government of the Qing Dynasty, and Russia's provocation and differentiation did not succeed.

On the surface the Golovin mission shouldered a peace mission of negotiation, but in fact it was a murderous expedition army. After their inducement and differentiation failed, they immediately resorted to force, launched a sudden attack against the Khalkha people of China, and implemented a bloody crackdown. On the excuse that the Russian troops had lost cattle, sheep and horses, Golovin slandered the Mongolian people as thieves. He ordered Russian troops to burst into the Mongolian rangeland and wantonly burn and loot. Golovin shouted hysterically that he wanted to "restrict volatility and theft by those ill-conceived border Mongolian residents", "to attack their Mongolian Ulus", and "destroy their tents and capture their wives and children in revenge". "Once our army arrives, Mongols will suffer."[50]

The Khalkha Mongolian people could not bear the ravages of the Russian troops and rose up in resistance. In early 1688 the Mongolian army and people defeated the Russian army in the Chukuboxing (Selenggesike) area.

Golovin hid in the castle of Chukuboxing and did not dare move. However, in the occasion that the Mongolian people won victory against Russia, under Russia's instigation and support Galdan, leader of the Junggar tribe and scum of Mongolia invaded Khalkha Mongolia on a large scale and attacked the Khalkha Mongolian army and people in coordination with military operations by the Russian army. Khalkha was defeated. Tuxietuhan and Zhebuzundanba led their subordinate army and people to flee southward and requested protection and assistance from the central government of the Qing Dynasty. At that time, Golovin took advantage of the conflagration to loot. He and Galdan echoed each other. He sent Russian troops on a large scale to "crusade against" Khalkha. He also absurdly proposed a "submission" clause, which required China's Mongolia to "eternally submit to the noble autocratic rule of His Majesty the Tsar", "collaborate with His Majesty the Tsar's army to fight", pay cattle and sheep tax to Russia, and "provide as many horses and camels as possible". He also threatened the Taiji and the herdsmen of Mongolian tribes to make them cut off all contacts with the Qing government, Tuxietuhan and Zhebuzundanba.[51] Although the Mongolian Taijis and people were under military from the Russian army, their hearts favored the motherland and they refused to yield. Some of them dispatched troops and some of them waited for an opportunity to flee. Golovin ruefully admitted his failure. He said that the Taijis and herdsmen were "obstinate and repeatedly prevaricated", "persisted in their opinions and were unwilling to acknowledge allegiance and serve Russia."[52]

The Qing government sent a negotiation mission headed by Suoetu, minister of internal defense, and Tong Guogang, commander-in-chief and imperial uncle to go to Chukuboxing via Mongolia. Before leaving, Emperor Kangxi showed his determination of regaining lost ground. He said that "the Nerchins, Yakesa, and Heilong River area as well as every river or stream leading to this river are all our territory, and we should not abandon them and give them to Russia."[53] When they got to Mongolia area, the Suoetu party encountered an attack from Galdan. The Khalkha Mongolian tribes fled southward and thus the road of the mission to the north was blocked and Suoetu ion had to turn back to Beijing.

In June 1689 (the 28th year of the Kangxi period) the Suoetu mission set off again, and the negotiation place was changed to Nerchinsk. At that time, because Galdan had defeated Khalkha Mongolia, his crimes of defying the central government and rebellion were very obvious. The Qing government urgently needed to spare resources to deal with Galdan. Therefore it hoped even more to keep peace with Russia to avoid further collusion between

Russia and Galdan. This important change in the northern border situation promoted the Qing government to re-study the negotiating position. The Qing government was willing to make more concessions. Emperor Kangxi said that in order to strive to reach an agreement and realize peace, he was ready to cede Nerchinsk city to Russia. He instructed Suoetu and other people that "now if Nerchinsk is used as the boundary line, Russia has no back-up place for sending envoys and trade, it is bound to be hard to communicate. When you first negotiate, you should still take Nerchinsk as boundary line. If Russia's envoy does not agree to Nerchinsk, you can take the Ergun River as the boundary line."[54]

It can be seen from the instructions received by the negotiation missions of the two countries that both China and Russia were busy with other affairs. They did not want to fight each other and hoped to achieve peace. The Russian government instructed: Yakesa can be ceded. The Chinese government instructed: Nerchinsk can be ceded. Thus there was a basis for reaching an agreement. The future boundary line was necessarily some line between Yakesa and Nerchinsk. This was a boundary line which could be accepted by both countries. Therefore foreign scholars such as Pavlovsky wrote as follows: "The instructions brought to Nerchinsk by the delegations of both parties show in the wording that they actually have common opinions."[55] Mancol also said that "continuous amendment to the instructions of each party provided a basis for agreement."[56]

Sino-Russian negotiations and the signing of the *Sino-Russian Treaty of Nerchinsk*

At the end of July 1689 (the 28th year of the Kangxi period) the Chinese mission arrived at Nerchinsk first. The mission included less than 3,000 officers and soldiers, sailors, servants and porters together with a great number of cattle, sheep and horses used for food and transportation. The mission traveled in two groups. One group was led by Suoetu and Tong Gugang. They left Beijing from Gubeikou, passed by Daerbo, the Kelulun River and the Wendu River and finally arrived at Nerchinsk. The other group was led by Langtan and Sabusu. They shipped from Aihui along the Heilong River, passed by Yakesa, and finally arrived at Nerchinsk.

At that time Golovin still remained on the east bank of Lake Baikal and did not go to Nerchinsk. On the one hand he was still crusading against the Khalkha Mongolians and trying to force Mongolian tribes to "come over and pledge allegiance" to Russia; on the other hand he was strengthening military force in Nerchinsk. He "ordered Ivan (i.e. Nerchinsk Governor Vlasov) to try his best to construct defense works in Nerchinsk and nearby."[57] He attempted to make use of the advantage of forces at the negotiation site to force the Chinese mission to submit.

The Chinese mission had been in Nerchinsk for 19 days. Golovin had still not arrived, but he sent messages to the station of the Chinese mission many times to make accusations and create difficulties. Golovin accused the Chinese mission of having no sincerity in negotiation and violating principles of international law. He said that the Chinese mission had brought too many people. "Do you come to fight? If you really want to make peace, I do not think that you would bring such a big troop."[58] He also said that the Chinese soldiers were violent. "Killing and violence also frequently happen."[59] When passing Yakesa, Chinese soldiers had killed two Russians. He also said that the station of the Chinese mission was too close to Nerchinsk city and required the Chinese mission to withdraw to the mouth of the Argun River.

Obviously, Golovin's accusation had no reason. The Chinese mission patiently explained its will for peace and also solemnly refuted the false charges of the Russian party. Suoetu explained that he "only brings attendants and offices and soldiers for the mission's use". In addition, "Sabusu, general stationed in Northeast China and other persons are personnel specializing in administration of the Heilong River area. After the demarcation issue is finished, those places will be delivered to them to manage. Therefore they also come to Nerchinsk from Yakesa by water."[60] The mission had come "not for fighting, but for the purpose of concluding a permanent peace treaty."[61] In fact the size of the army brought by the Chinese mission was less than 3,000, and the Russian army in Nerchinsk had 2,600 people. The military forces at the negotiation site were roughly equivalent. The Chinese party had no intention of threatening with more soldiers. Suoetu also pointed out: "in your letter last year, you said, 'take 500 officials and 50,000 soldiers to come for negotiation'."[62] It can be seen that it was Russia not China that was making a deceptive show of strength and assuming a fighting posture, and wanted to threaten the other side with more soldiers.

The Chinese mission pointed out to the Russian party that it had ordered officers and soldiers to strictly observe discipline. The so-called two Russians being killed at Yakesa had nothing to do with China. In fact, it was completely fabricated by Golovin. The Yakesa Russian authority also admitted that "the Chinese people quietly passed by Albajin (i.e. Yakesa) and did not seek a quarrel". The Chinese troops passing by Yakesa "seemed to be for negotiation, and the troops did not receive orders to take any action over crops planted in Albajin and nearby."[63] It was ridiculous that Golovin required the Chinese mission to withdraw to the mouth of the Argun River because the mouth of the Argun River was about 900 *li* away from Nerchinsk city. If the Chinese and Russian missions were so far apart, how could they negotiate? The Chinese mission pointed out that "since you and I are to meet to negotiate for reconciliation, living nearby was only for the convenience of communications and business discussions. There is no malice."[64] On the eve of the negotiations, all kinds of accusations and deliberate harassments raised by Golovin were spurned by the Chinese mission.

On August 19 the Golovin mission arrived at Nerchinsk. Then both parties consulted about time, place and way of negotiation, and determined that the negotiation should start from August 22 and would be held in a tent put up 200 sagene out of the Nerchinsk town. Each party could have 300 officers and soldiers at the negotiation site with knives and swords, but no firearms were allowed. In addition, Chinese vessels could carry 500 soldiers to berth 200 sagene away from the negotiation venue to balance with the Russian forces in Nerchinsk city.

On August 22, both parties entered the meeting venue. The Russian party forestalled China by showing its strength. When marching, their flags, weapons, etc. carried by guards of honor were in good order and drums and music were played. The tents of the Russian party were furnished luxuriously, and the three envoys (Golovin, Vlasov and Kornitsky) wore gorgeous clothes and had an air of arrogance. The Russian guards violated the agreement of no firearms, and hid grenades. The Chinese party put up a refined black tent, but there were not many ornaments and there was no guard of honor and band. Seven envoys (Suoetu, Tong Guogang, Langtan, Bandarshan, Sabusu, Mala and Wenda) sat together, showing a simple, natural, intimate and unanimous atmosphere.

As soon as the negotiations began, Suoetu and Golovin had a heated tit-for-tat debate. Golovin insisted that the Heilong River basin "has been owned by His Majesty the Tsar since ancient times", but he could not offer any evidence. In fact "since ancient times" just referred to the invasion activities of Boyakefu and Khabarovsk 40 years earlier. Golovin also made unfounded counter-charges. He accused China of "suddenly sending troops to invade the border of His Majesty the Tsar... provoking bloodshed" and "provoking a war owing to such small disputes."[65] He required the Chinese government to compensate for Russia's loss and punish the relevant personnel. Suoetu solemnly refuted the ridiculous false charge. He pointed out that "the Tsar has never owned land in the Heilong River area, and all the lands on the side of Lake Baikal belong to Chinese emperor."[66] He listed many facts, and illustrated that "both Onon and Nerchinsk are the original living places of our Maomingan and other tribes, and Yakesa is the living place of our official Aerbaxi and other people,"[67] and "hometown of our Daur Governor Beiler"[68] as well. The people on these lands have been paying taxes to the Chinese government. Their leaders and descendants are still alive and have fled to inland China because of the intrusions of the Russian Cossacks.

Suoetu briefly reviewed the history of the Russian invasion of the Heilong River region. He pointed out that local people of all nationalities of China "suffered unbearable ravages for years. Their property was stolen, their wifes and children were looted and they were killed."[69] Golovin lightly described the Russian army's crime of murdering and setting fires on Chinese territory as a "little dispute". It was really very ridiculous. The Chinese government had repeatedly persuaded and warned, but the Russian side had turned a deaf ear. Suoetu said that "For years, we waited for you to come to your senses". "Our majesty repeatedly wrote letters to announce orders, but he has not had any response. On the contrary, you invaded our border ceaselessly. Therefore we stationed troops in Heilongjiang and other places for defense."[70] The Chinese government could not take any more and so fought back in self-defense and expelled the aggressors. It was a just action. The responsibility of "provoking a war" lay in the invasion by Russia. If "punishing murderers" and "compensation" were to be discussed it should be that Russia punished murderers on its side and compensated the losses of the Chinese victims. Suoetu said that in order to strive to realize peace with Russia, China was only negotiating demarcation of the border and trying to reach an agreement, and did not put forward the requirement of "punishing murderers" and "compensation" to Russia.

This debate involved the ownership of the Heilong River, who was the aggressor, who started the war, and other major issues of principle. Golovin was unable to find a word to justify himself and was dumb as a fish in the face of facts and evidence.

Then Golovin put forward the first demarcation proposal, which is to use the Heilong River as the boundary line between China and Russia. Suoetu flatly rejected this ridiculous proposal, and put forward using the Lena River and Lake Baikal as the national boundary between China and Russia. Both parties clashed again, but no result was achieved.

On August 23 the second meeting was held. In the meeting, Golovin stuck to demarcation using the Heilong River and deployed a variety of tactics. Sometimes he blustered and swaggered, and sometimes he spoke sugared words. However the Chinese mission was not swayed. Finally, Golovin made a deliberate gesture and pretended to make a concession. He proposed to use the Niuman River as the boundary line. This proposal still put the northern bank of the upper and middle reaches of Heilong River under the jurisdiction of Russia. Of course, the Chinese mission would not agree. However Suoetu and other people mistakenly thought the Russian mission had been making a concession and immediately put forward a new proposal with Nerchinsk as boundary. The Chinese mission lacked diplomatic negotiation experience and did not have a program of gradual concession. It laid out the bottom line instructed by Emperor Kangxi all of a sudden, and ceded Nerchinsk to Russia. It hardly realized that it had swallowed the Golovin's and lost the room for maneuver. When hearing that the Chinese government was willing to cede Nerchinsk, Golovin was very happy because the preset purpose of the Russian government had been met. However in order to extort more interests at the negotiating table, he deliberately continued to get dispute with the Chinese mission and rejected China's demarcation proposal.

The Chinese mission did not realize Golovin's show was fake. When they saw their final proposal was rejected, they thought that the negotiations had broken down. They had nothing to say, was very disappointed and prepared to return to Beijing. Golovin persuaded the Chinese mission to stay in Nerchinsk and continue negotiation through Thomas Pereirain (Portuguese) and J. F. Gerbillon (French), two foreign missionaries serving as interpreters for the Chinese mission. Thomas Pereirain asserted: "there is still great hope for the conclusion a treaty."[71] J. F. Gerbillon said: "The Russians will abandon Yakesa."[72] From August 24 to September 6, the two missionaries went between the stations of the Chinese and Russian missions and carried out negotiation. With the help of Thomas Pereirain and J. F. Gerbillon, Golovin tied the Chinese mission down in Nerchinsk. On the one hand, he made sure the negotiation did not reach the point of breaking down out; on the other hand, he was reluctant to reach an agreement for a long time, bargained on all issues, and did his best to trick and blackmail. The Chinese mission was eager for the success of the negotiation. In addition to conceding Nerchinsk, the Chinese mission made many concessions as follows: First, the Chinese mission had proposed demarcation of the middle border between China and Russia, namely demarcation between China's Khalkha Mongolia region and Russia. Golovin feared that demarcation of the middle section would influence Russia's momentum of expanding southward, so he strongly objected to it. In order to rapidly demarcate the eastern border, the Chinese mission agreed to Golovin's request, and temporarily shelved demarcation of the middle border. According to Suoetu's account of the situation at the Nerchinsk negotiation eight months later, "I have declared the wish to determine the Khalkha issue through negotiation, but you said that Khalkha has not settled down and there is no imperial order from the Tsar, so temporarily it was not discussed and shall be discussed later."[73] Second the Chinese mission had ceded the boundary line at the northern bank of the upper reaches of the Heilong River to the Erbiqi River about four to five hundred li east to Nerchinsk, which was beyond the instructions of Emperor Kangxi. According to the missionary, it was said that "the imperial envoy had the Chinese emperor's final decree, that is, to demarcate the boundary along the Chuoerna River, but the imperial envoy demarcated the boundary to the Gerbiqi River behind the Chuoerna River, beyond the emperor's instructions."[74] Third, the Chinese mission also ceded the boundary at the southern bank of the upper reaches of the Heilong River to the Argun River. The mouth of Argun River was only 900 *li* away from Nerchinsk. This huge region had silver mines, salt lakes and vast farming lands and pastures and was a fertile region most coveted by the Tsar.

The Chinese mission made concessions step by step, and it really had nothing left to concede. However Golovin still played diplomacy and extorted endlessly. At that time, when they heard the news of arrival of Chinese mission, the Chinese people of various nationalities, who suffered Russia's oppression and had been driven in to the mountains and forests, successively came to look for relatives from the motherland. They brought along the old and the young, took tents, drove camels and sheep, broke through the blockade of the Russian army, and finally came near Nerchinsk. The Chinese mission "encountered a large number of Khalkha people, who were at least six to seven thousand in number. They had risen to resist against the Russians."[75] Golovin feared development of an anti-Russia struggle by Chinese people would burn all of Russia's colonial interests to ashes, so he quickly changed tactics and took out the demarcation proposal predetermined by the Tsarist government and quickly reached an agreement with the Chinese mission to avoid further development of the situation. Thus he hastily sent his messengers to the station of the Chinese mission in the middle of night, and agreed to withdraw from Yakesa.

Ownership of Nerchinsk and Yakesa was the focus of debate in the negotiation. China had agreed to cede Nerchinsk, and now Russia also agreed to withdraw from Yakesa. Thus the problem was resolved. After that a series of arduous and strenuous negotiations on other issues and specific details were carried out, and finally an agreement was reached. On December 7, 1689 (the 24th day of the 7th month of the 28th year of the Kangxi period), China and Russia formally signed the Treaty of Nerchinsk.

The *Sino-Russian Treaty of Nerchinsk* was the first treaty signed between China and Russia. The official version was the Latin version and was signed

Fig. 9.2. *Sino-Russian Treaty of Nerchinsk*, Latin version (part)

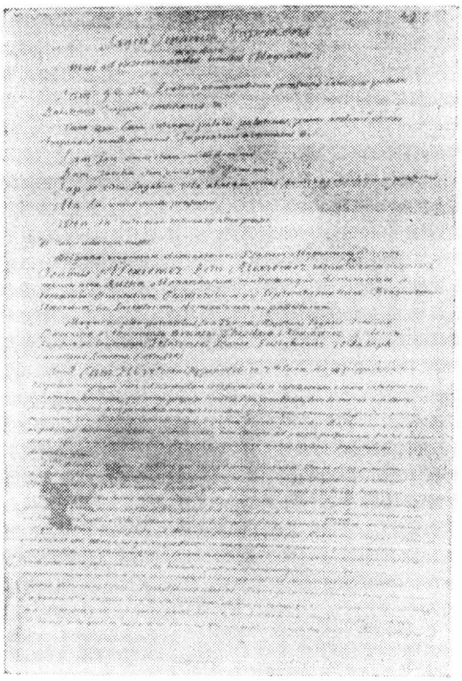

Fig. 9.3. *Sino-Russian Treaty of Nerchinsk*, Latin version (part)

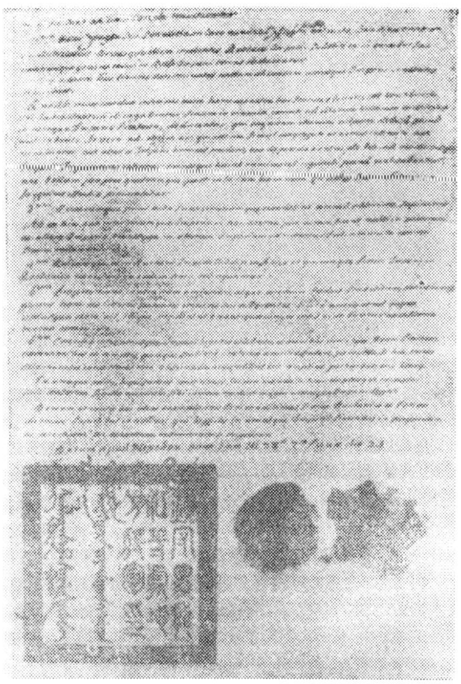

and sealed by the representatives of both parties. In addition, there was a Manchu version and a Russian version, but neither were official versions. The Treaty had six articles in total. Its substantive part included: demarcation of the eastern border between China and Russia, cross-border incursion and treatment of escapees, communications and trade between China and Russia and so on.

Demarcation of the eastern border between China and Russia was the most important part of the Treaty. The Treaty definitively stipulated that the Argun River, Shidaxingan Mountains (i.e. Waixingan Mountains) and E'erguna River were the boundary line between the two countries. It also stipulated that the region between the Waixingan Mountains and Wudi River was temporarily shelved for further negotiation. The Qing government made major concessions in territory. It ceded Nerchinsk and the territory west of Nerchinsk to Lake Baikal which originally belonged to China to Russia in exchange for the withdrawal of Russian troops from Yakesa. Therefore, in the Treaty, it stipulated that all the strongholds of Russia in Yakesa and the south bank of Argun River should be demolished and moved.

The *Sino-Russian Treaty of Nerchinsk* strictly prohibited cross-border incursions, and stated that both parties shall not house escapees in order to reduce border disputes. It also stipulated Russia's long-standing requirement. A French historian commented as follows: "due to growing administrative costs and wars carried out in the west, Russia's treasury was very empty and it was in urgent need of gold and silver. As long as an agreement can be reached between Russia and China, the consequent trade between the two countries will not be small and can bring considerable benefits for the Russian side."[76]

The *Sino-Russian Treaty of Nerchinsk* was an equal treaty. Representatives of both parties negotiated within the scope of prior instructions of their respective governments. They did not and also could not use force to impose their will on the other party, and the final agreement reached between China and Russia did not go beyond the scope that the Chinese and Russian governments were willing to accept. The Treaty clearly demarcated the eastern border between China and Russia. It confirmed that the vast areas of the Heilong River basin and Wusuli River basin were China's territory by law. The Treaty also met the requirements of Russsia in territory and trade. In some books of the Soviet Union it was said that "the Treaty of Nerchinsk signed in 1689 was essentially a great diplomatic victory of Moscow."[77] "The Nerchinsk negotiation was a formal and equal negotiation." "This treaty consolidated and expanded harmonious relations between the people of the

Fig. 9.4. *Sino-Russian Treaty of Nerchinsk*, Manchu version (part)

Fig. 9.5. *Sino-Russian Treaty of Nerchinsk*, Russian version (part)

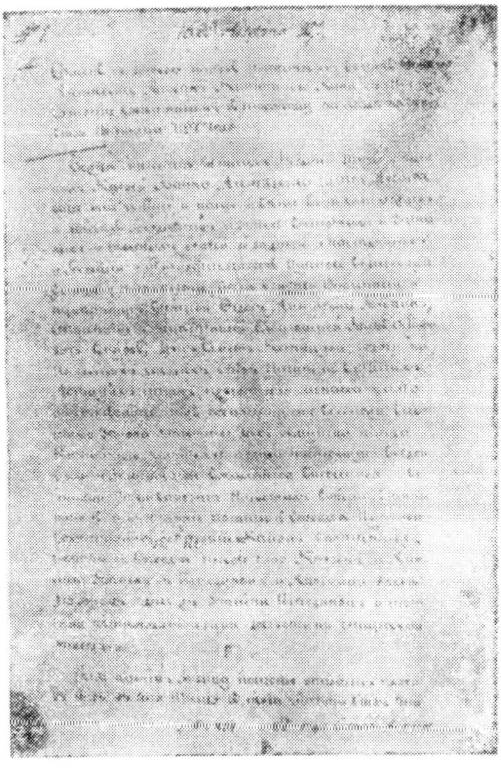

two countries."[78] In a period of time after the Treaty was signed, the eastern boundary between China and Russia was stabilized, the border was relatively calm, and peaceful communications and trade between the people of two countries also had some development.

The Signing of the *Sino-Russian Treaty of Kiakhta* and Aggression of Foreign Countries to China through Religions

The signing of the *Sino-Russian Treaty of Kiakhta*

The Mongolian region including the Lake Baikal area has been China's territory since ancient times. As early as the Warring States period, Huns of China established a powerful country of slavery here. In the Three Kingdoms, Northern Wei, Zhou and Sui Dynasties, Xianbei, Rouran and the Turks continued to rise and occupied the land. The Tang Dynasty defeated the Turks and established officials to administrate, and built the Anbei Frontier Command. In the Liao and Jin Dynasties, the Mongolian tribe originally living in the Argun River basin gradually moved westward. Genghis Khan rose here. He unified the area north to desert, made expeditions and established the Mongol Empire. The area north to the desert and Lake Baikal zone were under the jurisdiction of Lingbei province in the Yuan Dynasty. In the Ming Dynasty, it belonged to the Wala and Tatar of Mongolia, and in the late Ming Dynasty it became the area of the Khalkha. Khalkha Mongolia was divided into the three parts of Tuxietu Khan, Chechnya Khan and Zhasaketu Khan. They established close political and economic relations with the Qing Dynasty. In 1638 (the 11th year of the Chongzhen period of the Ming Dynasty, the 3rd year of Chongde of the Qing Dynasty), the three Khalkha Khans officially acknowledged allegiance to the Qing Dynasty, and paid tribute of the nine whites to the Qing government.[79]

While invading the Heilong River basin of Northeast China, Russia also invaded Mongolia. Russian troops built castles in Uddinsk, Selengesike (Chukuboxing) and Nerchinsk, and enslaved and suppressed the local Buryats and Khalkha. Tuxietuhan and other Mongolian leaders sent emissaries to Moscow and asked the Tsar to stop the invasion, but Russia shut its eyes to it. Mongolian soldiers and civilians could not stand it any longer and rose in revolt. In 1688 (the 27th year of the Kangxi period) Russia colluded with and supported Galdan of Junggar to attack from both sides and defeated

Khalkha Mongolia. The Khalkha suffered huge losses and successively moved southward. Russian troops took advantage of the conflagration to loot, deployed in large numbers, attacked southward and encroached on the northern territory of our country. As one scholar of Russian history said: "Cossacks of Selenge Ge Sike... successfully captured a piece of land quite far away to the south of Selenge Ge Sike. They first sent quartering soldiers to occupy the land, and then set up outposts. By using this method they specified the boundary of Selenge Ge Sike today. This boundary line was only to consolidate actual occupation in law, which was a national contribution of the Cossacks to the county."[80]

From the late 17th century to the early 18th century, on the one hand, due to the signing of the *Sino-Russian Treaty of Nerchinsk*, trade between two countries was greatly developed. Russian trade caravans frequently came to Beijing and sold a large number of furs. They also transported a large amount of silk, cloth and medicine out of China. Profits made by Russian businessmen were very big. For example, in 1705–1709, the trade caravan led by Peter Kutiyakv was said to make a profit as high as 270,000 rubles; on the other hand, Russian Cossacks continued to invade Mongolia, looted the population, plundered cattle and sheep, built houses in the land of China, and established strongholds. The situation on the middle border between China and Russia was increasingly tense. The Government constantly lodged protests with Russia, but the Russian government turned a deaf ear. In 1717 (the 56th year of the Kangxi period) Emperor Kangxi pointed out: "In order to determine and discuss the Khalkha issue, I have written to Chahan Khan (i.e. the Tsar), but there has been no response for more than ten years."[81] As Russia's invasion and harassment upon Mongolia, China became more and more serious, the Qing government decided to suspend trade from 1718.

In 1720 (the 59th year of the Kangxi period) the Russian government sent Special Envoy Lev Vasilevich Izmailov to Beijing to negotiate the issue of resuming Sino-Russian trade. Lev Vasilevich Izmailov was ordered to obtain a wide range of commercial and political interests for Russia, and seek to conclude "free trade treaty" with China. This mission stayed in Beijing for more than three months. Emperor Kangxi interviewed them more than 10 times, and expressed China's wish for peace to the mission over and over again. Emperor Kangxi said that: "I always want to keep a solid peace with your emperor. Moreover, is there any reason that our two countries must fight? ... Both countries have a lot of land. What benefit does a war bring to the two countries?"[82] He wanted to demarcate the boundary of China and Russia in the Mongolia region to maintain stability on the border. However,

Lev Vasilevich Izmailov avoided discussing this topic, and the demarcation issue continued to be delayed.

When the Lev Vasilevich Izmailov mission returned to their country, the Qing government allowed Lanck, secretary of the mission, to stay in Beijing. During his stay in Beijing Lanck brazenly carried out espionage activities. Meanwhile, Russia also carried out aggression and subversive activities in the Northwest region of our country. It attempted to tempt and force Tsewang Araptan, leader of the Junggar tribe, to "acknowledge allegiance" to Russia. When it heard this news the Qing government really could not endure it. In 1722 the Qing government announced a halt to Sino-Russian trade, and ordered Lanck to leave Beijing. Sino-Russian relations became tense again.

In 1722 Emperor Kangxi died and Yongzheng ascended to the throne. In 1725, Peter I also died of disease. In line with Peter's intentions before his death his wife, Catherine I, sent Savoie Fratislava as envoy to China to negotiate trade and border issues in China in 1725 (the 3rd year of the Yongzheng period). Prior to departure, in the instructions to Savoie, the Tsarist government said that he must ask China to cede the "Outer Baikal district, Uddinsk, Selengesike, Nerchinsk and other places;" "if the Chinese people insist on not ceding the places absolutely needed by Russia, the envoy must not make any compromise."[83] Savoie took a group of surveying and mapping personnel and Eastern Orthodox missionaries. In addition, he also took armed forces of 1,500 people, led by Colonel Buchholz who had been moving about with the Junggar tribe for many years. In 1726 (the 4th year of the Yongzheng period), Savoie reached the Chinese border and he wrote a secret letter to Jesuit missionary Dominique Parrenin and "asked him to provide assistance in intelligence information."[84] Through the string-pulling of Dominique Parrenin, Savoie bought off Great Academician Ma Qi and stole a large amount of confidential information of the Chinese government and negotiation delegation, putting the Chinese party in a very passive and disadvantaged position.

In the 11th month of 1726 (the 4th year of Yongzheng period) Savoie went to Beijing to congratulate Yongzheng on his ascent to the throne and to hold negotiations with the Chinese government. The representatives on the Chinese side who participated in the negotiation included Fubina, minister of the Ministry of Personnel, Tegutui, minister of the Ministry of Tribal Affairs, and Tulishen, vice minister of the Ministry of War. No specific agreement was reached in the negotiations in Beijing. Only general principles were discussed and it was agreed that a border negotiation would continue to be held at the Boer riverside. During the negotiations Ma Qi disclosed the Qing government's decision and intentions to Savoie, which provided all kinds of opportunities to the Russian side. Savoie reported to the Russian government that "it seems that things go smoothly. The Chinese emperor desires peace" and "old ministers of the Kangxi period have been replaced by incompetent young people."[85] However, despite this, Savoie also saw that China at that time still had the power to regain lost ground. Therefore he suggested that Russia should strengthen its strongholds in the occupied areas as soon as possible. "Troops of Her Majesty the Tsarina should be increased at the border, and he "hopes to make it serve for the highest interests of Her Majesty the Tsarina by threats or other means."[86]

In the 6th month of 1727 (the 5th year of the Yongzheng period) the boundary survey conference was held at the Boer riverside. The negotiators for China were Longkeduo and Tulishen. At that time Emperor Yongzheng had decided to get rid of Longkeduo, but he asked him to preside over the boundary negotiation. Moreover he said in advance that "if you have ulterior motives, want to ruin things, and the boundaries determined are not in line with the guidelines...I will surely punish you."[87] In addition there was a Galdan Daikichi hidden in Khalkha Mongolia who was bought off by Russia. Galdan Daikichi disclosed a lot of confidential information to the Russian side, so the work of the Chinese delegation was very difficult. During the early stage of negotiations, Longkeduo's attitude was firm and he refused Russia's unreasonable requirements. Through Ma Qi Savoie knew inside information of the Qing government very well, and he ordered Buchholz to seize strategic important places. He assumed a battle position and openly threatened China with force. Furthermore he threatened that: "Russia has ended its war in Europe. Now it can focus its attention on the boundaries on the other side."[88] Early in the 8th month, Emperor Yongzheng ordered Longkeduo dismissed from his position because he did not "sincerely render service. If he is left over there, it may result in him acting absurdly and cause trouble. There is no benefit at all."[89] Emperor Yongzheng sent Celing, a Duoluo Prefecture Prince and son-in-law of the emperor, and Bosige jointly with Tulishen to continue negotiations. In such a situation, the delegation accepted all the requirements of Russia and ceded the vast territory in the north to Kiakhta to Russia. On the 31st day of the 8th month of the same year, the *Sino-Russian Treaty of Kiakhta* was signed. Before the boundary had been officially demarcated Savoie not only built fortresses in Kiakhta, but also arranged troops and set up defenses to freely occupy China's territory.

After signing the treaty China and Russia sent officials of border issues to survey and divide the whole border of the middle part between China and Russia. On the 23rd day of the 10th month, 1727 (the 5th year of the

Yongzheng period), *Abahayitu Boundary Treaty* was signed and thus the border from Kiakhta east to the Argun River was demarcated; on the 7th day of the 11th month the *Selenge Boundary Treaty* was signed, and thus the border from Kiakhta west to Binbadabaha was demarcated.

Based on the negotiations in Beijing and by the Boer River, China and Russia signed the *Sino-Russian Treaty of Kyakhta* on the 25th day of the 6th month, 1728. This treaty was a general treaty confirming preceding articles, and stipulated the relationship between China and Russia in politics, economy, trade and religion. The Treaty had 11 articles in total. It confirmed the Sino-Russian border stipulated in the *Sino-Russian Treaty of Kiakhta*: Ebo between Kiakhta and Mount Erhuaitu is the starting point of the border between the two countries. The area south to the line from the Argun River in the east to Mount Shabinayi (i.e. Mount Shabindabaha) in the west belongs to China, and the area north of the above-mentioned line belongs to Russia; it reiterated that "since the Uda River and other rivers herein cannot be discussed, they shall be kept in their original state", and both parties shall not occupy this area. The *Sino-Russian Treaty of Kyakhta* stipulated that Russian businessmen could go to Beijing once every three years, and their numbers should be no more than 200. In addition, they could trade in Nerchinsk and Kiakhta. The Treaty also stipulated that Russia could send several Eastern Orthodox priests to Beijing. Meanwhile, China also accepted Russian students to learn the Chinese language in Beijing.

The *Sino-Russian Treaty of Kiakhta* and *Sino-Russian Treaty of Kiakhta* were very favorable to Russia. After the Treaty was signed, Savoie said that by the Treaty, "we not only make China cede a favorable zone at the border, but also lands which have never belonged to Russia are obtained and occupied by Russia"[90] in his memorial to Tsarina Catherine I. In the attestations of other officials of the Russian mission, it was said that the treaty areas were "very favorable" to Russia, and "now, all the counties where Russian people are are several days' travel deep in the territory of Mongolia, and some places are even as far as several weeks' distance. Currently, boundary tablets have been erected smoothly in these places. The boundary delineation makes the territory of Russia expand."[91] The Tsarist government was very satisfied with Savoie's success and appointed him minister of the Privy Council and awarded him a knighthood of the Saint Alexander Medal level.

The Russian Orthodox Church's aggression activities against China

As the Roman Empire split into two parts, Christianity also appeared in two centers of Rome and Constantinople and finally split openly in 1054. The

Western Church took Rome as the center and is known as the Roman Catholic Church or Catholic Church; the Eastern Church took Constantinople as the center and is known as the Eastern Orthodox Church or Orthodox Church.

Fig. 9.6. The North Hall

After the demise of the Eastern Roman Empire, the Russian Orthodox Church grew gradually stronger and was in a leadership position. In Russia, the Eastern Orthodox Church was an "ordinary tool of state and turned into a tool for internal oppression and external looting."[92] Wherever Russian aggressor troops went, priests of the Eastern Orthodox Church would follow. "The Russian Eastern Orthodox Church played a very important role in settling occupied regions."[93]

In 1665 (the 4th year of the Kangxi period), Russian aggressor troops siezed China's Yakesa, a strategic point along the Heilong River, and constructed Arbajin stronghold. Yermgen, an Eastern Orthodox priest following the troops, built a church in commemoration of the "Resurrection" in the stronghold. In 1671 (the 10th year of the Kangxi period) another "benevolent savior" church was built on high ground outside the stronghold. This was the earliest Eastern Orthodox Church built in China.

From the 1660s, during the fighting against the invading Russian aggressor in various places in the Northeast, Chinese soldiers and civilians successively captured a lot of Russian soldiers. The Chinese government showed leniency to such captives and surrendered Cossacks. Some captives and Cossacks were set free, some were settled in Shengjing and Beijing, and some were enlisted into the Qing army. Later, as their number increased, they were specially arranged into Russia Zuoling, which belonged to the Bordered Yellow Banner, and lived within the Dongzhimen gate. In order to let these Russian people live their original religious life, the Qing government gave them a temple place as a church. This was Nicholas church, commonly known as "Rakshasa Temple", also known as North Hall, or North Church. It was chaired by Leontyev, an Eastern Orthodox priest. The religious activities of these Russians who had joined the banner registration system were protected by the government, which reflected the policy that the Chinese government did not discriminate against proper religious beliefs. The Russian government attached great importance to the Eastern Orthodox Church in Beijing. In the imperial instruction, Peter I required that priests be sent to China. They attempted to make China's emperor, ministers and all the residents convert to the Eastern Orthodox. The Russian side party requested sending another priest to take over from Leontyev in the "North Hall" on the excuse that Leontyev was old. The Qing government agreed to this request. In 1715 (the 54th year of the Kangxi period), Tulishen and other persons were sent on a diplomatic mission to Turehute. When they passed by Russia, they took back ten "foreign monks doing missionary work"[94] including Laurent. These people established a missionary stronghold in the "Rakshasa Temple" to carry out activities.

The *Sino-Russian Treaty of Kyakhta* entitled Russia to send priests to Beijing. It was stipulated in the Treaty that: Russia may send several priests to Beijing and six students shall be allowed to go along with the priests. After that Santa Maria church, commonly known as "South Hall", was established in Dongjiangmi Lane (Dongjiaomin Lane). The Eastern Orthodox mission in South Hall was under the jurisdiction of the Ministry of Foreign Affairs of Russia, and was regularly rotated. The Qing government paid a part of their costs, the Russian government granted them generous subsidies, and the mission also accepted funding from Russian trade caravans. From the perspective of leadership, financial resources and activities, it was not an ordinary religious group, but was a very undisguised intelligence information agency of the Russian government.

From when the Russsian Eastern Orthodox Church in Beijing was established in 1715 (the 54th years of the Kangxi period), members of the mission actively engaged in stealing information on various aspects of China. In 1756 (the 21st year of the Qianlong period) Alexei Vladimir Kim, leader of the Russian trade caravan and former student of the second mission, together with members of Beijing mission, copied a set of province and capital maps of

China in accordance with the collection in the imperial palace of the Qing and delivered them to the Privy Council of Russia. Biqiulin , known as the Father of Russian Sinology, often put on ordinary clothes, surveyed everywhere, and drew a Beijing city map by using the method of eye measurement and pace measurement during the period 1809 (the 19th year of the Jiaqing period) to 1820 (the 25th year of the Jiaqing period) when he worked as leader of the ninth mission. When he left Beijing to return to Russia he carried away a large number of books and maps, and a total of 15 camels were used to transport his luggage.

Many of his works related to our border were very important intelligence information. Therefore someone said that Biqiulin "used his knowledge to serve the Asian Department of the (Russian) Ministry of Foreign Affairs established in 1819."[95]

In 1818 (the 23rd year of the Jiaqing period), the Tsarist government issued instructions to the mission as follows: "The main task in the future is not religious, but is to conduct a comprehensive study of China's economy and culture, and make timely reports on major events in China's political life to the Russian Ministry of Foreign Affairs."[96] The Eastern Orthodox mission actively carried this order. For example: political and military information collected by Tong Zhenghu, leader of the 12th mission, was called "be very thoughtful and meticulous". "When providing information for the Petersburg Ministry of Foreign Affairs, he apparently guided the course of action of the Ministry of Foreign Affairs."[97] Tong Zhenghu also kept on a close eye on China's market. He provide detailed information about tea, quality, price and marketing information of main products such as fur, cloth and tea in the trade between China and Russia. "He advised the Russian businessmen which goods can be sold in the Chinese market, and told them market conditions... He pointed out a course of action without any error to Russian businessmen ... He showed extraordinary talent and creativity.[98]

Before the middle of the 19th century, there was no foreign diplomatic bodies nor diplomatic representatives in Beijing. The Russian Eastern Orthodox Church was the only resident foreign organization in Beijing. Therefore its role in collecting information was very important. Later Babkov, the chief of staff of the Russian West Siberian Military District, said that "to establish this mission was an important measure in our country's foreign policy affairs with China", and "our government can get the most precise and the latest materials about China."[99]

In 1860 (the 10th year of the Xianfeng period), Russia established a legation in Beijing and the missions were restructured to come under the jurisdiction of the Ministry of Religious Affairs. The early activities of the Russian Orthodox mission in Beijing came to an end.

Agressessive Activities of Catholic Churches and the Qing Government's Prohibition of Missionary Activities

Jesuit missionary activities and the calendar dispute in the early Qing Dynasty

After the 15th century, European colonial countries expanded to the whole world. They established colonial rule and cruelly exploited local residents through brutal killing and bloody suppression. In this colonial wave sweeping the world, religion played a very important role. The military flags of European countries were usually raised in backward colonies together with the cross. A large number of missionaries were sent overseas. They would "not only follow the routes of those who conquered overseas, but also often sat in the same vessel with them."[100] In every place occupied by an invading army, the missionaries would act in the role of colonial administrators. "They administered residents who joined the Catholic Church and levied tax in money or in kind and spices tax,"[101] and used religious superstition to paralyze the enslaved people's will to resist.

However, the colonialists encountered another situation in China. China has a long history and splendid ancient civilization, and was a large and powerful country at that time. For quite a long period of time the fleets of the colonial countries could not open the gateway to China. Therefore traditional aggression methods used by missionaries who followed the troops were not applicable. Although many Catholic sects, such as Franciscans and Dominicans, still insisted on the idea of an armed mission and repeatedly called on the King of Spain to send troops to China, at the time no colonial country was capable of sending an expeditionary force which could fight with China. Therefore the idea of an armed mission to China was just a wild dream. These sects had also sent some missionaries to the Fujian and Guangdong coastal areas. As they did in other colonies, they carried their heads high and disregarded the laws and customs of China. Therefore they were strongly opposed by the Chinese people and government. The missionary activities of these sects in China had little success.

Only the Jesuits used a strategy very different from the other sects. The

Jesuit leaders thought that the traditional missionary way of force "cannot be used in the great empire in the Far East."[102] They advocated using indirect and moderate means, abiding by the decrees and laws of China, following Chinese rites and customs, learning Chinese language, and using the Western science and technology being developed to attract Chinese officials and intellectuals, carrying out peaceful penetration over time and so slowly influence and persuade the Chinese people. Because the Jesuits adopted such a strategy, its missionary activities won the support of some officials and intellectuals and made rapid progress. In the early 17th century Matteo Ricci, Sabatino de Ursis, Didaco de Pantoja, Nicolas Longobardi, Johann Adam Schall von Bell and other Jesuit missionaries worked in the Beijing Directorate of Astronomy. They revised the calendar, made artillery, translated books and manufactured instruments for the Ming government. These missionaries were familiar with the advanced results of Western science and technology. They spoke fluent Beijing dialect and wore the clothes and hats of Chinese Confucian scholars. They could talk about the doctrines of Confucius and Mencius, had contact with high officials and noble lords of the Ming court, and strangely combined Western Christianity, Confucian theory and contemporary advanced science and technology together to carry out their missionary activities. By the late Ming Dynasty they had built a lot of churches in different places in China, and admitted thousands of followers.

Founded in 1540, the Jesuits were a tool used by the Vatican to suppress Protestantism and implement overseas colonial expansion. They were well-organized and disciplined, and adopted a flexible strategy and diverse means. The Jesuits stipulated: the branch society of each place must report to the provincial society once a week, and each provincial society must report to the general society once a month, and each branch society must directly report to the general society. People called it a "legal spy system of top-down, bottom-up and in-depth."[103]

The Jesuits were protected and supported by the Kingdom of Portugal and Portugal deemed them a handy tool for overseas expansion. "Wherever Portuguese or other European robbers went, Jesuit missionaries would follow them." "There was no doubt that the authority of the Portuguese bayonet and the terror resulting from Portuguese bayonets made a great contribution to the great achievements made by Francois Xavier and his fellows."[104]

The fall of the Ming Dynasty and entering the Pass of the Qing Dynasty did not interrupt the activities of the Jesuits in China, and Johann Adam Schall von Bell staying in Beijing won the trust of the Qing Rulers very soon. Since the 13th century China had been using the calendar of Guo Shoujing. This calendar had been followed for a long time, and there were a lot of mistakes in the deduction and calculation. Matteo Ricci saw the problems existing in China's calendar. He began to make a new calendar, and Johann Schreck, Johann Adam Schall von Bell and other people continued this work. Entering the Pass by the Qing required a change of dynasty and calendar. The following year (the 2nd year of the Shunzhi period) the Qing court adopted the new calendar made by the missionaries. The calendar was called the Shoushi Calendar. The Qing court also appointed Johann Adam Schall von Bell to be in charge of the Directorate of Astronomy and conferred the title of Tongxuan Teacher on him. Johann Adam Schall von Bell and Emperor Shunzhi had close contacts. "Emperor Shunzhi favored Johann Adam Schall von Bell, and such favor was entirely different from the usual practice. When talking with him for a long time, the emperor was glad to hear what he said". Emperor Shunzhi often called Johann Adam Schall von Bell to the palace, and went to the church of Johann Adam Schall von Bell to visit and chat with him. "The emperor and Johann Adam Schall von Bell got along with each other happily and harmoniously, and their relationship was like father and son."[105] Johann Adam Schall von Bell came in and went out of the court, and took up with influential officials. His missionary work was developed greatly. In the later years of the Shunzhi period, there were the footprints of the missionaries in various provinces all over the country. Franz Furtado, deputy chief of the provincial society in China, wrote to the president of the Society of Jesus to ask to reward Adam Schall von Bell. In the letter he said that "his work and diligence and ardency in representing the general affairs of the Society of Jesuits in Beijing make all the things done by us in such a large country greatly possible to realize."[106]

The nature and role of Jesuit missionaries in China was a more complicated issue. On the one hand, because they used science and technology as a means of missionary work, they brought China mathematics, physics, astronomy, the calendar, mapping techniques, artillery building techniques, cartography and other advanced knowledge. This was a major exchange of Eastern and Western cultures before entering modern history. In this process, the missionaries played a useful role. On the other hand, as the advance team of colonialism, the Jesuits were also aggressive. Although they adopted a flexible strategy and trod the straight and narrow path and were careful on the surface, they collected information, stole secrets, interfered in China's domestic and foreign affairs, and also widely established churches, extensively accepted followers, and bullied and oppressed good people in different places. Therefore the activities of the missionaries had serious contradictions with the

Chinese people and the Qing government. Regarding a series of struggles that happened around the Jesuits, these cannot be generally treated with a simple affirmation or denial, but we should make a specific and detailed analysis.

In the early Qing Dynasty, the *"Shixian Calendar"* revised based on the Western calendar was used, causing an outcry from the conservatives. At the end of the Shunzhi period, Wu Mingxuan from Huihui Department and Xinanweiguansheng Yang Guangxian from the Directorate of Astronomy successively submitted letters to the throne to accuse Johann Adam Schall von Bell and other people of mistakes in making the calendar. However, in field measurement, the extent to which the Western calendar was consistent with the actual astronomical phenomena was better than the traditional calendar. Therefore Emperor Shunzhi did not take the advice of the conservatives.

After Emperor Shunzhi died Aobai implemented a dictatorship, and the political climate changed. Yang Guangxian submitted a written letter to the throne again and conducted a fiercer comprehensive attack on Johann Adam Schall von Bell and other Western missionaries. Yang Guangxian said that "the *Shixian Calendar* dares write the words 'made according to the Western new calendar' on the cover of the *Shixian Calendar*. It secretly steals the power of the new calendar promulgated by the emperor and clearly indicates that the Great Qing obeys the Western calendar, ruins the Confucianism of our country and only respects Catholicism."[107] He also accused Johann Adam Schall von Bell of "misusing Hongfan five elements in choosing the funeral date of Heshuo Prince of Rong", and said the "Hongfan five elements is scripture savages. It is sinister to use it."[108] He also said that Johann Adam Schall von Bell had only made the calendar of the "endless Great Qing" for 200 years, which meant that he wanted the Qing Dynasty to be short-lived. Yang Guangxian's attack was not only a criticism of the Western calendar; it was also linked to political issues. He sensationally accused missionaries of attempting to subvert the Qing Dynasty. They "secretly implement evil religion in the name of revising the calendar", "hide in Jinmen and spy on the secrets of the court", and "have 100,000 people in Macau, and occupy Macau as a nest to stand ready to assist overseas dealing". He asked to "execute Johann Adam Schall von Bell and other people according to law."[109] This demagogic incitement caused real concern in the Qing court, and traditional forces such as Confucianism and Buddhism, which were hostile to foreign religions, also came out in support and added fuel to the flames. The ruling Aobai group did not know the facts of the calendar dispute, but they were not satisfied with the open and progressive policy implemented by Emperor Shunzhi and were hostile to the missionaries who were put in important positions by Emperor Shunzhi, so they accepted the charge of Yang Guangxian and threw Missionary Johann Adam Schall von Bell and his assistants Ferdinand Verbiest, Lodovico Buglio and Gabriel de Magalhães as well Li Zubai and other officials from the Directorate of Astronomy into prison.

In the autumn and winter of the 3rd year of the Kangxi period, the Ministries of Personnel and Rites conducted a trial and investigation. This trial started from narrow exclusionism, and did not question whether it was right or wrong scientifically, so it was unjust. Yang Guangxian accused Johann Adam Schall von Bell of stationing troops in Macau and subverting the Qing Dynasty, which was pure fabrication. The Qing court sent people to investigate in Guangdong, and did not verify it. However the result of trial was that Yang Guangxian won the lawsuit and Johann Adam Schall von Bell and other persons were respectively sentenced to put to death by dismemberment or beheading, or banishment. Just at that time a strong earthquake took place in Beijing. The people in the capital were in a panic and thought that it was warning of astronomical phenomena for the unjust lawsuit. Furthermore Johann Adam Schall von Bell and other persons also had the support of the imperial palace. Empress Dowager Xiaozhuang, Kangxi's grandmother, intervened. "The ministers of political assistance reported the case of Johann Adam Schall von Bell to the Empress Dowager for her order. After reading the report, the Empress Dowager was not happy, so she threw the original report to the floor and blamed the ministers of political assistance as follows: 'Johann Adam Schall von Bell was always trusted by the late emperor, and was treated very well. How can you want to put him death?' She ordered him set free immediately."[110] The missionaries survived, but Li Zubai and another four Chinese officials were still put to death. At that time, Johann Adam Schall von Bell was old and suffered a stroke, and was dismissed from his position. Yang Guangxian took over as director of the Directorate of Astronomy. The Shixian Calendar was abandoned and the Datong Calendar was used again. Shortly after, because there were too many errors in the Datong Calendar, the Huihui Calendar was used.

Although Yang Guangxian won, he blindly rejected the Western calendar, and his actual calendar knowledge was very low. Once he worked for the Directorate of Astronomy the work of the Directorate fell into chaos, mistakenly measuring the time and date of solar terms and mistakenly forecasting solar and lunar eclipses repeatedly. Both the Datong Calenda and Huihui Calenda were outdated calendars and were not in conformity with the astronomical phenomena, so needed to be fundamentally revised, but neither Yang Guangxian nor Wu Mingxuan could undertake such a task.

Yang Guangxian knew that this task was beyond his ability, and he had to admit that "now methods for divining changes of solar terms have been lost for a long time. Please allow me to find learned and clever persons to make instruments to forecast them," and "up to now I have not found a person who can divine the changes of solar terms. I suffer wandering arthritis, and cannot supervise and manage."[111] He repeatedly asked to resign, but was not allowed to.

In 1668 (the 7th year of the Kangxi period), Emperor Kangxi had grown up. The contradictions between him and Aobai became increasingly acute, which was first shown in the sensitive issue of the calendar. By that time the talk of errors in the calendar work of the Directorate of Astronomy was been widespread all over the town, but the Aobai group still shielded and covered up. Emperor Kangxi convened Yang Guangxian, Wu Mingxuan and Ferdinand Verbiest to discuss the astronomy calendar together. "You must sincerely revise the astronomy calendar through investigation."[112] He ordered Grand Academician Li Wei to go to the observatory with them, and for them to forecast the place where the sun shadow stopped at noon. After three field tests on the 24th day, the 25th day and the 26th day of the 11th month (lunar calendar), the forecasts of Ferdinand Verbiest were correct but the forecasts of Yang Guangxian and Wu Mingxuan had errors. Emperor Kangxi ordered Ferdinand Verbiest to review the calendar made by Yang Guangxian and Wu Mingxuan. As a result, the mistake of the leap month setting was found. In the calendar, the leap 12th month of the 8th year of the Kangxi period should have been the first month of the 9th year of the Kangxi period, and two spring equinoxes and two autumn equinoxes were mistakenly set within one year. In order to test Ferdinand Verbiest, Emperor Kangxi arranged five tests including two solar terms of Beginning of Spring and Rain Water and the movements of the moon, Mars and Jupiter, and ordered ministers to observe these together. The result was that every item Ferdinand Verbiest said "conformed to the fact" and every opinion of Yang Guangxian and Wu Mingxuan "did not conform to the fact". The Western calendar won owing to its accuracy of actual measurement. Yang Guangxian was dismissed, but he still continued clamoring and refuting as follows: "Ferdinand Verbiest wanted to ruin instruments passed down from Yao and Shun. If the instruments of Yao and Shun can be ruined, all the poems, calligraphy, rites and music as well as articles and systems can be ruined."[113] Yang Guangxian did not acknowledge science and showed a stubborn and conservative attitude. Finally, he was reproached by Emperor Kangxi and was expelled to his hometown. On the way to his hometown, Yang Guangxian died of disease.

The result of the calendar dispute was that the missionaries won. Ferdinand Verbiest took over the position of director of the Directorate of Astronomy. After that many missionaries came to Beijing on the introduction and recommendation of Ferdinand Verbiest. Those missionaries with scientific and technical knowledge or artistic talent, such as Thomas Pereira, Joan Franciscus Gerbillon, Joachim Bouvet, Philippus Maria Grimaldi, J. F. M. A. de Moyriac de Mailla, Jean Baptiste Regis and Ignatius K Gler, worked in the Qing court. Some of them were engaged on the astronomy calendar, reformed Beijing Observatory, and made astronomical instruments; some of them came in and went out of the court and served as imperial teachers to teach Emperor Kangxi mathematics, astronomy and physics; some of them introduced European art after the Renaissance to China, and engaged in music, painting and sculpture; some of them instructed workers in making chime clocks and other machinery in the imperial workshop of the imperial palace; some of them assisted the Qing government to make a national map and were busy rushing around various provinces to conduct field mapping. Finally the famous *Imperial Map of China* was completed. This map was more accurate than pervious maps and more specifically recorded the territory, mountains and rivers of China.

Jesuit missionaries played a useful role in the dissemination of Western science and technology knowledge. They set up a bridge for cultural exchange between China and the Western countries, enabling the Chinese to see some sides of modern science in rapid development by pushing a little of the feudal curtain aside. Of course, due to religious bias, the missionaries could only use the part of scientific knowledge not in conflict with religious doctrines, and could not spread all of the advanced science, but they did bring a fresh breeze to the conservative and arrogant intellectual circles in China. Due to the social conditions in China at that time, Western science and culture introduced to China were only restricted to a narrow circle, were only known to a small number of intellectuals, and could not be widely used and promoted. Moreover the government and influential intellectual figures from the intellectual circles still put Neo-Confucianism and the eight-part essay in the most important position and deemed advanced science and technology as an exotic "insignificant skill". Therefore advanced science and technology did not and could not take root, blossom and bear fruit.

Of course, the missionaries were the advance team of Western colonial expansion. Dissemination of science and culture was only a means of publicizing Catholicism. While affirming their active role in spreading science and culture, we should also see the aggressive role of missionaries. They spied, stole information and intervened in internal affairs and foreign affairs. Many of the confidential documents of the Qing government were sent to foreign countries by missionaries. For example, the *Imperial Map of China*, which missionaries participated in drawing, was a confidential map at that time. However shortly after the map was completed, copies of this map appeared in Paris. Jesuit missionaries regularly wrote a secret report to their superiors, in which there was a large amount of important political, economic, military and diplomatic information. In the negotiations between the Qing government and Russia, the Jesuit missionaries served as interpreters and they disclosed China's internal secrets and strategies to the Russians. Moreover they even helped the Russians to buy over Chinese officials. For example, Missionary Dominique Parrenin bought Grand Academician Ma Qi for Russia, putting China in a very disadvantageous position in the negotiations of the Sino-Russian Treaty of Kiakhta. In the report of Russian Envoy Savoie to the Tsarist government he said: "During my stay in Beijing, I found some kind persons by using gifts through the Jesuit Fathers... Among these people Ma Qi, the current grand academician, provided me with great assistance and promised to assist me in the future. I sent him furs of 1,000 rubles as a gift, and gave priest Dominique Parrenin a hundred rubles."[114] Dominique Parrenin and Ma Qi colluded with each other for a long time. Every time a missionary broke the law and offended, Dominique Parrenin would ask Ma Qi to save him. Dominique Parrenin said: "Ma Qi has taken a shine to Westerners, especially to me. For 36 years he and I communicated with each other and established a friendship."[115]Another example is Ferdinand Verbiest. Ferdinand Verbiest made a large achievement in the dissemination of Western science and he was also humble and careful on the surface. Before his death, he submitted a written letter to Emperor Kangxi which said: "Emperor, I devoted my life to serving your Majesty, and I will die without regret."[116] However when he met Nicholas G. Spatary Milescu, envoy of the Tsar in Beijing, this Ferdinand Verbiest said that he was "glad to do his best to serve the Tsar" and that Emperor Kangxi was a "fickle person", and criticized China as a "savage nation."[117]

In his later years, Emperor Kangyi had been worried about the issue of appointing his successor. His sons fought overtly and covertly and fostered private cliques. The Jesuit missionaries also intervened and attempted to fish in troubled waters. They first wanted to draw in Crown Prince Yinreng. Missionary Jean de Fontaney once reported to the French Church as follows: "The Prince will ascend to the throne some day, and he is now inclined towards us, so it is very important to completely win him over.[118] After Yinreng lost power, the missionaries turned to the other princes and vainly hoped that once the prince supported by them got the upper hand, they could use the prince. After ascending the throne Emperor Yongzheng put Missionary Johanns Mouras to death because Johanns Mouras was involved in the struggles between the princes, and transmitted secret messages for Yintang. In the imperial edict by Emperor Yongzheng, it said: "Saiqihei (Yintang) received Westerner Johanns Mouras as his henchman, praised him, and tried to get the throne. It is universally known."[119] The Cardinal of the News Department of the Vatican issued No. 398 Memorandum, and also admitted that "the cause of the death of this priest owed much to intervention in imperial affairs, of which he was guilty. This issue will make the new emperor and ministers keep a sharp eye on us."[120]

Due to the long-term activities of the Jesuits, by the late Kangxi period there were nearly 300 Catholic Churches and nearly 300,000 Catholics in the whole country. In Beijing there were three churches and one public school. The churches raised funds from Chinese followers to do business. "Each Catholic church actually had businesses making money of 50,000 or 60,000 taels of silver." The three Catholic churches in Beijing had "a total of 700,000 francs, and an income of 180,000 francs each year."[121] Missionaries also made loans to followers, officials and civilians to implement usury exploitation. Even the envoy of the Vatican "condemned their exploitation through usury."[122] Missionaries in the provinces bought a lot of land, opened shops, extorted by trick or by force, and acted illegally. In 1715 (the 54th year of the Kangxi period), Missionary Gao Shangde from the Catholic Church in Zhending County, Zhili beat Zhang Fengshi, a Wu Juren (a military successful candidate in the imperial provincial examination) for rent, and "Fengshi was beaten so that he spit blood and fell down in a faint."[123] The missionaries from Beijing Directorate of Astronomy came forward to protect the missionary, so not only was he not found guilty he also continued to use force and ask Zhang Fengshi to pay mortgage money and rent. If they were so imperious towards a Wu Juren with scholarly honor, their attitude towards ordinary people can be imagined.

In short, although the missionaries brought some advanced scientific knowledge, they came in and went out of the imperial palace, took up with influential officials, stole information, disclosed confidential secrets, exploited with high interest, and oppressed good people. They often had conflicts with the Chinese people and government. In the early 18th century, the Qing government had to take measures to prohibit missionary work.

The Qing government prohibited missionary activities

China is a country with many religions and freedom of belief. Buddhism, Taoism, Islam and Shamanism have been spread freely in China for a long time. Each religion has its different idols and creeds, and many followers, and is not interfered with or restricted by the government. However China has a long culture, and various ethnic groups have their own traditional rites and customs. If a foreign religion wants to spread in China, it must appropriately adjust its doctrines and ceremonies according to China's situation in order to adapt to Chinese society. The introduction of Buddhism and Islam underwent a long adjustment process. When they first came to China the Jesuits also adopted a special missionary way and expressed respect for the Chinese rites and customs and for Confucianism. Some people from the ruling class in the Ming and Qing Dynasties misunderstood that the missionary work of the Jesuits was elucidation of the doctrines of Confucius and Mencius in another form. Someone praised Johann Adam Schall von Bellchall as follows: "Catholicism respects heaven, and Confucianism also respects heaven; Catholicism goes into truth thoroughly, and Confucianism goes into truth thoroughly...You are a Western Confucian scholar, that is to say a great Confucian scholar in China."[124] Jesuits often called themselves "vulgar overseas Confucian scholar." They tried their best to adapt their missionary way to Chinese rites and customs. It was precisely because of this that they could make a stand in China and achieve certain results in carrying out missionary activities. However the missionary methods of the Jesuits were fiercely opposed by other sects. In the late Ming Dynasty, other sects complained to the Pope that the preaching way of the Jesuits in China was against doctrines of Catholicism. In 1645 the Vatican ordered the Jesuits to change their methods. The Jesuits in China realized that if they adopted the missionary methods used in the colonies, then they could not make a stand in China, so they filed a defense to the Vatican. At that time the Jesuits were supported and sheltered by Portugal, and Portugal's overseas forces were very powerful and the Jesus monopolized religious activities in the Far East, so the Vatican had to listen to their views. In 1656 the Vatican issued an order and recognized the methods of the Jesus in China.

However it did not end there. As the situation developed, the overseas strength of Portugal and Spain gradually declined and the strength of the Netherlands, Britain and France grew. In overseas missionary work, the Portuguese also increasingly lost the right of control. With the support of France, the Vatican tried to put overseas missionary activities under its unified leadership. The Jesuits that had been sheltered by Portugal were impugned by the Vatican in Europe. Within the Jesuits there were more and more missionaries of non-Portuguese nationality, and they tried to get rid of Portuguese control.

Against such a background, the question of whether the missionary methods of the Jesuits in China were adequate was stirred up again.

Because among the missionaries there were a lot of complaints about the Jesuits, the Pope sent Margaret, a Catholic father of a French foreign mission, to China to investigate in the second half of the 17th century. Margaret objected extremely to the Jesuits' methods and accused them of confluence with heresy (refers to China's Confucianism and rituals and customs), and required them to change their missionary strategies and methods. The Jesuits did not accept this. Therefore the Vatican determined to intervene. In 1705 (the 44th year of the Kangxi period), Priest Charles-Thomas Maillard De Tournon as special envoy of the Pope came to Beijing with the order of the Pope. In the order, the Pope prohibited the Chinese who joined Catholism to worship Confucius and ancestors, and required missionaries to prevent confusing "God" and "Jehovah" with "heaven" and "the emperor" which were always worshiped by the Chinese people. After Charles-Thomas Maillard De Tournon arrived in Beijing, Emperor Kangxi received him several times. He explained to Charles-Thomas Maillard De Tournon that: worshiping Confucius means to respect the saint, worshiping ancestors is not to forget to be thankful for existence and upbringing, and respecting heaven and serving the emperor is "a universal truth and law under heaven."[125] These were traditional Chinese ethical concepts and customs, and must not be abandoned. Western countries should not ask the Chinese to act according to every sentence of the Bible doctrine, just as the Chinese people should not ask foreigners to act according to the Four Books and Five Classics. Missionaries in China must "strictly abide by the laws". Missionaries who were willing to obey Chinese laws could go and get a permit to stay in China, and missionaries who were not willing to obey Chinese laws should leave China and go back to their own countries. Emperor Kangxi alsos required Charles-Thomas Maillard De Tournon to temporarily defer announcement of the order. However, after he left Beijing and arrived in Nanjing, Charles-Thomas Maillard De Tournon announced the Pope's order. Emperor Kangxi was very angry and he ordered the arrest of Charles-Thomas Maillard De Tournon and escorted him to Macau for imprisonment.

When getting this news, the Vatican's attitude became tougher and it wanted to confront the Chinese government to the end. In 1715 the Pope reiterated a prohibition. He required that missionaries in the Far East must obey the prohibition, or they would be severely punished. In 1720 (the 59th year of the Kangxi period) Jiale, a special envoy of the Pope, came to Beijing to transmit the pope's order, and all the missionaries in China had to obey. Of course, Emperor Kangxi would not accept the order imposed by the Vatican and the relationship between the Qing government and the Vatican broke down. Emperor Kangxi, who formerly had quite a good impression of the Jesuits, realized the arrogance of Western church force and also dimly perceived that European countries would become a serious threat to China. He said that "missionary works of Westerners in China shall be prohibited to avoid making trouble."[126] He also said: "after a thousand or a hundred years, I am afraid that China will be threatened by overseas such as the Western countries."[127]

Due to the tough attitude of the Vatican the relationship between the church and the Qing government significantly deteriorated and missionaries in different places acted illegally. Officials of the Qing Dynasty were very vigilant. In 1717 (the 56th year of the Kangxi period) Chen Ang, regional commander of Jieshi Town, Guangdong reported to the throne as follows: "Catholicism came from Western countries. Now it has established churches in various provinces, and assembled miscreants. These missionaries nursed evil intentions. Currently, churches established in Guangzhou are all over inside and outside the city. In addition, foreign vessels from their countries cluster here. How can we know that they do not collude with each other to make trouble? I request an early total prohibition and not allow them to grow and spread."[128] The Qing court accepted the suggestion from Chen Ang and ordered that missionary work be prohibited. However this order was not vigorously implemented. After Yongzheng ascended to the throne, missionaries intervened in the internal struggle of the imperial family and supported Yintang and Yinti, so Emperor Yongzheng became determined to prohibit missionaries. In early 1724 (the 12th month of the first year of the Yongzheng period), after discussion, the Ministry of Rites responded to the memorial to the throne from Jueluo Man Bao, governor-general of Fujian and Zhenjiang, as follows: "Westerners establish Catholic Churches in various provinces and do missionary work by stealth. Our people are gradually drawn in, and there is no benefit. Except for Westerners in various provinces who are to be sent to Beijing to work, please arrange all the others in Macau as you requested. Catholic churches are to be changed into public offices. The people who join Catholicism by mistake shall be managed and controlled."[129] In the 7th month of this year, Emperor Yongzh eng expressed his determination of prohibiting missionaries to Pere Dominique Parenin and other missionaries. He said: "you want all Chinese become Catholic. This is the aim of your religion, and I know it well. If so, what kind of person shall I be? Shall I be subordinate to your king? The Catholic believers persuaded by you only have you in their eyes. Once something happens, they will only listen to you. I know nothing to fear today, but if thousands of foreign vessels come successively, it surely will cause trouble."[130] After that, except for a small number of missionaries who stayed in Beijing and worked in the Directorate of Astronomy, all the missionaries in various places were moved to Macau, the churches closed, and missionary activities stopped.

After Emperor Yongzheng prohibited missionaries, the missionaries did not give up and they sneaked in to operate in various places. "The number of Western missionaries who incessantly sneak into inland China is countless."[131] Therefore, in the three periods of Qianlong, Jiaqing and Daoguang, the order of prohibiting missionaries was reiterated again and again. As for the missionaries who stayed in Beijing, their number continued to decrease but they still actively collected information and delivered it to foreign countries. At the end of the 18th century, a lot of books about China published in Paris were all written by missionaries, and there was still a lot of information hidden in the archives of the churches in Europe. In 1805 (the 10th year of the Jiaqing period) it was discovered and seized in Jiangxi and was "escorted to Rehe and confined in Elute barracks". In 1811 (the 16th year of the Jiaqing period), the Qing court ordered again: "Except for missionaries engaging in deducing and calculating celestial phenomena and the calendar in the Directorate of Astronomy who are still ordered to hold office, other Western people are to be delivered to the Governor-General of Guangdong and Guangxi. As soon as a vessel from his country gets to Guangdong, the missionary shall be ordered to return to his country."[132] In 1837 (the 17th year of the Daoguang period) Gao Shuoqian, who served as the last director of the Directorate of Astronomy among the missionaries, returned to his country and Vice Director Gaetano Pires died of disease. After that there were no more foreign missionaries in the Directorate of Astronomy and the activities of Catholic missionaries in China in the early stage ended. Soon afterwards, the Opium War broke out. In the roaring of cannons the missionaries returned and the missionary activities of Western countries in China entered into another stage.

10

Chapter

Unification of Ethnic Minority Areas on the Frontier and the Consolidation and Development of a Multiethnic Country

The Qing Government Putting Down Galdan's Separatist Forces in the Junggar Area and Unifying the Northern Desert Region

Ethnic minorities on the frontier in Western and Northern China in the late seventeenth century

"China is a country with a large population composed of numbers of different peoples."[1] After the Qing Government crossed the Shanhaiguan and established its national rule, the ethnic minorities such as the Mongol, Tibetan, Hui, Uygur, Kazak and Brut, etc. distributed in the vast areas on western and northern borders of China established political and economic ties with the central Qing government, increasingly becoming integral members of our multi-ethnic country.

The Northern Desert, "five thousand *li* from east to west and three thousand from south to north,"[2] on China's northern border with Hulunbeier of Heilongjiang in the east, Hanhai in the south, the Altai Mountains in the west, and Russia to the north had long been the home and nomadic area of the Khalkha Mongolians in China. Khalkha leaders were of the royal clans of the Yuan Dynasty, namely the descendants of Gelie Senzha • Zhalaier, the youngest son of Dayan Khan who was the fifteenth generation descendant of Yuan Taizu. According to historical records after Dayan Khan died, his sons and grandsons occupied the whole territory of Mongolia; however, "only his son Gelie Senzha • Zhalaier decided to stay in his original land and named his branch the Khalkha. He prepared seven flags and distributed them to his seven sons who would then rule the more than 10,000 people of this branch."[3] This is referred to as "Khalkha • Duolun • Heshuo" (the Seven Khalkha Flags). Before the Qing Government crossed the Shanghaiguan the three major feudal lords, namely Tuxietu Khan, Zhasake Khan and Chechen Khan, had established a link with the Qing Government. In 1638 (the eleventh year of the Chongzhen Reign of the Ming Dynasty; the third year of the Chongde Reign of the Qing Dynasty), the three branches of the Khalkha "sent their emissaries to the Qing Government". The Qing Government specified that each of the three Khalkha branches must pay a tribute composed of "one white camel and eight white horses, which was called the tribute of nine whites."[4] This meant that the Khalkha officially belonged to the Qing Government. But in 1646 (the third year of the Shunzhi Reign), Shuolei who was the Chechen Khan enticed Tengjisi who was the leader of Sunite Branch of Inner Mongolia into launching an anti-Qing rebellion when the Qing army was invading Shanhaiguan and was unable to move into the northern border. Both Chechen Khan and Tuxietu Khan dispatched troops to assist in the rebellion. Since the Qing army was called out rapidly to suppress this rebellion, it was soon put down. In 1648 Tengjisi surrendered to the Qing Dynasty, and Shuolei the Chechen Khan and Bu the Tuxietu Khan paid a tribute of camel and horse again while "confessing their guilt by presenting an article."[5] In 1655 (the 12th year of the Shunzhi reign), Chahui Duoerji who was the son of Bu the Tuxietu Khan, Babu who was the son of Shuolei the Chechen Khan, Norbu the Zhasaketu Khan and Danjin Lama who was the leader of Saiyin Nuoyan "sent their people to pay tribute to the Qing Government;"[6] in the same year, the Qing Government established Bazha Sake in Khalkha and divided this into left and right wings. In this way, the political relationship between the Khalkha Mongolians and the central government of the Qing Dynasty was enhanced.

The region to the west of Khalkha was where Elute Mongolians moved about in search of pasture. They "all graze to the north of the Tianshan Mountains and to the south of the Altai Mountains"[7] and in the vast region to the east and south of Balkhash Lake.

The Elute Mongolians, as a branch of the Mongolian group in China, were called Hanyilati in the Yuan Dynasty, Wala in the Ming Dynasty and Weilate, Welate or Elute in the Qing Dynasty.[8] Western historians called the Elute the Galmeck, which was "not the way the Elute Mongolians called themselves"[9] but was borrowed by Europeans from the Turkic neighbors of the Elute and the Russians.[10] The Elute have long been a member of our multi-ethnic country—China. Before the establishment of the Yuan Dynasty the Woyilati submitted to the authority of Genghis Khan who had his daughter married to the leader of the Woyilati so as to establish generations of marriage relationship. As a result, the Woyilati became an important part of Mongolia in China. After the Yuan Dynasty was established, the central government set up the "Branch Department of State Affairs" in Woyilati pastoral areas in order to govern it and sent officials from the royal clans and ministers to govern Woyilati. The future generations of these royal clans and ministers became the leaders of the Elute branches and their lineage could be clearly analyzed even in Qing Dynasty.[11] After the end of the Yuan Dynasty the Ming government continued the sovereignty of central government in the Northwest region, setting up *Wei* (衛) and *Suo* (所) while proposing the official positions such as commander, Qianhu and Baihu, etc.[12] to Wala leaders; at the same time, the Wala continuously "paid tribute" to the central government of the Ming. In the reign of Yongle, Mahamu, Taiping and Batuboluo etc. who were the leaders of the Wala "came to the Ming and paid the tribute of horses", applying for titles. The Ming government made them the King of Shunning, the King of Xianyi and the King of Anle respectively and "presented the corresponding stamps and imperial mandate."[13] In the early 15th century, Yexian who was the grandson of Mahamu, the King of Shunning, established separatist forces and fought against the Ming Dynasty. His forces routed the Ming troops and captured Zhu Qizhen (Ming Yingzong) in Tumubao (Huailai County, Hebei Province) not far from Beijing. This event was called "the Change in Tumubao." Yexian ruled "the east half of Central Asia and admitted by himself that his rule was on behalf of China."[14] After the death of Yexian his descendents continued to send their envoys to pay tribute and obeyed the jurisdiction of the Ming Dynasty while keeping a close economic relationship with the central government of the Ming Dynasty. The Elute paid tribute of up to thousands of horses to the Ming Government every year so as to import grain, silk, cloth and iron hardware from the central plains area. The Ming government sent its envoys to collect taxes in Elute. In 1610 (the 38th year of Wanli reign), Tomilco Petrov who was the Russian messenger arrived in Elute and met an official sent by the Chinese government for tax collection in Elute. Petrov asked this official about the issues such as the land, population and religions of China.[15]

In about the late 16th century, the Elute was divided into four branches namely Heshuote, Junggar, Duerbote and Torghut. "They lived in pre-designated pastures"[16] and "elected their own leaders,"[17] "moving along rivers and pasture while living without town walls."[18] Their main activities were conducted in the Ili Valley, on both banks of the Irtysh River, and in the Tarbaghatai and Urumqi areas. Some tribes moved along the Irtysh River to the Ob River and Tara area. The Elute had long been holding an alliance conference called "Qigulgan" attended by the feudal aristocracy from the tribes so as to jointly decide internal and external policies and reconcile internal conflicts of interest. The Qigulgan had one or two leaders who were elected from the nobilities of Heshuote. In the early 17th century, Baibagasi from Heshuote was elected as the leader of the Qigulgan.

During this period the nomadic economy of the Elute developed rapidly and the population and number of herd animals increased by a large margin. As a result, the original pastures were not sufficient for distribution. Therefore conflicts happened frequently between the Elute and its neighbors such as the Khalkha Mongolians, Nogays and Kazakhs. At the same time, internal strife over pasture disputes happened frequently inside the Elute tribe. The Junggar moved about in search of pasture along the Ili River valley and had established a developed trading relationship with the central plains area of China, the Monan and Mobei Mongolians, Tibet, and Central Asia. The Junggar enjoyed the most rapid economic development and had the most powerful forces. Halahula who was the leader of the Junggar competed with Baibagasi and then jointly executed the power of Qigulgan leader.

When Batuer Huitaiji, the son of Halahula inherited the leadership, the power of the Junggar became stronger. Batuer Huitaiji relied on the increasingly prosperous animal husbandry economy while enforcing the development of agriculture and handicrafts, having the captured Bukhara people open up farmland and plant wheat and millet; in addition, Batuer Huitaiji owned a large number of carpenters, plasterers, smiths and armor craftsmen and established several residential towns based on Lama temples. Politically Batuer Huitaiji further consolidated his authority, forcing the four tribes of the Elute to obey his rule. Since Heeerleke, the leader of the Torghut who roved around Tarbahatai, had conflicts with Batuer Huitaiji and would not obey his rule, he led about 200,000 of his people to migrate to the western area in 1628 (the 1st year of the Chongzhen reign; the 2nd year of the Tiancong reign, Later Jin Dynasty) and reached the downstream area of River Volga after passing through many places. Subsequently Tulubaihu (namely the Gushi Khan), the brother of Baibagasi who was the leader of the Heshuote, led his people to move southeastward from the Urumchi area to Qinghai due to his conflict with Batuer Huitaiji in around 1637 (the 10th year of the Chongzhen Reign; the 2nd year of the Chongde Reign of the Qing). In 1640 (the 13th year of the Chongzhen reign; the 5th year of the Chongde reign of the Qing), in order to ease the internal contradictions between the sub-tribes of Mongolia, a conference was organized by Batuer Huitaiji and attended by the leaders of sub-tribes of the Elute including Heeerleke from the Torghut in the downstream area of the River Volga, Tulubaihu of the Heshuote in Qinghai, and the three Khans of Khalkha. Monan-Mongolia did not attend this conference. The conference issued the Mongolia-Weilate Code, adjusted the relationship between Mongolian tribes, consolidated the rights of the feudal aristocracy and herd owners to exploit herders, and ensured that unified deployment and mutual support should be realized in the case of wars against foreign forces. However the conflicts between Mongolian tribes remained extremely acute after the conference. Batuer Huitaiji fought with Altai Khan (also known as Aritan Khan), to which Zhasaketu Khan of Khalkha belonged, for several times. Additionally internal conflicts frequently occurred between Elute Mongolian tribes. In 1653 (the 10th year of the Shunzhi reign) Batuer Huitaiji died[19] and his son Sengge inherited the leadership of the Elute Qigulgan. At the same time, fierce conflicts occurred inside the Elute. Sengge and Eqiertu of Heshuote launched a fight against Zhuotebabatuer who was the brother of Sengge and Chechen Taiji and Abalai who was the younger brother of Eqiertu. In the first instance Sengge won the advantage in the struggle and consolidated his governance. However he was assassinated in 1670 (the 9th year of the Kangxi reign). The Junggar became acephalous. The sixth son of Batuer Huitaiji, Galdan had studied Lamaism in Tibet from his childhood. Immediately after Sengge was murdered Galdan hastened back to the Junggar, declaring that he would take Sengge's revenge upon the command of the Dalailama and put down the civil strife of the Junggar. He expelled Chechen Taiji, the enemy of Sengge, killed Suonuomu Alabutan, the son of Sengge, imprisoned his own uncle Chuhuer Wubashi and killed Eqiertu Chechen Khan, his father-in-law. On the principle of "those who resist shall perish" Galdan established a reign of terror by bloody means. He sent his troops to Qinghai to attack the Heshuote and then sent to Southern Tianshan to destroy Yerqiang while colluding with Tsarist Russia to attack Khalkha Mongolia. Galdan "called himself the Boshuoketu Khan and forced the Weitelas to follow his orders."[20] In the second half of the 17th century, the Junggar under the rule of Galdan had developed into a powerful separatist force that controlled the northern and southern parts of Tianshan Mountains while threatening Qinghai, Tibet and Khalkha Mongolia. As a result, the Junggar became a severe threat to the consolidation of national unity and national solidarity.

In the meantime the Yerqiang Khanate, a local feudal regime with the descendents of the Mongolian Chahatai Khan as the ruling class, was established in the Uighur region in South Tianshan and was called *Huibu* (回部) in the books written in the Qing period.[21] Immediately after the Qing Government crossed the Shanhaiguan, the Yerqiang Khanate established "tribute payment" and trade relations with the Qing Government. In the early years of the Shunzhi Reign, the Hami authority of Yerqiang supported the anti-Qing struggle launched by the Hui and Han people in Gansu and broke its ties with the Qing Government for a time. In the year 1656 (the 13th year of the Shunzhi reign), Abudule Khan of Yerqiang restored the ties with the Manchu court, "sending his special envoys to Shengjing. At first, he was willing to send ten envoys; finally, he assigned thirty envoys to have an audience with the emperor. The three hundred followers stayed in Suzhou, applying for grain and rewards". The envoys brought camels, horses and uncut jades. The Manchu court bestowed a reward of 338 pieces of satin and 720 pieces of silk. It was agreed that the tribute should be paid once every five years and that only thirty envoys were allowed to enter the capital and the others should stay in Gansu. "The goods carried were allowed to be stored in the warehouse in capital, and the frontier trade was conducted in due form."[22] The people of the Yerqiang Khanate had long before converted to Islamism. In the last years of the Ming

Dynasty in the reign of the Chahatai King Lashide Khan, a missionary named Mahedumi Azhamu went from Samarkand to Kashigaer to do missionary work. He called himself "Hezhuo", namely the shereef, and was worshiped by Lashide Khan who sincerely believed in Islamism. The offspring of Mahedumi Azhamu lived in Kashigaer and Yerqiang for generations and had great power and impact.[23] "*Huibu* treated them as the offsprings of lords and supported them."[24] The power of Mahedumi Azhamu's offspring kept increasing. Finally, Mahedumi Azhamu's families became the actual rulers of South Tianshan and the Chahataihou King was completely controlled by Hezhuo.

Sectarian disputes, namely the dispute between the "black mountain sect" and the "white mountain sect", were a long-term phenomenon during the dissemination of Islamism in the south of Xinjiang. This dispute became increasingly intense in the early Qing Dynasty. In the early years of the Kangxi reign, Izmir Khan the Chahataihou King supported the "black mountain sect" in expelling the "white mountain sect", whose leader Apaike had recourse to the Junggar to the north. This gave an opportunity to the Junggar in which the separatist force had been long been established to invade the south of Xinjiang. In the year 1678 (the 17th year of the Kangxi reign), Galdan who was then the leader of the Junggar took the opportunity to advance his troops, "subduing the Khans as offspring of the Yuan and forcing them to move to the northern part of Tianshan. Both *Huibu* and Kazak were under his control."[25] Thereafter the Yerqiang perished and the rule of the descendents of Chahatai in the Uighur region came to an end. The Junggar began to control South Tianshan.

Russia's invasion of China's western and northern regions and the anti-Qing wars initiated by Galden

"Beyond all doubt, Russia was an aggressive country."[26] Since the 16th century Russia had, under the drive of major serf owners and merchants, performed acts of aggression and expansion rapidly. Russia was at war with Poland, Lithuania and Sweden in Europe while moving into the East, crossing the Ural Mountains, subduing the Kazan Khanate, Astrakhan Khanate and Sibil Khanate, and marching into Siberia. After the mid-17th century, the forces of Tsarist Russia crossed Lake Baikal and Waixing'anling and broke into the Heilongjiang River basin in northeastern China while invading the Khalkha region in northern China and the Elute region in western China.

Tsarist Russia invaded Elute Mongolia by force of arms or "conciliation" means. When they felt that the swift and fierce nomads who moved about freely and quickly on the grassland were too powerful to "conquer", they would not use armed intrusion but "sent their envoys"[27] to entice the tribal leaders of the

Elute into "joining the Russian nationality" through intimidation and bribery so as to divide China and encroach on our territory. In 1607 (the 35th year of the Wanli reign in the Ming period), Gagarin who was then the Tara General sent a deputation to Junggar in accordance with the command from Moscow, inducing its leader to "join the Russian nationality". The Tsarist Russian government sent a deputation with Gerupin as the director from Tara to Junggar in 1609 (the 37th year of the Wanli period in the Ming Dynasty) and suggested that the Junggar should "swear loyalty to the Tsar and sign a corresponding treaty."[28] In 1616 (the 44th year of the Wanli period in the Ming Dynasty), the Tsarist Russian government sent a deputation with Petroff and Cunikin as the directors from Tobolsk so as to "induce its Taiji to yield surrender."[29] In the following year, the Tsarist Russian government sent Chavy Lev to Junggar to persuade it to agree. However the persuasion and unreasonable demands of the Tsarist Russian aggressors were rejected by Batuerhui Taiji, the leader of the Junggar. Subsequently, the increasingly powerful force of the Junggar attracted more attention from the Tsarist government. When the Junggar was under the rule of Sengge, the Tsarist government continued to dispatch envoys to ask Sengge to submit to the Tsarist Russian government. These requirements were sternly rejected by Sengge who a lodged strong protest against Russia's plundering of his people. In 1667 Sengge led more than four thousand of Junggar's armed forces and people to besiege Krasnoyarsk, which was the outpost of Tsarist Russia for invasion of the Junggar. The Tsarist Russian aggressors got their comeuppance from the angry armed force and people of the Junggar.

When invading Elute Mongolia, Tsarist Russia dispatched its troops to Khalkha Mongolia in the north of China. As early as in the first half of 17th century, the Tsarist government began to take aggressive steps against Khalkha Mongolia. In 1616 (the 44th year of the Wanli period in the Ming Dynasty), the local authority of Tobolsk (Russia) sent Cumannic and Petrov to the Altai Khanate[30] to conduct espionage. They gained quite a lot of information about the Ming Dynasty. In the year 1636 (the 9th year of the Chongzhen reign of the Ming Dynasty; the 1st year of the Chongde reign of the Qing Dynasty), the Tsarist Russian government successively sent Paijkullchaning and Starrkov to Altai Khanate as envoys in order to persuade Altai Khan to submit to Russia. In the 1640s after the Russian colonial forces crossed Lake Baikal, an "exploration crew" from Tsarist Russia forced an entrance to the Chechen tribe of Khalkha in 1647 (the 4th year of the Shunzhi reign). In the same year a secret agent by the name of Pohabov scurried to the court of the Chechen Khan, suggesting that the Chechen Khan take Tsarist Russian nationality. This suggestion was rejected by Chechen Khan. However the Tsarist Russian aggressors did not give up their ideas. "In order to continue the negotiation with Chechen Khan and present the gifts from the Tsar,"[31] the Tsarist Russian authority dispatched a diplomatic mission headed by Zabolotsky from Tobolsk in 1649 (the 6th year of the Shunzhi reign).Unfortunately Zabolotsky was shot by Buryat Mongolians who fought against the invasion. Led by Panfil Semyonov, the interpreter, the diplomatic mission arrived at the court of the Chechen Khan and tried to persuade Tayha, who was the widowed wife of Shuolei the Chechen Khan, to take Russian nationality. This suggestion was rejected again. In the second half of the 17th century, the invader forces of Tsarist Russia penetrated directly into the territory of Tuxietu Khan in the Selenga River basin and established military strong points such as Selengsk (Chukubaixing) and Irkustsk etc. successively. The invasion launched by Tsarist Russia against Khalkha was strongly protested by Tuxietu Khan, who was the leader of Khalkha Mongolia in China. Tuxietu Khan sent his envoys time and again to Moscow for negotiations, requiring the Russian forces to leave Chinese territory. In the year 1672 (the 11th year of the Kangxi reign), Tuxietu Khan and his younger brother Jebsundamba Khutuktu (the Lamaist leader of Khalkha Mongolia) sent their envoys to Moscow requiring that the Russian army leave Selengsk and notifying the Russian government that they would have friendly relations with Russia if the Russian government stopped the expansion, but that the Mongolians would rise to resist the invasion of the Russian government went on with the invasion. In 1675 another Mongolian diplomatic mission headed by Biliketu arrived in Moscow, remonstrating against the unjustifiable crimes of the Russian Cossacks who "attacked those who paid real tax of fur to us, seized a great many women, children and properties, and destroyed the residence of the Buriat people who paid real tax of fur to us, disturbing the lives of our people, forcing them to flee, and making them unable to work normally." The Cossacks "humiliated the Mongolians by every means, robbing and looting them, and beating them to death."[32] However the Russian aggressors turned a deaf ear to the remonstrations and warnings of the Mongolian authority and intensified their aggressive activities. The Mongolian soldiers and civilians came to the end of their endurance and conducted frequent anti-Russian struggles. For example, the Xieyigong Taiji of a Mongolian tribe attacked Russian aggression strongholds such as Balagansk in 1668; and in 1671 the Russian warlord of Yeniseysk received the plea for help from the Russian Cossacks in Nerchinsk. In the letter the Cossacks said they were "besieged in castles by Mongolians and nearly starving to death." The warlord then received a plea for help from Selengsk. In this letter, "the Russians called for more military service personnel so as to ward off the neighboring Mongolian Taiji."[33]

In 1684 the Qing government sent its troops to Heilongjiang, deciding to recover the territory seized by Tsarist Russia. The Jaxa War was thus of the utmost urgency. The Tuxietu Khan cooperated closely with the central Qing government to press ahead with the anti-Russian struggle, solemnly and justly requiring that the Russian troops withdraw from Mongolia. Their envoys warned the Russian colonial authority in Selengsk that "you must not reside in our territory and your castles will be destroyed", and pointed out that the Mongolian leaders had an ardent love for the motherland and would support the central government. "Our Woqilaisaiyin Khan (also known as the Tuxietu Khan) and Bogde Khan (also known as Emperor Kangxi) will cooperate with each other closely."[34]

The Russian government then sent a diplomatic mission headed by Golovin to China, negotiating with the Qing government about the establishment of the eastern boundary between China and Russia. Golovin together with two thousand soldiers arrived at Lake Baikal in 1687, invading the Khalkha tribes under the pretext that the Mongolians had stolen horses from the Russian troops and burning, killing and pillaging. As a result, the Mongolian ulus were ransacked. In addition, the Russians sent their envoy to require the Mongolian leaders to compensate for the "stolen" horses and to punish the "thieves". Golovin sent letters to Mongolian leaders, rattling the sabre. He declared that the Russian troops "would certainly attack their Mongolian ulus," "destroy the tents, take their wives and children prisoners, and take revenge." "The Mongolians would suffer disaster after the main forces come."[35]

The Mongolians in China had the strong will and brave spirit to fight against external invasion. No pressure and threat would overawe them. In order to take precautions against Russian troops, the Mongolian soldiers and civilians were rallied along the Eerhun River and faced the Russian troops. Although the Russian troops were provided with advanced weapons, the Mongolian soldiers and civilians rallied around Tuxietu Khan and Jebsundamba Khutuktu and fought bravely, shattering the Russian troops. The Russian troops scampered off like frightened rats. Golovin and the Russian troops were holed up in Selengsk castle. The Mongolian soldiers and civilians were roused greatly. When the Tsarist Russian troops were surrounded by the Khalkha Mongolians Galdan, the feudal lord of Junggar, suddenly attacked the Khalkha Mongolians as they fought against the Russian troops, leading his troops across the Hangai Mountains and attacking Tuxietu Khan, stabbing the Khalkha soldiers and civilians in the back.

At that time Galdan has unified the Junggar and occupied South Tianshan, exerting influence on Qinghai and Tibet. Galdan became increasingly ambitious, "looting the surrounding regions based on his powerful and prosperous tribes."[36] He had been planning an attack on the Khalkha for a long time. Prior to this, civil strife broke out among the Khalkha. Elinqin (also known as the Altai Khan) who was the feudal lord of the Zhasaketu tribe killed Wangshuke the Zhasaketu Khan. As a result, the tribes were in havoc. "The people broke ranks and most of them turned to Tuxietu Khan."[37] Chahuiduoerji (Woqilaisaiyin Khan) who was the Tuxietu Khan cooperated with Tenzin Lama who was the director of Saiyinnuoyan to defeat Elinqin who then went to the Junggar for shelter. Cheng, who was the son of Wangshuke, succeeded to the title of Zhasaketu Khan. After Cheng died his son Shala succeeded to the Khan title. The Zhasaketu tribe had been asking Tuxietu Khan to return its people and this request was rejected by Tuxietu Khan. This resulted in conflict between the Zhasaketu tribe and the Tuxietu tribe. Both the Qing government and the Dalai Lama sent envoys to mediate, but unfortunately this conflict was not resolved. Galdan who had long been "coveting the rich and populous" Khalkha took opportunity to intervene and stir up trouble through gossip, scheming for expansion. He sent Duoerjichabu, his younger brother, to "insult the Tuxietu Khan wantonly"[38] under the pretext that the Tuxietu Khan and his younger brother Jebsundamba Khutuktu "had not respected the envoy of the Dalai Lama". This exasperated Tuxietu Khan who then killed Duoerjichabu, and for this reason Galdan made a large-scale attack on Khalkha.

Galdan attacked Khalkha "suddenly when Tuxietu Khan was unprepared" since he was resisting the invasion of Tsarist Russia. The troops of Tuxietu Khan were taken by surprise and were caught between the hammer and the anvil. Although the Khalkha soldiers and civilians resisted the attack under the command of Tuxietu Khan, they were put to rout due to the fierce attack by Galdan's troops after "fighting hard for three days" in Eluohuinuoer. The civilians "abandoned their tents, utensils, horses, camels, cattle and sheep and headed south."[39] "The valley was filled with routed soldiers; even if you walk for five days, you would see soldiers."[40] "The migrants with trepidation swarmed together like ants and bees."[41] The Russian aggressors lured the elites of Khalkha or threatened them by force when the Khalkha was defeated and in disorder, requiring them to surrender to Russia to be shielded by Russia. At this critical juncture Jebsundamba Khutuktu threw himself into the breach and held to the patriotic policy, inspiring the Mongolian elite with the thought of national solidarity. He said, "Since the Russians do not believe in Buddhism and have different prevailing customs, languages and clothes from us, we should not surrender to them. We had better move inwards and surrender to the Great Emperor (referring to Kangxi) so as to enjoy the peace of thousands of years."

"The people kneeled agreeably to support the decision."[42] As a result, the conspiracy of the Russians to force the Khalkha Mongolians to surrender failed.

It should be pointed out that Galdan attacked Khalkha with the support and connivance of Tsarist Russia, which trained and used Galdan to invade China for the purposes of territorial expansion. Golovin pointed out in his report to the Russian Department of Foreign Affairs that an alliance between Russia and Junggar should be established, suggesting that "a diplomatic mission should be dispatched from Tobolsk to the Elute Khan (also known as Galdan)."[43] As a French historian said: although an official military alliance was not established between Russia and Junggar, "Russia has always supported and taken the part of its powerful neighbor (namely the Junggar) since the support of the Junggar was of great importance."[44] Therefore Golovin "decided to send the Tsarist Russian credentials and the gifts given by the Tsar to him (namely Galdan)"[45] and to actively support the separatist forces of Galdan. For the purpose of annexation of Khalkha Mongolia, Galdan relied on Tsarist Russia to split the motherland. From the year 1674 (the 13th year of the Kangxi Reign) to 1683 (the 22nd year of the Kangxi Reign), Galdan sent his envoys to Russia nearly every year "in the attempt to enter into a military alliance and require the Russians to give 'troops and arms'."[46] The Mission Diary of Golovin recorded the talks with the Mongolian seigniors. "Kaermeike Boshuoketu Khan (namely Galdan) launched the war under the royal instruction from your majesty (namely the Tsar). A large quantity of Russian troops with a large number of firearms and cannons cooperated with him. On the battlefield, the Kalmuck intimidated them in the name of royal troops (namely the Russian troops)."[47] In the year 1690 (the 29th year of the Kangxi reign), Golovin wrote in the letter to Galdan that, "you concentrated all your officials and soldiers for an armed attack on Khalkha Mongolia...His Majesty the Tsar launched the same armed attacks in which many Mongolian seigniors were put to rout by officials and soldiers following the plenipotentiary and others were captured."[48] It is thus evident that the Tsarist Russian aggressors launched an armed attack on Khalkha and participated directly in the Galdan Rebellion, committing a bloody crime against the Mongolians of China.

The war in Ulanbutong and the alliance of Duolun

In order to annex Khalkha thoroughly and further enhance his anti-Qing forces, Galdan fell back upon Tsarist Russia, sticking at nothing. When the Qing government was negotiating with Russia about Nerchinsk issues and requiring the Russian government to return the Chinese territory, Galdan secretly sent his envoy Daerhan Zaisang to visit Gisliangsky, the Irkutsk governor, and Golovin, asking Russia to send its troops to cooperate with Galdan's army. In his letter to Golovin Galdan asked that the Russian aggressor troops come "directly to the appointed place so as to fight shoulder-to-shoulder."[49] Galdan unscrupulously sold the holy territory of the motherland. He said in his instruction to the envoy that "Aerbajin (namely Yarkesha) originally belonged to Mongolia but not to Bogda Khan (referred to as the Qing emperor) and that it was him (Boshuoketu Khan) who ruled the Mongolians and this region. He also pointed out that the Boshuoketu Khan would like to transfer this region to the Tsar if the Tsar had a mind to build castles here."[50] In his reply Golovin "promised to support the attack of the Elute troops against Tuxietu with corresponding activities by Russian troops." Subsequently he sent Kibirev to follow Daerhan Zaisang to Galdan, "continuing the negotiation of the possibility of dispatching Russian troops to attack Tuxietu Khan and his supporters."[51]

The Qing government has long been wary of the Galdan rebellion. During the suppression of the the rebellions of the "Three Feudatories" and the resistance against Tsarist Russia in Northeast China, the Qing government had kept an eye on the deve lopment of Galdan's forces in northwest China. As early as in 1678 (the 17th year of the Kangxi reign), the Qing government sent its personnel to Gansu to find out "information about Galdan Taiji of the Helute Tribe and feed the information back from time to time."[52] In the first instance the Qing government was dedicated to the pacific settlement of dissension between minorities, trying to avoid war measures. In the year 1683 (the 22nd year of the Kangxi Reign), the Qing government sent Qitate, the Minister of Internal Affairs, to Junggar to placate Galdan and bestow gifts so as to have him obey the central command and get along with other tribes. At that time, Galdan was still a fledgling and not in real collusion with Russia, so he dare not show his willingness to rebel and pretended to be very respectful and submissive. Galdan "kneeled down to receive the edict"[53] and presented 400 horses, 60 camels, 300 pieces of marten fur and 4 Elute scatter guns. In the following year, Galdan sent a large team composed of 3000 people headed by Gurbanbai to Beijing to pay tribute and establish trade relations[54] and promised to obey the command from the central government of the Qing Dynasty, saying that "I do not dare escape the rule of the Chinese Emperor"[55] and that "I should be always under the control thereof and dare not presume."[56] However he played tricks secretly and pressed ahead with the collusion with Tsarist Russia, preparing for the attack on Khalkha Mongolia. Kangxi hoped to resolve the dissension through mediation even after Galdan attacked Khalkha and beat Tuxietu Khan. Kangxi suggested that the central government of the Qing Dynasty should hold a conference attended by the representatives of the Dalai Lama, Galdan and Tuxietu Khan etc. in which the Tuxietu Khan should offer an apology and Galdan should promise to stop the war and withdraw his troops, and return the seignory and people to Tuxietu Khan etc. Kangxi's suggestion was rejected. Galdan was insufferably arrogant, requiring that Kangxi hand over Tuxietu Khan and Jebsundamba Khutuktu, and shouting that "I will try to fight for five or six years and promise to exterminate Khalkha and capture Jebsundamba."[57]

In June 1690 (the 29th year of the Kangxi reign), with the support of Russia, Galdan felt emboldened to dispatch his troops south in the name of chasing the Khalkha and penetrated into Uzhumuchin of Inner Mongolia, defeating the cavalry led by Alani who was the minister of the Ministry of Tribal Affairs of the Qing government at the Uhui River. The Russian envoys billeted with Galdan recorded this battle. "Boshuoketu Khan (Galdan) led his troops to fight against the Chinese after ordering the arms and equipment in a sort of way. This battle lasted from the daybreak to the afternoon. Boshuoketu Khan killed many Chinese soldiers...He seized more than five hundred carts and all the supplies and gear of the army."[58] Galdan won the first war and held his head high. He threatened Ulanbutong (in the south of Keshiketeng Banner, Zhaowuda, Inner Mongolia) which was only 700 *li* from Beijing. The Qing government was shocked and people were in a panic. The government moved its forces in a hurry. "The government enforced the restrictions in the capital. Each Niru sent up to eight gunmen. Almost all the government offices were closed, and the rice price rose to more than three *liang*."[59] The Qing government divided its forces and made a joint attack. The emperor appointed Fuqian the Prince Yu (the elder brother of Kangxi) as the Fuyuan General who would lead the left wing of the Qing troops out of Gubeikou and appointed Changning the Prince Gong (the younger brother of Kangxi) as the Anbei General who should lead the right wing of the troops out of Xifengkou. Kangxi was willing to leave the boundary personally and go to the front. However he stopped in Boluohe Tun (Longhua County, Hebei Province) because of illness, and commanded the troops there.

Galdan arrayed his army in Ulanbutong. "Tens of thousands of cavalry were at the mountain foot, relying on the woods and stopping the water. Tens of thousands of camels lay on the ground with their feet tied and with cases stacked and wet felt on their backs. The arrangement was made like grille. The soldiers operated arrows and blunderbusses in the clearance between stacks. This is called the 'camel town'."[60] On August 1, the 29th year of the Kangxi reign, the Qing troops advanced to Ulanbutong, "organizing the array at the river bank. The soldiers in the front lines held firearms and attacked the core forces of the enemy."[61] This battle was extremely fierce. According to a foreign preacher, "this battle started with artillery and muskets followed by close fighting."[62] The two parties launched a fight unto the death. Under the heroic attack of the Qing troops, the "camel town" of Galdan was destroyed. "The array was broken down". The Qing troops followed up their victory with hot pursuit and utterly defeated the rebel forces. "Galdan ran away at night."[63] The Qing troops suffered heavy losses. Tong Guogang, the maternal uncle of Kangxi, was shot dead. Galdan sent his personnel to bargain with the Qing troops after being defeated, "suing for peace with humble words". Under the guiding ideology of avoiding war and of compromise, Fu Quan who was the front-line commander failed to follow up the victory with hot pursuit. As a result, Galdan escaped.

In order to further put down the Galdan rebellion under the support of Tsarist Russia and consolidate the northern border, the Qing government established barracks in Mulanwei and encouraged the soldiers to learn martial arts, "feeding the horses and sharpening the weapons, training the soldiers, practicing techniques for battles, encouraging the generals and soldiers, and drawing a clear-cut line between reward and punishment so as to improve morale and combat effectiveness; on the other hand, take timely measures for the Khalkha Mongolians who "were routed and submitted to the Qing government", requiring the people from the three Khalkha tribes "to be put out to pasture in the areas between the boundaries of the Sunit tribes and be provided with rice from Guihua."[64] After the battle of Ulanbutong, Kangxi established an alliance with tribe leaders of inner and outer Mongolias and combined the forces of the Khalkha tribes so as to further unify the Mobei region.

Dolon-nuur[65] which is located in the northwest of Chengde features an open and flat topography and plentiful water and grass, and was been the place for "internal and external jasaks who came to Beijing to have rest."[66] In May 1691 (April, the 30th year of the Kangxi reign), Kangxi together with the officials and soldiers of the "three upper banners" departed from Beijing out of Gubeikou, going up along the Luanhe River; the officers and soldiers of the "five lower banners" left by Dushikou and joined forces with the officials and soldiers of the "three upper banners" in Dolon-nuur. The Qing troops attending the meeting of sovereigns arranged the barracks and set up sentry posts, showing their mighty power and majestic momentum. It is recorded that "the troops of the three upper banners were in the middle; the two vanguard camps of the Eight Banners, the ten guards brigades and four firearms camps were divided into 28 *xun* (汛, station) and arranged around the emperor's camp."[67] The leaders of the Khalkha tribes and the dukes and Taiji of the 49 banners of Horqin in Inner Mongolia waited a long time "one hundred *li* away from the location of the meeting" for the imperial decree. First of all, Kangxi mediated the dissension between the three Khalkha tribes, pointing out that the Tuxietu Khan should not have annexed the pasture of Zhasaketu and killed Shala the Zhasaketu Khan. Tuxeitu Khan "prepared a memorial of apology". Kangxi appointed Cewangzhabu, the younger brother of Shala, as the leader of the Zhasaketu and made him the Heshuo Prince. After the disputes were successfully settled, the leaders of the three Khalkha tribes were led into the tent of Kangxi in succession by the officers of the Ministry of Tribal Affairs and the Frontier Minorities Temple to meet with Kangxi. "The internal and external lords, Beiles, their sons, the dukes and Taiji etc. were arranged on the left and Khalkha Khans were arranged on the right."[68] Together, they had a royal dinner at which music was played and tea was offered. The Alliance Ceremony was held in a solemn and harmonious atmosphere. The day after, Kangxi gave a dinner for 35 leaders such as Tuxietu Khan, Jebsundamba, Wumohe the Chechen Khan and Cewangzhabu etc. At the meeting Kangxi solemnly declared that the Khan titles of the three Khalkha tribes would be preserved and the titles such as Jinong and Nuoyan etc. of the Mongolian aristocrats should be abolished. The titles of Mongolian aristocrats would be in accordance with the rules of the Manchu aristocrats and include prince, county lord, Beile, son of Beile, Defender Duke, Fuguo Gong etc. The administrative system would be in accordance with the 49-banner system of Inner Mongolia, namely the jasak (banner head) system.[69] The Khalkha were divided into banner teams in accordance with the 49-banner system and provided with land". The Khalkha was divided into 34 banners under positions such as major and assistant commandant etc. which ended the confusion in which the Khalkha tribes "failed to abide by laws and impose restrictions, and bullied and robbed the weak,"[70] and strengthened and consolidated the rule of the central authority over the Khalkha tribes.

The Qing government ruled Mongolia through Lamaism. Therefore a huge lamasery called the "Huizong Temple" was established in Duolun after the meeting of sovereigns in response to the request of the Mongolian aristocrats to "build a temple to manifest the grand ceremony". This temple became the religious center of the Khalkha tribes that temporarily resided in Inner Mongolia. Jebsundamba Khutuktu hosted religious activities there and often led Mongolian aristocrats to the Mulan paddock which was 100 *li* to the east of Duolun to meet with Kangxi who "sometimes made his round every two years. The tribe leaders reported their work jointly here."[71] Later, Qianlong said, "My grandfather put down the rebellion in Khalkha and built the Huizong Temple in Duolun to satisfy the requirements of the people."[72] This reflects the purpose and role of the Huizong Temple built by Kangxi.

The meeting of sovereigns in Duolun was of great significance to the reinforcement of unification of China and the consolidation of the northern frontier defense, having further developed the relationship between the central government of the Qing and the Inner and Outer Mongolias and strengthening the management over the Khalkha tribe. Kangxi said, "The Qin Dynasty constructed the Great Wall in ancient times; now, my court bestows favor to the Khalkha, making it possible to take precautions against the northern forces. The relationship is stronger than the Great Wall."[73] In dealing with invasion by Tsarist Russia and the Galdan Rebellion, the measures taken by the Manchu court had a positive effect.

The war in Jagunmodo and the defeat of Galdan

After the failure in Ulanbutong Galdan fled to Hovd, gathering the remnants of his forces and recovering in an attempt to stage a comeback; he also sent personnel to Moscow, asking for the support of Tsarist Russia. In 1691 (the 30th year of the Kangxi reign), the Tobolsk general sent Matvey Eugene to "the Hovd River basin to meet with Galdan,"[74] continuing to stir up the rebellion.

In 1694 (the 33rd year of the Kangxi reign), with the hope of a peaceful settlement of the rebellion, Kangxi repeatedly asked Galdan to attend the meetings of sovereigns, requiring him to obey the command of the central government. However Galdan disobeyed the command of Kangxi while "invading Khalkha more frequently". He sent letters to the Manchu court asking the Qing government to hand over Tuxietu Khan and Jebsundamba and sent his envoys to rouse the Horqin tribes of Inner Mongolia to betray the Qing Dynasty. At the same time Tsarist Russia sent its envoys to meet with Galdan, promising to "dispatch one thousand scatter gunmen and on-cart cannons to the eastern boundary after the grass turns green."[75] In the year 1695 (the 34th year of the Kangxi reign), Galdan believed he was powerful enough and advanced to the east. He led 30,000 troopers to march along the Kerulen River to the Bayan Ulan areas, announcing openly that "he would rely on the 60,000 Russian scatter gunmen to invade the south of the desert in great force."[76] With the support from Tsarist Russia, Galdan lit the flame of war against the Qing government again.

It was extremely difficult for the Qing troops to go to the northern desert to do battle. As Kangxi said, "I led the army personally and was familiar with the situation to the north of the Great Wall. Since ancient times, it has been difficult to use military forces here. The land here is barren or sometimes short of water. The transport of grain is particularly hard in the sandy areas of Hanhai etc. In the rainy season, it is difficult to cook. We must make detailed plans for action."[77] The Qing government had to send forces to suppress Galdan's forces to ensure the security and unification of the frontier since Galdan was insufferably arrogant and colluded with Tsarist Russia to reject the amnesty and enlistment from the central government of the Manchu court. The Manchu court "called the military officers of Grade III or higher together and required them to present the plans for suppression of the rebellion in detail. All the officers believed it was difficult." Kangxi prevailed over all dissenting views, insisting on ironing out all the difficulties to advance troops to the north of the desert. "When I wanted to lead my army to suppress Galdan in the past, all the officers discouraged me and only Feiyanggu believed that Galdan should be crusaded against. The subsequent two suppressions were my own decision."[78] In 1696 (the 35th year of the Kangxi Reign), the Qing troops were divided into three military units. The troops of the three provinces in northeast China headed by Heilongjiang General Sabusu and the Horqin tribe of Inner Mongolia composed the Eastern Group which "advanced along the Kerulen River"; Imperator Feiyanggu and General Sun Sike "led the Shaanxi and Gansu troops to launch an attack from the west of Ningxia"; Kangxi "led the imperial guards to advance from Dushi", making a long drive forward while carrying the grain and implement a converging attack, hoping to capture the main force of the enemy and win a swift victory. In the meantime, the rebel forces of Galdan fled to the Kerulen River basin. When hearing that Kangxi was leading his army personally to suppress them, they "threw away all their tents and ran away through the night."[79] Kangxi secretly ordered Feiyanggu to intercept Galdan. The Qing troops encountered Galdan's rebel forces in Zhaomoduo and fought hard with them.

Zhaomoduo (which means big forest in Mongolian) is to the south of the Kente Mountains, to the east of the Han Mountains and to the north of the Tula River. With an open and flat topography, Zhaomoduo had been the battle field in the north of the desert from of old. Feiyanggu waited at his ease for the exhausted rebel forces of Galdan and lured the enemy deep into the ring of encirclement. According to the stratagem previously provided by Kangxi, Feiyanggu ordered the officers and soldiers to "get down from their horses and then to get into the saddle after hearing the clarion call." Galdan led more than ten thousand rebel forces to attack the Qing troops who "occupied the commanding position" and "relied on the natural barrier to attack the rebel forces. The crossbows and fire spears shot arrows and bullets repeatedly and then rattan shields were used. When moving forward, the Qing troops arranged the horses in the front for the reinforcement."[80] The two sides conducted a deadly combat. The Qing troops fought a bloody battle from noon to dusk and utterly defeated Galdan, having killed more than 3,000 soldiers of the rebel forces. Anu who was the wife of Galdan was brave and resourceful in battle. She was killed by shells during the charge. "Other soldiers were wound and ran away. Thousands of them died in the valley. Their corpses lay close together." Galdan "led only several troopers to flee". More than two thousand rebels surrendered to the Qing troops.

In the Zhaomoduo battle, the Qing troops basically annihilated the rebel forces of Galdan and achieved the decisive victory of the war.

After being defeated Galdan led the remnants of his forces to flee hither and thither in the Tamir River basin, becoming a group of gangsters who were driven from pillar to post and were approaching the end of their days. Yili, the foothold of Galdan, was taken by his nephew Cewang Alabu when he was attacking the Khalkha. Cewang Alabu sent his envoy to the Qing court to show his obedience to the central government and to declare that he had broken with Galdan. Galdan "had only less than 5,000 soldiers who had very few livestock. Many of them did not even have tents...When the winter was coming, they were in an extremely difficult situation since they had no food, shelter or a reliable source of supply."[81] However, Galdan was so stubborn that he refused to accept the amnesty of the Qing government, continuing to split China and putting up a last ditch struggle.

Kangxi believed that Galdan did great harm to the unification of the nation, saying that "we should make an end to Galdan as soon as possible"[82] and "exterminate his forces immediately after he is defeated."[83] Hence Kangxi decided to launch the third campaign to put down the rebellion in the year following the Zhaomoduo battle.

In 1697 (the 36th year of the Kangxi Reign) Kangxi went to Ningxia, ordering Feiyanggu and Masiha to dispatch troops to suppress the remnants of the forces of Galdan. In the meantime, most of the remnants of Galdan's forces fled. The five or six hundred rebels who had not fled had reached the bottom of the barrel. "They killed horses for food everyday."[84] Tsarist Russia was not interested in Galdan any more. Therefore, when Galdan "wanted to go to Russia, the Russian government rejected his request." Galdan was in an impossible position and knew that the final day would come; as a result, he died of a sudden attack of severe illness. At this point the rebellion of the separatist forces of Galdan with the support of Tsarist Russia was completely suppressed by the Qing government.

The Qing Government Pacified the Junggar Again and Its Rule over Tibet and Qinghai

Cewang Alabutan attacked Tibet and the Qing government escorted the 6th Dalai Lama to Tibet

The Galdan Rebellion was suppressed; however the struggle of the Qing government against the Junggar was not concluded. In the last years of the Kangxi Reign and in the Yongzheng Reign, the Junggar headed by Cewang Alabutan became increasingly powerful and had conflicts with the Qing government.

Tsewang Rabtan was the eldest son of Sengge and the nephew of Galdan. Since he and Galdan were contending for power after Galdan usurped the sovereignty of Junggar, Tsewang Rabtan has to flee from Junggar. According to Emperor Yongzheng, "due to the conflict with Yishu Galdan, Tsewang Rabtan led seven people to abscond to Turpan. Given the fact that Tsewang Rabtan escaped for fear of being murdered by Yishu Galdan, Emperor Kangxi bestowed beneficence upon him. For the Sacred Heart of Mercy, Emperor Kangxi could not bear to send troops to exterminate the remnant tribe of Galdan and he also dispatched an envoy to grant rewards to Tsewang Rabtan. At that time Tsewang Rabtan was obedient and submissive as he lacked power."[85] When Galdan was attacking the Khalkha, Tsewang Rabtan occupied Ili, the foothold of Galdan, and "took in all the remaining subordinates of his father and Galdan and rebuilt the tribe."[86]

After Tsewang Rabtan occupied Ili, he "paid respects and tribute to the Qing Government" and express his willingness to "devote himself to serving the Qing Government"[87] and to assist the Qing army in wiping out the rebel forces of Galdan. After Galdan's death he obeyed the order of the central government to hand in Galdan's ashes and Galdan's daughter Zhong Qihai. At the same time, he made efforts to foster the economic development of Junggar by expanding pasture, developing animal husbandry and encouraging a large number of Uyghur people to move from the south of Xinjiang to the Ili area in the north to engage in agricultural production. As a result, "crowds of farmers stood and looked at each other across the vast expanse of land"[88] and broad stretches of fertile fields appeared gradually in the Ili River basin and the Irtysh River basin as well as in the Urumchi area. Moreover he made effective use of foreign captives and craftsmen to develop the handicraft industry and therefore numerous handicraft workshops for making leather, cloth and woolen goods and for paper-making, printing, etc were successively established. Thanks to the above series of measures, Junggar's social and economic development grew rapidly and therefore the power of Tsewang Rabtan was strengthened gradually. As recorded in literature, Junggar "increasingly thrived during the ten years and became more and more arrogant."[89]

On the one hand, Tsewang Rabtan recuperated and rebuilt Junggar in an attempt to reinforce its internal strength. On the other hand he launched several wars with Tou Khan from the neighboring Kazak. He thereupon occupied the whole area of the Large Yuzi (along the Chu River and Talas River), most of the Middle Yuzi (along Syr Darya), and forced the Small Yuzi to escape to the west. Some cities such as Tashkent and Samarkand were also under his control. According to historical records, "an AQimu from Hui and a Haer Han from Oirat were quartered in the Tashkent city, which was a tradition passed down from Tsewang Rabtan's age."[90] At that time, Tsewang reported on the reasons for fighting against Tou Khan to the Qing court.

However with the increase in economic and military strength, the Junggar gradually changed its attitude towards the central Qing government. It became increasingly unwilling to accept the commands of the central government and requested an eastward expansion of pastures and coveted the reoccupation of the area to the east of the Altai Mountains and the area near Hami. In the year 1714 (the 53rd year of the Kangxi reign), the Junggar "attacked Hami with two thousand soldiers."[91] When Hami's Zhasake Daerhan Baikehemin reported an emergency to the Qing court, Kangxi sent troops to assist Hami and at the same time dispatched an envoy to Junggar. But Tsewang Rabtan refused the envoy's request for discussion of a peaceful settlement of the disputes on allocating pasture. Moreover taking the opportunity of the internal strife in Tibet, Tsewang launched an attack on Tibet in 1716 which revealed his ambition to annex Tibet and split the country. The Qing government dispatched a great army to Tibet in order to crack down on Cewang's separatist activities. The peace between the Qing government and the Junggars was broken and fighting broke out again.

Tsewang Rabtan's attack on Tibet was caused partly by the expansion of the separatist forces, and partly by the change of political situation in Tibet.

Tibet made early contact with Qing government before the Qing government crossed the Shanhaiguan. In 1639 (the third year of the Chongde reign) i.e. four years after the establishment of the Qing Dynasty, Emperor Taizong sent a letter to Dalai declaring that the Qing government admired the policy of Shamanism. At that time Gushi Khan, the leader of Khoshut of Oirat, moved to Qinghai and cooperated with the Shamanism leaders in Tibet, namely the 6th Dalai Lama and the 4th Panchen Lama, in invading Tibet. They defeated and killed the Zangba

Khan, who had dominated Tibet, and set up the joint rule of both Khoshut and Shamanism. The Panchen Lama became the supreme religious leader of Tibet, and the Dalai Lama and Gushi Khan jointly appointed the *"Diba"* (第巴) to take charge of Tibet's government affairs, while the Khan King of Khoshut held the actual power. Gushi Khan maintained close relations with the Qing government. In 1652 (the 9th year of Shunzhi reign), Gushi Khan introduced Ngawang Lobsang Gyatso, the 5th Dalai Lama, to visit the Emperor Shunzhi. The Qing court gave him a ceremonious reception, conferred a honorific title on Dalai Lama, and granted him golden books and seals.

After Gushi Khan passed away, his sons Dayan Khan and Dalai Khan were in charge of the Tibet's government affairs. Until 1701 (the 40th year of Kangxi reign) Dalai Khan died and then his son Lhabzang Khan succeeded. Having been governing Tibet's affairs for sixteen years, Khoshut's nobilities refused to surrender their privilege and therefore had inevitable conflicts with the upper class in Tibet. Meanwhile, Dalai Lama also expanded the power. In 1643, the Potala Palace was extended and became the sacred sites in Tibet. Moreover, through the forcible conversion of other religious sects, the Shamanism managed to strengthen its power, increase its monasteries and monks, and maintained direct contact with the Qing emperor. Whenever the Mongolian King Khan fell vacant, a *"Diba"* was nominated and had the right to appoint and dismiss administrators. In 1679 Sangy Gyatso, the trusted aide of the 5th Dali Lama, was appointed as *"Diba"*. In 1682 the 5th Dalai Lama passed away. But Sangy Gyatso concealed his death and "deceived others into believing that Dalai stayed in the high mansion and refused to see anyone except him. He then gave false orders in the name of Dalai."[92] Due to strict concealment, the 5th Dalai's death was hidden for as long as fifteen years. It was not until the defeat of Galdan that the Qing government learned of the passing of the 5th Dalai and rebuked Sangy Gyatso: "someone from Oirat informed me of Dalai's death. You have long concealed the fact and cheated others."[93] Given that the falsehood has been brought to light and the Qing court was furious, Sangy Gyatso sent a representative to the capital to apologize to the Emperor Kangxi by explaining that "it was for fear of the Tangut's rebellion that he hid the death of Dalai."[94] Although the emperor did not criticize him sternly, Kangxi was severely offended by the deception.

In 1697 (the 36th year of the Kangxi reign), Sangy Gyatso publicly announced the death of the 5th Dalai Lama and declared the official enthronement of Tsangyang Gyatso who was chosen by him as the reincarnated soul boy and as the 6th Dalai Lama. The Khan King of Khoshut was exacerbated by the news, believing that Sangy Gyatso was scheming and supporting a puppet in an attempt to crowd out his forces in Tibet. The contradictions between the Khan King and Sangy Gyatso became increasingly acute. Although exceptionally talented Tsangyang Gyatso, the newly appointed 6th Dalai Lama, was not a devout Buddhist but an elegant, romantic poet. He became tired of the ascetic, puritanical life in the Potala Palace and was obsessed with the pursuit of free and unrestricted love. So Lha-bzang Khan regarded him as a false Dalai Lama and reported his "misconduct" to the Qing court. In 1704 (the 43rd year of the Kangxi reign), as a result of the conflicts of both parties, Lhabzang Khan led troops from their base in northern Tibet to attack Lhasa. Fortunately, thanks to the mediation efforts of the representatives from the three major monasteries, an agreement was reached that Sangy Gyatso would abdicate and his son succeed as Diba. However the conflicts between the Khan King of Khoshut and the upper class of Tibet were not resolved. In 1705 war broke out again in which Tibetan soldiers were defeated and Sangy Gyatso was killed. Considering Sangy Gyatso's previous concealment of the 5th Dalai's death and his collaboration with Galdan, Emperor Kangxi sided with Lhabzang Khan during the battle and conferred on him the title of "devout religious follower and humble Khan". Lhabzang Khan arrested Tsangyang Gyatso, the 6th Dalai Lama, and sent him to Beijing, which aroused the anger of the Tibetan people. Afterwards Tsangyang Gyatso died on the journey to Qinghai.[95]

After the killing of Sangy Gyatso, Lhabzang Khan appointed Yixi Gyatso as the 6th Dalai Lama but the tribes of Qinghai and Mongolia did not obey him and instead selected Guotang Kelzang Gyatso as the real Dalai. In order to ease the conflicts between Qinghai and Tibet, the Qing government dispatched Kelzang Gyatso to live at the Ta'er Monastery in Xining to preside over diocesean affairs and sent Shilang Heshou to assist Lhabzang Khan in government affairs. Nevertheless, there were still strong opposition forces against Lhabzang Khan in Tibet and the situation was not stable.

Tsewang Rabtan had long been watching the turn of events in Tibet before he launched his premeditated invasion of Tibet. On the one hand, he was married to Lha-bzang Khan's sister and adopted Lhabzang Khan's eldest son as his son-in-law, thus utilizing intermarriage to reduce Lhabzang Khan's alertness. On the other hand, he secretly "took other measures to get in touch with the lamas (monks) of three major monasteries i.e. Sera, Zhaibung and Gandan" and "persuaded and bribed the lamas into supporting him, which brought a chain reaction among the ministers and attendants."[96] After a series of preparations, in 1716 (the 55th year of the Kangxi reign), Tsewang Rabtan asked his brother Tsering Dondup to "lead an army of 6000 that walked across the Gobi Desert and Tiannan snow-capped mountains around the clock, meeting many hardships and obstacles."[97] The next July when Lhabzang Khan was unprepared, they entered Tibet directly through the Teng Geli Sea. They then took Lhasa, besieged the Potala Palace, killed Lhabzang Khan, "captured his wife and looted the weapons of all the temples that afterwards were sent to Ili."[98] After the Junggar troops occupied Lhasa they went on a rampage that caused chaos in Tibet. According to the description of a missionary eyewitness, "As soon as Tsering Dondup stepped into the palace he ordered his troops to loot Lhasa. Being the most greedy and cruel robbers, those monks that joined his army intruded into the people's houses with weapons, and even rushed into the temples to sack the stored and hidden property. What is more they repeatedly broke into family houses, insulting and beating some people, whether young or old, and hanging some others from beams, torturing them into telling the places where treasure was stored. The looting and raping lasted for two days until every valuable thing had been taken away."[99] The invasion of the Junggar troops brought great calamity to the Tibetans.

On hearing the news of the invasion of Tibet the Qing government immediately sent Xi'an General Er Lunte and imperial bodyguard Seling to aid Tibet. However, owing to the hurried and inadequate preparations and weak forces, the Qing army lost the battle of Kala Wusu where General Er Lunte forfeited his life.

Emperor Kangxi believed that "Tibet was a shield for Qinghai, Yunnan and Sichuan; therefore, if it was occupied by the Junggar, there would be no peace in the border area."[100] For the maintenance of national unity and the stability of Tibet, Kangxi decided to dispatch a great army to crush the Junggar's rebellion. In 1718 (the 57th year of the Kangxi reign), he appointed the prince Yin Ti as the Fuyuan Great General, the commander-in-chief of the army, "to be stationed in Xining where he governed and paid for the enrolled troops"[101] and to direct the whole Qing army aimed at crushing the rebellion in Tibet. Nian Gengyao was appointed as the Governor-General of Sichuan to assist in military affairs, and Fu Edan and Fu Linan each led troops to regions such as Balikun and Altay so as to tie down the Junggar's reserve forces. In 1720 (the 57th year of the Kangxi reign), Generals Yanxin and Gaerbi led the Manchu, Chinese and Mongolian armies to enter Tibet respectively from Qinghai and Sichuan. The Qing army led by Yue Zhongqi took Chamuduo (Qamdo) from Litang and Batang, and finally occupied Lhasa. With the wide support of the Tibetans, the Qing army defeated the Junggar troops utterly. Tsering Dondup "fled in disorder"[102] and escaped to Ili with the remaining troops.

After the Qing army successfully entered Tibet, the Qing government officially granted the honorific title of "Hongfa Juezhong 6th Dalai Lama" to

Kelzang Gyatso who lived in Ta'er Monastery, and ordered that "Manchu, Chinese and Qinghai armies be sent to Tibet". On the 15th September of 1720 (the 57th year of the Kangxi reign), "the enthronement of Dalai Lama was held on a fine day"[103] conducted by General Yan Xin, which established the official status of the 6th Dalai Lama[104] and helped Tibet restore social order.

Russia's invasion of Junggar and the Junggar's fight against Russia

When Junggar was under the reign of Tsewang Rabtan Russia did not change its aggressive policy towards Junggar. At that time the Emperor of Russia Peter I the Great (1682–1725) was on the throne. Peter the Great was a "foresighted emperor who indicated various aggressive polices to his inheritors;"[105] therefore, ever since his reign, Russia embarked on a path of contending for world hegemony. Peter the Great and his successors launched a series of wars against European neighbors and meanwhile actively implemented the policy of expansion towards the Eastern countries.

In 1713 a Turkmen called Hezuo Naipusi arrived at Petersburg via Astrakhan, claiming that Amu Darya which empties into the Caspian Sea could "revitalize what the ancient geographers called the waterway between the Indian Ocean and the Caspian Sea"[106] and asserting that there was plenty of alluvial gold in the Amu Darya basin, which was confirmed by the envoy Azulborg from Kiva Kingdom in Petersburg.[107] At the same time, Peter the Great received a report from Gagarin, the Governor-General of Siberia, saying that the Yerqiang area in Southern Xinjiang, China was abundant in gold and suggesting that "Russia build some forts from the Irtysh River"[108] to the Yerqiang area. On hearing the news, Peter the Great was ecstatic and determined to commit aggression against the Kiva Kingdom in Central Asia and the Northwestern border area of China with the purpose of "revitalizing the path through India and realizing his ambition."

In order to achieve the aim of aggression, Peter I the Great organized two expeditions: one expedition of 60,600 led by Lieutenant Beikeweiqi of the Guard crossed the Caspian Sea in 1716 and established three forts along the coast;[109] another expedition, made up of more than 4,000 troops and commanded by Lieutenant Colonel Buhegelici went to the Irtysh River in 1715. Then the army led by Lieutenant Beikeweiqi was defeated by the people of Kiva Kingdom and the 6,000 soldiers were completely annihilated. The other army commanded by Lieutenant Colonel Buhegelici entered the middle and upper reaches of the Irtysh River, clandestinely arriving at the Yameishi Lake of Junggar, building forts, planning fortifications and preparing to spend the winter there.

Before the invasion of the army led by Buhegelici, at the request of Peter the

Great, Gagarin dispatched a courier to deliver a letter to Tsewang Rabtan, the leader of Junggar, so as to threaten and coerce him. He said in the letter that "it was unnecessary for you (referring to Tsewang Rabtan) to worry about the aim of the expedition," and "if you did not interfere with the army, you (referring to Tsewang Rabtan) could get support and assistance."[110]

Through contact with Russians the Junggar people had long before seen through Russia's sugar-coated promises and therefore did not believe their lies. In February 1716, sharing bitter hatred of the enemy, an assembled army of over 10,000 Junggar soldiers and civilians led by Tsering Dondup marched to the fortress at Yameishi Lake occupied by Russia and demanded that the invading army withdraw from Junggar. Tsering Dondup gave a warning to the aggressors that if they did not leave, "I will besiege the fortress so that your troops cannot get out... when you all run out of food and are starving I will take the city."[111] Buhegelici was not scared by the warning; on the contrary, he threatened the Junggar people that "he had plenty of supplies and reinforcements would soon arrive here from Tobolsk."[112]

After the failing of the warning and in the face of the Russian aggression, the Junggar soldiers and civilians had to take up their weapons to fight so as to safeguard the sacred territory of their motherland. They attacked the invading army with machetes, spears, bows and arrows, so that the Russian aggressors were utterly defeated. Moreover the courageous Junggar people also wiped out the reinforcements from Tobolsk. In April 1716, Buhegelici had no choice but to destroy the fortress at Yameshi Lake and lead the remnant troops to escape by boat along the Irtysh River. They finally arrived at the Om River and built the Omsk fortress.

The battle of Yameisi Lake was a just war of the Junggar people against Russia's invasion for the sake of safeguarding their own territory. It struck a heavy blow to the aggressive forces of Russia and wrote a glorious page in the history of the Chinese nation's struggle against foreign aggression.

Despite the failure at Yameisi Lake, the Russian aggressors did not give up their aggressive ambitions. In 1719 Peter the Great dispatched another invading army of 440 troops led by Liha Liefu that departed from Tobolsk and marched to Zaisang Lake where they built a fortress. Then the aggressors were again attacked by the 20,000 Junggar soldiers and civilians and had to retreat to Tobolsk.

During 1721 to 1722, Tsewang Rabtan's forces in Tibet were expelled by the Qing army. Consequently, in the face of the dilemma, he was willing to make concessions to Russia and keep peace with it in order to overcome adversity. The Russian government wrongly assumed that it could seize the opportunity and therefore immediately took aggressive action against Junggar again. Peter the Great sent Wenkowsky to Junggar to persuade it to surrender to Russia so that Russia "could protect Junggar from encroachment just as it protects its Russian subjects, and it could send a letter to persuade the Chinese emperor not to bully Tsewang Rabtan because he was a Russian subject. If the Chinese emperor did not listen to the persuasion, I would take steps to force him to agree."[113] Moreover Peter the Great also "tried to convince Tsewang Rabtan to cede territory to him so that he could build fortresses there and form a continuous line of fortresses connecting Siberia with outposts which could also defend the exploration team during their journey.[114] The demands of Russian government fully exposed its evil ideas of coveting China's territory and making mischief between the Qing government and the Junggar.

However Russia made wrong judgments about the Junggar people and Tsewang Rabtan, assuming that they must seek refuge with Russia after their defeat by the Qing government, which was absolutely not true. The Junggar people loved their motherland. Although Tsewang Rabtan set up a separatist regime in northwest China and got into a fight with the Qing government, with the support of the Junggar people he maintained a solemn and stern stand in the face of Russia's temptations and threats. Tsewang Rabtan "refused to take Russian nationality or to take the advice of Wenkowsky about the construction of fortresses on Junggar's land and the dispatch of garrisons there.[115] The mission led by Wenkowsky stayed in Junggar for two years, but "their results were vague and poor."[116]

The suppression of Lobsang Danjin's rebellion and the Qing government's administration of the Qinghai area

In 1723, the year after Kangxi's death and the first year of the Yongzheng reign, taking the opportunity of the Fuyuan General Yinti's return to Beijing for a funeral, a Khoshut-Oirat aristocrat of Qinghai called Lobsang Danjin launched an armed rebellion.

Lobsang Danjin was the grandson of Gushi Khan and the son of Dashibaertu.[117] In 1697 (the 36th year of the Kangxi reign) his father Dashibaertu, "together with all Taijs (title of the chief of a Mongol tribe), were presented to the Emperor". Emperor Kangxi "bestowed the emperor's garments and court beads on them" and granted the title of "Heshuo Prince" to Dashibaertu. In 1714 (the 53rd year of the Kangxi reign), Lobsang Danjin succeeded to his father's title. In 1720 (the 59th year of the Kangxi reign), as a Khoshut representative of Qinghai, he led troops to join the Qing army escorting Dalai Lama to Tibet.

There were profound historical reasons for Lobsang Danjin's rebellion against the Qing Dynasty. After Gushi Khan acquired control of the Qinghai and Tibet regions, his subordinates in Qinghai were divided into two wings led separately by his sons. During the reign of Gushi Khan, he insisted on paying tribute to the Qing government. But after his death in 1656 (the 13th year of the Shunzhi Reign), the Khoshut of Qinghai lost the binding force of unification. His sons quarreled constantly over territory and "led their troops to revolt against officers and soldiers and to loot the inner land", which "did not stop after the Qing court's constant prohibitions"[118] and became the "trouble on the frontier" of Northwest China of the Qing government. In 1697 (the 36th year of the Kangxi Reign) when Galdan's revolt had been put down, the Qing government was committed to offering amnesty in Qinghai. Emperor Kangxi sent his son-in-law Alabutan to meet Xining Lama Sangnanduoerji by the Chahantuoluo Sea and enroll the Khoshut Taijs of Qinghai into the Qing government. He then again, as mentioned before, granted the title of "Heshuo Prince" to the only living son of Gushi Khan who had been called to Beijing. In this way the Oirat-Mongol of Qinghai resumed a tributary relationship with the Qing government. However the Qing government did not install an administrative agency in Qinghai so that the local separatist forces were quite strong due to the loose administration by the central government. Lobsang Danjin's rebellion was a result of the local separatist forces triggered by the specific historical conditions.

It is necessary to note that, after the Qing army entered Tibet, the Qing government's strengthened administration of the Qinghai-Tibet area has a direct bearing on Lobsang Danjin's rebellion. In order to stabilize Tibet's social order, the Qing army organized the Tibetan local government after entering Tibet. The local government conferred the title of "*Beizi* (貝子, a knighthood)" on *Diba* Kangjiding and Aerbuba who submitted to the Qing court earliest, and the title of "Fuguo Gong" on Longbulaifeng, so that they could jointly govern the affairs of Anterior Tibet. "Biluoding Shouzalake, the first-rank Taij, was responsible for governing the Tsang affairs and was granted the title of Gabulun (title of Tibetan local government officials)."[119] From then on, the Oirat-Mongol's rule of Tibet came to an end.

In addition, the Qing government took relevant measures in Qinghai with a view to splitting the local forces and preventing them from becoming too powerful to control. Although credited for entering Tibet, Lobsang Danjin was only given a small reward of "additional salary of two hundred taels of silver and five pieces of satin", while the previous Junwang (a peerage) Chahandanjin (the great-grandson of Gushi Khan) was granted the title of "Qing Prince", the previous Beile (an imperial peerage) Erdene Elktogtod was granted the title of "Jun Prince", and the other Taijs were also given various hereditary titles of princes and dukes as well.

Originally, as the only "Qing Prince" among the Oirat-Mongol aristocrats in Qinghai, Lobsang Danjin was quite powerful and therefore harbored political ambitions of "regaining the ancestors' dominant position and acquiring control of all the tribes."[120] He also wanted to restore Khoshut' sovereignty over Tibet. It is recorded that "becoming the Tibetan king was his long-standing desire."[121] In the eyes of Lobsang Danjin, as the supreme leader of Khoshut aristocrats, he should have subrogated Lha-bzang Khan and gained domination of Tibet. However, to his great disappointment, the Qing government's measures in the Qinghai-Tibet region did not enable him to gain any power in Tibet, and the promotion of Chahandanjin and others further constrained and weakened his power in Qinghai. As a result, strongly dissatisfied with the central government, Lobsang Danjin as the representative of separatist forces in Qinghai waged armed rebellion against the Qing government.

The rebellion started in August 1723 (the first year of the Yongzheng reign) when Lobsang Danjin threatened Taijs in Qinghai to meet by the Barbaro Sea. Claiming to be Dalai Hui Taij, he forced all Taijs "to use their former names instead of the hereditary titles of princes and dukes."[122] The Jun Prince Erdene Elktogtod and the Qing Prince Chahandanjin were successively attacked by Lobsang Danjin because of their refusal to join the rebellion. Erdene Elktogtod, "whose subordinates were all captured", led his wife to "escape to Ganzhou"[123] for assistance; and "after the defeat by Lobsang Danjin", Chahandanjin also "led his wife and his remaining 40 subordinates to flee to Laoyaguan in Hezhou" so as to appeal to the Qing government for help.

At the news of the rebellion, the Qing government asked Nian Gengyao who was Governor-General of Sichuan and Shaanxi to quell the uprising and at the same time dispatched the assistant minister Changshou to Shalatu, where Lobsang Danjin was stationed, to declare the emperor's decree of "withdrawing troops and negotiating for peace."[124] Lobsang Danjin did not listen to the order but instead imprisoned Changshou and became increasingly aggressive with his cohorts Alaknuomuqi, Aerbutanwenbu and Zangbazhabu.[125]

In October 1723 the rebels first launched attacks in Nanchuan Shenzhongbao, Xichuan Zhenhaibao and Beichuan Xincheng near the capital Xining. "Two or three thousand rebels were scattered at each place, expelling soldiers, setting fires, burning houses and looting property. People in and outside Xining all suffered from their ravages."[126] Everywhere around Xining was on fire.

At the same time, incited by Lobsang Danjin, the monks of the lama monasteries near Xining also joined the revolt. "All the lamas of famous monasteries within 100 *li* of Xining led their tenants and monks to attack the city, looting and burning everywhere they went."[127] The revolt of the lama monasteries started with Lama Chahannuomen Khan of the Tar Lamasery. Chahannuomen Khan was a religious leader in Qinghai "with strong charisma and appealing power", therefore when he joined the side of the rebels"over 2,000 herdsman, officials and lamas from far and near joined the rebellion in response to his call."[128] Lamas from Guonong Temple and Guomang Temple[129] also joined the revolt.

In line with the situation at that time, the Qing government took immediate measures. It appointed Nian Gengyao as "Border Pacification General-in-Chief" who transferred some troops from Sichuan and Shaanxi to be stationed at Xining; and appointed the Sichuan prefect Yue Zhongqi as "Mighty General" to assist in military affairs. To prevent the rebels from invading the interior, some defensive Qing troops were quartered at Bunongji River in Yongchang and some soldiers were stationed in other places such as Batang, Litang and Huangshengguan so as to block the rebels' road to Tibet. Moreover others such as Fu Ningan were sent to Turpan and Gasijian to prevent the rebels from making contact with the Junggar. After the completion of all deployments, the Qing army attacked any rebels around Xining and "defeated all adherents of Lobsang Danjin" and forced him to escape westwards". Subsequently the Qing army recaptured Zhennan, Shengzhong, Nanchuan, Xichuan, Beichuan and other areas. In early 1724 (the second year of the Yongzheng reign), the uprising of lamas from Tar Lamasery and Guonong Temple were successively put down by the Qing army as well.

After the success of the peripheral battles the Qing army concentrated on quelling the rebels of Lobsang Danjin. On February 8, 1723, by using General Yue Zhongqi's fighting strategy of "taking the initiative to attack when the enemy was understrength and unprepared,"[130] Nian Gengyao sent three separate troops to catch the rebels: the troops led by Chief General Wu Zhangan marched in from the north; Huang Xilin's troops pressed on from the central way; and Yue Zhongqi and Dading led the army to advance from the south. They captured the rebel leaders Aerbutanwenbu, Zangbazhabu and Lobsang Danjin's mother. Wearing female dress as a disguise, Lobsang Danjin fled to Gaershun with his wife"[131] and subsequently escaped to Junggar, turning to Tsewang Rabtan for help.

The Qing army gained rapid victory in the battle. According to the official records of the Qing Dynasty, "the rebels were suppressed in only 15 days from February 8 1723 to February 22. The amazingly quick success was unprecedented in history."[132] Emperor Yongzheng also regarded the victory as the most "outstanding success during the ten years."[133]

After the suppression of Lobsang Danjin's rebellion, the Qing government adopted the suggestions of Nian Gengyao and took a series of rehabilitative measures.

First, it adopted the system of "Jasak" (a Mongolian term for governor) in all the Mongol tribes in the Qinghai area and established the banner system of military organization (organizing armies according to the different banners) with the smallest unit called the "assistant command" in each army. There were all together 19 banner armies. It also set the rules for meetings and tributary affairs. All banner armies should hold a meeting once a year chaired by the Xining minister "and elect obedient and experienced people as the leader for the meetings". The tributary system stipulated that "from the third year of the Yongzheng reign a selected team of Princes and Taijs, divided into three groups, should visit the capital Beijing to pay respects and tributes to the Qing government with their own horses and llamas." The visits should occur once every three years and last for one week over nine year.[134]

Second, in terms of economic development, the Qing government adopted measures to increase agricultural production and stabilize people's life. Efforts were made to reclaim the "arable land" around Xining and to transfer "military and civilian convicts" from Zhili, Shanxi, Henan, Shandong and Shaanxi to places such as Datong and Bunongjier to reclaim farmland. Meanwhile some peasants and the military families in the Xining area were recruited to take up farming with cattle, ploughs and seeds distributed by local government officials. They could also be exempt from land taxes during the first three years of farming.

There were also clear stipulations about the trade between Qinghai and the interior: people should trade at "the authorized fairs" in the Nalashala area outside Xining and Xichuan twice each year in February and August. Exceptionally, daily necessities such as tea, cloth and flour could be traded throughout the year to meet the basic needs of Mongolians.

Third, it vigorously carried out rectification and reorganization of the lama monasteries. Since the late Ming Dynasty and early Qing Dynasty, with the increasingly wide spread of Lamaism, the number of monasteries continued to increase. During the reign of Kangxi there were over 1000 lama monasteries in Qinghai so that "a large number of people committed crimes and tens of thousands of producers were idle with nothing to do."[135] According to Nian Gengyao, "the lama monasteries in Xining, consisting of two and three thousand monks at most and five or six hundreds at least, gradually became harbors for villains and bandits. The lamas demanded the masses pay tax to them, which was the same as paying tribute, and they privately collected armor and weapons"[136] which enabled them to join the rebellion afterwards. In view of this, the Qing government issued licenses to 300 selected lamas in the Tar Lamasery, which was an important stronghold for the rebels, and dismissed the remaining lamas. Moreover it stipulated that "there should be no more than 200 houses for a monastery and no more than 300 lamas and no less than tens of lamas in each monastery."[137] Later, when the Tar Lamasery again developed into a huge monastery with 7,000 houses and 3,000 monks, the Qing government carried out inspections of it twice each year. Through the above measures the Qing government acquired control of the lama monasteries which were vital backing for local separatist forces.

While implementing the above measures the Qing government also carried out major reforms of the administrative structure in the Qinghai-Tibet area. In 1725 (the third year of Yongzheng's reign), it changed the name "Xining Wei" into "Xining Fu" (an administrative division) and established "two counties, one *wei*", namely Xining county, Zhanbo county and Datong wei. Moreover, it appointed the Vice Commander-in-Chief Dading as the first "Minister responsible for directing the affairs of the Qinghai Mongol tribes" (Xining Banshi Minister for short) to manage the government affairs in Qinghai. From then on the Qinghai area was completely under the direct control of the central government.

The wars in Hetongbo and Guangxian Temple

In 1727 (the 5th year of the Yongzheng reign), Tsewang Rabtan died and his son Galdan Tseren succeed him as the Khun Tayishi (ruler) of the Junggar. Galdan Tseren basically followed his father's domestic and foreign policy. Internally, he made efforts to develop agricultural production, which brought about an increase in the proportion of the agricultural economy. Agriculture was quite developed in the areas alongside the Irtysh River, Emin River, and Ili River,"with the production of all kinds of spring-sown crops except rye."[138] As witnessed and recorded by a Russian major, Galdan Tseren possessed a manor which "was located by the Hashatunor Lake in Ili Valley and was enclosed with a brick wall. About five or more versts (a Russian measurement unit) away from the manor...there were some other brick buildings and cottages...and a few orchards and vegetable gardens."[139] Galdan Tseren also took measures to develop the handicraft industry, especially weapon manufacturing, the textile industry and the production of certain daily necessities. A captured Swedish officer was once in charge of some military production such as making artillery and even engaged in the mining of iron ore, silver ore and copper ore.

As Junggar lay to the south of Russia, Galdan Tseren was confronted with the threat of a strong and greedy neighbor which continued its southward expansion of territory and occupied the land of the Junggar. Galdan Tseren repeatedly protested against Russia's appropriation of Junggar's land. In 1729 he called the Russian envoy to account: "Look! Why do you built your city by the Irtysh and Ob River? That is all my territory!"[140] Then in 1742, Galdan Tseren sent an envoy to Petersburg (a Russian city later renamed as Leningrad) to deliver a letter which gave a detailed account of the history of border disputes. It was pointed out in the letter that the Junggar once came into an agreement with Russia to regard the Om River as the border, "but later during the reign of another Tsar (referring to the Russian emperor Peter the Great) you established fortresses outside the estuary of the Om River. In order to take the fortress and safeguard our own territory, we once sent troops and clashed with Russia (referring to Junggar's defeat of the Russian troops led by Buhegelici). Now you Russians again have taken our land where you are building fortresses, hunting, digging gold and mining copper ore... if you continue to stay in our land and seize it for your own use, I will not transfer the land to you... therefore, please gave an order to withdraw your people, as I will absolutely not allow them to live on my land."[141]

Confronting with great pressure from Russia in the north, Galdan Tseren neither stopped the continuous fight against Kazak in the west nor gave up the ambition to expand to Khalkha, and therefore there was tension with both the Qing government and Khalkha. In 1729 (the 7th year of the Yongzheng reign), because of Galdan Tseren's continual intrusions into Khalkha and his sheltering of Lobsang Danjin who was the rebel leader in Qinghai, the Qing court decided to send troops to attack him. The minister Fu Edan was appointed as Border Pacification General-in-Chief stationed at Altai and marched in from the northern side; and Yue Zhongqi, the Governor-General of Sichuan and Shaanxi, was appointed as Ningyuan General to be quartered at Balikun and pressed in from the western side. Galdan Tseren was frightened by the Qing court's move and dispatched Telei to the capital, claiming that he had meant to send Lobsang Danjin to the Qing court but had suspended the action when hearing the news of the Qing troop movements. He also falsely promised that if the Qing government could forgive his previous faults, he would obey the commands of the Qing court and surrender Lobsang Danjin. So Emperor Yongzheng "ordered Galdan Tseren to send the escapee and to delineate the border between Junggar and Khalkha, and then pardoned him for his previous guilt and promised a one-year suspension of sending troops."[142] Unexpectedly, during the time of suspension, 20,000 Junggar troops were dispatched to make a sudden assault on the base camp of the Qing army which incurred huge losses. As a result the

Qing government and the Junggar became further estranged.

In April 1731 (the 9th year of the Yongzheng reign), the Qing army led by Fu Edan was stationed at Hovd. After Galdan Tseren discovered this he ordered the Tsering Dondup brothers to lead an army of 3,000 to attack the Qing army from the north. First a Junggar came to pretend to surrender to Fu Edan's army and falsely alleged that the main troops of Galdan Tseren had not yet arrived yet and only the Little Tsering Dondu with less than "1,000 troops" was quartered at Chahanhada which was "three days journey from" the Qing army's camp. He also pretended that "due to sudden illness during the journey, the Elder Tsering Dondu had had to stay near the Hefuke Mountains". Being brave but incautious, Fu Edan believed the words of the enemy without verification and hastily sent 4,000 Qing troops to attack the Junggar. When the Qing army entered the encirclement of the Junggar, the more than 2,000 troops which had been hidden in the valley immediately attacked the Qing army. At that time, "the whistle of the fight resounded across the skies and the coats of armor overlapped like dark clouds."[143] After the vanguard of 4,000 troops was besieged in Hetongbo,[144] Fu Edan sent another 6,000 reinforcements. However the vanguard was routed and the Junggar "directly attacked the base camp of Fu Edan's army". Fu Edan dispatched Suolun (Daur) Mongolian troops to defend the camp but was still defeated. Finally, only a small part of the Manchu troops persisted in fighting hard and managed to escape to Hovd.

The Qing army suffered heavy losses in the Hetongbo battle where "Deputy General Basai and Cha Nabi were both killed,"[145] and only 2,000 troops returned to Hovd from the 3,000-strong Qing army. The failure of the battle was mainly caused by the "arrogance and pomposity of the generals". Being conceited and headstrong, Fu Edan underestimated the enemy and believed the false information of the spy. Moreover he stubbornly insisting on sending troops in a hurry and did not listen to the advice of his subordinates, such as the admonishments of "the Vice Commanders-in-Chief Ding Shou, Yong Guo and Hai Lan."[146] As a result, his rash action finally led to the annihilation of his troops.

The victory in the Hetongbo battle further fed Galdan Tseren's ambition of expanding his power. He deployed troops from both the west and the east. On the one hand he "sent Taijs (chiefs of Mongol tribes) to Urumqi so as to examine the situation of the Qing army from the western side"; on the other hand, with the main direction of attack on Khalkha, he also "dispatched garrison troops to open up wasteland and grow food grain by the Ertix River"[147] for the purpose of detecting the situation of the Qing army from the eastern side. Later, 26,000 troops led by the Tsering Dondup brothers were sent to invade Khalkha. Given that places like Hovd and Chahansouer were "well-defended with strong troops" they did not dare to take direct action and therefore marched to Herlen, attacking places such as the Er Sea and Karausu. The Khalkha prince Danjin Duoerji and Celing jointly defeated the Junggar troops in Edengchule and dealt them a heavy blow, which forced them to retreat.

However, the failure in the Edengchule battle did not change Galdan Tseren's ambition to attack Khalkha. In June 1732 (the 10th year of the Yongzheng reign), he sent 3,000 troops led by Little Tsering Dondu to Erdeni Bilaseqin. The Khalkha prince Celing, "together with General Taerdaiqing, guarded against them in the Benbotu Mountains."[148] After discovering that Celing had led troops to the Benbotu Mountains, the Junggar waged a sneak attack on Celing's grazing land by the Tamir River and "captured his children and livestock." On hearing the news Celing became furious, "cutting off his hair and the tail of his horse to swear to God" that he would immediately "return to save his children" and soon reported to Shunchen Junwang (a peerage) Chibao to "appeal for help". Then Celing led 20,000 Mongolian soldiers to "take shortcuts across the back of the mountains at night and on the next morning pressed on all the way from the peak. Roused from sleep, the Junggar troops abandoned their military supplies and "fled in panic".[149] Celing's army continued to closely pursue the Junggar and finally arrived at Guangxian Temple by Orhon River after over 10 battles in different places one after another. Since the area was "blocked by mountains on the left and by river on the right", the Junggar troops had nowhere to escape to. Then Celing's army "took advantage of the special terrain to capture the Junggar and killed thousands of soldiers, so that the valley was strewn with corpses and the river was stained with blood."[150] The Little Tsering Dondu broke through at night and then fled westward from the Tui River.

Due to distinguished service in the battle of Guangxian Temple the Qing government conferred the honorific title of "Chaoyong (very courageous) Prince" on Celing, allowed him to wear a yellow girdle (a symbol of the Imperial Clansmen consisting of those who traced their descent direct from the founder of the Qing Dynasty), and permitted him to "wear the stamp standing for Left Deputy General Who Secures the Frontier, to be stationed at Hovd with power to act at his discretion."[151] Furthermore the Qing government transferred twenty-one *Qi* (army unit) from Tuxietu Khan to be attached to the Saiyinnuo tribe of Celing. "Consequently the Saiyinnuo tribe adopted the system of jasak and enjoyed the same status with the three other Khan tribes."

After the debilitating battle of Guangxian Temple, the Junggar suffered heavy losses and therefore intended to make peace with the Qing government. And because of the long-term fighting, the Qing government also felt the need to recuperate and rebuild itself. Therefore from 1734 (the 12th year of the Yongzheng reign) to 1739 (the 4th year of the Qianlong reign), both parties sent people to negotiate several times and eventually agreed to take the Altai Mountains as the pastoral boundary between the Khalkha and the Junggar, which meant that the Junggar could only move about in search of pasture on the west of the Altai Mountains and the Khalkhas could only herd in pasture on the east of the Altai Mountains. So the tension between the Qing government and the Junggar separatist forces was temporarily eased and peace was maintained for nearly 20 years.

The Qing government's Unification of the North and South of Tianshan

The internal division of the Junggar and the Qing government's suppression of Amursanaa's rebellion

After the death of Galdan Tseren, the Khan of the Junggar Khanate, in 1745 (the 10th year of the Qianlong reign) the Junggar aristocrats began to fight each other for the succession. Galdan Tseren left three sons: the eldest son called Lamdarjaa who was 19 years old; the second son called Tsewang-Dorji-Namjil who was 13 years old; the youngest son named Tsewang Dash who was just seven. The eldest Lamdarjaa did not succeed because of his common blood. His younger brother Tsewang-Dorji-Namjil "inherited the throne owing to his mother's blue blood."[152] The youngest, Tsewang Dash, was supported by the prestigious Tsering Dondup brothers. However, being "fatuous and incompetent", the Junggar ruler Tsewang-Dorji-Namjil indulged in sensual pleasures and did not listen to the exhortations of his sister Elanbayaer. He even slandered his sister by bringing a false accusation that "she planed to serve Russia and to declare herself as Kouke Khan (empress); and then arrested and seized his sister."[153] He also turned a deaf ear to the dissuasion of the Zaergu (council of the tribe) and "executed many *Zaisang*,"[154] which aroused the dissatisfaction of the most of the Junggar aristocrats. In 1750 (the 15th year of the Qianlong reign), Tsewang-Dorji-Namjil's brother-in-law Saqiboleke "assisted Lamdarjaa in attacking and murdering Tsewang-Dorji-Namjil."[155] So Lamdarjaa seized the throne from his younger brother.

Although Lamdarjaa gained the rule of Junggar, the fighting for the throne did not come to an end and another new struggle grew behind the scenes. Since Lamdarjaa was of humble origin his succession was unpopular and suffered opposition from some Junggar aristocrats. In order to seize the throne, the Dash Dava (son of Little Tsering Dondup) from the Tsering Dondup Family, who had been supporting Tsewang Dash, conspired with Taij Amursanaa of the Huite tribe who had a close blood relationship with the Tongcuoluosi Famlily and Taij Banzhuer of Khoshut to jointly plot to hail Tsewang Dash as the new Khong Tayiji (ruler of Junggar). But Lamdarjaa discovered the scheme and then killed his younger brother Tsewang Dash and the Dash Dava, which resulted in greater turmoil in Junggar. The confused situation in Junggar caused by the aristocrats' internal struggle for power provided an excellent chance for Amursanaa from Huite tribe.

Originally as a Taij of the Huite tribe, Amursanaa was the grand-son of Tsewang Rabtan and had a close blood relationship with the nobility of Junggar. After the failure of Tsewang Dash, Amursanaa was turned to supporting another noble, Dawaachi.

Dawaachi was the son of Taij Batuerhui and the grandson of the Older Tsering Dondup. "According to the traditions, Dawaachi has the legal right to succeed as Khan."[157] After Amursanaa turned to Dawaachi they established an alliance against Lamdarjaa and conspired in the Middle Yuzi of Kazak. Then in 1752 (the 17th year of the Qianlong reign), "they led 1,500 crack troops equipped with weapons and food to take shortcuts to enter Ili and attacked its camp at the dead of night. At that time Lamdarjaa was sitting around a fire and drinking with his concubine, and Amursanaa went forward and killed him. After that Amursanaa pacified Lamdarjaa's subordinates and hailed Dawaachi as the new ruler."[158] After that, since Dawaachi's and Amursanaa's alliance was in fact a kind of taking advantage of each other, after the defeat of their common rival they fought each other and their conflicts became increasingly fierce. Amursanaa used to stay in the Taerbahatai area, but in order to expand his forces he murdered his father-in-law and transferred to the Irtysh River. Therefore he clashed with Dawaachi's forces in Ili. According to the records of Russian profiles, the fight between Dawaachi and Amursanaa occurred "at the source of Irtysh River" between the spring and summer of 1754 (the 19th year of the Qianlong reign). In the beginning Amursanaa "summoned about 6,000 soldiers from various areas" to attack Dawaachi, who also "levied large number of troops". The two armies fought closely with each other and finally Amursanaa was utterly defeated.[159] He led over 20,000 of his subordinates to surrender to the Qing government.

The submission of Amursanaa was due to his desire to take advantage of the Qing government's military forces to eliminate his political rival Dawaachi. In the winter of 1754, Amursanaa was receive by Emperor Qianlong in the

Summer Villa of Rakog and was granted the honorific title of Qing Prince. He tried to show that "it was advisable to take Ili" and requested the Qing court to send troops to attack Dawaachi.

The Qing government was quite concerned about the unrest in Junggar. Ever since the 17th century the Junggar had arisen in the Northwest and set up a separatist reign by force of arms that had long disobeyed the Qing government and repeatedly attacked Khalkha, Qinghai and Tibet. The Junggar were a great harassment to the Qing government during the ten years and became the major obstacle to realizing national unification and stability. Emperor Qianlong believed that the suppression of the Junggar separatist forces was of primary importance and was "an arranged but unfinished event" during his grandfather and father's era (referring to Kangxi and Yongzheng's reign). "Peace and stability could not occur with the existence of the Junggar separatist forces."[160] However under the rule of Tsewang Rabtan and Galdan Tseren, Junggar enjoyed a stable political situation and a strong military force. If the Qing government rashly sent troops to attack Junggar it would be difficult to win because of the long arduous journey and insufficient supplies. The failure in the Hetongbo battle in the 9th year of the Yongzheng era was a lesson that the Qing government had learned. Therefore in the early years of the Qianlong reign it could only agree to delineate the pastoral boundary with the Junggar to seek a temporary peace. After the death of Galdan Tseren, the situation in Junggar was chaotic due to internal strife. And the rule of Dawaachi worsened the situation. As an incompetent but greedy and cruel ruler, Dawaachi attacked several tribes, killing and looting in order to capture their property and pasture. Many herdsmen suffered greatly and a few noble ranchers also suffered Dawaachi's plunder As a result, Dawaachi was utterly isolated by his relatives and subordinates. There was a growing tendency among the masses and upper class in Junggar to surrender to the Qing and uphold national unification, since they all desired to get rid of Dawaachi's arbitrary rule and to bring the chaotic situation to an end. This trend provided the precondition for the Qing government to launch a war of pacification and to unify the northwest border area. Long before the submission of Amursanaa, quite a few Oirat-Mongols broke away from the rule of Dawaachi and surrendered to the Qing.

Zaisang Salale of Dash Dava's tribe surrendered Qing court at the earliest moment. In 1750 (the 15th year of the Qianlong reign) when Dash Dava was killed in factional strife, Salale escaped from Junggar and submitted to the Qing. In 1753, Dawaachi laid waste to the Duerbote tribe. The chief of the Duerbote tribe Cheling and Taij Cheling Wubashi and Cheling Mengke "summoned the clansman, claiming that it was wiser to surrender to the Qing government than to rely on Junggar."[161] They then led subordinates of over 3,000 households and 10,000 people to leave their original pasture by the Irtysh River, climb across the Altai Mountains and finally arrive at Uliastay where the Left Deputy General Who Secures the Frontier was stationed. In the long-standing fight between the Qing government and the Junggar separatist forces this was the first large-scale domestic movement of the Oirat-Mongol, which reflected the great dissatisfaction of Oirat-Mongol herdsmen with the chaos and wars caused by the Junggar's rule and also revealed their strong desire for unity and stability. Qianlong greatly valued the submission of the three Chelings from the Duerbote tribe and therefore made proper arrangements for them, offering them 500 head of cattle, 2,100 sheep and 2,000 pecks of grain. In May 1754 (the 19th year of the Qianlong reign), Qianlong gave a ceremonious reception for the three Chelings at the Summer Villa of Rakog and appointed Cheling as Qing Prince, Cheling Wubashi as Jun Prince and Cheling Mengke as Belei. With a better knowledge about the internal situation in Junggar from the three Chelings, Emperor Qianlong determined to put down the Junggar separatist forces. He declared that "today Cheling and Cheling Wubashi came here and I asked them about the situation in Junggar and found that the Junggars were divided and not united. I therefore decided to take the chance and attack next year from Altai and Balikun."[162] Soon Amursanaa surrendered to the Qing, which further strengthened Qianlong's determination to suppressing the Junggar.

In the spring of 1755 (the 20th year of the Qianlong reign), one North-Route army jointly led by Ban Di who was appointed as General Who Secures the East and Amursanaa, the Left Deputy General Who Secures the Frontier, attacked from Uliastay; another West-Route army led by Yong Chang who was appointed as General Who Secures the West and Salale, the Right Deputy General Who Secures the Frontier, marched from Balikun. The two armies met at the Boro Tala River. Under the attack of the two armies, the Junggar troops yielded to the Qing one after another. "As the Qing army pressed on, a large number of the Junggar headed by the Etuoke (name for the tribal chief) surrendered to the Qing."[163] "The surrendered tribes, among which some large tribes had thousands of households and the small ones had hundreds of households, all carried with them their wine and sheep"[164] to submit to the Qing army. The collapsed Dawaachi's army was unable to resist, so the Qing army won a victory without firing a shot with its vanguard made up of the surrendered Oirat-Mongol soldiers.

Fig. 10.1. Emperor Qianlong entertaining the three Chelings to dinner at Wanshu Garden

In view of the dangerous situation, Dawaachi retreated to the Gedeng Mountains and camped there to resist the Qing with the mountains and waters as the shelter. The Qing army continued to fight against him and smashed his camp so that Dawaachi's troops fled in confusion and over 6,000 surrendered. The remaining ten soldiers, together with Dawaachi, escaped to the South Xinjiang. Then the Uygurs in South Xinjiang actively responded to the call of the Qing army to extricate themselves from Dawaachi's rule. So when Dawaachi escaped via Wushi, Huo Qis, the chief of the Uygur, captured him and sent him to the camp of the Qing army. Junggar's separatist regime then came to an end. But after his capture Emperor Qianlong pardoned his previous sins, granted him the title of Qing Prince, and provided preferential treatment to him in Beijing.

With the suppression of Dawaachi's separatist forces, Amursanaa gradually revealed his hidden ambition of usurping the power of Oirat, which was against the basic policy of national unity of the Qing government. Originally Emperor Qianlong wanted to adopt the principle of "decentralizing power" and appointed "four Khans in Oirat to separately govern the four tribes."[165] However, because of his strong desire to "become the head of Taijs and the tyrant of the west,"[166] Amursanaa used a series of plots and tricks to gain the Qing court's recognition of him as the head of the four Khans. Although the Qing government granted him the additional title of "Shuang Qing Prince" and paid him double salary, his greed was hard to satisfy and his ambition for national separation expanded. Being autocratic and arbitrary he conducted killing and looting at will, and refused to wear the official robe of the Qing Dynasty and to use the Qing official seal. Instead he "used his own Hun Taij printed seal with patterns of chrysanthemum,"[167] and "called himself the head of the four Khans" when he wrote to all the tribes. Moreover he dispatched his subordinates to raise an army and meanwhile strove to expand the separatist forces in active preparation for an insurrection.

Since Amursanaa's separatist ambition was obvious, the Qing government took countermeasures and ordered him to present himself to the Emperor at the Summer Villa of Rakog in September 1755 (the 20th year of the Qianlong reign) in an attempt to lure him away from his base and to wage an attack. But the crafty Amursanaa saw through the Qing court's intention and therefore continuously dragged out his journey to Rakog. When he arrived at Wunongu River, he "said falsely uttered that he was turning back in order to purchasing things necessary for the long journey" and gave his seal of Deputy General to his companion Elinqin Duoerji, the Khalkha Prince. He used shortcuts to flee back to Taerbahatai, which revealed his ambition to rebel against the Qing government.

At that time most of the Qing troops in the North Xinjiang area withdrew except for 500 soldiers led by Ban Di and Erongansuo who were stationed at Ili and besieged by Amursanaa's rebels. They were hopelessly outnumbered and defeated in the battle, and Ban Di and Erongansuo committed suicide because of their failure. In spite of the possession of thousands of brigades in Urumchi, the West-Route army led by Yongchang did not dare to assist them, which led to continuous upheavals in the regions to the north and south of the Tianshan Mountains.

Shortly after the rebellion of Amursanaa, Chingünjav, the feudal lord of the Hetuohuite tribe of Khalkha, joined the rebellious action. Owing to his merits in the suppression of separatist forces in Ili, Chingünjav was appointed as Deputy General of Khalkha and was granted the title of Jun Prince. During the attack in Ili, when he witnessed Amursanaa's "rebellious ambition and separatist moves, he conceived similar disloyalty to the Qing government"[168] and afterwards colluded with Amursanaa. In the battle to pacify the Junggar, the Qing government enlisted soldiers and horses in the Khalkha area which led to great discontent among the masses of the people. Chingünjav made use of people's dissatisfaction to launch a rebellion especially when Elinqin Duoerji, the brother of Khalkha' Grand Living Buddha Hutuketu, was executed by the Qing court because of his release of Amursanaa.[169] This aroused greater apprehension and upset among the feudal lords in Khalkha. Chingünjav "secretly fled from the Qing camp and withdrew all the troops in Carens (posts) and stations."[170] As a result the Qing government's stations along the north route, from the 10th to the 26th , were all paralyzed, which resulted in the interruption of communication.

Taking the chaotic situation in Khalkha and Junggar areas into consideration, the Qing government took corresponding measures to put down the rebellion. The Qing army led by Chenggunzhabu and others rapidly quelled Chingünjav's uprising and stabilized the situation in Khalkha. In 1757 (the 22nd year of the Qianlong reign) Chengzhabu, with the appointment of Qing court as the General Who Secures the Frontier, and Shuhede, the grand minister consultant, jointly led troops from the north route; Zhaohui, with the appointment of the Qing court as Ili General, and Fude, the grand minister consultant, jointly led troops from the west route to suppress Amursanaa. It happened that a "plague raged for months in the Junggar area which led to many deaths,"[171] and therefore the Qing army drove straight in with irresistible force. Under the attack Amursanaa escaped in confusion to Kazak and soon fled north, with several companions, to seek refuge with the Russians.

It should be noted that Qing government's suppression of the Junggar separatist forces played a significant role in restoring national unity and maintaining defense in the northwestern areas. However, just as with many progressive causes in human history, there was a heavy price. The Qing government also adopted fairly inhuman means to realize national unity. Since there had been separatist forces in Junggar for a long time, the rulers of Qing Dynasty harbored deep rooted distrust and hostility against it. So as soon as civil strife happened in Jungar, the Qing army took the chance to march in and to conduct killing and looting of anyone including the innocents. The number of Junggars killed by the Qing army exceeded the death toll in average warfare. "Any places in Junggar where there could be living creatures were being looted completely", so that "all edible things were destroyed including plants and animals."[172] Some tribes had already surrendered, but the Qing army still massacred them due to unnecessary suspicions and brought great disaster to Junggar. The brutal means adopted by the Qing army deserved exposure and criticism.

The Qing government was deeply worried about the escape of Amursanaa. Emperor Qianlong thought that "the objective of securing the west could not be regarded as completed unless the traitor (referring to Amursanaa) was captured,"[173] and he made up his mind to arrest Amursanaa. When hearing that Amursanaa had fled to Russia he became increasingly anxious. Qianlong believed that "since the Russians had taken Amursanaa in, they must have taken him for their own use."[174] Therefore Qianlong asked the Ministry of Tribal Affairs to send letters repeatedly to the Russian government requiring Russia to "comply with the previous agreement on not hiding escapees"[175] and to extradite Amursanaa to the Qing. But the Russian government hesitated to reply and made a false statement that Amursanaa "has already died from drowning". In fact, after Amursanaa escaped to Russia, the Governor of Siberia Gelabolian Loff "for fear of the revelation of Amursanaa, decided to help him settle down in a house located in a discarded Kudusik brewery which was about 20 versts (Russian measure of length) away from Tobolsk."[176] Later Amursana died there of smallpox. After several negotiations with the Qing government, the Russian government brought the frozen body of Amursanaa to Kyakhta for the Qing officials to see.

The revolt of Burhanidin and Hojajahan, and the Qing government's unification of the south of Tianshan

As soon as the rebellion of Junggar separatist forces was put down by the Qing government, the revolt of Burhanidin and Hojajahan broke out in the south of the Tianshan Mountains in the Uighur region. Burhanidin and Hojajahan were the sons of Mahedumi Aizhamu Khawaja. When Galdan attacked the south of the Tianshan Mountains, their grandfather Abudushite was transferred to Ili in the north of Xinjiang. After the defeat of Galdan, Abudushite extricated himself and returned. The Qing Government sent him back. The family of Tsewang Rabtan set up a separatist regime by force of arms in Xinjiang. Mahanmutewei Khawaja, who was the son of Abudushite, "was highly respected by the Uygurs" and "was ordered to come back."[177] Mahanmute was captured by Galdan Tseren and taken to Ili since he had attempted to break away from the control of the Junggar aristocracy. Mahanmute had two sons, of which the elder one was Burhanidin and the younger Hojajahan. They were called the "Hezhuo brothers". After Mahanmute's death, the Hojajahan brothers were still confined in Ili. When the Qing army put down the separatist forces of Dawaachi, the Hojajahan brothers were set free. Since the Qing government regarded them as "leaders of the Huibu" it sent Burhanidin back to Yerqiang so that he could "govern the Huibu" and sent Hojajaha back to Ili to take charge of Islamic affairs.

When the insurrection in Ili was fomented by Amursanaa, Hojajahan led the public in assisting the revolt. After the revolt of Amursanaa was put down, Hojajahan escaped from Ili to Yerqiang and suborned his brother Burhanidin to conspire a revolt.

To unify the south of Xinjiang peacefully, the Qing Government sought to make the most of the religious influence of Hojajahan brothers so that "the people of Yerqiang and Kashigaer would summit to the Qing."[178] Burhanidin originally tried to obey the rules from central government, "called up people from all the cities, and waited for orders. But Hojajahan did not obey."[179]

Desirous of power, Hojajahan underestimated the strength and determination of the Qing Government to unify the country. He urged Burhanidin that: "If we obeyed the emperor's order, one of us must be called to Beijing, which means that we would be confined. But if we revolt against China, because of the long distance, the Qing soldiers have to spend much time and energy on coming here. Moreover they would have difficulty transporting grain here so they can do nothing about us. Since the Junggar no longer exist there are no strong neighbors near us, so we can successively capture all the cities and set up an independent regime."[180] Unfortunately, the separatist ideas took the lead and Burhanidin was forced to participate in the revolt. In 1757 (the 22nd year of the Qianlong reign), the Qing envoys Amindao and others who were sent to northern Xinjiang were killed. So the revolt in South Xinjiang spread immediately.

In 1758 the Qing Government appointed Yaerhashan as General Who Pacifies Rebels. He led thousands of soldiers from Turpan to Kuqa which was a "threshold" to "Huibu". As long as Kuqa was taken, "the rest of the cities would be under control". So Kuqa was a strategic area which the Qing Government had to take. But "surrounded by hummocks, the city was enclosed by willows and sandy soil."[181] The city's buildings were strong and therefore it was easy to defend but hard to attack. The Qing army attempted to attack it but failed several times. Then when Hojajahan led troops to assist the rebels, he was blocked by the Qing army and lost more than half of his troops. So he moved back to Kuqa for defense. The Qing Government failed to take a strong offensive to wipe out Hojajahan's troops when Hojajahan returned to Kuqa. Instead Yaerhashan "stayed in the Qing camp" and "did not take any measures to block Hojajahan's way"[182] so that Hojajahan was able to escape during the night. The Qing government cancelled Yaerhashan's military appointment as his faults had led to the delay of fulfillment of the Qing army's plan, and then appointed Zhaohui who had just put down the revolt in the north of the Tianshan Mountains to lead an army to marchAfter Hojajahan withdrew from Kuqa he escaped to Aksu, but was "refused by the Uygurs in Aksu." Since the chief of Aksu, Eduiboke had surrendered to the Qing army long ago, Aksu people warmly welcomed the return of their chief. Then Hojajahan had to flee to Wushi where Bokchuoji also "closed the city door and refused to let him enter" and dispatched people to greet the Qing army. After that, Hojajahan returned to Yerqiang and Burhanidin returned to Kashigaer. They both attempted to occupy a city and to put up a last-ditch struggle against each other. In October 1758 (the 23rd year of the Qianlong reign), Zhaohui led the Qing army to attack Yerqiang. Hojajahan fortified the defense works outside Yerqiang so as to leave nothing usable to the invading Qing enemy. Thirteen thousand rebels defended Yerqiang[183] while there were only three thousand Qing troops led by Zhaohui. So when the weak Qing army penetrated into the rebels' territory they were unable to take it and were then "stationed at the place by the Heishui River to the east of Yerqiang where there was some water grass." The rebels then dispatched large numbers of troops and besieged the Qing army. But the Qing troops "built up strong entrenchments" and "long enclosures to maintain confrontation with the rebels."[184] They persisted in a long-standing fight with over 10,000 rebels, which was known as the siege of Heishui River. The rebels adopted every means to attack the Qing army such as bombardments, water flooding and sneak raids. However the Qing troops struck back courageously and kept fighting for up to three months by the Heishui River with the Qing camp remaining intact.

In 1759 (the 24th year of the Qianlong reign), Fude, the Right Deputy General Who Secures the Frontier, led Qing troops from Urumchi to South Xinjiang to give aid to Zhaohu's army. Then under the converging attack of Qing troops, the Hojajahan rebels collapsed and fled in desperation. Therefore, the predicament in Heishui River was solved.

In the summer of 1759 the Qing army started to attack via two routes. One troop led by Zhaohui proceeded from Wushi to attack Kashigaer; the other troops led by Fude started from Hetian to assault Yerqiang. Under the attack of the Qing army, the Hojajahan brothers abandoned the cities and fled in confusion. Then the Qing army vigorously followed up a victory with hot pursuit, repeatedly defeated the run-away troops, and finally annihilated all the rebels on both sides of Yixierkuer beside the Badakshan. The Hojajahan brothers were captured and killed by the chief of Badakshan. The rebellion of the Hojajahan brothers was thus put down by the Qing government.

After suppressing the rebellions in Junggar and "Huibu" and unifying the regions north and south of the Tianshan Mountains, the Qing government established a military administrative system and set up a form of direct military rule over these regions. In 1762 (the 27th year of the Qianlong reign), the Qing government established the post of Ili General, headquartered at the fort of Huiyuan (the so-called "Manchu Kuldja", or Yili). The Ili General had the power to "deploy all officers and soldiers in Urumchi and Balikun, whether they are Manchus, Suoluns, Chahaers or Yellow Banners. He was also concurrently in charge of the officers and soldiers stationed at Yerqiang, Kashigaer and Qomul (Hami). Local affairs were governed by the quartered ministers as before. And since some cities such as Yerqiang and Kashigaer were located on the frontier, when it was necessary to allocate some officers and soldiers from Ili the ministers in those cities were permitted to consult with the Ili General to transfer nearby assistance."[185] It was clear that the Ili General was the supreme military and political officer who "exercised unified military and administrative jurisdiction over the regions south and north in Xinjiang." Inferior to the Ili General, the post of Dutong was established in Urumchi to govern the garrisons in Urumchi, Gucheng, Balikun and Turpan; the post of Grand Minister Consultant was set up in Kumbum Bahatai to govern the garrisons in regions of Kumbum. In the south of Xinjiang the Qing government established the posts of "Banshi Minister" and "Lingdui Minister" in cities such as Kashigashi, Yerqiang, Yingjishaer, Hedian, Wushi, Aksu, Kuqa and Bizhan to exercise military rule over the local Uygurs. The"Banshi Minister"and"Lingdui Minister" were "under the jurisdiction of the Grand Minister Consultant in Kashigaer," who was further under the direct command of the Ili General. The implementation of the military administrative system not only improved the relationship between the Xinjiang area and the central government, and strengthened the Qing government's rule and defense of the northwestern regions, but also, objectively speaking, played a positive role in maintaining national unity and territorial integrity.

The Torghuts' struggle against Russian oppression and their fight for the return to the motherland

Since the late twenties in 17th century, over 50,000 nomadic households of the Torghut (or Turhute tribe) led by Kho Orluk separated from the other Oirats and moved to the southwest. They expelled the Nogays, crossed the Kazakh Steppe and the Urals, and finally arrived at the unexploited "and sparsely populated coastal areas of the lower reaches of the Volga and its tributaries."[186] The Torghuts settled down here, "made use of the water grass to pasture and hunt animals,"[187] and "established Etuoke and Zaisang (administrative posts),"[188] forming an independent nomadic tribe.

However downstream of the Volga River was not the Torghuts' ideal "paradise". Although they had driven away the declining Nogai to the west of the Volga River, to their north was aggressive Tsarist Russia. In order to strengthen its control of the newly conquered countries Kazan and Astrakhan, Russia expanded its forces of aggression to the Volga River and Don River drainage areas, and the nomadic Torghuts in the Volga River downstream area became a target of Russia's aggression. But it was not easy for Tsarist Russia to fully master these strong and valiant nomads. From the end of the 17th Century to the early 18th Century, the Russian government persuaded the Torghuts to sign six treaties by the means of threats and promises. The Torghuts gradually

Fig. 10.2. **Monument of the *Torghuts' Complete Submission to the Qing Dynasty***

came under Russia's control after receiving favorable political and economic privileges. But they did not yield to the Russian government's control. They rebelled many times and took part in the fights in which people of all nationalities struggled against Tsarist rule int the Volga River drainage area.

Early in the 1660s, after the rebellion of peasants who were in the Don River drainage area, led by the famous peasant leader in Russian history Racine people of all nationalities on both sides of Volga River actively participated in rebellion.[190] At the end of the 17th Century Bashkris broke out in revolt, again in Volga River drainage area. The Torghuts "turned to support Bashkris"[189] under the leadership of the Khan. In 1706, Astrakan broke out revolt as well. The Russian government asked the Khan to send out troops to repress the revolt. But he made an alliance with the Bashkris attack against Penza and Tambov towns which were under Tsarist rule in 1708. People continued to fight against the Russia government so that Russia's ruler was unable to conquer the Torghuts completely. The Torghuts maintained their political independence.

Nevertheless, under the frequent invasion and threats from Tsarist Russia, the Torghut people were still missing their homeland. They had wanted to return to the motherland many times after they migrated to the downstream of Volga River, but due to the distance and the hard journey, this idea could not be acted on. However they still kept in close touch with the Eleut Mongolian tribes.

In 1634 Batuerhuitaiji held a chiefs meeting in Tarbaghatai between the Khalkha and Eleut Mongolian tribes. The chief of the Torghut Tribe, He'erleke, led his sons to attend the meeting from ten thousand miles away. The Torghut tribe in the Volga River region had been in close contact with other Eleut Mongols living in the north of the Tianshan Mountains. He'erleke's daughter married Batuerhuitaiji, and then He'erleke's grandson Pengchuke married the daughter of Batuerhuitaiji. Pengchuke's son Ayuqi had lived in the place of Batuerhuitaiji since he was young. Later Cewangalabutan married Ayuqi's daughter. These frequent marriages were the reflection of the close political contacts between the two tribes.

After Torghut migrated west to the downstream of the Volga River, they had been in close touch with the central government of the Qing Dynasty. Early in the Shunzhi Reign, the Torghut constantly dispatched ambassadors to offer tributes. In 1655 (the 12th year of the Shunzhi reign), the oldest son of He'erleke, Shukeerdaiqing, sent ambassador Xilabueerbu to submit the tribute list to the Qing Dynasty. In 1657 (the 14th year of the Shunzhi period), Luobocangnuoyan and his son Duoerji from Torghut dispatched Shake Xibu Te offering "more than 200 camels and thousands of horses for doing business in Guihua City."[191] The Qing Government agreed to their request to conduct horse business transactions. In the Kangxi reign, the relationship between the Torghut and Qing Dynasty became closer. In 1697 (the 36th year of the Kangxi Reign), after the Qing Dynasty had pacified Galdan's uprising, the Torghut tribe Ayuqi sent Nuoyan and Shuiqi following Cewangalabutan as ambassadors to "celebrate the defeat". Cewangalabutan occupied Xinjiang, stopping the tribute road from Junggar to Jiayuguan. However the Torghut still had not cut off contact with the central government of the Qing Dynasty. In 1712 (the 51th year of the Kangxi reign), Ayuqi dispatched Samutan and other ambassadors to "borrow the Russian road to reach the capital for offering tributes."[192] To show concern for the Torghut tribe which was outside the motherland and lived in another land from Kangxi, the minister Sidutulizhen asembled an ambassador group which was dispatched by Kangxi to the downstream of the Volga River to visit the Torghut Tribe. Tulichen started in the summer of 1712, passing Lenggesike, Tuoboersike and Kashan, and arrived in Ayuqi Han's station on the downstream of Volga River in June 1714, receiving a warm welcome and prosperous entertainment. "There were constant feasts during their stay for more than ten days."[193] Ayuqi asked Tulizhen about the political and economic situation of the motherland in detail, expressing the endless desire of the Torghut Mongolians for the motherland. The ambassador group returned to Beijing at the end of April in 1715 (the 54th year of the Kangxi reign). Later

Tulizhen wrote a book named *Record of Exotic Place* in the Manchu and Han languages, recording the experiences of this visit. After the 1720s, although the Tsarist Russian government strengthened its control over the Torghut, the Torghut broke through all kinds of obstacles, keeping in touch with the Qing Dynasty. In 1756 (the 21st year of the Qianlong reign), Torghut Dunluobulashe dispatched ambassador Chuzhabu through Russia. After a hard three-year journey they came back to meet with the Qing Dynasty. Emporer Qianlong received Chuizhabu hospitably in the Wanshu Garden in the Chende Mountain Resort. In the following year, Qianlong met him in Beijing. Chuzhabu stressed the hard stance of the Torghut people under Tsarist Russian rule. He said: "the Torghut are only attached to Russia, they have not surrendered to it, so how will they be willing to serve Tsarist Russia without an order from the Emporer of the Qing Dynasty?"[194] This statement of Chuizhabu's to Qianlong showed that although the Torghut was away from the motherland, they were sure that they were one of the members of the multiracial country and kept a relationship with the Qing Dynasty as one of its subjects all the time.

In 1724, the Tsarist Russia authorhe ities availed themselves of Ayuka Khan's death to obtain the privilege of appointing the new Khan of Torghut.[195] After that the control by Tsarist Russia of the Torghut became more and more pressing in the aspects of politics, economy and religion etc. In the 1860s when Ubasi (the great-grandson of Ayuka Khan) took power, by making use of the turbulent situation owing to the change in power once again, the Tsarist Russian authorities carried out an unprecedented policy of suppression so as to totally control the whole tribe.

First of all, the Tsarist Russian authorities restricted the Khan King's power by reorganizing the Zaergu the council of the tribe . The Zaergu was an organ of authority originally set up under the domination of the Khan King of Torghut, and it was composed by eight nobles who were trusted by their Khan King. "In fact, they were ministers and assistants affiliated to the Khan King."[196] According to the *Code of Oirat-Mongol in 1640*, "All the decisions of the Zaergu could come into force only through the Khan King's approval."[197] But the new Zaergu regulations enacted by the Tsarist Russian authorities on August 20, 1726 stipulated: the members of the Zaergu cannot be appointed by their Khan King, "its constitution must be approved by the Tsarist Russian government" and the Khan King cannot change the Zaergu's resolution at will. Such regulations tremendously weakened Ubasi Khan's power.

Moreover under the camouflage of "reformation", Tsarist Russia attempted to prop up the Torghut noble—Dun Dukov Family,[198] which had converted to the Orthodox Christian Church, so as to take over Ubasi's domination.

"Let Dun Dukov rebuild the Torghut regime" and then make Torghut "a new administrative area of Tsarist Russia."[199] Furthermore, the Tsarist Russian authorities endlessly recruited soldiers by force from the Torghut during the war with its neighbouring countries Sweden and Turkey, which brought great catastrophe to the Torghut. After 1765 the Tsarist Russian authorities "recruited soldiers from the Torghut for the wars with its neighbouring countries,"[200] "making the ones from Torghut the vanguards in the wars". Tens of thousands of people died in the wars, and "just a few people survived and returned."[201] This situation made "everyone feel worried and apprehensive", and the whole tribe was in a turmoil. The Tsarist Russian authorities' ruthless persecution undoubtedly caused the strong protests by the whole tribe and strengthened their determination to return to the motherland.

On January 5, 1771 (the 36th year of the Qianlong reign), Ubasi launched an armed uprising against Tsarist Russia after thorough preparation with the Taij and Lama of Torghut. He led his tribe with more than thirty-three thousand families, about one hundred and sixty thousand people, to march back to their motherland. As recorded in the *Torghuts' Complete Submission to the Qing Dynasty* written by Emperor Qianlong, "(Ubasi) continuously recruited troops in Russia and recently appointed his son to lead soldiers. Russia's religion was not shamanism (yellow hat), so he could conspired with Taijs from other tribes and formed an alliance with other places so that the forces of shamanism (yellow hat) thrived." For the convenience of marching, they threw away utensils such as pots and stoves. It took them only eight days to go through the grasslands between the Volga River and the Urals. They crossed the Urals after capturing the Russian fortress in Kulajinna, and then rapidly entered the snow-covered Kazakh Steppe.

When the Tsarist Russian authorities learnt the critical intelligence that the Turhute tribe had moved east, they immediately dispatched large numbers of cossack soldiers under their leader Matrosoff's command to pursue Turhute tribe closely. The Turhute's troops heroically beat back the pursuing Russian army, but the move back east was not smooth sailing. After entering the Kazakh Steppe, difficulties came one upon the heels of another. The difficulties on the long journey and the lack of water, plants and other supplies brought the tribe unprecedented misery — hunger and cold epidemic disease a sharp decline in population, and a large amount of dead livestock. Moreover Russia's Orenburg authority dispatched pursuing forces again, and recruited Kazak chief Nur Alihan. Together with attacks by Bashkirs from time to time this brought even greater losses to the Turhute tribe. However the Torghut Mongols proved to be a valiant race. Under the leadership of Ubasi they not only overcame all sorts of difficulties, but also overcame the enemy's interception and siege through quick-witted strategies and indomitable spirit, and "crossing Caren (post on the Russian frontier)"[202] they finally crossed the Chinese border and realized their glorious dream of coming back to their motherland.

After crossing the Chinese border, the Turhute tribe went south along Balkhash Lake, passed the Zaysan Lake, and finally arrived in the Shala Burrel area. They then began to get in touch with the local authorities of the Qing government. The Qing government's Ili General Yiletu received Ubasi and other leaders. Ubasi and his group "respectfully presented the Qing government with a privy seal made in the 8th year of the Yongle reign (referring to the reign of Yongle Emperor Zhu Di) in the early Ming Dynasty,"[203] which showed their patriotism in returning back to the motherland and their firm attitude of submitting to the Qing government.

The Qing government attached great importance to the Turhute tribe's submission. Emperor Qianlong had an interview with Ubasi and his group. He gave them a banquet in the Garden of Ten Thousand Trees after returning to the Mountain Resort. At that time the imitation of the Potala Palace in Tibet — the Putuo Zongcheng Temple built in Chengde by the Qing government- happened to be completed so the two stone tablets the *Torghuts' Complete Submission to the Qing Dynasty* and *Preferential Treatment for the Torghuts* were set up in the temple, for which Emperor Qianlong wrote the inscriptions personally. The two stone tablets recorded the whole process of the Turhute tribe's hard journey back to its motherland. The Qing government made suitable arrangements for the Turhute tribe's leaders and its massive troops. Ubasi was granted the title of Zuoliketu Khan, and other lesser leaders were also granted the titles of prince, chief of county, Beile, duke, Fuguo Gong, Taij etc. The Turhute tribe was divided into the new and the old, and jasaks were established in each part. The old part was commanded by Ubasi and included four groups — the east, the west, the south, and the north; there were ten banner armies in all, and it was under the command of the General of Ili. The new part was commanded by the chief of county Sheleng and comprised two groups, and was controlled by the Left Deputy General Who Stabilizes the Frontier. In order to relieve the massive troops, the Qing government adopted the policy of "making everyone have his own food and clothes,"[204] and dealt out 200,000 silver dollars for them to buy a large quantity of daily necessities, such as domestic animals, rice, tea, cloth, felt etc.

The Tsarist Russia government was very angry about both the Torghut's patriotic action in returning back to their own motherland and the Qing Dynasty's proper arrangements made for the Turhute tribe, and wrote to ask the Qing government to return the Torghut. It even made the rude and unreasonable proposition that if the Qing government could not return the Torghut, "there will be endless wars and people will never enjoy a good and prosperous life."[205] The Qing government answered clearly that, "Ubasi and his whole Turhute tribe are very different from you (meaning the Tsarist Russian authorities), and they did not originally belong to you". They returned to their homeland because "they could not endure your heavy taxes and levies any more." To Tsarist Russia's bluff of force, the Qing government made it clear that, "choose fighting or peace, just do as you wish."[206] The above declaration indicated the Qing government's solemn attitude that they would never yield to Tsarist Russia's bluff of force.

The great migration of the Turhute tribe's return to the homeland finished between January and August 1771. It lasted over eight months, and during the whole journey they had traveled for more than 10,000 miles, experienced many battles, and overcome a variety of difficulties. When finally arriving in Ili its remaining population was only about 70,000, "which was just half of that at the beginning."[207] The Turhute people had made great sacrifices in order to revolt against Tsarist Russia's oppression and devote themselves to their motherland. Their epic deeds are a brilliant chapter in the history of our country's ethnic relations; their heroic achievement is praiseworthy.

The Qing Government Reinforced Its Domination in the Southwest and Its Reform of Tibet's Political and Religious System

"Bureaucratization of Native Officers"

"Bureaucratization of Native Officers" was a step taken by the Qing government to abolish the Native Chieftain System (or Tusi System) of the southwestern ethnic minorities and let officials appointed by the central government dominate. This kind of measure was introduced in the Ming Dynasty, and was carried out on a large scale in the southwest in the Yongzheng reign of the Qing Dynasty.

Southwest China's Yunnan, Guizhou, Guangxi, Sichuan, Hunan and other areas had always been the areas where ethnic minorities lived together with the Han ethnic group. From the very early ancient times the Miao, Yao, Zhuang, Bai, Yi and other fraternal nations had been laboring, living and multiplying on this vast region. Since the Yuan and Ming Dynasties, the ruling class of our country's central government had been ruling the ethnic minorities in these areas through the Native Chieftain System.

The Native Chieftain System involved two ruling systems—Chieftain and local officials. The former included Xuanwei Si, Xuan Fusi, An Fusi etc. These official posts, although invested by the central government, were actually separated regime of local authorities; the latter included local prefects, Zhizhou and local magistrates which were official posts held by minority nationalities' leaders of governments, states or counties established in accordance with the Han administrative institutions. This kind of Native Chieftain System was a system aiming at "winning over" and a special hierarchy carried out by the central government after the military conquest or political pacification based on the south-west minorities' backward economy and lack of transportation. Although it had its practical side in the beginning, with social and economic development and further intensification of political, economic and cultural relations with China proper, such a system not only hampered the development of social productivity in minority areas but also went against the unification of the multinational country. Therefore, from the Ming Dynasty onwards, the chieftains gave place to liuguan (officers appointed by central government) in some areas where the conditions were right and the same administrative system used in China proper was implemented. This change was called "Bureaucratization of Native Officers."

In the early years of the Qing Dynasty, while consolidating national unification and fighting against Russia's invasion, the central government was too busy to strengthen its domination in the southwest and continued to use the old Native Chieftain System. In the early years of the Kangxi reign, although "Bureaucratization of Native Officers" was implemented in some areas, the entire Southwest region was still in such a disordered situation with a mix of original native officers and officers appointed by central government, and the administrative system was chaotic. Some powerful Chieftains, who owned thousands of soldiers and had a jurisdiction of hundreds of *li*, were cruel and fierce. They ran riot everywhere and broke the laws. With regard to the people under their domination, the chieftains "can get domestic fowl, take children, and live freely. Local people under their oppression bore their exploitation, felt angry but failed to express this."[208] Chieftains offered the imperial court "both money and grain no more than three hundred *liang* (Chinese unit of weight), but a hundred times as many as that they extorted from local people. The local people were ordered to hand in a certain amount of *qian* (small amount of money) to the chieftain four times each year and a certain amount of *liang* (large amount of money) every three years. If chieftains got married, local people could not enter into marriage for three years. If local people were killed, their relatives had to pay dozens of *liang* to the chieftain and they all kept living without light all their lives."[209] Some areas adopted "Bureaucratization of Native Officers," but the Chieftains' power was deeply ingrained and tenacious. "The native officers forcibly occupied the area with both civil and military forces, so that no one would dare to reclaim 400 *li* of fertile fields."

With the development of political and economic relations in both the central plains and remote areas, and the enhancement of the Qing Dynasty's domination, people of all nationalities felt it more and more urgent to break down the uncultured and cruel Native Chieftain System, and the Qing Dynasty also did not allow unruly independent kingdoms to exist in their own territory. Thus the "Bureaucratization of Native Officers" was again put on the agenda. In 1726 (the 4th year of the Yongzheng reign), the Governor-General of Yunnan-Guizhou Eertai requested to put the three original native officers' residences of Dongchuan, Wumeng and Zhenxiong, which originally belonged to Sichuan, under Yunnan's administration, and carried out "Bureaucratization of Native Officers." Then throughout a widespread region, "Bureaucratization of Native Officers" was constantly pursued in Yunnan, Sichuan, Guizhou, Guangxi, Hubei and Hunan. According to incomplete statistics, in Yongzheng reign alone, more than 60 Tusi such as the original native prefectures and residences were bureaucratized. After getting rid of the chieftains the Qing government set up official residences, offices, states and counties in different places, appointed non-hereditary Liuguan (officers appointed by the central government) to rule during certain tenure, and implemented the same political system as that in the rest of China.

The implementation of "Bureaucratization of Native Officers" involved a serious struggle and caused many armed rebellions by various chieftains. The Native Chieftain System preserved the original backward political and economic structure in these areas, and maintained the upper class's hereditary status and privileges in the ethnic groups. It enabled them to control the local authorities, live a life of luxury, and cruelly exploit and oppress the local people. "Bureaucratization of Native Officers" meant the cancellation of their hereditary status and the limitation of their privileges, so this kind of system would undoubtedly meet with violent opposition from the ethnic groups' upper class, who even started rebellions in order to frustrate the implementation of "Bureaucratization of Native Officers".

According to the different situations of different places and the different attitudes held by chieftains about this policy, Eertai adopted the following two means — peaceful pacification and armed suppression. While the former was taken as the principal path he said that: "During the implementation of the policy of "Bureaucratization of Native Officers" it was better to convince the native officers with tactics than to capture them by force, and it was better to persuade them to surrender than to force them."[210] During the whole process of "Bureaucratization of Native Officers" Guangxi, Sichuan and Huguang adopted the former means for the most part, but Yunnan and Guizhou resorted to arms on a large scale.

The government of the Qing Dynasty first put Dongchuan, Wumeng and Zhenxiong, which had formerly belonged to Sichuan Province, under the administration of Yunnan Province and made the change from tribal authorities to regular officials. The Tusi of Wumeng, Lu Wanzhong, and the Tusi of Zhenxiong, Long Qinghou, then rose in armed rebellion. Eertai sent two of his generals Liu Qiyuan and Ha Yuansheng to put down the rebellion. Before long Dao Ruzhen, a lower official of Zhenyuan, "murdered government officials and committed burning and looting;" and Cen Yingchen, tribal prefect of Sicheng of Guangxi, "connived at looting by his staff". They were soon suppressed. The Tusis in Yunnan were very powerful and fights among them were particularly fierce. When Lu Wanzhong rebelled, his uncle Lu Dingkun surrendered to the Qing Dynasty and therefore his troops remained mostly intact. He resented the "nomination of magistrates" and "coveted the hereditary tribal position, so he rejected the assigned command."[211] He bode his time and was plotting insurgence. Liu Qiyuan, the commander-in-chief transferred to Wumeng, was corrupt, ruthless and cruel, and his army had slack military discipline. He "privately imposed taxes, embezzled provisions and funds for the troops, employed trickery, robbed citizens and locked up tribal chiefs."[212] His atrocities stirred up the anger of the minority groups. Lu Dingkun took advantage of and appealed to discontent of people, launching a rebellion in 1730 (the 8th year of the Yongzheng reign) together with his clansmen Lu Dingxin and Lu Wanfu. The rebels killed Liu Qiyuan and seized Wumeng. They were"welcomed by people and tribal chiefs of villages on the south of the Jinshajiang River, including Liangshan, Xiafang and Alv, as well as villages on the north of the Jinshajiang River, including Qiaojiaying, Zhejiahai and Dongchuan...They killed Xuntang soldiers (basic units of the army), seized army provisions, blocked strategic passes, destroyed bridges, and assembled as rebels in local places."[213] Eertai assembled a troop of over 10,000 soldiers to suppress the rebellion. The troops were divided into three parts for three routes: Commander-in-Chief Wei Zhuguo attacked Dongchuan, Commander-in-Chief Ha Yuansheng attacked Weining, Assistant Brigade Commander Han Xun attacked Zhenxiong. The battles were fierce and the Qing soldiers indulged in a killing spree. Eertai "supervised the troops in person,"[214] and finally put down the rebellion of the Lu's Tusi. While in the south of Yunnan, after the Qing army quelled the rebellion of Dao Ruzhen, they marched deep into the lower reaches of the Lancang River. "The army blazed a trail with axes and shovels, burning down fences and filling up ditches. They captured one and another strategic passes and reached Mengyang...They marched thousands of miles to the depths of the province and searched every place of strategic importance. Places on the south of the river belonged to Cheli Tusi, while those on the north received regular officials. Puer was upgraded to prefecture level. Troops and adjutants were stationed in Yuanjiang, Simao and Ganlanba."[215]

Guizhou was a settlement of the Miao nationality. It was also a place where the central government had weak control. In particular, in regions where the population consisted of "pure Miao people" and "no sovereign has been established", effective authority was nothing but a castle in the air, no matter whether the rulers were Tusi or regular officials sent by the central government. In 1726 (the 4th year of the Yongzheng reign), the Qing government attacked Zhongjiamiao. Commander-in-Chief Shi Liha and other generals led troops to capture Changzhai village in Guangshun Prefecture, west of Guizhou. After crushing the local Miao people's resistance, the army followed the victory and brought pacification to some one thousand Miao villages in Guangshun, Dingfan, Zhenning, Yongning, Yongfeng, and Anshun. The situation in the south, north and west of Guizhou gradually became stable. Eertai then mustered superior forces and marched to the Miaoling Mountains on the east of Guizhou, as well as the river basins of the Qingjiang River and the Dujiang River. The region was well-known as "Miaojiang (territory of Miao People)" of Guizhou. According to Eertai, "Tusis in Guizhou had no responsibility for governing the Miao people. The Miao plague was even worse than that of the Tusi. Miaojiang covers an area of over 3,000 *li*, containing more than 1,300 villages surrounding Guizhou. By the Qingjiang River on the west, local people could reach Hebei; by the Dujiang River on the east, they could travel to Guangdong. They occupied an isolated area and became alienated from civilization. If the central government wants to smooth the way to Guizhou and Guangdong by river, we must deploy troops deep in the region and suppress the people thoroughly."[216] It is obvious that the region was of great importance for the Qing government's rule in the Southwest and for transport between the South and the North. In 1728 (the 6th year of the Yongzheng reign), Eertai appointed Zhang Guangsi, who was familiar with local geographic conditions, to lead a troop to "Dujun, Liping, Zhenyuan and Qingping to instruct and guide the Miao people, and take every opportunity to quash revolts by force and implement pacification measures."[217] Zhang Guangsi suggested stationing troops in Zhugeying, a strategic post in the mountains, to "control the area by clutching the throat", and resorted to arms to quell the Miao villages which refused to surrender. As a result, the situation in regions in eastern Guizhou where the Miao people lived gradually became stable. The Qing government sent officials and stationed troops in various places, and opened land and water transport to Hunan and Guangdong.

However the officers and generals who were sent to the Miao area bullied the Miao people and brutally collected money and grain, which caused turmoil among the Miao again. In 1735 (the 13th year of the Yongzheng reign) the Miao people in Qingjiang and Taigong rose up against the oppression of the officials, resulted in the defeat of Carey and Huang Ping Chau. Miao had an earthquake, and the majority of the Miao areas set off a climax of anti-Qing struggle. Book of Board of punishments Zhang Zhao was then appointed to put down the struggle of Miao people in Guizhou Province. Zhang Zhao was opposed to the policy of "Bureaucratization of Native Officers" proposed by Eertai. He "secretly presented a memorial to the emperor on the defects of this policy and sent letters to many generals that advocated abandoning the policy."[218] Moreover, being weak in military planning and deployment of troops, he caused continuous chaos and led a host of soldiers with no achievement. When Qianlong succeeded to the throne he immediately fired Zhang Zhao and sent Zhang Guangsi to Guizhou province in order to govern the Miao. Zhang Guangsi "temporarily pacified the familiar Miao people and ordered them to hand in their weapons so as to weaken the strength of the strange Miao people."[219] He divided his forces into three, burning and killing the Miao people. The Miao people retreated into a forbidding mountain valley. The Qing soldiers bottled it up, moved towards it, and finally made a breakthrough. More than ten thousand people were killed. Then the Qing soldiers slaughtered the Miao people who had already surrendered. "Making use of their military power they searched for and wiped out the Miao people, whether they had surrendered or not, and divided the people into the three categories of principal culprit, secondary culprit and accomplice under duress. Through their "mopping-up" campaigns they destroyed 1,224 Miao stockade villages, granted amnesty to 224 stockade villages, executed about 17,600 people and captured approximately 25,000 people."[220] The Miao areas in Guizhou province were submerged in a pool of blood in the holocaust launched by the Qing forces.

The Liang mountain area in Sichuan province is inhabited by the Yi. Ningyuan, Yue, Ebian, Leibo and Mabian were the places where the Yi people worked and lived. Native Chieftains and hereditary headmen were living at the places not deep into the mountains at the junction of the Han and the Yi, while the Yi people were scattered in remote places deep in the mountains. The Qing government implemented "Bureaucratization of Native Officers" in Yunnan and Guizhou provinces, and sent troops into the Liang Mountains at the same time. "They marched on from many places along the Jinsha River where the Native Chieftain System prevailed such as Shama, Leibo, Tundu and Huanglang. Then they arrived at Jianchan, quartering there for thousands of *li*."[221] The Qing government assigned Liuguan (officials appointed by the central government) and dismissed some of the native chieftains and hereditary headmen.

The power of the native Chieftains was impaired in the Miao areas in the west of Hunan as well as in the native Chieftains area in Guangxi, since these areas had experienced a period of time when "they were governed by both Liuguan and native chieftains". In the Yongzheng reign, "Bureaucratization of Native Officers" displayed impressive influence. The Qing government resorted to force to suppress Wumeng in Yunnan, the Zhenxiong native Chieftains, and the Miao area in Guizhou. Thus most of the other native Chieftains had to take an affirmative attitude towards the "Bureaucratization of Native Officers". On the whole, from the forth year to the ninth year of the Yongzheng period, the Qing government had carried out "Bureaucratization of Native Officers" in large areas in Yunnan, Guizhou, Sichuan, Hunan and Guilin.

The "Bureaucratization of Native Officers" inevitably led to national oppression. The Qing forces burned, killed and pillaged in the battle to suppress the rebellions of the native Chieftains, which brought disaster to the minorities. However, from a long-term historical perspective, "Bureaucratization of Native Officers" played an active role. It attacked and restricted the separatist forces and privileges of native Chieftains. Moreover it strengthened the relationship between central and local government, consolidated national unity, enhanced the economic and cultural contacts among various nationalities, and had a positive influence upon the production of national minorities as well as the improvement of their life.

Pacification of the Greater and Smaller Jinchuan

The Greater and Smaller Jinchuan (meaning River of Gold) refer to two branches of the upper reaches of the Dadu River. Located in the northwest of Sichuan, it earned its name from the gold mines in the mountains along the river. The Jinchuan area was a Tibetan settlement with "numerous towering mountains surrounded by tumultuous narrow and winding rivers that can only be crossed by boats and tight bridges."[222] The terrain was dangerous and rough, making it an isolated place without transport to the outside world. The local people all lived in stone-built houses. Adjacent to the realms of the Major Nine Tusis, such as Chuosijiabu, it was under the jurisdiction of the Zagu Pacification Commissioner in the Ming Dynasty. In 1650 (the 7th year of the Shunzhi reign) the Qing government appointed tribal chief of Smaller Jinchuan Buerjixi as Tusi. In 1666 (the 5th year of the Kangxi reign), the government granted the seal of "Master of Change" to Jialetaerba. In 1723 (the 1st year of the Yongzheng reign), the government appointed Shaluoben, grandson of Jialetaerba, as Pacification Commissioner for his success in pacifying Tibetan rebels with Yue Zhongqi. So he became Greater Jinchuan Tusi and the former Tusi Zewang still governed Smaller Jinchuan.

After Shaluoben was named Pacification Commissioner, his powers grew stronger and he planned to invade and occupy Smaller Jinchuan. He first married his daughter Akou to Zewang, Tusi of Smaller Jinchuan. Zewang was weak and controlled by his wife. In 1746 (the 11th year of the Qianlong reign), Shaluoben took over Zewang's jurisdiction and his seal. He refused to "return the land to Zewang" until the Governor-General of Sichuan reprimanded him. In 1747 (the 12th year of the Qianlong reign), Shaluoben launched a rebellion and attacked Luegebushizha Tusi and Mingzheng Tusi. Sichuan governor Ji Shan sent out troops, but the troops were defeated by the rebels. On hearing the report, the Qing government ordered the Governor-general of Yunnan and Guizhou Zhang Guangsi, who had gained merit in the expeditions against the Miao people, to suppress the rebellion.

Zhang Guangsi assembled a troop of 30,000 soldiers and branched out into two columns to attack the Jinchuan area. "The first column attacked east of the river from the west of Sichuan and the second attacked west of the river from the east of Sichuan."[223] Zhang expected a one-off victory. However the army was "halted and stopped", and confronted with "various defeats and failures" due to the steep mountains, dangerous paths, lines of fortress and posts, and the forceful resistance of the rebels. The central government then sent grand secretary Naqin to supervise the army, along with Yue Zhongqi who had been deposed but was then appointed prefect. Capitalizing on his high rank, the arrogant Naqin ordered when he got to the frontline that "the army should capture Guaerya Cliff in three days. Generals or soldiers who objected were punished by military law. The entire army was shocked and frightened. They spared no efforts in the battle and suffered great losses. Naqin succumbed to the defeat and dared not give any orders. He hid inside his room every time before a battle and gave instructions from a remote distance. All laughed at him, so the army's prestige was deteriorating day by day. One day a troop of 3000 soldiers attacked a fortress and was confronted with only scores of enemies, who shouted they would attack. All the soldiers then scattered like birds and beasts."[224] Naqin swallowed his defeats and had to pin his hopes on Zhang Guangsi. Zhang "looked down upon Naqin, for the latter knew nothing about military affairs, but Naqin had superior authority. So he showed outward meekness but harbored inner hatred. All the generals did not know whose orders to follow, so they sat on the fence on every issue."[225] Zhang Guangsi relied on Liangerji as his guide, but Liangerji was a spy sent by Shaluoben. He secretly sent information about the army to Shaluoben and thus Shaluoben knew all the army's actions beforehand. As a result, "the troops were losing morale and gained no merits after half a year's siege."[226] Emperor Qianlong was furious. He executed Zhang Guangsi and Naqin, and sent Grand Secretary Fu Heng as minister commander. Fu Heng assembled 35,000 elite soldiers and accepted Yue Zhongqi's plan to attack the enemy in two columns. At that time the Qing government had been at war in Jinchuan for two years. The troops were tired and funds had been spent in vain. Naqin and Zhang Guangsi were executed, and Generals Ha Yuansheng and Dong Fang were removed from their posts. It was like a lion fighting with rabbits. Although the empire has had exerted its full efforts, no satisfactory results were seen. Emperor Qianlong wanted to stop the war, ordering Fu Heng to retreat. His decree said: "My intention of the war in Jinchuan was not to exploit the land and people, but to bring an end to atrocity and pacify the remote minority groups…In my opinion, how can the trivial minority groups withstand the attack of our mighty imperial army? Grand minister commander Fu Heng is one of the top-ranking ministers in the imperial court. He spent so long a time outside the court tackling the clowns in remote areas. Even if we sweep their base, it cannot redeem the laborious hours Fu Heng has spent!"[227] Fu Heng thought that he could soon pacify Jinchuan and applied to take military action. But Emperor Qianlong refused. The emperor wrote three pieces of poetry for Fu Heng, saying "An ambitious heart need not to be in restless pursuit", and "Return to the Imperial Court quickly for compliments and honor." Yue Zhongqi had led troops to attack Lewuwei, the den of Shaluoben. Shaluoben was afraid as he was once a subordinate of Yue Zhongqi and went on the expedition to Tibet with Yue. He begged to surrender. Yue Zhongqi seized the opportunity, meeting with Shaluoben at the enemy's camp with an entourage of only 13 cavalry. Shaluoben "kowtowed and worshiped Yue with a grand welcoming ceremony,"[228] "and expressed the intention of submission and vowed before religious doctrines."[229] The Qing government won a victory without firing a shot and pacified Jinchuan. Shaluoben was spared and resumed his post as Tusi.

After that the Greater and Smaller Jinchuan were still under the jurisdiction of Tusis and battles and fights always flared up between Tusi. The issue was not fully resolved. As a result, after more than a decade, rebellions on larger scale broke out.

In the middle of the Qianlong reign, the Greater Jinchuan Tusi Shaluoben was old. His nephew Langka was in charge of all Tusi affairs. Langka continued to invade and harry neighboring Tusis. In 1758 (the 23rd year of the Qianlong reign), he seized Smaller Jinchuan and Gebushizha Tusi. Aertai, Governor-General of Sichuan, tried to dissuade Langka from doing so but he "would not stop invading the neighboring realms."[230] In 1766 (the 31st year of the Qianlong reign), the Qing government ordered Governor-General of Sichuan Aertai to call up the soldiers of the "Nine Major Tusi"[231] neighboring Greater Jinchuan Tusi to join submit. Aertai hoped to make concessions to avoid trouble and mediated; he also allowed a "marriage" between Langka and Chuosijiabu Tusi. Langka also married his daughter to Senggesang, son of Smaller Jinchuan Zewang. In this way, the Greater and Smaller Jinchuan Tusi, who "had old grudges and a gulf between each other" were joined together by "marriage", and "the neighboring 18 Tusis elected the two Jinchuan Tusi head."[232] In 1771 (the 36th year of the Qianlong reign) Suonuomu, grandson of Shaluoben, trapped and killed Gebushizha Tusi. Smaller Jinchuan Senggesang also attacked Ekeshi and Mingzheng Tusi, and openly fought against the reinforcements sent by the Qing government. Aertai led a troop to crack down on them, but he spent half a year on the siege of Jianlu. Emperor Qianlong was upset and ordered Aertai to commit suicide, ordering Grand Secretary Wen Fu to transfer from Yunnan to Sichuan to supervise the army. He also appointed Minister Gui Lin to replace Aertai as Governor-General of Sichuan and continue the pacification. In the beginning, the Qing army had a few victories. They took over the military passes one after another, approaching Meinu where the Smaller Jinchuan Tusi was stationed. Senggesang fled to Greater Jinchuan and joined forces with Suonuomu. The central government again appointed Wen Fu to be Frontier Pacification General-in-Chief, and Agui and Feng Shene to be adjutants for attacking the Greater Jinchuan. Suonuomu "exerted all his forces to resist the attack. He built ten times more fortress and passes than those in Smaller Jinchuan."[233] The army sent by the government attacked in six columns. However the General-in-Chief Wen Fu "was perversely persistent and would not ask for others' opinions."[234] He repeated the old methods of Zhang Guangsi, building fortresses to fight against fortresses. He built over one thousand fortresses and his 20,000 soldiers were divided up, resulting in insufficient military strength on the frontier. In the summer of 1773 (the 38th year of the Qianlong reign), Wen Fu was stationed at Muguomu, east of Greater Jinchuan, but he "drank all day with generals such as Prefect Dong Tianbi."[235] Suonuomu sent out troops to cut off his provisions transport and attacked Muguomu camp as well as the fortresses. Wen Fu died in the battle and "the army was defeated and fled in disorder. Soldiers trampled on each other. And the miserable sounds were heard even through the entire night. When the soldiers were passing over a steel cable bridge they pushed each other, causing the collapse of the bridge and thousands of deaths."[236]

The Qing government refused to swallow the defeat and deployed military forces. The government appointed Agui to be General of Pacification of the West, and Feng Shene and Mingliang as adjutants, calling up Scouting Brigade, Firearm Brigade and Suolun soldiers into the battle. The attacking force was thus significantly reinforced. After the Qing army seized Smaller Jinchuan they marched to Greater Jinchuan, which required far more arduous efforts. Suonuomu took advantage of the geographical conditions and relied on stone fortresses for defense. The troops engaged in bitter battles, capturing the fortresses one by one, and finally approached Lewuwei. Suonuomu poisoned Senggesang and surrendered to the Qing army with the body as a pledge. Agui rejected surrender and continued the attack. The army spent half a year and took Xunkezong Fortress, an exterior fortress of Lewuwei. Lewuwei "has strong fortresses and thick walls. It faces a big river on the west and has a Praying Tower on the south that forms a corner against the camp. The picket fences and stone blocks are about 500 meters long. On the east, it sits at the foot of a mountain that has eight layers of cliffs. Fortresses were built on each layer of the cliffs and the retreating enemies of the first cliff would gather and station on the second one."[237] The Qing army first broke the fences and blocks to weaken the defense, then destroyed bridges in case the enemy fled, and bombarded their camp with canons. On Mid-autumn Day of 1775 (the 40th year of the Qianlong reign) the Qing army breached Lewuwei. Before that Suonuomu has escaped to Guaerya Cliff (Geer Cliff). In early 1776 the Qing army surrounded Guaerya Cliff. Suonuomu was cornered and had to surrender together with his grandfather Shaluoben and 2,000 of his followers. After the pacification of Greater and Smaller Jinchuan, the Qing government set up Maogong Prefecture.

The establishment of high commissionerships and the reform of the Tibetan administrative system

Soon after Qing government reshuffled the local government of Tibet (Kashag former local government of Tibet) in the late years of the Kangxi Emperor, there emerged new struggles for wealth and power within the Tibetan nobles in power in Emperor Yongzheng's time. A small group of nobles led by Al

Bubba attempted to seize power from Kang Jinai who supported the central government of the Qing Dynasty, which made their struggle with Kang Jinai and Po Luonai increasingly fierce. When the struggle was known by the Qing government in 1727 (the 5th year of the Yongzheng reign), Emperor Yongzheng officially nominated the academician of the Grand Secretariat Zeng Ge and Vice Commander-in-Chief Ma La as high commissioners to go directly to the area where Dalai Lama resided so as to supervise the local government of Tibet and reconcile the interior conflicts among the Tibetan nobles. However, before the two high commissioners reachedcame to Tibet, Al Bubba had colluded with Long Bunai, Qiu Ernai and others and had launched a rebellion. As a result, they killed Kang Jinai and attacked Po Luonai who was in charge of the Tsang governmental affairs. Po Luonai led his subordinates to rise up in resistance and defeated and captured all the rebels, Al Bubba included. Meanwhile the, Qing government had dispatched the Left-Court Censor Cha Lang to lead more than 5,000 soldiers to go to Tibet and put down the rebellion, and the two high commissioners had arrived in Lhasa. The Qing government had given the order to execute the leading figures of this rebellion and praised Po Luonai by making him prefectural governor to take over Kang Jinai's position.

The establishment of the high commissionerships strengthened the Qing government's governance of Tibet. Meanwhile, in handling Tibetan affairs, Po Luonai had showed "faithful loyalty and wholehearted dedication"[238] and had positively safeguarded the unification of the whole country and maintained over 20-year stability of Tibet.

In 1747 (the 12th year of the Emperor Qianlong), Po Luonai died from disease and his second son Zhuer Mote Namu Zhale succeeded his position. However, in contrast to his father, he attempted to seize total power for himself and had conflicts with Dalai Lama. He also evaded the Qing government's control and accused the high commissioner Ji Shan, aiming to splitting Tibet from Qing government. Ji Shan made a proposal to the Qing government to deploy Zhuer Mote's older brother Ce Budeng who was in charge of the Ali region of Tsang to Lhasa to jointly govern the Tibetan political affairs together with the purpose of removing total power fromseparating Zhuer Mote's total power. Unfortunately, Zhuer Mote gained the initiative by sending somebody to the Ali region to kill his older brother and attack his brother's troops. Later, he "arranged lots of spies around Ji Shan. Therefore if once Ji Shan planned any moves, he would take action to find out what it was and deal with it immediately. He forbade the postmen to send letters and made them give any information to him, while he secretly ganged up with outside assistance. If there was somebody opposed to his reign, he would remove him right away. His commanding force could be compared with that of Dalai Lama who used to be the leading figure controlling the Tibet."[239] At that time, the Qing government captured the ambassador heading for Junggar sent by Zhuer Mote, and seized his rebellion letter and all articles of tribute. All of this made the Emperor Qianlong so furious and agitated that he secretly named Fu Qing as the new high commissioner and gave him a confidential letter stating that Zhuer Mote Namu Zhale was surly, cunning and treacherous. If kept alive, he would be a trouble in the future. There were two ways to kill him. One was that since he attempts to dispatch troops to fight against his brother, you can appoint the Governor-General of Sichuan Ce Leng to lead the army to take the chance of capturing or killing him on the pretense of aiding him. The other is that when Zhangjia Hutu Ketu heads for Tibet to collect teas, you pretend to send the Governor-General of Sichuan to escort him to Tibet and try to find a chance to kill him. As to which method is more convenient and reliable, you can respond according to the exact situation once you arrive at Tibet. You can plan this matter skillfully and cautiously, and then report to me in detail. Taking the secret letter written by the Emperor Qianlong and knowing that he must kill Zhuer Mote, Fu Qing reached Lhasa, followed by another high commissioner La Budun.

Right at that moment the real situation in Tibet was extremely desperate because of the armed rebellions. So Fu Qing and La Budeng discussed this and decided to take the risk of trapping and killing Zhuer Mote rather than waiting helplessly for death and letting rebellion spread. In November 1750 (the 15th year of Qianlong's reign), in the name of announcing that there was an imperial edict calling Zhuer Mote to the high commissioners' Yamen (governmental residence as well as office) to discuss official business, the two high commissioners enticed Zhuer Mote to the upstairs of their residence and killed him. Knowing that Zhuer Mote had been trapped in the Yanmen, gangs of Zhuer Mote's accomplices besieged the Yamen and "attacked it with cannons and circled all the walls of it. But all the walls of the Yamen were so high and solid that none of them could breach them. Later these accomplices changed their plan and began to pile stacks beneath the walls and lit these stacks. In a moment the Yamen was a sea of flame and was burned at last. Seeing that the Yamen was burned, these accomplices climbed the walls and broke into the yard."[240] Fu Qing committed suicide and La Budeng jumped down from the upstairs and fought against the rebels, and was finally killed by them.

When the Qing government was informed of the rebellion in Tibet, Emperor Qianlong dispatched the Governor-General of Sichuan Ce Leng and Prefect Yue Zhongqi to lead the army to Tibet so as to put down the rebellion. However before the army arrived in Tibet, the 7th Dalai Lama Kelzang Gyatso and the

Tibetan monks had already defeated the rebels and pacified the Tibetans. After the army arrived the leaders arrested the head of this rebellion and rewarded Dalai Lama and others who had helped in putting down this rebellion. Later, in honor of Fu Qing and La Budeng, the Qing government built a "Double Allegiance Temple" both in Beijing and Lhasa to praise them for their dedication and achievements in defending the unification of the country. Zhuer Mote Namu Zhale's willful persecution and ferocious misdeeds were condemned by the Tibetans. Therefore the story of Fu Qing and La Budeng sacrificing themselves to remove the rebels was admired by all Tibetans, and they are deeply respected by the Tibetans. It was said later by Fu Kangan that forty years after this incident he could still see the scene that "while time flies by, endless Tibetan pilgrims still continue" in front of the "Double Allegiance Temple".

From the rebellion led by Zhuer Mote Namu Zhale the Qing government realized that the reason why he could be so fearless and treacherous as to start this rebellion lay in the increasing power of the Tibetan feudal serf- owners. They owned "a large range of land and a group of powerful soldiers as well as holding unified power in all kinds of affairs"[241] so that they did not need to obey the orders given by the central government. So in order to prevent the Tibetan nobles from gaining excessive centralized power, the Qing government conducted a political reform from 1750 to 1751 (the 15th and 16th year of Qianlong's reign) on the principle of "nominating multiple leaders to weaken their separate power". The main contents of this reform was to abolish the Fungnembi of conferring a Tibetan Prefectural Governor and to stipulate that the Tibetan government—Kashag should be composed of four Galoins (Tibetan officials renowned for meritorious service) and all the governmental affairs of the Galoin should not be disposed of by one person. According to *The Regulations for the Better Governing of Tibet* reported by the Governor-General of Sichuan Ce Leng in 1751 (the 16th year of Qianlong reign), the Qing government made some specific stipulations. The main points were as follows:

First, it was stipulated that the number of Galoins in the Tibetan local government remained four as usual. But one Galoin who had a good knowledge of Shamanism should be chosen to follow Jasak Lama and help him, and thus the chosen Galoin could "cooperate with other three Galoins in disposing Tibetan affairs."[242]

Second, the Galoins should deal with all the political affairs from the Kashag's Yamen (location of the official department) instead of "from their own residences." They would be deprived of their previous "privilege of nominating officers privately." In disposing affairs, all minor affairs should be "discussed by all the Galoins justly and then handled properly." In the case of important affairs that needed to be reported to the central government, the Galoins should "ask for instructions from Dalai Lama and the high commissioners and then handle them appropriately."[243]

Third, when nominating Diba leaders, the Galoins should not add them privately. Instead they should report it to Dalai Lama and discuss it with the high commissioners before making the final decision. When it came to the dismissal of officers who had committed crimes, the Galoins should "find out the truth impartially and write the statements clearly, and then report them to Dalai Lama and the high commissioners before implementing the final results as instructed by them."[244]

Fourth, all the temples should be designated a Lama Khenpo. If there were not enough Lama Khenpo, Dalai Lama would be responsible for the shortage of Lamas and they had the right the designate properly. Galoins "should not act on their own authority to designate Lamas solely and privately according to incomplete regulations."[245]

This reform involved some other administrative aspects that were all recorded in *The Regulations for the Better Governing of Tibet* reported by Ce Leng.

While carrying out these administrative system reforms, the Qing government also decided to deploy 1,500 soldiers to garrison Tibet permanently and ordered the prefectural officers to lead them. The soldiers would have a three-year tour and after that they would become permanent soldiers.

In 1757 (the 22th year of Qianlong reign), the 7th Dalai Lama Kelzang Gyatso died of disease. Nobody was capable of dealing with all the governmental affairs and the newly-designated 8th Dalai was too young to control the government. The Qing government immediately ordered Dimu Nuomen Hutu Ketu to exercise Dalai's power for the moment and told the incumbent high commissioners Wu Mitai and Sa Lashan to keep an eye on him. If they came across any issues they should "discuss with Dimu Hutu Ketu by treating him as Dalai instead of letting the Galoins surpass their power and raise trouble."[246] The establishment of such a kind of affairs-regent was to prevent the autocracy of the Galoins. In other words this regulation was a supplement to the above reform.

Although the additional reform of the Tibetan administrative system by the Qing government at this time was not perfect, it did limit and weaken the Galoins' powers and highlight the power of the high commissioners as well as strengthening the central government's control of Tibet.

Since the putting down of the rebellion led by Zhuer Mote, the Tibetan government had gone through nearly 40 years' of political stability. It was not until the end of the 18th century when the Gurkha invaded Tibet that political turmoil arose again in Tibet.

The Qing troops repelled the Gurkha invasion and the conclusion of the *Tibet Regulation Made by Imperial Order*

In the mid-18th century the Gurkhas ruled Nepal, founded a new dynasty, and continued to expand. In 1788 (the 53rd year of the Qianlong reign), the Gurkha sent troops to invade Nyalam, Zongga, Jilong and other regions in Tibet, which ruined the long-term friendly relationship between Tibet and Nepal. The Qing Government sent troops led by Ba Zhong to Tibet. Unexpectedly Ba Zhong muddled his work and ordered the local authorities to make peace with the Gurkha. "The Gurkha did not agree to return Nyalam, Zongga and Jilong on the grounds that they took them themselves. Then some local officials promised to give three hundred local ingots as land rent (9,300 taels of inland ingots) and ordered them to return the land."[247] Ba Zhong bought back the occupied territory with land rent in this way, but lied to the Qing Government that Gurkha had submitted to him and withdrawn their forces. In 1791 (the 56th year of Qianlong), theGurkha attacked again to claim the "land rent". Earlier than this, the 6th Panchen Lama was presented to Emperor Qianlong and was received in state in the 45th year of Qianlong. The Qing Government built the "Temple of Sumeru Happiness and Longevity" in Chengde similar in structure to the Tashilhunpo Monastery in Shigatse as the temporary palace for the 6th Panchen Lama. Later, the 6th Panchen Lama died of smallpox in Xihuang Temple in Beijing. "Over hundreds of thousands of jin of gold and silver, numerous tiaras, prayer beads, bowls made of crystal and jade, gold-threaded cassocks, sandalwood, ornamental flags, china, silk, and pearls"[248] awarded by Emperor Qianlong and offered by princes and dukes in Beijing and Inner and Outer Mongolia were all seized by Tonpa Khutukhtu, brother of the 6th Panchen Lama, while Sarmarpa, another brother of the 6th Panchen Lama and the Living Budda of Kagyupa, did not have a share due to his exclusion from Gelugpa. Sarmarpa was very angry about this. He fled to Nepal and incited and led the invading troops of the Gurkha to attack Tibet. They fought their way into Shigatse, occupied the Tashilhunpo Monastery, seized the possessions and ritual impliments left by the 6th Panchen Lama, and burnt, killed and looted wherever they went, which brought great disaster to both monks and ordinary people in Tibet. On hearing of the Gurkha's invasion Bao Tai, the High Commissioner in Tibet, was "scared to death" and even planned to "move Dalai and Panchen to Taining", which further caused public instability. The Qing Government then appointed Fu Kang'an the general, and Hai Lancha and Kui Lin the counsellors, to lead forces into Tibet and fight against the invaders. Wherever the Qing troops went they were warmly received and supported by the local residents. Dalai Lama "led monks and ordinary people to take care of gunpowder, leather boots lined with wula sedge and other errands"[249] to support the anti-invasion war of the Qing forces. Soon the Qing forces "expelled the Gurkhas from Tibet and made them flee across the Himalayas to Nava Cote, only twenty miles away from Katmandu". The Gurkha rulers agreed to return all the possessions they had taken from the Tashilhunpo Monastery, and promised the Qing Government that they would never invade Tibet. Fu Kang'an accepted the armistice terms, withdrew his troops and returned to Tibet.

Although the Qing Government had beaten the Gurkha invaders, there were also problems in the following two aspects: one was the extreme corruption of the Tibetan government which was unable to put an end to the internal conflicts or to fight against external attack; the other was the imperfect local political system. For example, there was no clear line between the relations and duties among Dalai, Panchen and the Tibetan government, and there were also some malpractices in the political, military, financial, religious and diplomatic systems. In sum, the Qing Government had not formed a powerful political center in the Tibetan area. In such circumstances, the Qing Government was determined to regulate and reform the political and religious systems of Tibet.

In 1792 (the 57th year of Qianlong reign), the Qing Government ordered Fu Kang'an to negotiate the regulations on Tibetan affairs with the 8th Dalai Lama and the 7th Panchen Lama. One hundred and two terms were proposed after October 1792. After revision by the Qing Government, twenty-nine were officially approved and implemented. This was the famous *Tibet Regulation Made by Imperial Order* (hereinafter called *The Regulation*). *The Regulation* not only used some old effective systems but also made great improvement and reform of these, and this became the supreme law made by the central government for the Tibetan local authority.

The main contents of *The Regulation* can be summarized as follows:

(1) The most important term in *The Regulation* is the one re-stipulating the authority and status of the High Commissioners in Tibet, Dalai Lama and Panchen Lama. The first term in *The Regulation* states that: "The High Commissioners in Tibet are in charge of the internal affairs of Tibet and enjoy the same power and obligations as Dalai Lama and Panchen Erdeni". All the Galoins and those below them are subordinate to High Commissioners in Tibet. "All affairs should be presented to the High Commissioners to deal with". This regulation greatly improved the power of the High Commissioners in Tibet. It actually put the Tibetan government under the supervision and management of

the High Commissioners in Tibe t, which was of huge importance in preventing serf-owners and nobles from grasping all the authority and separating Tibet from China.

(2) *The Regulation* also stipulated that the High Commissioners in Tibet were entitled to choose the local officials. Any vacancy in the officials under. Galoins, Deboins[250] and Shang Zhuo Bate[251], "the High Commissioners in Tibet will report to the Qing Government and choose officials together with Dalai Lama." Given the fact that former local officials "are promoted or demoted at any time and have no status at all", the official system was in disorder. *The Regulation* also prescribes the official ranks e.g. Galoin is in the third rank, Deboin and Shang Zhuo Bate are in the fourth rank. Promotion, demotion, reward and punishment of local officials were all administered by the High Commissioners in Tibet.

(3) *The Regulation* stipulated that the incarnation of Dalai, Panchen and Khutukhtus of Gelugpa[252] should be determined by a lottery of golden vase and conducted under the supervision of the High Commissioners in Tibet i.e. the system of the "Golden Tibetan Vase". In the past, when the older generation of Dalai, Panchen and other Living Buddas passed away, the new "Xubilgan", namely the "reincarnated soul boy" was "decided by the wizard."[253] This tradition had been observed for such a long time that some feudal serf-owners and nobles began to take advantage of it. They bribed or enticed wizards to their side, in order to make their offspring the "Xubilgan" and take both religious and political power to control the whole political situation, which has led to a situation where "from the Xubilgan of Dalai Lama and Panchen Erdeni to all the Khutukhtus honored by the four tribes in Khalkha, all are hereditary."[254] This system was unfavorable for the Qing Government's administration of Tibetan politics and religion, and easily expanded the separatist power of Tibetan serf-owners. Therefore the Qing Government stated clearly in *The Regulation* that when Dalai or Panchen passed away, the names and dates of birth of reported Xubilgan would be submitted to the High Commissioners in Tibet. Then they would be written on a toothpick in the Manchu, Chinese and Tibetan languages and put in the golden vase awarded by the Qing Government. The draw was conducted under the supervision of the High Commissioners in Tibet, and the chosen candidate would be the new "Xubilgan". He must attend the "installation ceremony" held by the High Commissioners in Tibet when he grew up.

(4) In accordance with the need to strengthen national defense, it was stipulated in *The Regulation* that a local standing army should be built up. Considering the situation that "former Tibetan soldiers escaped or fled" in the face of the Gurkha's two invasions, the Qing Government decided to "offer

Fig. 10.3. Gold Tibetan vase

provisions and rations and training"[255] to the Tibetan army. 1,000 Tibetan soldiers were stationed at Anterior Tibet and Tsang, and 500 Tibetan soldiers were stationed at strategic passes such as Ding Tong and Jiang Zi. There were altogether 3,000 soldiers stationed in Tibet. A series of systems concerning military organization, provisions, funds, rewards and punishments were also prescribed in *The Regulation.*

(5) In terms of the foreign affairs of Tibet, *The Regulation* stipulated: "The High Commissioner in Tibet is in charge of all foreign affairs." For instance, letters to Dalai and Panchen from Gurkha, Bulu Bake, Dremojong and other bordering states should all be "reported to the High Commissioners in Tibet and translated for further checking. The High Commissioners in Tibet will decide on the reply to them". Galoins and officials below them coul not "write letters to foreign countries privately". Foreign businessmen who "came to Tibet for alms giving and feast days" should be "permitted by the High Commissioners in Tibet after reporting their number to the official in charge of the border. When their business is done and the number checked, then the documents can be returned and they shall leave".

(6) In terms of the financial system, *The Regulation* stipulated that the fiscal revenues of Tibet should "all be in the charge of the High Commissioners in Tibet". An organization was set up to make coins and to unify the purity and exchange rate of currency.

We can see from the main contents above that the Qing Government made great reforms to the systems of Tibetan politics and religion. The reform strengthened the administration of the central government over Tibet and the relationship between the people in the central plains and people in Tibet, and played an active role in consolidating national defense and social order.

The Qing Government's Ethnic Ruling Policy and Exploration of Border Areas

The ethnic ruling policy of Qing government

China is a multi-national country with many minority nationalities. More than half of China's territory is vast border areas inhabited mostly by minority nationalities. Policy towards them is closely connected with national stability and unity, and with whether society will progress. Previous feudal rulers made nationality policies in accordance with their own interests and the balance of power at the time, which were inevitably of the nature of strong class and nationality oppression, and the Qing Government was no exception. However the Qing regime was established by a minority nationality—the aristocrats of the Manchu, and it was in close and lasting alliance with another important minority nationality—the Mongolians. The Qing regime has learnt from the experience of previous nationality ruling and formulated a comparatively complete and effective nationality policy, which gradually strengthened its administration of the border areas. There is no doubt that the Qing regime also launched brutal wars and slaughtered minority nationalities, and there was ethnic oppression and discrimination. However, when compared with previous dynasties with their successive wars, troubles on the frontier, mutual confrontation of separatist regimes, overturning of regimes and destroyed social economy, the situation in the Qing Dynasty was much better. Generally speaking, the nationality ruling policy was relatively successful in the Qing Dynasty. It enhanced the unity among nationalities, promoted economic and cultural development in border areas, maintained national unity, and laid a solid foundation for the vast territory of the People's Republic of China. Zhou Enlai once put a premium on the important role of Qing Dynasty in promoting the process of multi-national unification: "China was more united in the Qing Dynasty than in any other dynasties before it."[256]

The fundamental principle of the nationality ruling policy in Qing Dynasty was: "Cultivate them but do not change their customs, govern their politics but not change its advantages". This meant to maintain the social customs and religions of all minority nationalities, and making use of members from the upper class to govern and manage different ethnic groups according to different situations. The key of the Qing Government's nationality work was Mongolian affairs, including Inner and Outer Mongolia and Oirad Mongolia. They had a large population and a complicated tribal system with great power and vast lands, and lived from Great Khingan, Hulun Buir, to the areas near the desert and the Tianshan Mountains. They also controlled the Hui nationality, Qinghai and Tibet. The area inhabited and controlled by them occupied about half the territory of China. Wars and peace with Mongolia constituted the major part of the nationality issue in the Qing Dynasty, and were also the key to the change in political pattern in the early and middle Qing Dynasty. The Qing Government attached great importance to nationality issues and established the Court of Colonial Affairs (originally known as the Mongol Yamen) to deal with affairs concerning Mongolia and other minority nationalities. It enjoyed the same status as the Six Boards.

The main contents of the Qing Government's nationality ruling policy were as follows:

(1) Establishing different administrative agencies according to the situation in different regions, and strengthening the central government's management of minority nationality areas. For example, sending troops to guard the northeastern and northwestern areas which were coveted by Tsarist Russia and where wars had been launched. The Army's Office system was adopted in these areas and generals were appointed to be in charge of both military and civil affairs. The Mukden General was stationed in Shengjing, the Jilin General in Wula, Jilin, and the Heilongjiang General in Qiqihar. Cities were built in many regions with officials and troops. For example, magistrates were appointed in the government offices at Hulun Buir and Butha; vice commanders-in-chief were appointed in Aihui, Mo'ergen, Bodune, Ningguta and Sanxing, and soldiers were mostly picked from local the Soren, Daur, Oroqen and Ewenki nationalities and then assigned into the Eight Banners and ordered to be fully equipped to guard the country. Heads of counties Kala Da and tribes Gashan Da were appointed to other minority nationalities in remote areas which were not categorized into Eight Banners according to the original regional organizations and clans. Early in the 18th century, Mamiya Rinzõ, a Japanese who had been to the lower reaches of the Heilong River and Sakhalin Island once said: "The east of Tartary (the lower reaches of the Heilong River) was inhabited by Feiya Ga, Shan Dan, Hezhe, Jimen A Yinuoand other nationalities, most of which were governed by respective Nada and Gashan Da."[257] The majority of these posts were hereditary, commanded by the Vice Commander-in-Chief of Sanxing, and were responsible for timely tribute, service for official errands, peace-keeping and implementation of the Qing Government's decrees.

The Ili General was appointed in the northwest to handle the military and civil affairs in the areas around the Tianshan Mountains. Troops were also sent to be stationed in all regions. Grand Minister Consultants, Grand Minister Superintendents and Grand Minister Captains were all appointed to these regions. Although they were responsible for commanding troops, they were not subject to the military system as were the vice commanders-in-chief in northeast area. To the south of the Tianshan Mountains where the Uyghur nationality lived, the traditional Boke system continued to be adopted. Officials ranging from the third rank to the seventh rank were appointed by the Qing Government to manage civil affairs. In Urumqi, Balikun and other regions where many Han people had moved in, the system of prefecture/sub-prefecture/county like as in the central regions was adopted. Urumqi was renamed Dihua Sub-prefecture, and Balikun Zhenxi Prefecture.

After the Junngar forces were put down, there were basically no Qing troops in Inner and Outer Mongolia. Only the Vice General, Pacifier of the Frontier of Uliastay, was appointed in the border area of Outer Mongolia to defend against Tsarist Russia. The League Banner system was adopted in the whole of Mongolia. "Banners" were set up on the basis of former territory, each of which was governed by a Jasak. The Jasak was taken from the upper class of the Banner. Unlike the former lords, the Jasak was the country's administrator who took the designated job from the Qing Government without the power to deal with political affairs independently. A League was higher than a Banner and governed by the commander of the League who was selected by the Ministry of Tribal Affairs from the nobility in the League. With a view to preventing the dictatorship of the commander of the League, he was forbidden to give orders directly to affiliated Banners but he could monitor their political affairs. There was a fixed date and venue for the meeting of the League. The establishment of the League Banner system marked the enhancement of the central government's rule of the Mongolian areas. There were altogether 19 Leagues, 203 Banners with six Leagues and 49 Banners in Inner Mongolia, four Leagues and 86 Banners in Outer Mongolia, and nine Leagues and 61 Banners in Qinghai and Zungar. However even within the same Mongolian area, policies were very flexible. In some regions a commander-in-chief was appointed instead of a Jasak because these regions used to fight against Qing Government and were deprived of the rights of autonomy, such as Chahar, Tumet in Guihua City, Zungar and some areas in Hulun Buir.

The local administration of Tibet has been discussed in the previous sections. It was a system of unification of state and religion realized through the upper class of Tibet. The authority of Dalai Lama was built up while the Tibetan

Kings were abolished and the power of the noble serf-owners was suppressed. The Tibetan local government system managed by Dalai and the High Commissioners in Tibet together was also further improved.

(2) Winning over and making use of the upper class of minority nationalities. The Qing Government made great efforts to win over the upper class of minority nationalities. Generally, the rights of their own nationality were preserved and acknowledged; tax and corvée was abated; and a generous salary and hereditary bannerets were awarded to them to ensure that their interests and privileges could run in the family. Noble titles such as Prince, Governor, Beile and Beise usually given to Manchu nobles (in the early Qing Dynasty only a few people of Han nationality were awarded with nobility, such as Wu Sangui) were especially given to the Mongolian nobles. Some Mongolian nobles who had made great contributions could enjoy the double salary of Prince. The imperial court of the Qing Dynasty was connected with the Mongolian nationality by marriage. The emperors and Manchu nobility often married the daughters of Mongolian nobles and Mongolian women, while the princesses were married to Mongolian men. This kind of marital relationship strengthened their political connection. The Qing Government always emphasized "the unification of Manchu and Mongolia". It was the loyalty of many upper-class Mongolians that contributed to the stability of the Qing regime, administration of its vast territory, and the unification of the country.

In order to reach out to the upper class of all nationalities and increase their political centralism, the Qing Government formulated the systems of "annual audience" and "paddock audience". All the upper-class members from minority nationalities who had had smallpox should in turn go to Beijing to be presented to the emperor at a fixed interval. This was called the "annual audience". Others who had not had smallpox should not go to Beijing because they might easily get smallpox due to the different climate in Beijing. They would go to the Mulan Paddock in turn to accompany the emperor for hunting and be presented to the emperor at the Summer Villa, which was called the "paddock audience". All of them would be accommodated by the Qing Government and awarded with gold and silk. Thus hunting in the Mulan Paddock did not only train soldiers in horsemanship and archery but also played an important role in keeping in touch with minority nationalities. The Qianlong Emperor once said: "Ever since the Qin Dynasty built the Great Wall in the north to guard against minority nationalities, the stricter the defense, the wider the gap between minority nationalities and us. In the Qing Dynasty all the nationalities are a family and they will be our servants for generations. When previous emperors stayed in the Summer Villa, all the Mongolians who had not had smallpox could be presented and rewarded. The more kindness they are shown, the greater their affection. This is indeed a good idea which should be passed on forever."[258]

(3) Based on the principle of "cultivate them but do not change their custom" the Qing Government made great efforts to promote Lamaism among the Mongolian and Tibetan nationalities. As the Qianlong Emperor said, "To promote Gelugpa will appease the Mongolians, which matters a lot and has to be maintained."[259] As a result the Qing Government started to build Lama temples all over China, namely the Xihuang Temple and Yonghe Lama Temple in Beijing, the Temple of the Potaraka Doctrine, Temple of Sumeru Happiness and Longevity, Anyuan Temple, Puning Temple and Pule Temple in Chengde, the Huizong Temple and Shanyin Temple in Duolun, the Qingning Temple in Outer Mongolia, the Huiyuan Temple in Litang, and the Xiantong Temple in the Wutai Mountains. Millions were spent to build these splendid temples which boasted a large number of Lamas, Tibetan serfs, livestock and wealth. The Living Buddhas and upper-class Lamas were awarded titles and privileges from the Qing Government, and they could control the life and thoughts of the Lamas and herdsmen in the lower classes. Anyone who chose to become Lama could be exempted from tax and corvée, and thus more and more people became Lamas and the temples had more power. A large force of theocracy was formed. There were four leaders of Lamaism in China, namely Dalai Lama, Panchen Erdeni, Khutukhtus and Zhangjia Living Budda. They were in charge of the religious affairs in anterior Tibet, Tsang, the north of the desert and the south of the desert respectively. The reason why the Qing Dynasty respected Lamaism was to adapt and make use of the original religious faith of minority nationalities and use it as a tool for ideological dominance. Some critics said that the Qing Government's attitude towards Lamaism was "Whenever the emperor prayed for rain and snow or protected people from solar and lunar eclipse, religious rites were held. There were hundreds of lamas serving the imperial residence all year long. They rampaged through the streets but no one could stop them; they deceived ordinary people and performed no good deeds at all. That is because when the Qing Dynasty was established, Lama was the first to submit; Lamaism prevailed in the east of China and was always honored by all Mongolian tribes. As a result the Qing Government decided to respect Lamaism to control all the vassal states."[260] The Qing Government took advantage of Lamaism to comply with the faith of minority nationalities and bring closer relations between the central government and minority nationalities, which maintained the stable and united situation to some extent. However it eventually had serious negative effects. People's thoughts were anaesthetized and corrupted, and the monks' power within minority nationalities expanded considerably. The number of

Lama who did not participate in production and fertility rose greatly, which hindered the economic and cultural development of Mongolia.

(4) Establishing Karun to strengthen frontier defense. In order to protect the minority nationality regions and to protect people from foreign attack, the Qing Government etsblished a series of military sentry posts called "Karun" in the northeast, Outer Mongolia, and border areas in the northwest. Some were permanent sentry posts with garrisons; some were "mobile sentry posts" and "temporary sentry posts" which were established, removed or moved with different seasons. Many Karun in the northeast were along the Heilong River and on the east side of the Ergun River. For example, Huma Karun was a "temporary sentry post" located on the island at the confluence of the Huma River and Heilong River. "On the island, there was a land of grass on which stood three cone-shaped shacks and one cottage, all roofed with straw. There lived Manchu officials and a small group of soldiers who were stationed in Huma Karun until the river was frozen. Once the river was frozen, the army would march to Aihui for winter."[261] Wulusumudan Karun, located in the lower reaches of Huma Karun, was a permanent Karun. "There was one official and seventeen soldiers." It was set up during the reign of Kangxi on the north bank of the Heilong River, 300 *li* away in the northwest of Aihui. In the mid-19th century when Tsarist Russia attacked the Heilong River valley, this Karun was pulled down and the official and soldiers were all banished. According to Russian records, "This station was also a gathering place for all frontier defense Karuns. Usually all Karuns gathered here in the middle of May, and then went upstream along the Amur River (i.e. the Heilong River) to go to the Gorbitsa River."[262] On the Niuman River (Bureya River today) valley, on the north bank of the Heilong River, there was Butha Karun set up to check marten hunters. "Troops were sent in March and stayed there until the river was frozen."[263] Twelve Karuns were set up around Hulun Buir on the east bank of the Ergun River. Each Karun was equipped with one official and thirty soldiers who were responsible for patrolling along the border. "When there were people trying to cross the border illegally or steal livestock, they should report it to the commander-in-chief."[264] The patrolling system was adopted in the northeast area. Troops were sent out from Qiqihar, Mergen and Aihui each June to patrol along the Gorbitsa River and Ergun River; Butha Yamen appointed soldiers to patrol along the upper reaches of the Jingqili River, Niuman River and Xilinmudan River and the Outer Xing'an Mountains every three years. Every patrolling official and soldier "had their own name, title and patrolling date written on the wooden board and buried it on the mountain. Soldiers in charge of patrolling would take it back every year and hand it over to the general and

vice commander-in-chief. Then they would bury theirs for the future check. This was fixed as a rule."[265] In 1765 (the 30th year of Qianlong reign) Aisenga, General of Heilongjiang, restated the regulation of border patrolling. "(The Commander-in-Chief of Butha) will send a secretary, lieutenant and soldiers in June to arrive together with the marten hunters by water at Tuoke and Yinken, two mouths of the river, to patrol along the Elexi River and Xilimudi River and report to the commander-in-chief and general. The vice commander-in-chief, assistant commander and lieutenant will be sent out every three years by water to arrive at the Xing'an Mountains (Outer Xing'an Mountains) to patrol once and report when they come back. Officials and soldiers of Heilongjiang would do the same job as well."[266]

Along the boundary line in the north, "from the north of Khalkha, Du'erbote, and the Wuliang Sea in Altai, to the east to Hulun Buir", Karuns were set up and garrisoned with Mongolian soldiers who patrolled regularly. The Grand Minister Superintendent of Kulun was in charge of the defense affairs of the north and would deal with them together with Vice General Pacifier of the Frontier and the Grand Minister Superintendent of Hovd.

In the northwestern frontier, Karuns were also set up in mountain passes and along the main roads. The vast area beyond the Karuns was patrolled by soldiers from Yili, Tacheng, Hovd and other places. The district of the Balkhash Lake and Issyk-Kul Lake was the patrolling region. In the middle of Qianlong's reign the frontier troops expelled invaders from Tsarist Russia who had crossed the border illegally and entered the Hatun River valley administered by the Grand Minister Superintendent of Hovd. The Qing troops "demolished all the houses built by Russia." In order to prevent future intrusions, the Qing Government changed the patrol from once every three years to once every year, and ordered that if the frontier forces found any Russians who had clandestinely entered China's territory they should "immediately expel them."

(5) Establishing stations to facilitate post routes. The Qing Government established stations and opened up post routes in border areas so as to facilitate transportation. The post routes in northeast China were opened up during Kangxi's reign. They started from Shengjing and led to Jilin, Qiqihar, Aihui, Sanxing etc. The Qing Government dredged the waterway from the Liao River to the Yitun River (Yitong River), Songhua River and Heilong River. This was the artery of communication which connected all the regions in the northeast part of China.

The stations in Mongolia were set up during Kangxi's reign, and more were added during Yongzheng and Qianlong's period to form a dense network of stations. "Nine stations were built from Gubeikou to Wuzhumuqin, nine from Dushikou to Haoqite, five from Zhangjiakou to the Sizi Tribe, six from Zhangjiangkou to Guihua City, nine from Shahukou to Wulate, eight from Guihua City to Erdos, and sixteen from Xifengkou to Zhalaite". Stations in Outer Mongolia were located on the east route, west route and the back route. Roads led to all the Karuns via Altay Station.

There were two routes from Beijing to the northwest part of China, and both crossed Jiayuguan. The southern one took a course through the backland and reached Jiayuguan (called Huanghua station) via Baoding, Taiyun, Xi'an, and Lanzhou; the northern one followed the edges of Mongolia and also reached Jiayuguan (called the Station of Report of Success) via Zhangjiakou, Datong, the north of Shanxi Province, and Ningxia, and then it went westwards to Hami or took the north road of the Tianshan Mountains and arrived at Urumqi, Yili and Tacheng; or took the south Tianshan road and reached Kashgar via Turfan.

Explorations of border areas

The border areas in China are inhabited by minority nationalities. Through the efforts of generations of all nationalities, the economy and culture in these areas have made great achievements. In the wake of the stable political situation in the Qing Dynasty, the border areas made peace with the central government one after another. This created favorable conditions for further economic development.

The development situation in border areas during the early and middle period of Qing Dynasty was as follows:

(1) The northeast area. This was originally the cradle of the Qing Dynasty, but a large amount of the population and wealth from the northeast area was brought inside Shanhaiguan after the Qing Dynasty entered the Shanhaiguan, which caused economic depression in this region. Later, the Qing Government diverted soldiers from the Eight Banners to guard the northeast area and exiled many criminals into this area. Many people of Han nationality, in particular, had to cross the Bohai Sea or pass through the Shanhaiguan to reclaim wasteland in the northeast part of China. As a result the population in the northeast increased sharply and the depressed economy was restored and developed.

It should be pointed out that the Qing Government attempted to take the economic benefits of the northeast area exclusively and sever the relationship between the lower-class Manchu and the Han nationality. The Qing Government regarded the northeast as "the place of origin of the dragon" and forbade people of Han nationality from entering this region. During the reign of Shunzhi, the Qing Government "repaired the border trench and planted willow along the trench"[267] based on the border walls built during the Ming Dynasty in the east area of the Liao River. The government also established the "Willow Palisade" to prevent people from entering. Anyone who wanted to go outside the Shanhaiguan had to hold an official "stamp". Although the Qing Government went out of its way to close the northeast area, people still resorted to various means to break the ban and go there to make a living. For example, during Kangxi's reign, "more than ten thousand people annually"[268] went to the forests in the northeast area to pick ginseng illegally. Later, more and more people came outside the Shanhaiguan to cultivate the wasteland and the Qing Government's ban was practically useless. Han people who went and settled there "would not come back to their home and invited their friends to settle down with them, and more and more people came to live there."[269] The local officials were glad to have more people to exploit, and turned a blind eye to people who settled there "under the pretext that they have already settled down with local people, so it is hard to expel them. The local officials approved of their settlement."[270]

Through the joint efforts of all nationalities, agriculture in the northeast area enjoyed rapid development and the area of cultivated land increased quickly. In Fengtian Banner for example there were 460 thousand *shang* (about 15 *mu*) during Shunzhi's reign, 1.16 million *shang* in the middle of Kangxi's reign, 2.36 million *shang* in Yongzheng's reign, and 2.89 million *shang* in the middle of Qianlong's reign. In Jilin there were 8,000 *qing* of Banner land and 200 *qing* of civil land; in the 46th year of Qianlong, Banner land increased to 240 thousand *qing* and civil land increased to 110 thousand *qing*. The land in Heilongjiang was allocated for combat food when fighting against Tsarist Russia during Kangxi's reign. The government opened up military colony land on the east bank of the Heilong River near Aihui where "the land was fertile and people need not worry about flood or drought. The annual yield of each *shang* was twice that of the land on the right bank of the river."[271] Later it developed into the famous "Sixty-four Stations on the east of the river". In the east of the Wusuli River, many people were involved in ginseng-picking, hunting and cultivation. In the middle of the 19th century, agriculture in this area achieved a very high level. Viniukov, a Russian who came here in 1858, wrote in his record that: "There were many Chinese engaged in agriculture along the river for 75 miles from the origin of Fujin River to its confluence with Sandaogou. They planted millet, barley, wheat, oat, marijuana, potato, cucumber, pumpkin and other vegetables, which met their needs and those of the ginseng-pickers. People in China worked on the land with uniquely hard."[272]

With the increasing population and development of agriculture, a series of rising military and civil strongholds and commercial cities appeared in the northeast area. There were the "Seven Towns Outside Shanhaiguan": Wula in Jilin, Qiqihar, Ningguta, Bodune, Sanxing, Mergen and Aihui. Wula was the station of the General of Jilin, and the ship-building industry here was flourishing. "Wula was built with wood and rested near the river. There were altogether 2,000 old and new Manchu soldiers, and thousands of households had moved from Zhili and other provinces. Over forty warships have been built, including two-masted boats and Jinkou warships. There were also fifty river boats with masts which practiced battle on water in preparation for the Russian invasion."[273] During Kangxi's reign it was very bustling: "Thousands of households came from the central plains. Shops, pavilions and theaters could all be found there, and it was already a metropolis outside the Shanhaiguan."[274] Other places such as Ningguta were "densely populated. Commodities and traders come here in an endless stream,"[275] while in Qiqihar, "the streets were lined with shops and full of bustle and hustle."[276]

Besides the rising cities there were other special forms of trade among all the nationalities. For example there was an annual "Chulehan" in the suburbs of Qiqihar. "Every May, the Qiqihar government would present marten. Those not picked as the tribute would be sold on the market called 'Chulehan', which means a meeting."[277] Hunters and herdsmen from the Heilong River, Songhua River, Nenjiang River, Great Khingan and Hulun Buir prairie carried all kinds of goods and there to trade for production tools and the necessities for the next year. "Chulehan" was very important for the economic life of minority nationalities living in border areas. According to the survey by the Qing Government in the last years of Qianlong's reign, "hunters would come to the marten trade meeting (i.e. Chulehan) and brought their wives and children. Swarms of merchants came here to buy all the stuff they needed for the next year."[278]

(2) Inner and Outer Mongolia. These two areas had long established a close relationship with the central government of the Qing Dynasty and the political situation here was always stable. The Qing Government adopted some measures to promote production in this region, such as Banner boundaries, establishing pastures, relieving famine, building storage and appointing people to teach farming techniques and hand out farm tools and seeds. Through the hard work of the Mongolian people, the economy progressed rapidly. Prosperous grasslands and herds of cows and sheep could be found everywhere. Some nobles owned thousands or tens of thousands of livestock. Han farmers from the central plains swarmed into Mongolia to cultivate wasteland. According to the imperial edict in 1707 (the 46th year of Kangxi reign), outside the Gubeikou "there were people from Shandong everywhere. There were more than 10,000 people engaged in commerce or farming."[279] The Qing Government also closed

the Mongolian area as it did to the northeast area. Han people were forbidden to go to Mongolia and a nationality separation policy was adopted. However due to the serious feudal exploitation, continuous disasters and rising population in the central plains, it was hard for to people to make a living there and more and more Han people went to border areas where there was much uncultivated land. This was the irresistible historical trend which the government's ban could not reverse. People tried all means to break the ban, while the Mongolian nobles were glad to turn pastureland into farming land and rent it to Han people to increase their income, so more and more Han farmers settled down in Mongolia. For example, in the early days of the Qing Government, there were no Han people in the north of Jehol. The number increased to 550 thousand in 1784 (the 49th year of Qianlong reign), and reached 880 thousand in 1825 (the 5th year of Daoguang reign). During the Qing Dynasty many Han people moved to live in the area from the Great Wall and Erdos, via Tumet Banner in Guihua, Chahar, Jostu League, and Zhaowuda League to the east of Horqin, creating a vast semi-agricultural and semi-pastoral area inhabited by Mongolian and Han people.

The agricultural development improved the economic life of the Mongolian people. Due to the exchange between animal husbandry and agriculture in production and techniques, people living in pastoral region had access to more food and other agricultural products and gradually changed their habit of relying on meat. The development of agriculture also provided much straw, which to some extent met the need for fodder and fuel in winter and facilitated the development of animal husbandry. Many regions constructed houses and created the conditions for the transition to permanent settlement or semi-permanent settlement.

There was some farming land in Outer Mongolia, but it took up a small proportion of the whole economy. The Qing Government had opened up military colony land and the stationed troops took turns to cultivate this to provide combat food. After suppressing the Junggar, the land became waste and did not play an important role in the economy in Outer Mongolia. In addition, Tushetu Khan and Khutukhtu gathered the Han farmers to cultivate their own manors.

Inner and Outer Mongolia had established frequent trade links with the central plains. Mongolian princes, nobles and Taijs would bring caravans and local products for business when they came to Beijing to visit the Emperor. They made the inner chamber (in Dongjiaomin Lane) and the outer chamber (outside of Andingmen) in the Ministry of Tribal Affairs a flourishing market for business deals between Han and Mongolian people. Han merchants also went to Mongolia taking food, cloth, tea, silk, bronze ware and ironware, and bringing back furs, animals and medicines. Some regular bazaars were formed near temples or stations, based on which larger commercial cities were built up. For example commerce in Zhangjiangkou, the main artery from Mongolia to Beijing, developed at a rapid rate. According to the records there were only something over ten shops in Kangxi's period but over 90 in Yongzheng's reign, about 190 at the end of Qianlong's reign, and more than 230 in the late years of Jiaqing's reign. "Most cows and horses in central plains were bought from here. And the businessmen were mostly from Shanxi. All the deals were done with tea and cloth."[280] Guihua was also filled with merchants. Since the old city was too small, a new city called Suiyuan was built five miles away from the old one. Later the two were renamed Guisui, which was the basis of today's Huhhot. Duolun was a bazaar centered around temples. After the 18th century, some merchants and farmers came to settle down here, making it an important religious and commercial center in Inner Mongolia.

(3) The south and north areas of the Tianshan Mountains. After suppressing the Junggar, the Qing Government made great efforts to develop agriculture and open up military colony land, especially in northern Xinjiang, promoting economic recovery and development in this area. There were many kinds of military colony land: soldier stations (Luying Army), Banner stations (Eight Banners Army), Hui stations (Uyghur nationality), transfer stations (exiled criminals), civil stations (immigrants from the central plains) etc. The scale and results of reclamation was much greater than in previous dynasties. According to the statistics in 1777 (the 42nd year of Qianlong) there were over 287 thousand *mu* of soldier stations, Banner stations and transfer stations, and 280 thousand *mu* of civil stations,[281] which were all in northern Xinjiang. After Qianlong the area of civil stations increased quickly, while the other kinds of colony land did not expand. For example in 1775 (the 40th year of Qianlong) there were 150 thousand *mu* of civil stations in Urumqi, 680 thousand *mu* in 1808 (the 13th year of Jiaqing). Hui stations were colony land cultivated by Uyghur people who came from southern Xinjiang to Yili in the middle of the Qianlong period. These farmers had always had farming techniques, and when they moved to the Yili River valley "they were divided into nine stations and built Ningyuan City to live in. They also chose Aqimu Boke to take charge of affairs in the Hui stations."[282] Their offspring were called the "Talanqi" people and their population increased to over 340 thousand. The area of reclaimed land was vast. "From Ningyuan for three hundred *li* to the east, the land was all the Hui's (Hui stations)."[283] In southern Xinjiang there were no large-scale military colony stations but there were traditional agricultural areas with a dense population. Since the middle of the Qianlong period this area

witnessed rapid development due to the stable social order. According to the records of that time, Aksu "had fertile land. Sesame, barley, wheat, corn, bean, broomcorn millet and cotton were all over the land; peach, apricot, mulberry, pear, pomegranate, grape, pingpo, melon and vegetables filled the orchards". Kashgar was also "a fertile land with plenty of grain and vegetables". Khotan "had vast and fertile land stretching thousands of miles. Many households lived there... vegetables and fruits were sufficient... men were engaged in farming while women were engaged in handwork." Turfan "was abundant with wheat, corn, flax, and muskmelon, watermelon, grapes and other fruits could all be found there. All these species were the best in the west part of China. The fertile land here was also good for cotton and bean."[284] Qomul "had fertile land and the climate there was favorable. The spring water was sweet and the region was indeed prosperous."[285] From these records we can see that agriculture and products were plentiful in those areas.

Xinjiang also had handicraft industry. The Qing Government relocated thirty Uyghur households who were familiar with iron mining from Aksu to Suoguo'er, south of the Yili River, in 1773 (the 38th year of the Qianlong reign), in order to mine for iron. Southern Xinjiang had abundant gold and jade, and "the Hui tribe produced gold and jade, and the jade was extremely good."[286] "The Hui tribe in Kashgar practiced techniques in polishing jade and gold which were very delicate."[287] The textile industry was also well developed. For example, Khotan "was abundant with original silk and oak silk, and the cloth made from it was very precious."[288] Most of northern Xinjiang's piece goods came from southern Xinjiang and some from the central plains.

With the development of production, business in the south and north of the Tianshan Mountains was booming. The Qing Government encouraged merchants from the central plains to go there for business. Anyone who was willing to leave the frontier "would be given an official document exempting them from being charged by the officials on the way" and commercial tax would also be decreased. Qianlong wrote in the imperial edict that "after quelling the Hui tribe, businessmen from central plains would not be delayed on their way via post routes and the Hui tribes. If the merchants would come to do business here, this place would become one larger area with Qomul and Turfan, which is also good for officials and soldiers."[289] At that time some commercial cities emerged in southern and northern Xinjiang. Yili, for example, was the station of the highest military official, and the political and military center, and also the commercial center. From every March to September, people of Kazak and Bulut nationality would come to the cities in Yili with plenty of animals to exchange for silk, tea, piece goods and china imported from central plains.

Hong Liangji, who was exiled during the Qianlong period, wrote a poem to describe the situation there: "people go out on camels in the morning and come back in evening, word has it that Bulut people come here with tens of thousands of cattle and sheep, the road in the west of the city will be crowded for three days". According to Zhaoyi, "people from central plains vied with one another to come to Yili. Counties were connected with each other. Herds of sheep and horses could be found in the streets and lanes. Where leather and grain were sold, merchants swarmed there. Shaoxing wine and Kunqu opera also attracted many people."[290] In the other cities business also flourished. For example, "wide streets were packed with shops and people" in Urumqi which "was even richer than the cities beyond the Shanhaiguan."[291] In Aksu "merchants and people from the central plains, and traders from the vassal states, spread all over the place. When there was a bazaar, people jostled each other in the crowd and goods were crowded as dense as fog."[292] In Ye'erqiang, "many merchants from Shanxi, Shaanxi, Jiangsu and Zhejiang took great trouble to sell goods there, while people from minority nationality areas such as Anjiyan, Tuibaite, Guohan, Kashmir and other places all went there to do business."[293]

(4) Tibet and the southwest area. In the Qing Dynasty Tibet was still controlled by the serf system. The economy was underdeveloped, and the high and cold climate was not appropriate for crops, thus people could only plant Tibetan barley, beans, wheat etc. in the river valleys which were lower and warmer, and grazed sheep, horse and yak on the grassland on the high plateau. Through the hard work of the Tibetan people and enhanced management by the Qing Government, Tibet enjoyed long-term stable social order which promoted economic development. "Gelugpa was more developed, and people's livelihood was much better." The economic and cultural relationships between Tibet and the central plains were enhanced day by day. Monks and laymen from Tibet often came to Beijing to pay tribute and have an audience with the emperor. Mongolians went to Tibet to "make a pilgrimage" and "boil tea". Han officials and soldiers took turns in the garrison, and traders from various regions came to Tibet to sell goods. The connection between Tibet and other parts of China became closer and closer. Silk, piece goods and tea from the central plains were transported into Tibet, while furs and other local specialties were transported to every part of China. Due to the strengthened political and economic relationship, people travelled frequently along several roads between Sichuan, Qinghai, Yunnan, southern Xinjiang and Tibet. A series of cities were formed along the way. For instance, Dajianlu "was inhabited by Han and other nationalities, and was the only way leading to Tibet. It was well stocked with all kinds of groceries and business here was booming." "The annual volume of

trade was more than several thousands of gold, thus Dajianlu was called 'Little Chengdu' by people."[294]

Some remote areas in the southwest area got rid of the tyranny of the chieftains of Tibet after the land reform during Yongzheng's reign, which changed some backward regulations and systems of minority nationalities and promoted local economic development. Much land which used to be monopolized and closed off by the chieftains was given to local working people of minority nationality through recruitment. Han people from central plains were also allowed to reclaim in the banned remote areas. For example the Wumeng Government distributed the land seized by chieftains to ordinary people. "All the land was divided into four categories: irrigated land, dry land, uncultivated land and long-cultivated land, and distributed to soldiers, ordinary people and farmers."[295] In some remote regions of Yunnan, "people from Chu, Shu, Qian and Yue all endured the hardship of traveling and came with their family"[296] to "settle down near the mountain and cultivate the wasteland."[297] In Pingyuan and Anshun, which were in the common border area of Yunnan and Guizhou, people there "cultivated the wasteland and burnt forests, and the yield of long-wasted land increased several times."[298] In western Hunan, "people came to settle on the newly-cultivated land with their families and planted in rows."[299] In the Large and Small Jinchuan regions which had been tortured by long-term war, "the number of households increased on a daily basis and there was almost no space between cultivated lands."[300] Han people from the central plains moved to southwestern area to earn a living, and brought with them advanced know-how and production tools. For example, they built water conservancy projects and terraces, made compost, strengthened crop management, improved farming techniques, and promoted high-yield crops and cash crops, boosting economic development in the southwestern area. For instance Pu'er Prefecture in Yunnan learned the tea-planting techniques of the central plains and opened up tea gardens, and the tea produced here was good in both quality and quantity. As a result, Pu'er became a famous tea-producing area with "tens of thousands of people working on the mountains"[301] from all nationalities. Yunnan and Guizhou were also abundant in bronze, tin, silver and lead. In their heyday there were many ore yards here with tens of thousands workers, most of whom came from Hubei, Hunan, Sichuan, Jiangxi etc.

On basis of developed agriculture, commerce in the southwest area flourished even more. Han businessmen went there in an endless stream. There were tycoons arriving with ships of goods and also vendors carrying commodities themselves. Although they pursued much more intermediate exploitation, they also played an active role in exchanging commodities, connecting with all nationalities and satisfying people's needs. In Yunnan for example, "people from the central plains came here to do business in an endless stream every year."[302] In Hunan, "Miao nationality people in Chenzhou carried crops, silk and cloth on the back of cattle and horses, in order to go to the market and exchange with the Han people for salt, silkworm eggs and all kinds of implements that they needed."[303] In the mountainous district inhabited by the Miao nationality in eastern Guizhou, after the land reform the Qing Government "hired hundreds of Miao ships to purchase cloth, grain and other groceries in Hunan. The transportation was much more convenient than before and buyers all came here."[304]

(5) Taiwan. In 1661 (the 18th year of Shunzhi reign), Zheng Chenggong recovered Taiwan and put an end to Holland's colonial rule of Taiwan. This beautiful and prosperous island returned to the embrace of the motherland. Before Zheng Chenggong's recovery of Taiwan it was meagerly populated with vast uncultivated wasteland and backward production. There were even no iron agricultural implements. "When visiting the cultivated land, farmers know nothing about the efficiency of plow, harrow, hoe and ax."[305] Zheng Chenggong and his successors offered reward to induce immigrants to cultivate land, build water conservancy projects, and spread agricultural techniques in Taiwan. Taiwan's economy enjoyed a rapid development. Twenty years later, when the Qing Government united Taiwan, Shi Lang reported to the government on the abundant resources in Taiwan: "By imperial decree, I came to subjugate the rebellion in Taiwan. Wherever I went I saw fertile land and abundant resources. People were farming in the land side by side. Taiwan was also rich in sea salt. The mountains were covered with thriving trees and bamboos. Sulfur, water cane, sugar, buckskin and all daily necessities were amply provided. Taiwan used to be lacking in cloth and silk, now it abounds in silk-cotton trees which provide material for weaving and knitting. Wherever a ship arrived, cloth and silk would follow. Although the regulation was strict, the government still could not prohibit it completely. Taiwan was indeed a prosperous and dangerous region."[306] After that the Qing Government began to set up prefectures in Taiwan and appointed officials and soldiers. The ban on maritime trade was lifted and people were encouraged to engage in cultivation. The land in Taiwan was very fertile, and the climate was suitable for crops, so agriculture developed at a rapid rate. "When the land of Taiwan was cultivated, it was extremely fertile. Three and four crops could be harvested from the land. People from Fujian and Guangdong all swarmed to Taiwan."[307] Some wealthy landlords "dig ponds and ditches, build water conservancy projects, and hire tenant farmers to cultivate the wasteland". They also "paid to hire tenants to build villages and dams."[308]

Poor people from the central plains crossed the ocean to rent and cultivate the land. Many "Han Farms" appeared in many places, "each of which had 80 or 90 percent tenants from outside Taiwan. Most of them had no family. Tenants from Quanzhou were called Hakka, and they called the landlord boss. At first, the boss recruited tenants for reclamation. Gradually the tenants invited their friends and thousands of people came to Taiwan."[309] The staple crops in Taiwan were rice and sugar cane. According to officials of the Qing Dynasty, "Taiwan had a vast territory with sparse population. The annual yield of rice was enough for four to five years."[310] Surplus rice was sold in Fujian, Guangdong, Zhejiang and other provinces short of food, or in Southeast Asia. The sucrose industry was also booming. "It was the staple industry of Taiwan, and no other industry could compete with it."[311]

Under the influence of Han people's agricultural reclamation, the farming level of the local Ganshan nationality also improved greatly. Most of them planted their own "land". They "were also aware of the importance of sowing and reaping,. All the old land was mown and opened up for reclamation.""They also learned from Han people how to build dams to use rivers for irrigation."[312] "The tools they used for sowing and plowing were all similar to those of the Han people."[313]

Due to the rapid progress in agriculture, the commodity economy was very active. The marine traffic between Taiwan and the Chinese mainland or Southeast Asia was well-developed. Taiwan Prefecture, Lugang Port and Mengjia were the three largest ports. A large number of ships plied between Amoy and Quanzhou, and many tycoons engaged in ocean trade: "all had access to large amount of wealth to win the game. Convoys of ships traveled between Southeast Asia and Tianjin, Niuzhuang, Yantai and Shanghai."[314] The rice and sucrose from Taiwan were transported and sold at home and abroad, while piece goods, silk, china, ironware and groceries were imported from the Chinese mainland.

In sum, due to the political unification in the Qing Dynasty, the social order in border areas was comparatively stable and thus great progress was achieved in the economy. It was the result of hard working by people from all nationalities, and the result of economic and cultural exchange between the Han nationality and minority nationalities.

11 Chapter

Cultural Policy and the Development of Sinology in the Qing Dynasty

The Cultural Policy of the Qing Dynasty

Advocating Neo-Confucianism and compiling books

The Qing Dynasty was a joint dictatorship of Manchu and Han landlords were based on the monarch's close relatives and trusted followers of the Manchu. On the one hand it adopted various military and political measures to suppress the resistance struggles of people from the Han and other nationalities. On the other hand, it focused on using the Confucianism of the Han and the Lamaism of the Zang and Mongol nationalies to enhance its control in the ideological sphere, in order to consolidate its rule. The Qing Dynasty tried hard to absorb and use the ideology and culture of the Han and other nationalities to fulfil its requirements of domination. In this respect, it cost it more effort to establish a dynasty than any other, but it obtained more results as well.

Soon after the entry of the Qing Dynasty into the Shanhaiguan it held the imperial competitive examination and advocated rigorously respecting Confucius and reading the classics. It respected Confucius as "Dachengzhisheng Wenxuan Great Teacher" [大成至聖文宣光師, afterwards "Zhisheng Great Teacher" (至聖光師)], and renovated Confucian temples. It also held a memorial ceremony for Confucius every year, giving the Yan Holy Duke (the descendant of Confucius) various honors and privileges while allocating additional lands to Confucius mansions and awarding treasures. On Kangxi's southern tour, when he went to the Confucian temples, he paid his respects and called together officials and Confucian scholars to talk about the Confucian classics. He even kneeled down and kowtowed towards Confucius. He was respectful to all the important representative figures of the Confucians in successive dynasties, building temples and memorial archways for them and awarding them horizontal inscribed boards. The descendants of "Deceased Confucians" inherited the Five Classics Scholar, being favored greatly. In 1670, or the ninth year of Kangxi, he formulated and issued sixteen "edicts" according to Confucianism as people's standard of behavior. They were as follows. 1) Highly esteem filial piety and the proper relations among brothers, in order to give due importance to social relations. 2) Give due weight to kinship in order to promote harmony and peace. 3) Maintain good relations within the neighborhood in order to prevent quarrels and lawsuits. 4) Give due importance to farming and the cultivation of mulberry trees, in order to ensure sufficient clothing and food. 5) Be moderate and economical in order to avoid wasting away your livelihood. 6) Make the most of schools and academies in order to honor the ways of scholars. 7) Denounce strange beliefs in order to elevate the true doctrine. 8) Explain laws and regulations in order to warn the ignorant and obstinate. 9) Show propriety and courtesy to improve customs and manners. 10) Work hard in your professions in order to quiet your ambitions. 11) Instruct sons and younger brothers in order to prevent their committing any wrong. 12) Put a stop to false accusations in order to protect the good and honest. 13) Warn against giving shelter to deserters in order to avoid punishment with them. 14) Promptly and fully pay your taxes in order to avoid forced requisition. 15) Get together in groups of ten or a hundred in order to put an end to theft and robbery. 16) Free yourself from resentment and anger in order to show respect for your body and life. Yongzheng made notes on the sixteen edicts which were called *The Sacred Edicts*. It was the political and moral admonishment given by the rulers of the feudal autocracy to the ruled people in the patriarchal society, and typified Confucian social ideals and beliefs. In the second year of the reign of Emperor Yongzheng he issued *The Sacred Edicts* to the whole country, and propagandized them widely. The Ministry of Official Personnel Affairs informed the civil and military governors of all provinces to select a Xiucai (someone who had passed the imperial examination at the county level) in their locality to preach them: "they need to explain all the sentences and words, and to explicate their pronunciations and meanings, without doing it in a perfunctory manner". For example, in Huolu county in Zhili province, "the first and the fifteenth day of every lunar month is the date to explain the edicts, and the place is outside the West gate. The board of edicts is laid and the platform is placed in the middle. One Xiucai is Yuezheng (people who explain the edicts), and two are selected to be on monthly duty. In the morning of the right day, the county magistrate leads his subordinates and common people to gather together in the place to give a salute, and asks the Yuezheng to explain the sixteen edicts...In the countryside, the location to explain the edicts is set up in a place which has a dense population, or near to the schools (private or community-run schools charging no tuition). The Yuezheng selected in this county and the teacher of literature will preach them together."[1] The Qing Dynasty tried its best to implement Confucianism countrywide.

The Qing Dynasty tried its best to advocate Cheng-Zhu Neo-Confucianism. Kangxi respected Zhu Xi very much. He said, "The Song Confucians and Zhu Xi annotated the classics and explicated the truth. All the books they have written or compiled are clear, precise and impartial. For about five hundred years, no scholars dare to criticize and discuss them. I think that after Confucius and Mencius, the appearance of scholars is all due to Zhu Xi."[2] He also said that "Zhu Xi's articles and discourse are all about the healthy atmosphere and the great truth. Only when I read their books and understand their principles can I know the secret of the relationship between human beings and heaven, administer the country from the imperial palace, apply a policy of kindness and benevolence, and unify the country."[3] Moreover he elevated Zhu Xi from the side room of the Confucian temple and put him next to the Four Pei and Ten Zhe in the Dacheng Hall, making him the eleventh Zhe. In the imperial examinations of the Qing Dynasty, the notes of Zhu Xi were considered as principles in the examinations on the Four Books and Five Classics. Therefore Neo-Confucianism became the official philosophy and was quite popular. Li Guangdi, who was good at flattery, tried to read the emperor's mind and preached that Zhu Xi carried on the Confucian orthodoxy of Yao, Shun, Yu, Tang, Wen, Wu, Chou Kung, Confucius and Mencius,"in five hundred years, an emperor must appear","from Zhu Xi to our emperor it was five hundred years, so this must be the time far an emperor to appear to carry out the study of sages...our emperor is undertaking the order from the heaven, and using Confucian orthodoxy to realize his merits."[4] Li Guangdi said that Kangxi continued the Confucian orthodoxy and combined it with the orthodoxy of managing a country. When Kangxi heard about this he was very happy, and said, "Guangdi and I know each other very well."[5] Under the rewards and promotions system of the Qing Dynasty, besides Li Guangdi, a large number of "Neo-Confucian ministers" who believed in Neo-Confucianism, such as Wei Yijie, Xiong Cilu, Tang Bing and Zhang Boxing were all in the highest rank and were put in important positions. The reason why the Qing Dynasty tried hard to respect Confucius and advocated Confucianism was to consolidate the feudal order and to enhance its autocratic rule. Emperor Yongzheng pointed out clearly that: "If there is no guidance from Confucius... the situation will be that the small overrides the big, the young overwhelms the old, the inferior hinders the superior; there would be a lack of due regard for precedence; social status would be disordered; status would be offended; and the faith violated. What is called an emperor is not like an emperor; a minister is not like a minister; a father is not like a father; a son is not like a son. Although there is grain, how can I eat it? The damage caused to the way of the world and the heart of a human being is too much that I cannot figure out!"[6]

In order to win over the Han intellectuals, the Qing Dynasty advocated "learning what happened in the past and paying attention to culture and education, while respecting Confucianism and setting up schools", and recruited a large number of intellectuals to collect, compile and annotate ancient books and records. The Four Books and Five Classics which belonged to the Confucian classics were naturally the focus. A great number of annotated classical works "compiled by the emperor" and "made by imperial order" were published in succession. In the reign of Shunzhi he ordered the annotation of

The Chinese Classic of Family Reverence. Kangxi ordered the compilation of *The Notes on the Books of Changes* and *Daily Discussion on the Explanation of the Four Books*, and ordered the drawing up of *The Pandects of the Book of Songs*, *The Pandects of the Book of History*, and *The Pandects of the Spring and Autumn Annals*. Yongzheng ordered the compilation of *The Annotation of the Chinese Classic of Family Reverence*. Qianlong ordered the compilation of *The Annotation of the Book of Changes*, *The Notes of Shiyi*, and *The Annotation of the Spring and Autumn Annals*. He ordered the drawing up of *The Annotation of Zhouguan*, *The Annotation of the Etiquette*, and *The Annotation of the Book of Rites*. He also revised *The History of the Ming Dynasty*, expanded three books of general knowledge, and redacted general plans. In addition, compilation of *The Integration of Ancient and Modern Books* was managed by Chen Menglei. This book gathered together a great number of books and was a large-sized reference book. It selected and extracted from every kind of ancient books and records according to their categories, and assembled them all in one book. However it did not record every book completely. *The Integration of Ancient and Modern Books* was divided into six collections utilizing thirty-two ancient works. The whole book contained 10,000 volumes and the work cotinued through the Kangxi and Yongzheng reigns until it was finished.

The largest scale of compilation was the *Siku Quanshu* (The Complete Library in Four Branches of Literature) in the reign of Qianlong. This was the biggest series of books in our history. It copied the important ancient books and records completely, and compiled them under forty-four categories of Classics, History, Masters and Collections. It collected 3,457 kinds of books and 79,070 volumes, which covered a vast and plentiful area and was the collection of our ancient ideological and cultural heritage. Compilation began in 1773, or the thirty-eighth year of Qianlong, the year in which the Siku Quanshu Hall was set up, and was finished fifteen years later in 1787, or the fifty-second year of Qianlong. Then they checked the content of the books, proofread mistakes and omissions, and added a batch of books into the *Siku*. In 1793, or the fifty-eighth year of Qianlong, the compilation was complete. There were seven copies of the *Siku Quanshu* in total plus another copy for the record. They were stored in the Forbidden City's Wenyuan Pavilion, The Old Summer Palace's Wenyuan Pavilion, Shenyang Wenshu Pavilion, The Mountain Resort in Chengde Wenjin Pavilion, Yangzhou Wenhui Pavilion, Zhenjiang Wenzong Pavilion, and Hangzhou Wenlan Pavilion. The copy for the record was stored in the Imperial Academy in Beijing.[7] There were 360 officials and intellectuals took part in the compilation, concentrating a large number of celebrities and scholars. Among them people who made great contributions and had a high reputation were Yu

Minzhong, Jin Jian, Ji Yun, Lu Xixiong, Ren Dachun, Lu Feichi, Dai Zhen, Shao Jinhan, Cheng Jinfang, Zhou Yongnian, Zhu Yun, Yao Nai, Weng Fanggang and Wang Niansun. A small part of the books recorded in the *Siku Quanshu* were written by the emperor, and official books written on the order of the emperor, the others were all classics of the past dynasties collected countrywide. The sources were: collected books in the imperial palace, books selected from various provinces, and books donated by officials in various places and book collectors. Some books were ancient scattered books renovated from the *Great Encyclopedia in the Yongle Reign* in the Ming Dynasty. In the process of compilation, Ji Yun and other people wrote *The General Summary of the Siku Quanshu*, 200 chapters in total. They introduced and commented on 3,457 recorded books and 6,766 unrecorded but catalogued books. They also narrated the contents of every book, commented on their advantages and disadvantages, and discussed their academic origin and the differences in different editions. Ruan Yuan gave his comment: "Gaozong Chun Emperor ordered compilation of the *Siku Quanshu*, and Ji Yun assumed overall responsibility and brought it to completion. The mistakes in the notes of the six classics, the differences in the records in various history, and the branches of these classics were all picked out and sources were traced. The general summary was up to nearly 10,000 catergories. When studying ancient things one must respect their principles, and when presenting an argument one must keep it fair."[8] The *Siku Quanshu* took up an important position in China's academic and cultural history. China's ancient books were damaged seriously by war and social instability, so the Qing government put a great amount of manpower and material resources into collecting books nationwide and compiled scattered books, which saved many valued ancient books. However it should be pointed out that even when the rulers of the feudal despotism were doing some good things, at the same time they were doing bad things. Using the opportunity of compiling the *Siku Quanshu*, Emperor Qianlong carried out a large-scale check-up of books countrywide and banned, destroyed and deleted and changed many books of so-called "rebellion" and "prohibition". In the second year of setting up the Siku Quanshu Hall and seeking missing books countrywide, or 1774 (the thirty-ninth year of Qianlong), the imperial edict put forward: "at the end of the Ming Dynasty there were many unofficial histories, which vilified arbitrarily and spread dissenting words. Within them there must be words which defame this dynasty. Now is the right time to investigate, destroy, and put an end to these adverse words, in order to correct people's ideology and customs. This cannot be ignored."[9] Thereafter various regions "posted the imperial edict everywhere to spread it" and persuaded people to hand in books of "prohibition". On the one hand, the local authorities sent people to investigate everywhere, and examined every kind of book, and then they delivered the banned books to Beijing. On the other hand, the Siku Quanshu Hall sorted out the banned books from among the books collected. Banned books from the two sources were all sent to the Grand Council and then scrutinized by the Hanlin Academy. The "offensive" places were written on yellow labels and pasted on the top of the page. After looking over by and permission from Emperor Qianlong, the banned books were burned. The scope of banned books became larger. "At the beginning of issuing this edict, the unofficial history of the Ming Dynasty was hated. Then the Siku Quanshu Hall discussed that if the Song's words to Liao, Jin and Yuan, and the Ming's words to Yuan had extreme prejudice, they should burned...After Longqing, all books written by generals and ministers of the late Ming Dynasty have disappeared."[10] At the period of the late Ming and early Qing, the books written by Huang Daozhou, Zhang Huangyan, Yuan Jixian, Qian Sule, Gu Yanwu, Huang Zongxi and Sun Qifeng were all banned. Then the scope was relaxed, and in the case of some people's books if "the taboo words and sentences are changed, they do not need to be burned". However the books of Qian Qianyi, Lu Liuliang, Qu Dajun, Jin Bao, Dai Mingshi, Wang Xihou and Yin Jiaquan were strictly banned. The books destroyed in the reign of Emperor Qianlong "were nearly 3,000 kinds, and more than 60,000 or 70,000 volumes, which was nearly equal to the amount of current recorded kinds in the *Siku Quanshu*."[11]

The literary inquisition

Besides destroying and distorting books which went against its regime, the Qing Dynasty implemented a literary inquisition in order to exterminate heresy and restrain people's thought. The literary inquisition convicted on literary works, and most literary inquisitions were interpreted without real understanding using hearsay evidence and arbitrary fabrication. The literary inquisition was the inevitable product of the feudal society which had no political democracy

Fig. 11.1. Some printed copies of the *Siku Quanshu*

Fig. 11.2. Wenlan Pavilion

and freedom of speech, and was an important method used by the autocratic emperors to frighten officials and intellectuals. In the more than 2,000 year feudal society, literary inquisitions were often seen. However the frequency, breadth and cruel punishment of the literary inquisition in the Qing Dynasty surpassed all past dynasties.

The literary inquisition in the Qing Dynasty began in the reign of Emperor Kangxi. In the reign of Emperor Shunzhi, the armed struggle to suppressing the South Ming was fierce and so the prohibitions in cultural and ideology fields were not severe. Although many works of poetry opposed the rule of the Qing Dynasty and preached national thought, they were seldom convicted of literary heresy. Through the cases of "Tonghai", "Zouxiao" and "Kechang" the Qing government struck at Han officials and intellectuals many times, but it had no time to check up the contents of these poems because it was busily engaged in warfare. The strict control in the fields of culture and ideology was implemented when its rule was relatively stable.

The earliest literary inquisition was a reaction to the national ideology and the anti-Qing Dynasty consciousness which was popular in the early years of the Qing Dynasty, and was a severe measure used to stop the ideological trend of overturning the Qing Dynasty and reinstating the Ming Dynasty. However, in the reign of Emperor Kangxi, there were few literary inquisitions. The biggest cases were Zhuang Ting and *The History of the Ming Dynasty*, and Dai Mingshi and the *South Mountain Collection*, both of which were inspired by the national consciousness of favoring the Ming Dynasty.

The case of *The History of the Ming Dynasty* happened in the second year of the reign of Emperor Kangxi, when Ao Bai was in power. Zhuang Ting, a rich man in Zhejiang province, bought *The History of the Ming Dynasty* written by Zhu Guozhen who lived in the late Ming. He stole this book as his own and wrote the history of the reign of Chongzhen and Southern Ming. He named Hongguang, Longwu, and Yongli of Southern Ming the first day of that year, and there were words and sentences reproving the Qing Dynasty, which were reported and led to a big case. At that time Zhuang Ting had died and he was cut coffins and desecrated the corpse. His brother Tingyue was put to death. This case involved many people, "221 celebrities were executed. Zhuang and Zhu (Zhu Youming from Nanxun was involved in this case) were both rich people. Impeaching these celebrities was used to show their importance. So it was handed down that among these two hundred people, half of them did not take part in compiling books but they were involved just because of their great reputation."[12]

The case of the *South Mountain Collection* happened in the late reign of Emperor Kangxi. The *South Mountain Collection* was written by Dai Mingshi, an editing official in the Hanlin Academy. In this book he discussed the historical affairs of the Southern Ming and used the reign titles of the Southern Ming's emperors according to Fang Xiaobiao's *The Record of Dian Qian*, which violated the taboo. In the fiftieth year of Kangxi, Zhao Shenqiao, Zuodu Yushi (an official title in the Qing Dynasty), reported Dai Mingshi for "stealing other's book arbitrarily, and being proud and insolent because of his talent...he made collections privately, said whatever he wanted, confused right and wrong, and spoke rudely". Kangxi inquired into the roots of this case and carried it forward resolutely. Besides the clansmen of Dai Mingshi and Fang Xiaobiao it also involved many people who wrote the preface for the *South Mountain Collection*, inscribed and sold the book, and who were in frequent contact with Dai Mingshi. All were arrested and punished including such celebrities as Fang Bao and Wang Yuan. But when the case was closed he was more lenient, and except for Dai Mingshi most of other people were released.

In the reign of Emperor Yongzheng, the inner contradictions of the ruling class were intensified. Literary inquisition was not only used to suppress intellectuals who had the ideology of opposing the Qing government, but also became a weapon of infighting within the inner ruling class. The number of cases increased, and the charges became severe and exacting. The rulers were also captious and framed up crimes deliberately. Many cases were not merely because of the words used but were an excuse for Yongzheng to strike at his dissident forces in politics. For example, the senior general Nian Gengyao presumed upon his contributions and was haughty and imperious. Yongzheng intended to kill him, so he fabricated many crimes for him. An important one was that Nian Gengyao transposed the order of the words "Zhao Qian Xi Ti" in the memorial to the throne. Yongzheng criticized that "Nian Gengyao is not a careless person, and he just will not give the 'diligence in work' to me...from this, I can see that Nian Gengyao is self-assured for having made contributions, and shows his heart of disloyalty. His abnormal words and deeds were not casual."[13] This was obvious a way to fabricate a crime. Wang Jiangqi, who wrote *The Desultory Essay of Going on a Campaign to the West*, was executed because of writing words and sentences mocking Kangxi in his essay; Qian Mingshi was a celebrity at that time, and Yongzheng hated him very much, so he gave him a horizontal inscribed board on which was written "the sinner of Confucian Ethical Code" to humiliate him. In fact Wang and Qian were both adherents of Nian Gengyao, and Wang was his Jishi (an official title), while Qian flattered Nian in his poem, so this was the real reason for their punishment. Zha Siting, the examiner, set a theme "things that the common people won't do" which was considered to be cutting off the head of the two words "Yongzheng"; *The Great Learning* annotated by Xie Jishi was reported to defame Neo-Confucianism; *The Record of Tongjian* written by Lu Shengnan objected to the system of prefectures and counties, and praised the system of enfeoffment. In fact these cases were related to the struggle between parties. Zha Siting followed Long Keduo, and Xie Jishi and Lu Shengnan followed Li Fu and Cai Ting. Through these cases Yongzheng wanted to punish officials and intellectuals and teach them not to give allegiance to influential officials' families, collude with cliques, or censure the affairs of state, and so they were punished severely.

The most important literary inquisition was the case of Zeng Jing and Zhang Xi. In 1728, or the sixth year of the Yongzheng reign, Zeng Jing from Hunan ordered his apprentice Zhang Xi to give a letter to Yue Zhongqi, the viceroy of Sichuan and Shanxi, and said that he was the descendant of Yue Fei to persuade him to revolt against the Qing government. He listed Yongzheng's crimes of killing his father and brothers for the throne. Yue Zhongqi reported him to the government, and investigated the instigator. He found that the ideology of overturning the Qing was generated by reading the works of Lu Liuliang, and his criticism of Yongzheng came from the eunuchs of Yongzheng's brothers Yin Si and Yin Tang who had been suppressed. Therefore Yongzheng turned his attack on the descendants and followers of Lu Liuliang and the remaining confederates of Yin Si and Yin Tang.

Fig. 11.3. A Portrait of Lu Liuliang

Lu Liuliang, who had died forty years previously, was a famous scholar in the early years of the Qing Dynasty. There was a strong ideology of overturning the Qing in his works and he did his utmost to declare the distinction between Chinese and barbarians, considering that was more important than the righteousness between the emperor and the minister. He also attacked the rule of the Qing Dynasty and said that "such a difficult position has not been seen since Xi Huang", which was a popular idea in the first years of the Qing Dynasty. In order to prevent the common people from revolting with the call of overturning the Qing Dynasty and reinstating the Ming Dynasty, and removing the national consciousness of Han nationality, Yongzheng made a big fuss about this case, issued many edicts and then inscribed and published these edicts as *Dayi juemi lu*. This book tried its best to refute the traditional distinction between Hua and Yi, saying that this distinction was because the territory was not vast in ancient China. In fact Hua and Yi were all of the same family. "In the last three generations what was Miao, Jingchu, Yun are now Hunan, Hubei and Shanxi. Can we call them barbarians?" Shun was from Dongyi, and Zhou Wenwang was from Xiyi, "the Qing Dynasty is Manchu, which is where China has its native place". Manchu and Han were an organic whole. Opinions and evaluations of people should obey the Five Cardinal Relationships rather than distinguishing people by their nationalities. "Just people with morality can be the emperor of the country. We founded our country in the east, and spread the morality widely. Depending on the mandate of heaven, we become the master of the people, so the subjects should not be unfaithful because of Huaxia."[14] The idea suggested by Yongzheng was reasonable, reflecting the closeness of the relationship between different regions' politics, economy and culture, and the different nationalities, which was different from the distinction of the traditional Confucian Hua and Yi. However his aim in issuing these edicts was to consolidate his dominant position, to strike at the counterforce, and to make use of this to elaborate his own ideas.

Yongzheng treated the family of Lu Liuliang and his disciples severely. The coffins of Lu Liuliang and his oldest son Lu Baozhong were opened and the corpses poked. His disciple Yan Hongkui died in jail and his corpse was poked and the head cut off in public. Another son Lu Yizhong and another disciple Shen Zaikuan were beheaded. In addition, his disciples who had not taken lessons directly under the master himself, and people who inscribed, sold and hid Lu Liuliang's book, were beheaded, sent into exile or whipped. Women and young boys in the Lu, Yan and Shen clans were given to meritorious statesmen as slaves. Strangely, the prime culprits Zeng Jing and Zhang Xi were released without punishment. According to Yongzheng's explanation, Zeng Jing and Zhang Xi trusted Lu Liuliang's heresy and the gossip of Yin Si and Yin Tang's remaining confederates by mistake, which made them confused accessory criminals, so they were released without punishment and were given the chance to turn over a new leaf. He declared at the same time that "my sons and grandsons cannot be sought out and killed because they have defamed me". However, when Qianlong became the emperor, he neglected Yongzheng's last words and put Zeng Jing and Zhang Xi to death.

The Emperor Yongzheng started a bad precedent. He went in for the literary inquisition and used it as a method to control ideology, hit out at his political enemies and enhance his authority. From then on, the Qing Dynasty always convicted people for words and punished them as monstrous crimes involving many people. In the reign of Emperor Qianlong, literary inquisitions were common and the number of cases was four times more than in the reigns of Kangxi and Yongzheng together. In the reigns of Kangxi and Yongzheng, the main targets of the literary inquisition were literati and officialdom with the ideology of overturning the Qing Dynasty, or political opponents, so most of the people punished were officials and superior intellectuals. Although they were framed, the emporers still had some reasons to punish them. In the reign of Emperor Qianlong he took the words too literally and ran after shadows, accusing them groundlessly. Most of the people punished were lower-class intellectuals. Apart from some cases which traced the ideology of overturning the dynasty to the works of people in the early years of the Qing Dynasty, most literary inquisitions had no political slant of overturning the Qing Dynasty but punished people by deliberately misinterpreting the law and committed indiscriminate slaughter. The only aim was to create an unpleasant atmosphere for intellectuals and to show the emperor's despotic power in depriving people of life and property.

At that time it was easy to violate taboo while reciting poems and writing articles, and disasters came from the sky without reason. For example, "Ming" and "Qing" were two common words, but if they were used in poems and articles they were always explained as overturning the Qing Dynasty and reinstating the Ming Dynasty, and attracted fatal disaster and led to the extermination of an entire family. *The Collection of Jianmosheng Poems* of Hu Zhongzao contained the phrase "using my heart to distinguish the turbid and the clear (Qing)"; the *Poetry Anthology of Taohuan Pavilion* of Fang Fen included "who has the ambition to turn the muddy world into an honest and upright society?" and "A reed wants to explain the innocence of the dew, and hears a swan goose lamenting in dream until the dawn (Ming) comes"; in the *Poetry Anthology of Yi Zhu Lou* Xu Shukui wrote "The Ming Dynasty hopes to flap its wings and conquer the capital of the Qing Dynasty", and his *Chanting the Poetry of Zhengdebei* said "Emperors of the Ming Dynasty again, let us put the pot (hu'er) aside"; the *Poetry Anthology of Biluo Houren* of Dai Yixiao contained the line "A promising future (reinstating the Ming Dynasty) is not easy to attain"; *The Collection of Li Qiufeng* included "Raising my head to wait for the brightness (Ming)". All the above poems were considered to denigrate and curse the Qing Dynasty and show the intention of reinstating the Ming Dynasty, which composed the treason. Zhuo Changling in Hangzhou wrote the *Poetry Anthology Recalling the Song*. In this title "Song" and "Ming" was homophonic in Chinese, so it was said to refer to the Ming Dynasty and was intended to hatch a sinister plot. The Emperor Qianlong hated the Zhuo family and called them "conscienceless, bereft of heavenly principles and cannot be borne".

In this atmosphere of interpreting without real understanding and punishing people deliberately, it was possible to be misinterpreted when composing an essay or writing a poem. "Short hair cannot hold the hairpin, so they hate wearing a cap on the head" was said to be against tonsure; "Gown, full sleeve and Haoran headband" was said to oppose the dress of the Qing Dynasty; "The heaven and the earth are one river, always pouring into itself" was explained as hoping the whole country would be in tumult because heaven and earth were flat, so how could they pour; "The Buddha is in health now, and orders not to open the door" was said to satirize the emperor not going to the court. Qianlong said "I hold court every day and call in ministers, when do I say not to open the door?"[15]; someone who lamented because of storms leading to a high rice price and wrote *Sympathy in the Current Time* was reprimanded for "living in a prosperous time but having the audacity to use the theme of sympathy in the current time"[16]; another person who wrote a historical book *The Sequel of the Three-Character Classic* to teach children was said to "have revolt in his heart, and be bold to comment on and appraise arbitrarily the emperors of successive dynasties."[17]

Some sentences were specifically used by the autocratic emperor. So if people misused these words and sentences they overstepped the mark and violated the emperor's authority. Wang Eryang from Shanxi wrote an epitaph for another's father and used "Huang Kao", which was an idiomatic expression. In Qu Yuan's *The Lament* and Ou Yangxiu's *The Memorial to the Emperor of Longgangmo*, they both called the father "Huang Kao", but were rebuked because "making free with the word Huang under the word Kao was overstepping;"[18] Wei Yuzhen inscribed a brief biography of his father which said "to the poor tenants, he remitted the additional interest", but the word "remit" could only be used by the emperor so Wei Yuzhen was denounced as "being presumptuous to use the word 'remit';"[19] Li Daben of Jiansheng in Hunan celebrated the birthday of his mother and wrote an essay including the words "Yao Shun of Women", and was reprimanded for "intending to go against the status", so he was banished to Urumqi; Cheng Ming, a Xiucai in Hubei, wrote an essay to celebrate someone's birthday which said that "Shao Fang was born in Hebei and established his great cause in Henan", and the words "established his great cause" were misinterpreted as becoming emperor, so Cheng Ming was beheaded because of "language rebellion"; Yin Jiaquan, Qingyin of the Grand Court, who were over seventy, called himself "Guxi old man", which was a common title according to the poem of Du Fu "A man seldom lives to be seventy years old". However Qianlong also called himself "Guxi old man" so he offended against the emperor's name, constituting a heavy crime of"overstepping and intending to revolt". Others who violated the temple taboos, the emperor's name or referred to the emperor without changing the line and writing in the next line were all convicted of this crime. Liu E from Henan compiled *The Record of the Emperors' Taboo* to tell people how to avoid these taboos, so he wrote and inscribed all the emperors' names in the Qing Dynasty "according to the original characters and standard form" and was accused of great disrespect to the emperors. He was decapitated.

The literary inquisition in the reign of Emperor Qianlong could not just be considered as having the real ideology of revolting against the Qing Dynasty. Some cases were even because of singing the praises of the rulers of the Qing Dynasty, and donating books and giving suggestions. However if they flattered in a wrong way, they would also be killed. Zhi Tianbao, a roving doctor in Rongcheng, Zhili province, compiled a *Perpetual Calendar* to wish the Qing Dynasty would last for a long time. He said "the Zhou Dynasty governed for just fifty-seven years, and the Qing Dynasty must govern much longer than the Zhou Dynasty". However in this perpetual calendar he only compiled the year of the Qing Dynasty to the fifty-seventh year, which offended the taboo, and was considered as cursing Qianlong to be short-lived. "He is of the most heinous guilt, and only dismemberment can cover his crime". He was put to death. There were a Xiucai, An Nengjing from Jizhou, who wrote a poem to praise the Qing Dynasty, including the words "we have the emperor's grace for a long time, but we can only offer our services for one time; we know that the emperor has much anxiety, but who can help him exclude the difficulty and anxiety." This poem was interpreted to curse the emperor with difficulties and anxiety with no one able to assist him. However as An Nengjing said when he was interrogated "I would have praised the emperor, but I did not know how to express myself". We can at most say that the poem was not a good one, but how could they say it defamed others? There were many groundless and unjust cases in literary inquisitions in the reign of Emperor Qianlong.

In places where there were big literary inquisitions the officials of local governments were accused of the crime of "oversight". Therefore, once places had this kind of cases, officials placed importance on them and were scared to neglect them. They arrested people and searched their houses as if they were facing a formidable enemy. They would rather involve more people than fewer, and dealt with such cases seriously lest they were considered by the emperor to have covered up for the criminals had not tried their best to handle the cases. Liu Zhenyu presented *The New Policy of Zhiping*, "praising the emperor's keen intelligence and excellent judgment, with no words about rebellion and defamation". He just made some pedantic discussion which should not have been any barrier to publication. Fan Shishou, the Grand Coordinator of Hunan, removed his qualification as Xiucai and gave him 100 lashes, preventing him from being an official. This was convicting him of a heavy crime deliberately, but Qianlong still thought the accusation was too light and he executed Liu Zhenyu. He also rebuked Fan Shishou, saying that "you only plan to beat this criminal with cudgels, which is not righteous; he needs to be punished seriously."[20] Ten years previously Liu Zhenyu had presented *The New Policy of Zhiping* to Sai Lenge, the Grand Coordinator of Jiangxi, who did not find any problems with it and praised him. When this case took place Sai Lenge had long been dead but Qianlong was angry and said "Sai Lenge was the commander of border provinces, but he praised this book and was conscienceless. If he were alive now I would have to convict him of shielding a rebel and put him to death."[21] The case of Yin Baoshan happened in Jiangsu. Qianlong scolded that "the local officials treat these things with indifference in ordinary days" and tongue-lashed the viceroys and grand coordinators stating "What things they should take charge of, and what crime they should be convicted of". He also asked to investigate the responsibilities of officials in different levels of departments, Dao, Fu and County, who "were all to be punished together."[22] In this situation scholars were anxious and fearful, and officials at different levels were also terrified. People "always keep small grievances in mind, and make use of some words with problems to attack others' poems and essays. They pick faults and criticize words and sentences, and stir up trouble with very little cause. They also investigate many people, leading to the involvement of teachers and students, relatives and friends, and a family is ruined at last."[23] For example Qi Zhouhua in Tiantai, Zhejiang, was put to death by dismemberment because of writing books such as *Famous Mountain Cang* with "many revolting words", and his sons and grandsons were given the death sentence with reprieve. His younger male cousin, Qi Shaonan, who was a famous geographer and was the former Shilang of the Ministry of Rites, was involved and was sentenced to confinement in his native place. His family property was confiscated. Another twenty people who had echoed Qi Zhouhua's poem, their families were confiscated. In Xie Jishi's family the book *The Notes of Mei Village* was discovered: "most discussions are absurd, and the words are sad and melancholy". In Lu Fu's family, they found *The Picture of Shengxue*, and *The Picture of Yiguan*, "Although there are no words about rebellion, most words are collected from mixed books, giving strained interpretations and drawing farfetched analogies." In Li Fu's family, a poem containing "resentment and ridicule" was found. Although the above three people had died, their sons and nephews were dragged in who nearly suffered a fatal disaster. In addition, they did not find anything in Fang Yan's home, but Fang Yan admitted that he had wrote the preface for Qi Zhouhua's poems and essays and had given accommodation to Qi Zhouhua, so Fan Yan was banished to Yili to be the slave of farming soldiers. The case of Zhou Lihua involved tens of families.

In the eighteenth century, Chinese intellectuals were under the control of cultural autocracy. It was easy for them to be punished when they wrote something, so they were in fear of discussing contemporary social problems and compiling histories. Therefore they kept outside society and escaped from the reality. They were only wrapped up in a heap of musty old books and developed the scholastic style of study, which suffocated their thinking and destroyed talents. At that time some people said that "people who write essays nowadays are afraid of being involved in the country's affairs...people are sailing with the wind, and avoid problems out of fear. They consider an eel a snake, and consider a mouse a tiger. Their uprightness disappears, while their feminine side appears. This relates to the way of the world and the heart of a human being."[24] In the 1780s, about 1782 or the 47th year of Qianlong, the literary inquisition was relaxed. This was mainly because the class contradictions were sharp and people in various areas revolted. The control of the Qing Dynasty was not stable. The Qing government was focused on suppressing the armed uprising and did not have time to cavil about written language to create something out of nothing. At the same time the rulers loosened control over the literary world in order to ease the conflicts and win over the intellectuals in opposing the resistance of the inferior people. At this time the attitude of Qianlong to the literary inquisition changed considerably. For example, in 1782 or the 47th year of Qianlong, they searched and seized sutras and books of the Huis because "most words are offensive and absurd", and according to the regular rule the people involved would be traced and punished for serious crimes. However the uprising of the Huis had at that time been suppressed and the Qing government was afraid of arousing the Huis resistance because of the trivial matters such as words. Therefore Qianlong said "Most words in books are vulgar, so we cannot consider them as surliness and rebellion. These kinds of Huis are stupid and ignorant, and praise their own religions. If we bring all of them to justice, we will be too much bothered...if we make a strained interpretation and judge too harshly these books of the Islam, it means I am too hard on them. So...these cases can be neglected. Afterwards, when civil and military governors meet such vulgar books, they do not need to investigate and deal with them."[25] It was obvious to say that if the rulers wanted to investigate and ascertain thoroughly these kinds of cases, the cases would be piled up like a mountain and involve a lot of people, and the government would "be too much bothered". When the people were in armed revolt against the government the Qing government had to restrain their despotic power and be lenient in deal with literary crimes.

Some officials of the Qing Dynasty still adhered to the regulations formulated in the middle time of Qianlong, and caviled about written language. In order to ease social conflicts and turn around the overcritical atmosphere rapidly, Qianlong rebuked these officials. In the 47th year of Qianlong there was the case of *The Record of Canglang County* compiled by Gao Zhiqing. Li Shijie, the Grand Coordinator of Hunan, picked on the so-called "rebellious and illegal words and sentences", which were all interpreted without real understanding, and cooked up charges. Qianlong pointed out that such a sentence "in the book as 'the morality and kindness are broad and wide, and the country is at peace' is to praise the country, but this grand coordinator picked them up. Such words of praise are banned, is it reasonable? Such examples are numerous. Every province searches banned books, if they all cavil and pick faults and criticize books falsely, how will people write books? The reason for this case is that Li Shijie's unity and coherence in writing are illogical, so the case is handled improperly". He also said "Li Shijie allowed these mediocre advisers to pick up words and sentences falsely...and make trouble for the village. If all officials deal with local affairs so carelessly, how can they be competent to be the local governors?"[26] Li Shijie was given a good dressing down, and other officials did not dare to be overcritical of words.

At the end of the eighteenth century there was a period of armed struggle, and people's uprising was like a raging fire. The rulers of the Qing Dynasty had to change their strong-arm tactics and relax restrictions on the literary world. Literary inquisitions decreased a lot. The atmosphere in the intellectual circles, where no one dared to discuss the reality, changed slightly. But even so, until the beginning of the nineteenth century, the shadow of the literary inquisition still enveloped the literary world and the intellectuals still had a lingering fear, so Gong Zizhen sighed that "people avoid and fear to hear about literary inquisitions, and books are all about grant", and "it is grievous that ten thousand horses are mute".

The Prevalence of Sinology

The evolution of Sinology

Emperor Kangxi advocated Neo-Confucianism. Because of the support of the political power, Neo-Confucianism was popular and took the eminent place. However after the Neo-Confucianism in the Song and Ming Dynasties was criticized by the advanced thinkers in the first years of the Qing Dynasty, it had gone through its zenith and could not rally and recover. There were no first-rate thinkers and scholars, or new creations, in the Qing Dynasty's Neo-Confucianism. As Zhang Taiyan said, "Neo-Confucianism in the Qing Dynasty has no outstanding achievements."[27]

The mainstream of ideology in the Qing Dynasty and the Neo-Confucianism of the Song and Ming took different paths, and it tried hard to leave and get rid of the Neo-Confucianism. It developed from the ideological trend in the first years of the Qing Dynasty which was represented by Gu Yanwu and Huang Zongxi. Of course, this development was not a simple repetition; it changed gradually according to the current social and political conditions. During the process of being used and spread by some class, an ethos must be changed and evolved along with this class' interests and desires. While some ideas which fit the interests and will of the ruling class were kept and developed, others which were in conflict with these were revised or discarded. At the beginning of the eighteenth century, the thinking and academic circles were in the process of evolution: in the first years of the Qing Dynasty, the academic thinking and style were bold, dealing with concrete issues and objecting to empty talk, and then they became plain, focusing on real evidence. However they revolved around the tedious Sinology or textology of the Qing Dynasty.

At this time, the control of the Qing Dynasty was stable and the economy was recovering gradually. The national conflicts between Manchu and Han were relaxed. The old die-hards who called themselves ministers or princes of the Ming Dynasty had all died and a new generation of intellectuals was emerging under the rule of the Qing Dynasty. The intellectual circles admitted the validity of the Qing's rule, and changed from wanting to overturn the Qing Dynasty to subordinating themselves to the Qing Dynasty. Ideology and words full of enthusiastic and intense anti-Manchu consciousness became fewer and fewer and those who offered policies to the Qing Dynasty became more and more. The political diversion in the intellectual circles reflected the change in academic content and style. At the same time, the autocratic cultural control of the Qing Dynasty throttled the vivid and vigorous situation in thinking circles in the first years of the Qing Dynasty, and people became timid and overcautious. They were afraid of discussing the affairs of the country, and did not dare to touch on the reality or write about history. The field of study became very narrow, and the intellectuals' intelligence and wisdom was focused on sorting out and annotating the ancient literature.

Yan Ruoqu, Hu Wei, Mao Qiling, Chen Qiyuan, Yao Jiheng, Wan Sitong and Gu Zuyu were the pioneers of Sinology in the Qing Dynasty, which was the way-station transiting from the ideology in the first years of the Qing Dynasty to the Sinology of the eighteenth century. The features of their ideology and academic thought were as follows:

1. They differed from the advanced thinkers in the first years of the Qing Dynasty, and their anti-Manchu consciousness was gradually disappearing. Although they were different from the Neo-Confucians Wei Yijie, Li Guangdi and Zhang Boxing, who were high-ranking officials of the Qing Dynasty, and still kept the appearance of "cloth gown" and "hermit", actually they were hand

in glove with the Qing Dynasty. Yan Ruoqu, Hu Wei and Gu Zuyu were all the hangers-on of high-ranking officials in the Qing Dynasty, and they all took part in the office of unifying a country's record which was set up by the Grand Secretary Xu Qianxue by imperial order. Yan Ruoqu was invited into service by Yinzhen, the Prince Yong, in his old age and he went into his mansion. When he died, Yinzhen held the funeral for him. On Kangxi's fourth Southern tour Wu Wei, seventy-one years old, welcomed his coming and received a horizontal inscribed board written by Kangxi with "Diligent in Study in Old Age", which was considered a great honor. Wan Sitong accepted the invitation of Shangshu Xu Yuanwen and took part in the Ming history office, but still signed himself "Cloth gown Mr. Wan". Mao Qiling had taken part in the struggle against the Qing, and then participated in the examination for high scholars held by the Qing Dynasty, and became the Jian Tao (an official title in ancient China). He presented books and sang the praises of the Qing emperor, and was proud of getting the new ruler's favor. Zhang Taiyan said that "He lost his virtue in old age, and flattered the new emperor". There was no trace of any resistance to the Qing government in their books.

2. They generally inherited the style of study of the thinkers in the first years of the Qing Dynasty of emphasizing reading and objecting to empty talk. Huang Zongxi had said that "reading little books cannot prove the change of truth"; and Gu Yanwu advocated "erudition from essays" and that "studying more means remembering more firmly". Their followers were all diligent and studied widely. Yan Ruoqu inscribed a couplet about himself saying that "I am ashamed of myself for being ignorant of one thing; when I meet something I do not understand, I always find others, it never stops." From this we can see his style of study. Mao Qiling had read hundreds of thousands of books and had a wide range of knowledge; Gu Zuyu "can recite classics and history fluently;"[28] Wan Sitong "is proficient in history, and is especially familiar with the anecdotes of the Ming Dynasty, and can recite the records from Hongwu to Tianqi."[29] However, though they were diligent and had read lots of books, the spirit of "Putting what is learned into Practice" became neglected. They made a penetrating study of ancient books and devoted themselves to textual research of the words and sentences, not daring to inquire into the current political and economic problems. For example Gu Yanwu studied geography, and wrote *The Medical Certificate of the World's Countries*. It expounded the terrain of mountains, cities and passes seen from the angle of the reality. His followers were all good at geography. Gu Zuyu wrote the 130 volumes of *The Summary of Reading History and Areas* which can be called a monumental work; Hu Wei wrote the *Yugong Zhuizhi* and Yan Ruoqu wrote *The Four Books Explaining*

the Earth, which were called masterpieces. However they all annotated ancient books and history, and did textual research on the ancient geography, leaving aside the aim of putting what is learned into practice.

3. Yan, Hu and others had a suspicious spirit and the method of textual research became precise gradually. They took part in specific research and formed a different study style from the Song and Ming Neo-Confucians which talked about heavenly principles, nature and life. After Yan Ruoqu and Hu Wei used concrete evidence to dismantle the fake ancient Chinese *Shangshu*, and distinguished *Heto Luoshu* (the ancient Chinese mythological fiction), Yao Jiheng wrote *The Research on the Ancient and Modern Fake Books* and listed ten kinds of fake books, opening the way to the detection of forgeries in learning. He said "people who made fake books have appeared from the ancient time to now, so there are so many fake books. Even scholars cannot distinguish the true from the false, so how can they call themselves a well-read person? Therefore the most important thing in reading books is to distinguish between them."[30] In the feudal era people considered ancient classics as the first source of knowledge, but now these classics were proved to be fake books and this could not but arouse a shock in intellectual circles. Mao Lingqi picked faults and criticized Zhu Xi, and wrote *Correcting Mistakes of the Four Books*. He said "there is no right in the Four Books...however, reading the Four Books and the annotation of the Four Books every day, and writing the eight-legged essay according to these annotations also makes mistakes...which means even gathering iron from all over the world cannot make such mistake."[31] They reviewed the past with a suspicious spirit and mainly put forward many questions about the spreading classics and Confucian annotations and comments on the classics after Song, Ming and Weijin, hoping to explore the true features of these classics. *The Piece of Mao Poems and Researching Ancient Affairs* written by Chen Qiyuan was a typical book. The study of *The Book of Songs* was divided into two schools. Some people respected, trusted and praised highly the preface of poems, Mao's biography and Zheng Kangcheng's annotation, while others depreciated and opposed them. Zheng Qiao and Zhu Xi belonged to the latter school. *The Biography of Collections* written by Zhu Xi took the position of Neo-Confucianism, annotated *The Book of Songs*, and summarised poets' praise and satire and the motivation for composing verse. There were many misinterpretations and they neglected to make exegesis and explain the name and description of a thing. Zhu Xi's book was praised by the government and became a popular book, so there were few people who studied the annotation of poems, Mao's biography, and Zheng's annotations. Chen Qiyuan reversed the attitude of Zhu Xi and respected the annotation of

poems, the Mao's biography and Zheng's annotation. He also focused on the textual research of the name and description of a thing, and disproved the Zhu Xi School. *The General Summary of the Siku Quanshu* gave a comment on Chen Qiyuan's *The Piece of Mao Poems and Researching Ancient Affairs*: "the standard of the explanations of words in ancient books was all *Erya*, the standard of articles was all *The Foreword of Mao Shi*, and the standard of the annotations of the classics was all Mao's' Biography, and Zheng's annotation was used to assist it. The name and description of a thing always took Lu Ji's commentary as the example...they always identified and corrected Zhu Zi's *Collections*...and mainly attacked Liu Jin's The Explanation of *The Song Collections*, and Fu Guang's *Poem of A Child's Question* took second place (Fu Guang and Liu Jin both inherited and passed on Zhu Xi School and their books all clarified the thinking of *The Song Collections*)...between them, they insisted on Sinology, and did not allow any discrepancy. Although there were deviations to some extent, the citations were broad and profound, and their explanations were complete and explicit. All had something to discuss."[32] From Chen Qiyuan's work we can see the trait of successive specialization of the Han scholars.

At the beginning of Sinology, the most typical representatives were Hu Wei and Yan Ruoqu.

Hu Wei (1633-1714, or the sixth year of Chongzhen reign in the Ming Dynasty to the 53rd year of Kangxi reign in the Qing Dynasty), also named Feiming, was born in Deqing, Zhejiang. He wrote *The Discrimination of Yitu, Yugong Zhuizhi* and *The Correct and Sensible View of Hongfan*, while the former was especially famous. *The Book of Changes* was a divining book in ancient China and contained no pictures. Chen Chuan, a Taoist priest, composed the *Hetu Luoshu* and then passed it on to Li Zhicai, Shao Yong, and Zhou Dunyi. It was said that it was carried by dragon, horse and holy turtle, and there were so called Tai Ji, Wu Ji, inborn, and the day after tomorrow, giving a strained interpretation, which was all mixed with *The Book of Changes* and connected with Fu Xi, Wenwang, Zhougong and Confucius. The annotation of *The Book of Changes* was mysterious with a bad atmosphere. Zhu Xi wrote *Yi Benyi*, which used these views, so the Taoist priest's statement of change was popular for many hundreds of years. Hu Wei's *The Discrimination of Yitu*, proved that the *Hetu Luoshu* was just a Taoist priest's practice of asceticism and appeared in late Song Dynasty, "it cited the old essays and proved each by the other, in order to suppress the people who depended on it". He said that "the *Book of Songs, Shangshu*, the *Book of Ceremonial*, and *Spring and Autumn* must have pictures, but only *The Book of Changes* does not need pictures. The sixty-four divinatory symbols, Yin and Yang, six Yao are all pictures."[33] The textual research of Hu Wei was a heavy blow to the Neo-Confucianism of the Song and Ming Dynasties. Liang Qichao said, "The so-called Tai Ji, Wu Ji and *Hetu Luoshu* were the core of the Neo-Confucianism in the Song Dynasty. The Confucianism in the Song Dynasty talked about reason, the spirit, fate, density, the heart and the nature, which developed another theory. Zhou Dunyi said that 'he had obtained non-public knowledge from the remaining classics'. The ancestors of Cheng-Zhu Neo-Confucianism narrated it and it depended on the Confucian orthodoxy. So it had taken up the thoughts of intellectuals for five or six hundred years, and its authority was nearly equal to that of the classics. This book refuted Xi, Wen, Zhou and Confucius with Yi, and refuted Chen Shao with pictures, which was not an excessive attack but the Song School was mortally wounded."[34] It was still wrong that Hu Wei refuted Xi, Wen, Zhou and Confucius with Yi, but it was right to refute Chen (Tuan) Shao (Yong) with pictures, which eliminated the additional mystical viewpoint in the study of *The Book of Changes* to a great extent.

Yan Ruoqu (1636-1704, or from the ninth year of Chongzhen reign in the Ming Dynasty to the forty-third year of Kangxi reign) was also named Baishi, and his ancestral home was Taiyuan, Shanxi, but he was born and raised in Huaian. He wrote eight volumes of *The Ancient Chinese Prose of the Explanation of Shangshu*. After the big fire in the Qin Dynasty, *Shangshu* had twenty-eight sections passed down by Fu Sheng in the Western Han Dynasty plus the *Taishi*, so there were twenty-nine pieces in total which formed the current edition. Then the ancient Chinese prose of *Shangshu* was obtained from the Confucian wall, which was sixteen pieces more than the current book. By the end of the Eastern Han Dynasty, th e sixteen pieces were missing. Mei Ze in the Eastern Jin Dynasty donated a *Shangshu* which had twenty-five pieces and also included *The Biography of Kong Anguo*. Kong Ying in the Tang Dynasty wrote *Justice*, including the twenty-five pieces in it, but there were suspicions about the ancient Chinese prose of the *Shangshu* in successive dynasties. Yan Ruoqu proved that the twenty-five pieces and *The Biography of Kong Anguo* were both fake. He cited evidence from the aspects of the number, name of pieces, the words and sentences, handwriting and examples, and also cited *The Mencius, Shiji* and *Shuowen* as the side witnesses. Through Yan Ruoqu's textual research, the ancient Chinese prose of *Shangshu* was proved fake which was an ironical case and was unshakable. *The General Summary of the Siku Quanshu* said that by "citing the classics, and using ancient essays as evidence, he stated its contradictions and so the faking of the ancient Chinese prose was clear", and by "discriminating repeatedly, and removing a big doubt that had existed for many years, so textual research was more consolidated than before."[35] The fake ancient Chinese prose of *Shangshu* had been studied for more than 1,000 years and was considered a holy classic, which was also important evidence to the scholars of Neo-Confucianism in the Song and Ming Dynasty. For example, the thirty-one words "Human hearts are evil; the heart of nature has its profound and unknown details; the heart and the nature are unified and harmonious; the speech and act keep to the center", which had been passed down from generation to generation by Confucians were from *The Plan of Da Yu* in the fake ancient Chinese prose of *Shangshu*. Since the *Shangshu* was a fake book, and the so called "theory passed from generation to generation by Confucians" which used to cheat people was exposed, the scholars of Neo-Confucianism were kept hanging and were in a difficult position. Therefore Yan Ruoqu's *The Ancient Chinese Prose of the Explanation of Shangshu* and Hu Wei's *The Discrimination of Yitu* were the same in having value in textual research and in clarifying literature. Moreover they also attacked the Neo-Confucianism of the Song and Ming Dynasties. They even touched on the authority of the Confucian classics, and their influence on thinking was profound.

The formation of Sinology—The Wu School represented by Hui Dong

Hu Wei and Yan Ruoqu were both transitional figures. They focused on the pronunciation of the word and specific evidences, but they neither flew the flag of "Sinology", nor did they completely get rid of the influence of the Song and Ming Neo-Confucianism. At that time the Song School and Sinology were still divided and until the next age, which meant the reign of Emperor Qianlong, they were sharply divided. Zhang Taiyan said that Hu Wei and Yan Ruoqu "were both academicians, however at that time they had just started to establish Sinology, so sometimes they might mix slanders of the Song and Ming. From the Qianlong Dynasty there were scholars who studied it systematically;"[36] Pi Xirui also said: "at the beginning of this dynasty, Sinology had just started and was based on the Song School. They did not divide the schools but used their advantages, which absorbed both Sinology and Song. In the Qianlong reign Xu (Shen) and Zheng (Kangcheng)'s study was formed, and the scholars of Song had passed away. The theories and classics both advocated using real evidence and they did not only talk about the argumentation, which was specialized Sinology."[37]

Any academic school of thought which creates a system of its own and establishes its own school of thought has its own tenets, ways of pursuing studies, studying emphasis, and academic style, which are built up over a log time. By the time of Hui Dong all this was provided and had built the strong position of "Sinology", forming the situation of contending against the Song School. Hui Dong and his students were all from the South and were called the "Wu School" in the Sinology of the Qing Dynasty.

Hui Dong (1697–1758, or from the 36th year of Kangxi to the 23rd year of Qianlong reign), also called Ding Yu, was from Wu county, Jiangsu. His grandfather Hui Zhouti and his father Hui Shiqi together with Hui Dong were all famous scholars. They imparted classics for generations, and were erudite through paternal teaching and influence. The Hui family inherited the tradition passed down from Gu Yanwu and they started study of the classics from the ancient Chinese, focusing on sound exegesis, in order to pursue the meaning of the classics. Hui Shiqi said: "The classics of ceremony came from the walls of a house, which were mainly the ancient words and pronunciations. The meaning of classics existed in exegesis. After learning the word and knowing its pronunciation, we can know its meaning, so the ancient exegesis cannot be changed."[38] Dai Zhen said of the way of pursuing studies that "If one wanted to learn teacher Song Ya (Hui Dong)'s classics, he had to study the ancient exegesis of the Confucian classics teacher of Sinology in order to examine the institutions and systems in ancient times, and ascertain reasons and meanings which all had evidence to support them."[39] The Huis said that pursuing the truth from words and pronunciations was the common principle believed by the Sinologists, which was the feature of study distinguishing them from the scholars of Neo-Confucianism. Wang Mingsheng and Qian Daxin, who were scholars of a younger age of Hui Dong stated this clearly. Wang Mingsheng said that"studying classics can help to know the doctrine, but the spiritual seekers do not need to just pursue the reasons and meanings. However they need to study the words, distinguish the pronunciations, explain the gloss and know the classics, so that they can see the reasons and meanings naturally, and the doctrine in it."[40] Qian Daxin said that "the six classics are the sage's words. Seeking for the meanings is according to their words, and all begins with the explanations of the ancient books."[41] The Sinologists outside the Wu School including Dai Zhen all held the same viewpoint so Fang Dongshu, the opposition faction of Sinology, said that "this is a tenet of Sinology, which is unbreakable". "This tenet is the most believable, and its opinion is the most powerful. The tenet he indicated and the limitation he insisted on are convincing. It is reasonable and cannot be changed."[42] The principle, which was respected and emphasized repeatedly, was absolutely right. In order to understand the ideological content of the ancient classics, the pronunciation and meanings of the words should be found. However after the Wei and Jin Dynasties, people could not understand the ancient Chinese and did not know the pronunciations and meanings. Some people gave a strained interpretation, and others changed the ancient Chinese into the popular form of characters, falsifying the ancient books. From Gu Yanwu to Hui Dong and Dai Zhen, they just used this undesirable style of study to emphasize that clarifying the ancient literature should start from the basic skills of pronunciation, exegesis, emendation and textual research, which could remove the misunderstandings and misinterpretation of ancient books which had been added over thousands of years and realize their original meanings. This was the scientific method and attitude of study. This opinion changed the temperament of empty talk of scholars from the Song and Ming Dynasty, and their bad habit of not taking notice of abandoned books. Some people said: "in the middle of the reign of Emperor Qianlong, scholars throughout the country all study intensively the ancient significances. From the Han-Confucians, traditional philology, and exegesis up to the descendants of the seventy teachers and people who study the six Confucian classics, all are guided by Ding Yu."[43] Of course pronunciation, exegesis, emendation and textual research were just methods used to study the ancient classics. If their function was emphasized improperly in order to replace and exclude the study of the ideological content, this would become scholastic academia which attended to trifles and neglected the essentials.

Another important trait in Hui Dong's study was to respect and adhere to the classics of Han Confucianism. Thus, the whole school after Hui Dong was called "Sinology". This name could not express the whole school's attitude and way of study completely, and especially could not represent the development after Dai Zhen, but it did reflect the trait of scholars in the Wu School which was represented by Hui Dong. Hui Shiqi, Hui Dong's father, had focused on the Han annotations to the classics and said: "*The Book of Changes* began with Fu Xi, flourished in the reign of Wenwang, was fully prepared by Confucius, and its theory existed in the Han Dynasty". He also said: "Kang Cheng's Three Rites and He Xiu's *Gongyang* are mostly cited from Han law, which was not far from the ancient times."[44] However Hui Shiqi did not especially respect Sinology. Hui Dong held high the flag of "Sinology", "the ancient theory must be true, and the Han theory must be good", and rejected the classics after the Wei and Jin Dynasties, going back to the time before the Han Dynasty. Therefore Jiao Xun said: "if scholars from the Hu School talked about Yi, the father and son held different opinions. If Hui Shiqi referred to Yi, he only expressed his own opinion. But his son Zi Dong's *The Narration of Zhou Yi* stuck to the old theory."[45]

It was the inevitable outcome of the development of the academic thinking since the first years of the Qing Dynasty that scholars in the Qing Dynasty went back to the classics of Han Confucianism. Although the Qing government tried its best to advocate Cheng-Zhu Neo-Confucianism, the authority of Neo-Confucianism had collapsed. People saw that when the Confucians of the Song commented on the classics they did not make clear the words and regulations on things in the classics and they even could not tell the true from the false classics, which was just like taking a part of the whole and guessing and assessing. The intellectual circles could not reestablish the devout faith in the Song Confucianism again, so escaping its constraints and getting rid of its influence was the general trend in the ideology. Clever intellectuals rushed out from the restraints of Song Confucian classics which had enveloped them for hundreds of years, but where would they go? The new gate of modern thesaurus was still closed, and they could not open it. Therefore they explored the source and went back to the ancient times. They hoped to find out the foundation of thinking from the remote past. From their point of view, the Han Dynasty was not far away from the present and the theories still existed, which were the secret for pursuing knowledge. In order to find out the true features of these ancient books, they had to go back to the classics of Han Confucianism. Hui Dong criticized academia after the Wei and Jin Dynasties, saying that "since the Wei and Jin Dynasties, the principle of Confucian classics and teachers has been lost. Wang Su defamed Zheng Shi and the ceremony of sacrificing to the earliest ancestors and the god was perverse. Yuan Zhun destroyed the clothes of Cai, and the system of the palace (in ancient times, a place for an emperor to declare punishment and rewards or issue instructions) was died out. Zou Zhan ridiculed Xun Xu and the study of Zhou Yi became obscure. With the distorted interpretation and all following one leader, why should they blame the following generations' confused discussion?"[46] He also praised highly the Confucian classics in the Han Dynasty, "Han Confucians had their own principle which was used to explain the classics, so there were teachers of the five classics. The study of explanations of words in ancient books was all passed on through oral instruction and then was written on bamboo tablets and textiles. So the theory of the teachers of Han classics kept a foothold in the teaching of officials, who paralleled the classics...only Confucian classics teachers could distinguish the ancient words from pronunciations...so the ancient precepts could not be changed and Confucian classics teachers could not be ignored."[47] Opposing Song and reviving Han was a general trend in the development of academic ideology in the earlier stage of the Qing Dynasty, and the Wu School was the peak of this phase.

Opposing Song and reviving Han were two aspects of the ideological trend at that time, which were related to each other. Opposing Song meant getting rid of traditional thought, which was an expression of ideological emancipation to some extent. The result of opposing Song must be to go back to Sinology in order to confront Song Confucianism with an equal authority. However it should be pointed that abandoning Song Confucianism and going back to the Sinology, which expressed the academic ideology, took a new branch road and was the premature death of ideological emancipation. Song Confucianism gave a farfetched interpretation, which was academia serving feudalism, and Sinology also drew wrong conclusions through false analogy and misinterpretation, which served feudalism as well. The social conditions at that time had not matured enough to break out of the restraints of feudal thought. Therefore leaving by on way but returning by another was the circular path taken in feudal studies of the classics. This was the limitation of the Wu School. Generally speaking, it was also the limitation of the whole Qing Dynasty's Sinology.

Hui Dong, the representative of the Wu School, was proficient in Zhou Yi and wrote *The Narration of Zhou Yi, Yi Sinology, The Example of Yi, The Ancient Meaning of the Nine Classics*, and *The Investigation of Ancient Chinese Shangshu*. He oppose Yi as stated by the Song people and was also against Wang Bi and Han Kangbo in the Wei and Jin Dynasties who respected Lao Zi and Zhuang Zi and used empty talk to annotate Yi, and "he especially respected Yu Zhongxiang (Yu Fan), and studied the meanings of Xun (Shuang) and Zheng (Kangcheng). Using its aim as the annotation and deducing its theory as notes, Sinology's extinction lasted for more than five hundred years but is reviving again."[48] Hui Dong's attention was concentrated on the establishment of a strong basis for Sinology and he tried his best to search and examine Han theories of Yi. In Han Confucianism's classics there was essence and also useless things, but Hui Dong did not distinguish and choose between them and inherited all of them instead. The Confucian classics were represented by both ancient Chinese and current Chinese. Hui Dong respected the ancient Chinese classics, and also adopted the current Chinese theories, swallowing anything and everything even though some parts conflicted with others. The Han classics were full of Yin, Yang, calamities, and the theory of augury. Hui Dong's works were influenced by these and his thinking was messy and complex, emphasizing excessively the recovery of Sinology, which would inevitably produce abuses. *The General Summary of the Siku Quanshu* commented on Hui Dong that "his advantages were to use wide knowledge, but his disadvantages were also to adopt excessive knowledge; his advantages were focusing on the ancient books, while his disadvantages were to obstinately follow tradition."[49] Wang Yinzhi said that "although Hui Dingyu was diligent in investigating ancient books, he had little discrimination and a careless attitude. If he saw something different from the current books he followed it without distinguishing the true from the false...he held on stubbornly to Sinology without seeking for the truth and did not make his own judgment."[50]

Contrary to the empty talk of Song Confucianism, Hui Dong's study of classics involved "respect for and connection to the ancient meanings, and he seldom has his own opinions."[51] However this did not mean that he never expressed his own thoughts. In his *Record of Ming Tang and Correct Reasons* he praised himself for having made clear the true features of the system of ancient Ming Tang. In fact he just expressed his political ideal according to Han theories, "establishing Ming Tang as the law to govern the country". He also noted "the reason" in *Comments on Yi*, and cited *Han Feizi, Jie Lao*, and said "the word 'reason' has two meanings. A person's nature is formed when he was born, and must have two aspects. In heaven it is called Yin and Yang, while on the ground it is called softness and unyielding and in people it is called benevolence and righteousness." This used the universal principle that everything has an opposite to explain the word "reason", which was totally different from the "reason" in Song Confucianism. He also said that "karma and justice are called heavenly principles...the later generations depend on the god, and the principle of nature and human desires should be opposite. He also said that 'god is reason', which is especially wrong."[52] This refuted Cheng-Zhu Neo-Confucianism directly and approached Dai Zhen's theory about the principle of nature and human desires.

Shen Tong, Jiang Sheng, Yu Xiaoke, Wang Mingsheng, Qian Daxin and Qian Daxin's brothers and nephews Qian Dazhao, Qian Tang and Qian Dian were all Hui Dong's friends and students. They were all from the south of Jiangsu province. They abided by the tenet of respecting Han Confucianism and were called the Wu School in Sinology. Dai Zhen said: "Hui Dong asked his son to keep his followers, if Jiang Qintao (Jiang Sheng) and Yu Zhonglin (Yu Xiaoke) are both faithful to what they have learned, they still imitate ...but the talented people and scholars of younger age in the Wu School are all refined and courteous, and pay attention to the passing on of teachings from a master to his disciples."[53]

Shen Tong's representative work was *The Study on Zhou Officials' Farmland.* Ouyang Xiu suspected the *Rites of Zhou* and he thought that according to the narration in the *Rites of Zhou* there were more officials than farmland so there was insufficient farmland for salaries. Shen Tong investigated the conditions of its implementation in order to solve Ouyang Xiu's puzzle. Hui Dong said of this book that "various opinions for 2,000 years have been solved in one day."[54] In fact the *Rites of Zhou* was finished in the Warring States Period. All the contents of this book refer to the Western Zhou Dynasty and may not represent the real situation in the Western Zhou Dynasty. Shen Tong took it as the real system in the Western Zhou Dynasty and investigated and proved it, which rigidly adhered to formalities. It was also the disadvantage of the ancient principles. Yu Xiaoke wrote *The Investigation on the Explanation of Ancient Classics*, and sought the missing classics from before the Tang Dynasty. He opened the way to sort out the missing literature, but the book was written hastily without careful examination. Wang Mingsheng, who was a scholar at that time, criticized this book as "being keen on ancient books but not making choices", "one book was gathered by the later generations, and another was abandoned from the Han exegesis."[55] Dai Zhen also criticized the name of this book "Gou Chen": "some hooks were not sunk, and some were sunk without hooks."[56] Jiang Sheng and Wang Mingsheng were all experts in the study of *Shangshu* and their style of study was the same as Hui Dong. Their respect for the Han and the ancient books was even stronger. Jiang Sheng wrote *The Annotation of the Phonetic Notation to Shangshu*, and "collected the annotations of Ma (Rong) and Zheng (Xuan) and the biography (the biography of Fu Sheng), the contrary opinion (Xu Shen's *Contrary Opinion of the Five Classics*), and consulted and deliberated over them. He also collected books which were referred to in the *Shangshu*, in order to benefit his book."[57] Jiang Sheng was addicted to ancient books, "he did not write the regular script, even in his writing to other people he wrote in seal characters. People were always surprised and considered them as sealed books and talismans."[58] Wang Mingsheng also respected Han and trusted the ancient books. He wrote *Postcase of Shangshu*, which respected Zheng Xuan especially and extremely admired Zheng Xuan. He said "why did I write *Postcase of Shangshu*? I wanted to express Zheng Kangcheng's theory."[59] Hang Shijun wrote the preface for him and he also called Wang Mingsheng the "person who can study Zheng theory at this period", "he studied intensively various books, collecting and picking up widely. Once he found one word and character coming from Zheng, he discriminated and recorded them, and gathered hundreds of thousands of words, in order to let people know the annotations of Zheng and make people know the theory of Zheng."[60] The advantage of Wang Mingsheng was to select carefully and that he respected the passing on of teachings from a master to his disciples. He avoided the shortcoming of swallowing anything and everything and mixing ancient and current Chinese like Hui Dong. However he only respected Zheng, and he neither paid attention to other people's study nor did he have his own opinion. He followed Zheng Kangcheng completely. He said that "studying the classics but being in fear of refuting classics...although the classics are difficult to understand I had to obey the Han principle, following him without changing my mind."[61] We can see that his attitude to study was very conservative without any creativity. Wang Mingsheng also used the same method to study history. He wrote *The Discussion of Seventeen Histories*. "He mainly collated this book, correcting mistakes and slips. He examined the truth of the achievement, and distinguished the disparities in biographies. He was good at local officials, institutions and systems. He disliked appraising people and considered this as empty talk without benefits."[62]

Fig. 11.4. A Portrait of Qian Daxin

Among the scholars of the Wu School, Qian Daxin had the widest knowledge and made the biggest achievements. His field of study was quite wide. He was proficient in Confucian classics, history, astronomy, the celestial almanac, rhyme, exegesis, inscriptions and poetry and prose, "he did not specialize in one classic, but knew all the classics; he did not major in one skill, but mastered all skills."[63] Although he stuck to the tenet of Sinologists, he did not think in absolute terms like other scholars in the Wu School. He thought that: for ancient people's theories, one could not slander them easily, and also should not hold on to them excessively. "I think that scholarship is a great thing for thousands of years. Revising mistakes does not defame the forefathers, and has benefits to the later study,"[64] "only through seeking truth from facts, and cherishing ancient people's pains, we can communicate throughout the country."[65] He wrote *The Differences between Twenty-two Histories*, doing textual research of the"history books written in biographical style" systematically and carefully. He collated different editions of twenty-two histories and compared them with other books and tablets. He figured out mistakes, gaps and omissions, and contradictions in the "history books written in biographical style", correcting the mistakes in copying and inscribing. Qian Daxin did not talk about argumentation; however, there was occasionally some thinking which broke out of the restraint of feudalism in his released comments. For example, in feudal society the emperor was the most honorable, so killing the emperor was a monstrous crime. However in Qian Daxin's comments on the history of killing emperors frequently in the Spring and Autumn Period, he thought that the emperors who were killed were all shallow. If the emperor was sagacious, treacherous ministers and traitors would not appear, "if the emperor was honest and wise, how could he be killed."[66] Another example was that feudal ethics demanded a woman be faithful to her husband until death without remarriage. However Qian Daxin thought that if there were no love between man and wife,"remarriage could not be called forfeiting her integrity...marrying another person did not mean that she was not a good woman, and there was no use to keeping her by force, which made the situation between man and wife painful."[67] These concepts were advanced and bold under the circumstances at that time. However Qian Daxin was conservative on some issues. For example, he did not admit the superiority of Western culture. He was proficient in mathematics, but he only respected ancient Chinese mathematics and looked down on Western mathematics. Jiang Yong made achievements in Western mathematics but Qian Daxin did not approve of him. He satirized Jiang Yong as being "used by Western people."[68] Another example was that Fanqie (a traditional method of indicating the pronunciation of a Chinese character) was a progress in phonetics which was related to the spread of Buddhism and was influenced by the phonetic transcription of the Buddhist sutras' Sanskrit. Qian Daxin denied this point, and insisted that the seeds of Fanqie had appeared in *The Book of Songs*. He did not admit that in aspects foreign culture was better than that of China. He said, "The wisdom of the ancient sages and men of virtue could not come from Buddhism", "I know the doctrine of six classics, which is complete, and later generations' wisdom could not exceed that of sages and men of virtue."[69] This opinion reflected Chinese intellectual circles' conservative attitude and arrogance. Qian Daxin, however, was outstanding among scholars of the Qing Dynasty. Jiang Fan praised that "his scholarship was broad and profound, and he was widely read. Since the country was founded, he was a Confucian of this generation. He was a Han Confucian who was followed Gao Mi (Zheng Kangcheng), but even Jia Kui and Fu Qian fell behind him."[70]

Academic achievements of Dai Zhen, scholar of the Wan School

In Sinology in the Qing Dynasty the Wan School, which was represented by Dai Zhen, was named like the Wu School. "Wu" and "Wan" were both names of places. Scholars of the Wu School were all from the south of Jiangsu province, while some of scholars of Wan were from Anhui (such as Jiang Yong, Dai Zhen, Jin Bang, Cheng Yaotian, Hong Bang and Ling Tingkan). Others were not from Anhui (such as Dai Yucai, Wang Niansun, Wang Yinzhi, Wang Zhong, Jiao Xun and Ruan Yuan) but they were either Dai Zhen's students, or people who studied personally under Dai Zhen, so they were always included in the Wan School.

The Wu School and Wan School were not two opposite schools and there were many common points of academic opinions between the two. Therefore they influenced each other, and were each other's teachers and friends. Later the academic achievements of the Wan School surpassed those of the Wu School. The Wu School mostly studied *The Book of Changes* and *Shangshu*, while the Wan School was good at traditional philology and the celestial almanac, and especially the three Rites. The Wu School advocated reviving the ancient, considering Han as the best, while the Wan School focused on pursuing the truth using sophisticated methods and careful examination. Wang Mingsheng talked about the differences between Hui Dong and Dai Zhen: "scholars in the current time praised them highly. When Hui Dong studied classics, he pursued ancient books, while Dai Zhen pursued the truth. After all, if the ancient knowledge was abandoned the truth could not be pursued."[71] Wang Mingsheng was a scholar of Hui School who favored returning to the ancients, thinking that the closer to the ancient, the nearer to the truth. This was prejudice. However the opinion that Hui Dong's "pursuing the ancient" and Dai Zhen's "pursuing the truth" were different styles of study said by Wang Mingsheng was insightful. When Zhang Taiyan talked of the differences between the two Schools he said that "the Wu School began with Hui Dong, who had wide knowledge and a respected reputation; the Wan School began with Dai Zhen, who put form and name together and allowed others to make their decision. This was their difference". He also said that the Wu School "all stated Erya, and had a broad and profound knowledge of exegesis", but "Dai studied widely, and their analysis and methods were close, tracing back to the ancient meanings to back up their own principles, which was different from the Schools in Suzhou."[72] Zhang Taiyan's view was close to that of Wang Mingsheng.

The appearance of the Wan School was the peak of Sinology in the Qing Dynasty. Although the Wu School could make rival claims as an equal with Song Confucianism, it could not elbow it out. After the appearance of the Wan School, this situation changed. "When Zhen (Dai Zhen) began to work in Siku Hall, all Confucians were shocked and wanted to be his disciples... Zhen wrote *Interpretation of Mencius Concepts* to show its nature. Scholars became estranged from Cheng-Zhu Neo-Confucianism naturally."[73] Thereafter Neo-Confucianism lost its attraction. Sinology took the place of the Song Confucianism, becoming the cultural and academic mainstream. In intellectual circles, scholars "hold on stubbornly to textual research and discuss the failings of the Song Confucians. The books of Lian, Luo, Guan, Min (Four Schools of Neo-Confucianism in the Song Dynasty) had no readers."[74]

The reason why Sinology could dominate the academic circles was inseparable with the social conditions at that time and the cultural policy of the Qing Dynasty. In the reign of Emperor Qianlong, the control of the Qing Dynasty had lasted more than one hundred of years and was in its heyday. At that time politics were stable and the economy was prosperous, so a peaceful and rich society provided good conditions for academic study. In Beijing, Yangzhou, Suzhou, and Hangzhou politics and the economy developed well and talented men emerged in succession. Academies of classical learning stood in great numbers, and inscribing and collecting books were popular. However in the reigns of Emperors Yong and Qian the literary inquisition was much stricter, and the intellectuals immersed themselves in heaps of musty old books. They were fearful of discussing politics and compiling history, and only studied ancient classics intensively. The official policies of the Qing Dynasty also advocated the classics. After *Boxue Hongci Ke* (an examination outside the imperial examination system to win over intellectuals), in the fourteenth year of Qianlong, he ordered scholars who "devote themselves to the classics" to submit their works and summoned them to the Qinzheng Palace. If one can say that in the reign of Emperor Kangxi, Cheng-Zhu Neo-Confucianism was specially respected, by the reign of Emperor Qianlong the ruler had realized that Neo-Confucianism could not hold the intellectual circle together so Sinology had to be advocated at the same time, making the two Schools serve for his control. Ruan Yuan said: "sages in this dynasty all possessed morality, and included the ancient opinions. They respected the humanity and natural law in Song Confucianism and enriched it with Han Confucian classics. Classics indicated by the two Schools were popular throughout the country."[75] On the suggestion of Sinologists, the Qing government compiled the *Siku Quanshu*. Many famous Sinologists took part in the compilation, which also included a group of officials who occupied important positions such as Zhu Jun, Zhu Gui, Ji Yun, Wang Chang, Bi Yuan, Lu Jianzeng and Ruan Yuan. They were accomplished Sinologists themselves who did their utmost to encourage and advocate Sinology. Therefore, "since the reign of Emperor Qianlong, people all talked about and respected Xu, Zheng and Jia Ma, the Eastern Sinology was quite influential."[76]

Dai Zhen (1723–1777, or the first year of Yongzheng to the forty-second year of Qianlong), named Dong Yuan, was the representative of the Wan School and was from Xiuning, Anhui province. His family was poor. He had been a small retailer, and then worked as a teacher. In his youth he followed the famous scholar Jiang Yong, "Yong has studied classics for ten years, and is proficient in the three Rites and mathematics, temperament, phonology and the evolution of place names. He learned widely, and was a great master."[77] One of Jiang Yong's contributions was to the Rites. He wrote *The Outline of Rites* which was included in the *Siku Quanshu* and which was called "the work of essence". His other contribution was in phonology. Jiang Yong criticized Gu Yanwu's study of phonology that "studies more on investigating the ancient and less on examining the phonology,"[78] and changed Gu's ten archaic rhymes into thirteen. He managed the celestial almanac, correcting Mei Wending's theory on the growth and decline of the year. Besides Dai Zhen, Jiang Yong's students also included Jin Bang and Cheng Yaotian, who were both logicians in the study of the Rites. Dai Zhen respected Jiang Yong very much. He stated "there are few people who can match his talent and learning since Jiang Cheng, a teacher of Han Confucianism."[79] Dai Zhen was inspired and influenced by Jiang Yong academically. In the twentieth year of Qianlong, Dai Zhen was thirty-three years old. At that time he was a poor Xiucai and escaped to Beijing, in order to avoid his enemy's trap. He was poor, "getting into trouble, and with not enough food to eat; people consider him as a bohemian young scholar."[80] He brought his work to the young scholar Qian Daxin, and Qian praised him as "an unusually talented person". After that Dai Zhen became acquainted with a group of Jinshi, scholars such as Wang Mingsheng, Qian Daxin, Lu Wenchao, Wang Chang, Ji Yun and Zhu Jun. They all admired Dai Zhen's knowledge and "are attracted to visit him by his reputation. They learned his knowledge, listened to his speech, and read his books, and all admired him greatly. Therefore he acquired a reputation in the capital, and famous aristocrats swarmed to associate with him."[81] Qin Huitian, *Silang* of the Ministry of Punishments, invited him to compile *The Encyclopedia of Five Rites* and Wang Anguo, Shangshu of the Ministry of Official Personnel Affairs, appointed him to teach his son Wang Niansun. In the twenty-second year of Qianlong, Dai Zhen visited Yangzhou, lived in the Salt Transportation official Lu Jianzeng's Yayu Hall, and met Hui Dong. "Hui and Dai met each other in Yangzhou, and have a high regard for each other."[82] Dai Zhen became *Juren* when he was forty years old, and did not pass the metropolitan examination. He then traveled about in Jiangxi, Jiangsu, Zhili and Shanxi, invited by officials to compile books. When he was fifty-five years old, he was summoned and became an official compiling the *Siku Quanshu* as *Juren*. He failed in the metropolitan examination again when he was fifty-three years old, but was specially permitted to take part in the final imperial examination and awarded Shu Jishi (an official name) in the Imperial Academy. He died in his fifty-fifth year. He had many students. For example Duan Yucai, Wang Niansun, Ren Dachun and Kong Guangsen had all studied with him.

Dai Zhen's academic achievements were excellent among the scholars in the middle Qing Dynasty. He studied widely and his judgment and solutions were careful. His difference from other Sinologists was that he wrote many theoretical articles which attacked Cheng-Zhu Neo-Confucianism, and explicated his thought creatively. Wang Zhong, a scholar in later times, commented on the academics of the Qing Dynasty, "many scholars emerged suddenly, which was a new beginning after 2,000 years' of abandonment...Ting Lin (Gu Yanwu) was the first; the legend of *Hetu Luoshu* was insufficient for Hu Shi (Hu Wei); Chinese and Western ways of calculating celestial phenomena and the calendar were precise to Mei Shi (Mei Wending); Yan Shi (Yan Ruoqu) tried hard to study ancient essays; Hui Shi (Hui Dong) specialized in Han Confucianism; and Dong Yuan (Dai Zhen) epitomized them."[83] Wang Zhong's respect for Dai Zhen was not exaggerated.

Dai Zhen's academic achievements were also expressed in the fields of phonology and characters. He made contributions to the division of archaic rhyme and the analysis of the category of sounds. Gu Yanwu divided the archaic rhyme into ten parts, while Jiang Yong divided it into thirteen parts, and Dai Zhen divided it into nine categories and twenty-five parts. He was good at examining pronunciations. He started from examining pronunciations and then divided the categories of sounds, matching pronunciations and sounds, and balancing the rhyme group. He inherited Gu Yanwu and Jiang Yong's theories and made creative progress. He also inquired into the meanings from ancient characters' pronunciations and sounds, and he established the principle that "pronunciations and sounds influenced each other very much." He said: "books of characters were mainly about exegesis, and books of rhythm were mainly about sound, but both of them always had a relationship. Some sounds did not change according to the exegesis, which were one sound with more than one meaning; some sounds changed according to the exegesis, which were one character with more sounds. Generally one word had one original meaning; in addition, this pronunciation and meaning was extended and were all phonetic loan characters in the six categories of Chinese characters. Its category and meaning came from its pronunciation...or with the same pronunciation and different meanings...or with different pronunciations and different meanings... the method of phonetic loan characters in the six categories of Chinese characters could be inferred by examples."[84] He explained that in order to make clear the meaning of much ancient Chinese it was necessary to use sounds to find synonymous characters and phonetic loan characters. Because Dai Zhen was good at traditional philology, and started from the basic skill of rhyme and exegesis, he made great achievements in the study of the classics. When Dai Zhen summarized his method of classics study he said that "this study was nothing more than using words to examine the classics, and using classics to examine words,"[85] "if one wanted to know the meaning of one word, he should read through a group of classics, use the six categories of Chinese characters, and then fix the meaning."[86] Ji Yun praised that "Dai understands ancient people's traditional philology, so his textual research on the meaning of words cannot be held back by Han Confucianism, and therefore he pursues the sages' remaining classics and is more inventive."[87]

Besides phonology and exegesis, Dai Zhen did much textual research on the name of things, systems and classics, for example, the book *Pictures of the Kaogong Record* used many parts of the original book of *The Record of Kaogong* and the annotations of Zheng Kangcheng. Another example was that in *Shangshu, Yao Standard* no one suspected the phrase "*Guang Bei Si Biao* (光被四表)", but Dai Zhen thought that "*Guang* (光)" was a wrong character and should be written "*Heng* (横)" according to *The Biography of Kong Anguo*, and *Erya*. He said that in ancient times,"*Heng*" was equal to"*Guang* (桄)", so"*Guang*" was miswritten as "*Guang* (光)", and "*Heng Bei* (横被)" was "*Guang Bei* (廣被)". He concluded that "in the ancient Yao Standard it must have *Heng Bei Si Biao* (横被四表). "[88] Several years after he put forward this opinion, his friends, students and relatives discovered some examples of"*Heng Bei Si Biao*" or "*Heng Bei*", which proved Dai Zhen's judgment.

Dai Zhen also made achievements in the study of the ancient celestial almanac. He combined the theory of ancient astronomy with related material in the ancient classics, which solved some difficulties in the ancient celestial almanac. For example, he did textual research on "astronomical sphere and jade weighing apparatus", and also collected many ancient calculation books from the *Great Encyclopedia in the Yongle Reign*, revealing the ancient mathematical theory which had long been lost. In the aspect of ancient geography, Dai Zhen sorted out Li Daoyuan's *Water Classic and Commentary*, which mixed up scripts and annotations, and could not be read clearly. Dai Zhen sorted out this book, "examining its examples according to their geographic locations, and consulting different books."[89] He separated scripts and annotations carefully and mainly recovered the true features of the *Water Classic and Commentary*.[90]

Dai Zhen was not only an excellent textual criticism scholar, but also a distinguished philosopher. Besides annotating the classics he also explicated materialistic philosophy, and set out anti-feudal thinking. On the one hand he focused on textual research and explanation of phonology, exegesis, the name of a thing, and systems, and said: "people in the current time do not learn words when they read books, so it was not strange that they always looked at the explanations of words in ancient books. The reason might be that if they knew little about the words, they could not learn their language; if they knew little about the language, they could not learn their quintessence."[91] He thought that only if the words, name of things, and systems in ancient books were all made clear could one understand these books' meaning. On the other hand, he did not stop with phonology, exegesis, and textual research, but emphasized the ideological content of the work, which was the so-called "argumentation" and "foundation". He described himself as "focusing on learning some principles", and said that annotations and textual research were just methods of "learning some principles". Although he was the leader of the Sinologists, he was dissatisfied with most Sinologists who adhered to ancient exegesis of classics, avoiding mentioning "argumentation". He said "argumentation is the source of articles and evaluations. Being familiar with argumentation, one can do the textual research, and then learn the articles;"[92] "a noble man should devote his efforts to learning principles. People who have wide knowledge, and can write articles and are good at textual research in current days do not focus on learning principles, but just hold on stubbornly to pre-Confucian theories."[93] He disapproved of this attitude to study which only did textual research and stuck to accepted theories without talking about ideological content. He thought that other people would obliterate his published philosophical and social thinking with his achievements in annotations and textual research. Therefore he declared: "things of the six books and Jiushu (name of ancient algorithm) are like Jiaofu who were used to carry sedan chairs. If one thinks that the six books and Jiushu are my only achievements, it is like considering the sedan bearer as the people who are in the sedan."[94] The *Interpretation of Mencius Concepts* was Dai Zhen's most important philosophical work. Dai Zhen said: "the *Interpretation of Mencius Concepts* is my most important book, which is used to correct people's thinking."[95] However ordinary people including Dai Zhen's friends and students could not understand Dai Zhen's academic tenet and always respected his achievements on textual research but paid no attention to his ideological thinking.

Dai Zhen inherited the materialistic tradition of the first years of the Qing Dynasty, and fiercely attacked idealistic Cheng-Zhu Neo-Confucianism. He opposed the Confucians' theory that "the principle comes before the material", he thought "material" was primary and was the origin of the cosmic inventory, and the occurrence and development of the nature was "the moving procedure of Yin and Yang", in other words, it was the movement of material. He said: "the moving procedure of Yin and Yang will continue and multiply forever, which is called principle. Yi said that Yin and Yang were called principle. In the Hongfan five elements, the first one was water; the second one was fire; the third one was wood, the forth one was gold, and the fifth one was soil. Xing was the general name of them."[96] "Dao" and "Yin and Yang, and the five elements" he said were all materials. In Dai Zhen's opinion, "principle" was only the moving rule of "material", and was secondary. "Occurrence is the origin of change, while occurrence with methods makes the change develop,"[97] "principle" was the method of material, which could only exist in every specific material, not on or outside material, so it was also called "divided principles". He said: "material does not have additional principles, but all material has its own principle", "material means things. Talking about things is inextricably linked with daily bread. Abandoning material to talk about 'principle' was not the 'principle' meant by ancient sages."[98] Dai Zhen opposed fiercely the "principle" which was above everything excessively praised by Confucians. He thought this mysterious and empty "principle" did not exist and was copied from Buddhism: "thinking 'principle' is the master of 'material' is like Buddhism considering 'spirit' as the master of 'material'; thinking 'principle' can make 'material' is like Buddhism considering 'spirit' can make 'material'."[99]

From the materialistic position, Dai Zhen put forward the theory of human nature and human desire, which was the most splendid and militant part of his thinking. He objected to dividing human nature into "the nature of argumentation" and "the nature of material" as put forward by Song Confucians. The Song Confucians considered "the nature of argumentation" as a sink of iniquity which produced "human desires", but Dai Zhen disagreed with this point of view. He thought that "nature" was the partition of the natural world, and "the difference between nature and things was that nature was divided into Yin, Yang and the five elements with blood and heart", "blood and heart were the entity of the nature."[100] Therefore nature was "the nature of temperament", the congenital "nature of argumentation" highly praised by Song Confucians did not exist. Human beings had their nature, and things had their nature too. The human nature was "Quan" naturally, and the nature of things was "Qu" naturally, so the human nature was "kindness". Dai Zhen respected human nature very much, and he thought that human nature included desire, emotion and judgment. "Desire" was the wish to experience sound, color and smell; "emotion" was the feelings of pleasure, anger, sorrow and joy; "judgment" was the ability to distinguish between beauty and ugliness. He said: "after their birth, people start to have desire, emotion and judgment. The three parts are produced by blood and heart naturally. People who have desire, have sound, color and smell, so they have love and fear; people will generate emotions, and they have pleasure, anger, sorrow and joy, so they have tragedy and comfort; people who have judgment can distinguish beauty from ugliness, so they have likes and dislikes. The desire for sound, color and smell can help to keep one in good health, and the feelings of pleasure, anger, sorrow and joy have a relationship with things; the judgment of beauty and ugliness can connect with the world...all are the nature."[101] He thought that when the human body was formed there was desire, emotion and judgment. Therefore, he opposed the Song Confucians' "pursuing heavenly principles, and destroying human nature" and "curbing people's temper and desires". In Dai Zhen's opinion, "desire" was a natural physiological requirement which possessed by everyone, and could not be destroyed. "Desire" was not "the root of all evil" which was the opinion of Confucians. So long as the "desire" was under the guidance of reason, developed according to the principle, and was fulfilled abstemiously, it was "kindness" and "humanity". He said: "desire is about the nature...if the desire was not before privacy, it was humanity;" "if people's desire has a relationship with the world's desire, it is humanity;" "sages administered the world, and investigated people's condition, so if they satisfied people's desire, it was a benevolent government."[102] Dai Zhen's morality was opposite to that of the Confucians. His was based on respecting human nature, and admitted people's desire. He thought that Cheng-Zhu Neo-Confucianism considered common people's "hunger, cold, anxiety and resentment" and "reason and hidden feelings" as extremely evil "human desire", so it obliterated common people's proper demand for survival. This was very cruel and hypocritical. According to Zhu Xi's theory that "heavenly principles and human desire cannot exist at the same time", he put forward the theory that "reason depends on desires,"[103] "action comes before desires, and the action which is proper and cannot be changed is called principle. How reasonable is the theory of no desire and action?"[104]

Dai Zhen exposed the so called "principle" of Neo-Confucians boldly, pointing out that their "principle" was not the truth but their own subjective prejudice, and an excuse for the stronger to bully and oppress the weaker. He pointed out that in the real world power was the general acknowledged truth, and criticized and lashed out at the feudal system and feudal Neo-Confucianism. He said:

> When a foolish person who was perverse and reckless handled something or censured a person, he always talked about the principle. This started to become a custom in the Song Dynasty, so they considered principles as material, getting them from the heaven and keeping them in mind, so they just complied with their opinion. Therefore for those who were strong and eloquent, their principles could be extended; those who were weak and did not have a glib tongue could not appeal to good reasoning. Alas! Who called it a rule, and it is not reasonable to govern people with it![105]
>
> The superior blamed the inferior using principle; the old blamed the young using principle; the noble blamed the ignoble using principle, and although they were wrong, they had to be obeyed. The inferior, the old, the young and the ignoble argued with them, and although they were right they were called disobedient...the upper used principles to blame the lower, and the lower was scolded by everyone. If a person died of the law, someone might sympathize with him, but if he died of principles, who would sympathize with him?[106]
>
> The later Confucians knew nothing about it and did not have any resentment, which was called principles. However people who called it principles used it like the cruel officials' law. Cruel officials used the law to kill people, and the later Confucians killed people with principles. Then the law was abandoned gradually. It was hopeless...the later Confucians calmed down and pursued principles. They focused on the law of Shang and Han, so when they learned their law, they did not know the conditions of the people. Since then there were more and more scholars who were behind the times, and when they blamed common people, people could not argue and refute them. These scholars thought of themselves as mastering principles, but many people were victimized.[107]

This was terrible and we did not know how many innocent weak people were sacrificed in the name of "principle". "Later Confucians killed people with principles", accused and attacked drastically according to feudal ethical code, and hit the crucial point of Neo-Confucianism. Besides suppressing people's resistance with military force directly, the feudal autocracy bound people's hands and feet with law and the feudal ethical code. Dai Zhen mentioned feudal "law" and "principle" in the same breath and considered them as the butcher's knife of the rulers, which was a very deep and bold view on politics.

It should be noted that Dai Zhen lived in the reign of Emperors Yongzheng and Qianlong, when the feudal autocracy controlled culture strictly and literary inquisitions emerged endlessly. Cheng-Zhu Neo-Confucianism was the ideological pillar of the Qing Dynasty's regime and the tool to maintain the old system and suppress new things. The Qing Dynasty respected Neo-Confucianism vigorously and several literary inquisitions happened because of opposing Cheng-Zhu Neo-Confucianism. Dai Zhen's criticism of Cheng-Zhu Neo-Confucianism was not only a struggle in thinking and academics, but also a political fight in a clever form of annotating *The Mencius*. The cutting edge of his criticism was actually aimed at the feudal autocracy and the cruel domination of the Qing Dynasty. Zhang Taiyan pointed out it exactly, "Dai Zhen...was born in the joint time of Yongzheng and Qianlong, and saw their imperial decree exile people, so he used Chen-Zhu exordium to trifle with the law. People would lose their heads, so he wrote *Yuanshan*, and *Interpretation of Mencius Concepts* to bitterly attack that moral principles and human desires were different from the truth...in order to get the effect of aiming at a pigeon and shooting at a crow."[108]

Of course, Dai Zhen was a naïve materialist and did not have a clear understanding of some issues. For example, he did not understand the objectivity of truth and said "something could be called principles if they are the same as what are in mind."[109] He did not pay attention to practice either, and said "it is not Confucian learning if practice comes before knowledge."[110] Especially when he referred to social and historical issues, he sank into idealism. Dai Zhen deviated from human beings' social and class nature, and assigned people with natural lust abstractly, which was not scientific. Therefore he could not explain human beings' nature, morality and desire correctly. Dai Zhen struggled with the feudal code of ethics and Cheng-Zhu Neo-Confucianism, and he strived for the liberation of individuality in his thinking. But generally speaking, Dai Zhen was still a thinker of the feudal class. He respected Confucius and Mencius, and considered himself as recovering and inheriting Confucian learning. His scope of study was limited to the Confucian classics, and could not break out of the cage of feudal academia.

The continuation of Sinology

When an academic school and thinking trend arrives at its peak, it will become divided. People who stand outside this school and trend will attack it, and those who belong to this school and trend will hold different positions and have different understanding and evaluation of the tenets of their own school as times change in order to correct, improve and even disintegrate and create new schools and trends during the practice of study. Ideology and academia develop constantly. Every kind of view debates with each other and the elitists join together, moving forward forever.

Dai Zhen was the peak of the Sinology in the Qing Dynasty. He not only opened up a new academic method which was different from Song and Ming Confucianism, established a new style and made new contributions with his profound knowledge and precise textual research, but he also criticized Cheng-Zhu Neo-Confucianism's idealistic preaching with his profound and careful thinking, which enraged a batch of Neo-Confucianism apologists. They had to admit Dai Zhen's achievements in textual research, but they opposed his "theory of argumentation". Weng Fanggang, a poet who was contemporary with Dai Zhen, said: "in recent days, Dai Zhen of Xiuning city has tried hard on the study of the name of things and Xiangshu, profound and diligent, but actually he just did textual research on one aspect of it! However, he was not content with his contributions on textual research and wanted to talk about human desires, in order to hold an unconventional point of view which was different from Cheng-Zhu."[111] Yao Nai, another five classics scholar of the Tongcheng School, attacked Dai Zhen saying that "because of not reading Song Confucian books, although his study was wide, his mind might be despicable and his acts might be abnormal."[112] "It is good for Dai Dongyuan to study textual research, but he intends to talk about argumentation and fight for the seat of Luo Min, which can be called going beyond his depth."[113] Yao Nai was dissatisfied with Dai Zhen's criticism of Cheng-Zhu and he even cursed that "Cheng-Zhu is like my teacher. Maybe there are mistakes, but one can correct them. However correcting while slandering and ridiculing is defaming my Master...so he is hated by others. Therefore, Mao Dake (Qi Ling), Li Gangzhu (Gong), Cheng Mianzhuang (Tingzuo), Dai Dongyuan (Zhen) will all die without descendants."[114]

Dai Zhen was attacked by Song scholars, and there were different understandings of Dai Zhen's academic tenets within Sinologists. After Dai Zhen's death his student Hong Bang wrote a *Biographical Sketch* of him. He recorded completely *A Letter to Answer Peng Yunchu*, which was written one month before Dai Zhen's death. This book clarified thinking on Materialism, and exposed the idealistic essence of Buddhism, Taoism, Cheng-Zhu and Lu and Wang. Zhu Jun, who admired Dai Zhen's textual research deeply, was opposed to recording this book in *Biographical Sketch* and said: "it should not be recorded, because we cannot listen to his opinion on human nature and natural law. How can we think about there are expositions and argumentation except Cheng-Zhu? This is not what we should write in Dai's biography."[115] Therefore Hong Bang wrote a letter to Zhu Jun and debated with him. It could be seen that among Dai Zhen's friends and students there were different opinions. Many people just adopted Dai Zhen's contributions on the celestial almanac, exegesis, the name of things and institutions. Zhang Xuecheng, a famous historian who was Zhu Jun's student and Dai Zhen's friend, stood outside the Sinological camp and was the earliest to criticize Sinology. His attitude to Dai Zhen was different from that of Zhu Jun. Zhang Xuecheng said "all study of Dai Zhen is proficient in exegesis, and he knows principles before the system of name of things, which is helpful to understand the principles. Fang Gui who had profound knowledge and was contemporary with Dai Zhen did textual research, and when he saw Dai Zhen's exegesis and name of things, he thought they were good and considered them as Dai's highest attainments. When Dai wrote *The Discussion of Nature* and *Yuanshan*, his point of view about heaven, humanity, principles and argumentation really were new opinions which had not previously been talked about, but people who were contemporary with Dai Zhen considered them as empty and useless argumentation which was not essential. They did not understand Dai Zhen's thinking."[116] It seems that this paragraph of discussion was written aimed at his teacher Zhu Jun.

Although Sinology was much criticized, it still took up the leading position in academic thinking circles, which was termed "every person talked about Xu and Zheng, while every family focused on Jia and Ma", and the later scholars were strongly influenced by Sinology. In the academic circles of the late 18th century: one school such as Duan Yucai, Wang Niansun and his son Wang Yinzhi inherited Dai Zhen's exegesis and textual research using a stricter method with excellent results, but they did not refer to abstract "argumentation" and gave up anti-Song study; another school such as Eang Zhong, Ling Tingkan, Jiao Xun and Ruan Yuan studied both exegesis and textual research, and argumentation, developing Dai Zhen's philosophical thinking continuously, but their discussion was more moderate and Sinology and Song thinking were moving together; another school such as Zhuang Cunyu and Kong Guangsen separated from Sinology, moved from respecting the Eastern Han's ancient Chinese classics to current Chinese classics, and made a fresh start and created new schools; one school such as Zhang Xuecheng always stood outside Sinology and criticized textual research, establishing their own thinking system; another school such as Wang Fenggang and Yao Nai to Fang Dongshu andDang Jian stood on the position of the Song scholars and did their utmost to attack Sinology.

Dai Zhen's lineal disciples were Duan Yucai, Wang Niansun and his son Wang Yinzhi. They studied widely with a strict attitude to study and scientific methods, and pushed exegesis and textual research to a new peak. Duan and Wang were both good at "recounting the general idea", which meant they sought "regulations" from numerous and complicated ancient books with the method of induction, and then made deductions based on the "regulations" in order to make clear the ancient Chinese characters' pronunciations and exegesis and correct mistakes in ancient books. Through this method they made great achievements, restoring a lot of ancient literature.

Duan Yucai (1735–1815, from the thirteenth year of Yongzheng reign to the twentieth year of Jiaqing), named Ruoying, was from Jintan, Jiangsu province. His most important work was *The Annotation of the Origin of Chinese Characters. The Origin of Chinese Characters* was written by Xu Shen in the Eastern Han. It contained more than nine thousand three hundred characters, and explained their meaning, pattern and pronunciation, which was an important tool for later generations to read ancient literature and study ancient characters. Duan Yucai made a detailed annotation of Xu Shen's book, corrected his mistakes, and clarified his phonology and exegesis. Lu Wenchao said that Duan's *The Annotation of the Origin of Chinese Characters* "all has evidence, which is different from assumptions. He did a thorough investigation and debated widely, and no other previous books of the same type of literature were better than this book."[117] Wang Niansun said that "there had been no such works in thousands of years."[118] Wang Guowei also praised the book, saying that "he has judicious judgment through the ages, and no other people who wrote the same form of literature could explain so clearly within 2,000 years."[119]

Wang Niansun (1722–1832, from the ninth year of Qianlong to the twelfth year of Daoguang), named Huai Zu, was from Gaoyou, Jiangsu province. He wrote eighty-two volumes of *The Record of Reading* and twenty-two volumes of *Interpretation of Guangya. The Record of Reading* examined and corrected character mistakes and exegesis in various ancient books combined with Wang's wide knowledge and method of emendation and grammar analysis, "in order to improve on characters, he invoked hundreds of thousands of books, making careful explanation, which could not be expected from others."[120] "When someone establishes a theory they must list ancient books, used wide evidence, and then make final decision. It can then be convincing, if there is no powerful disproof it cannot be refuted. The success of textual research in the Qing Dynasty was because of its precise method, and this book was a representative."[121] For example, in the book of *Huainaizi*, there were many omissions and errors. Wang Niansun corrected more than nine hundred

Fig. 11.5. Portraits of Duan Yucai (left) and Wang Niansun (right)

mistakes based on Taoism's collected scriptures and the Ming copy, and using other quotations in other carving copies and ancient books for reference. He also summarized several reasons which led to these mistakes. The *Interpretation of Guangya* was a book to collate and explain Zhang Yi's *Guangya*, and corrected 580 wrongly written characters, 490 missing characters, 39 redundant characters, 132 perversions and 69 confused texts and pronunciations in the original book. According to the principle that ancient characters with similar pronunciations and meaning could replace each other, he did textual research from a character's exegesis, "extending meaning, and containing many categories", and connected many characters, finding out their connections. Ruan Yuan said: "before the Han Dynasty, Cang and Ya both gathered and proved them. The exegesis originally focused on pronunciation, and sought the ancient meanings with ancient pronunciations, extended in meaning, which expanded outside the *Erya* and *The Origin of Chinese Characters*. He seemed to penetrate everywhere, but the part on pronunciations and characters was strict without disorder. He made use of Zhang Yi's book to take in every theory, adding much content unknown by Zhang Yi, and Hui Dingyu and Dai Dongyuan as well."[122]

Wang Yinzhi (1766–1834, from the thirtieth year of Qianlong to the fourteenth year of Daoguang), named Bo Shen, was Wang Niansun's son. He was the Shangshu of the Ministry of Works and wrote ten volumes of

The Explanation of Function Words and thirty-two volumes of the *Study on Classics*. *The Explanation of Function Words* was to study ancient function words in works, and recorded 160 words. He did textual research on the source and evolution, explaining meaning and functions; the *Study on Classics* was to study phonology and exegesis and correct omissions and errors, however this book was written from fragmentary results into a systematical academic essay. Because most of the study results were cited from his father Niansun's theories, Wang Yinzhi named it the *Study on Classics*. Wang Niansun and Wang Yinzhi made great contributions on language, characters and emendations. Their works were all conclusions reached through summing up a great number of materials, and had high scientific value. Ruan Yuan said "no one can match the knowledge of Wang of Gaoyou city."[123] Zhang Taiyan said: "the Wangs of Gaoyou city explained Han's ancient books with their erudition, and no other people within thousands of years were like them."[124] People who held the position of attacking Sinology had to admire Wang's academic achievements. Fang Dongshu said in the *Discussion and Consideration of Sinology* that "the *Study on Classics* of the Wangs of Gaoyou city make Zheng and Zhu bow their heads, and no people can compare with them since the Han and Tang Dynasties."[125]

Other scholars differed from Duan and Wang. They took part in annotations and textual research, but were not limited to textual research and also talked about "argumentation". Their method of study was similar to that of Dai Zhen and although they did not learn from Dai Zhen directly, they all admired Dai Zhen and most of them were Dai's disciples who had not taken lessons directly under the master himself. They were Wang Zhong, Ling Tingkan, Jiao Xun and Ruan Yuan.

Wang Zhong (1744–1794, from the ninth year of Qianlong to the 59th year of Qianlong), named Rong Fu, was from Jiangdu of Jiangsu province. He was born into a poor intellectual family, and his father died when he was young. He was raised by his mother, and led a hard life. He had been an apprentice in a bookshop, so he had the chance to read books. When he became Bagong (a kind of intellectual who went into the Imperial College from local provinces in the imperial examination system), he gave up becoming a Juzi in order to earn his living. He became the guest and adviser of high officials for a long time. He also studied emendation and exegesis, and focused on practice. He said in his tenet of study that "people who studied personally under the master, Guningren and recluses had put forward the tenet of six classics, which were suitable for use in the world. As to the study of archaeology, we must be practical and realistic, but not stick to convention."[126] He inherited the tradition of anti-Confucianism and pointed out that the *Great Learning* which was respected by Confucians was not written by Confucius. He said "when the disciples refer to Confucius's words, they say 'Zi says', 'Zi talks about it', 'Confucius says', and 'the teacher says that' to stress Confucius. We do not know who wrote the *Great Learning*, but just assume it was written by Confucius without evidence."[127] Wang Zhong thought that in order to control academic thinking, the Song-Confucians had put the *Great Learning* at the head of the Four Books and stubbornly insisted on it as the teaching essence of Confucianism. He also attacked the old feudal ethical code, and objected to asking women to maintain chastity after the death of their husband or to die with their husband. Wang Zhong paid more attention to the study of the philosophers. He collated and examined Lao Zi, Mo Zi, Xun Zi, the new book of Jia Yi, and the Spring and Autumn annals of the Lu family, and opened up the scope of study. He highly praised Xun Zi, and thought that Xun Zi was the real inheritor of the theory of Confucius. He spoke in defense of Mo Zi and thought that it was slander that Mencius called Mo Study "no father". Wang Zhong had the courage to appraise and discuss people in ancient and modern society, so his thinking was unfettered for the times and therefore he was envied and hated by some people. Lu Wenchao said that he "did not forgive ancient people and figured out their mistakes; let alone people in current time. People feared his words and wanted to kill him."[128] Wang Zhong intended to write an academic study on ancient history on a great scale, and its name was *A Statement on Study*, but unfortunately he did not finish it. The extant book entitled *A Statement on Study* is a collection of all Wang Zhong's articles by his son, which was not as what Wong Zhong intended.

Ling Tingkan (1755–1809, from the 20th year of Qianlong to the 14th year of Jiaqing), named Ci Chong, was from Shexian, Anhui province. He tried hard to respect his fellow academics from Anhui Jiang Yong, and Dai Zhen's academy, and opposed Song-Ming Confucianism. He thought that Zhu Xi and Wang Yangming had both stolen from Buddhism and Lao Zi's ideology, which violated the legitimacy of Confucianism. He said in his poem that "the study of Yangming was just the study of Kao Ting, and they stole the book and the country. Now the two schools scold each other and are ignorant when investigating ancient explanations."[129] Lin Tingkan studied rites carefully, and wrote three pieces of *Reply to Rites*. He thought that rites were psychic principle, and standard of behavior, "the morality of sages was just one rite."[130] He opposed the "reason" advocated by Neo-Confucians, and held the opinion that using "rites" to take place of "reasons", "the sages sought rites instead of reasons, people who pursued reasons must become self-approbation, but people who pursued rites could recover their human nature."[131] Lin Tingkan could be called the reserving force of anti-Song Confucianism, but he advocated going back to pedantic "rites", and still not jumped over the barrier of feudal ideology. Lin Tingkan wrote *The Annotation of the Rites Classic*, and he thought that the seventeen pieces of the *Ritual* were "impressive, dignified, and complicated. When reading them, one could find that they were all in an orderly way with main points", and that one must read through the book using inductive methods to find out "examples" in the book. The "example" was the main point of this book, "its macroscopic outline and detailed items were all based on examples."[132] In addition, he also studied ancient music and investigated Yan music in the Tang Dynasty, writing *The Investigation on Yan Music*.

Jiao Xun (1763–1820 or from the 28th year of Qianlong to the 20th year of Jiaqing), named Li Tang, was from Ganquan, Jiangsu province. He became a Juren in his middle age and then gave up taking part in the imperial examination. He did not want to become an official and closed the door in order to read books. He admired Dai Zhen, and described himself as "reading Dai Dongyuan's book and admiring his *Interpretation of Mencius Concepts*."[133] He was proficient in astronomy, mathematics and exegesis, and studied Mao Poems, Three Rites, *The Analects,* and *Mencius*. He was especially good at *Yi*, and wrote *The General Explanation of Yi, The Brief Drawing of Yi,* and *The Chapters of Yi*, which were called the *Three Books of Yi*. He thought that"Xiangcuo","Pangtong" and "Shixing" were the three principles of the *Yi* Classics which continued through the whole book. "Xiangcuo" was the unification with opposite things; "Pangtong" meant changing with a harmonious order; "Shixing" was the circulation of change. Jiao Xun established his own philosophical thinking system based on the classics, and he admitted contradictions and emphasized change, but he also tended to the theory of coordination and cycle. Most Sinologists at that time only focused on textual research, and playing with the words, so Jiao Xun was out of the ordinary. He made use of his knowledge of mathematics in the study of *Yi*, "using the proportion of number to find out the proportion of *Yi*", and he also paid attention to "actual measurement". He said that"*Yi* is like the heaven. We cannot know the heaven, but we can know it from actual measurement...based on the degree of operation to do the measurement, the heaven will be clear. Based on classics to do the measurement, *Yi* will be clear. Empty reason cannot be used, and the unfaithful mind cannot be used to measure it."[134] His study method broke the barrier of exegesis over successive dynasties, and therefore he made new achievements. Wang Yinzhi praised him highly as "talking about *Yi* with books in hand. He made *Yi* clear and could be called a select man. He weighed every word, and pursued precisely and exactly. He used proportion in his method. Proportion was not in other books but was in his book."[135]

Jiao Xun's philosophy was a changing philosophy. He respected "flexibility", and thought "kindheartedness and justice are flexible. People are flexible, so they are kind; things are not flexible, so they are not kind."[136] Because of the changing of the world, institutions, systems and sages' speech were all conditional, and were not the final truth, "well fields and feudalism were systems of the sages, but were not usable in later generations, so the sage words were no definitive. They were definite for a while, but were not the truth forever. Some were definitive in one place but not in other places; some were suitable for one people, but not usable by everyone; this was the reason why sages focused on flexibility."[137] He realized that things had two contradictory aspects and he asked for holding on to the two aspects to get full comprehension. He said "the heretic persists in one aspect, and people who persist in one aspect just know one aspect but do not know the other,"[138] "those persisting in one aspect were heretics, but those persisting in two aspects were sages."[139] His academic tenet was to blend public theories and to absorb anything and everything. He opposed uniting with those of the same views but alienating those with different views. He said "everybody has his strong points. It is better to take them rather than get rid of them."[140] Jiao Xun belonged to the Sinologist camp but was dissatisfied with those who only defended Sinologists' works, and said that "those defenders trusted the ancient, and thought that ancient works were all the truth. They just protect their theories without thinking about them, and they dare not discuss them...their disadvantage was to be narrow and limited."[141] Therefore he tended towards reconciling Sinology and Song Confucianism.

Ruan Yuan (1764–1849, from the 29th year of Qianlong to the 29th year of Daoguan), was named Bo Yuan and his alias was Yun Tai. He was from Zhengyi in Jiangsu province. He was a Jinshi, and had been in the position of civil and military governor, finally becoming the grand secretary of Tirenge. He advocated academic study actively, and compiled and printed books. He also established an academy of classical learning and rewarded talented people. His method of pursuing studies was similar to that of Dai Zhen. He also advocated the clarification of the meaning of the ancient classics through phonology and exegesis, in order to find out its "argumentation". He said "the principles of sages existed in the classics. Without exegesis it is difficult to make the classics clear, and the Han's classics were close to those of the sages."[142] However Ruan Yuan was different from Duan Yucai and Wang Niansun. Duan and Wang did not talk about "argumentation", and as a school their disadvantage was that they were trivial and narrow; Ruan Yuan considered phonology and exegesis as a necessary tool to seek "argumentation", and his final aim was to pursue

Fig. 11.6. A Portrait of Ruan Yuan

"argumentation". He said "the sages' principle was like the palace wall. Characters and exegesis were its approach and if the approach was wrong, all steps were wrong, so how could they have profound scholarship? Or they only pursued the name of things without seeking sages' principles, which was like sleeping between the gate and the side room, and didn't know there was a hall and other rooms!"[143]

Ruan Yuan made textual criticisms and explanations of the word "benevolence" using his own method. He counted that there were one hundred and five meanings and usage of the word "benevolence" in *The Analects of Confucius*, and he thought that the original meaning of "benevolence" was "the encounter between people", which pointed out the relationship between people. This was a method of pursuing ancient exegesis with ancient meaning. He objected to the Song scholars' empty explanation that "life and growth was called benevolence" and was also against pursing benevolence with action. He said "benevolence must be experienced in person, and two people are also necessary. If just one person closes the door and sits quietly with closed eyes, although there may be morality and principle in his mind, this could not be called the sages' benevolence."[144] Ruan Yuan said some words to reconcile Sinology and Song Confucianism, and he did not criticize Cheng-Zhu directly, but his thinking was different from the scholars of Neo-Confucianism. His textual criticisms and explanations of "nature" and "life" had the significance of anti-Neo-Confucianism. He took the usage and meaning of life in *Zhaogao* and *Mencius, With all Heart* as examples, and then put the classics and ancient exegesis in order, and he thought "nature" in the ancient classics was different from the explanation of scholars of Neo-Confucianism. Ruan Yuan said "nature comes from the heart, which means blood, breath and mind;" "taste, color, sound, smell, pleasure, anger, sorrow and joy are all from human nature, and generated from feeling."[145] However scholars of Neo-Confucianism said "nature is without desire" and "desire is the evil", and advocated "guarding against losing one's temper and repressing one's sexual passion." Ruan Yuan refuted that "desire generated from emotion and in the nature. We couldn't say that there were no desire in nature, but the desire had nothing to do with evil. Since people were born with blood, breath and mind, they couldn't live without desire, and only Buddhism said there was no desire...so Mencius said taste, color, sound and smell all belonged to nature."[146] Ruan Yuan admitted the rationality of sexual passion, which obviously came down in one continuous line with Dai Zhen's thinking.

Notes

Chapter 8

1. "Karl Marx," in *Selected Works of Lenin*, vol. 2 (People's Publishing House, 1972), 587.
2. "The Communist Manifesto," in *Selected Works of Marx and Engels*, vol. 1, 251.
3. Footnote of "The Land Program of the Russian Social Democratic Party," in *Collected Works of Lenin*, vol. 6, 93.
4. *Qianlong Xupu xian zhi*, vol. 9, 2.
5. *Qianlong Tongxiang xian zhi*, vol. 7, 2
6. The so-called "violation of imperial edict and law" refers to the provision that "Anyone who deliberately violates the imperial edicts shall be given 100 strokes of the cane" stipulated in the official law, formula and imperial edicts in the *Great Qing Legal Code*.
7. *Daiqing lüli tongkao*, vol. 27, 44.
8. Refer to the volume 2 of this series, 103.
9. *Qianlong Guangshan xian zhi*, vol. 19.
10. *Yuhua Tang liangjiang shigao*, 57.
11. Zhang Xintai, *Yueyao xiaoshi*, vol. 3.
12. "Report of Shan Censor of the Censorate on Manchu and Han Volumes," *Neige daku dang'an*.
13. *Qing Renzong shilu*, vol. 97 (the 4th month of the 7th year).
14. "Yongzheng period," *Donghua lu*, vol. 9 (the 11th month of the 4th year).
15. Quoted from *Manzu jianshi*, 84.
16. *Qingchao wenxian tongkao*, vol. 5.
17. *Qingchao wenxian tongkao*, vol. 198.
18. Documents on which the Ministry of Justice consulted the Imperial Household Department, files of *Neiwufu laiwen*, (the 6th month of the 25th year of the Qianlong period).
19. *Yongzheng zhupi yuzhi*, vol. 39, 89.
20. "Yongzheng period," *Donghua lu*, vol. 10 (the 4th month of the 5th year).
21. *Qing Shizong shilu*, vol. 81 (the 5th month of the 7th year).
22. "Yongzheng period," *Donghua lu*, vol. 2 (the 3rd month of the 1st year).
23. Ibid., 10 (the 4th month of the 5th year).
24. *Qing Shizong shilu*, vol. 81 (the 5th month of the 7th year).
25. Ibid., vol. 94, the 5th month of the 8th year.
26. Chen Hongmou, "Letter to Yang Jingsu," *Huangchao jingxi wenbian*, vol. 66.
27. "Annals of District and County," *Tongzhi Suzhou fu zhi*, preface of vol. 3.
28. Zhang Haishan, "On Inhabit Together," *Huangchao jingxi wenbian*, vol. 58.
29. *Guangzhu Shitai Dushi zongpu*, vol. 1.
30. See *Qufu Kongshi dangan shiliao xuanbian*, 3rd edition, vol. 1, 6, 1124.1.
31. Ibid.

32. "Clan Village of the Lujiang Zhang Family," *Wei Yuan ji*, vol. 2, 502.
33. "Clan Norm," *Yunyang Tushi zupu*, vol. 11.
34. Gu Donggao, "Discussions on Grandson Burying Grandparents," *Huangchao jingxi wenbian*, vol. 64.
35. "Sacrifice in Spring," *Jingzhao Guishi shipu*, vol. 1.
36. "Clan Norm," *Yunyang Tushi zupu*, vol. 11.
37. "Punishing Evil," *Chenshi zongpu*, vol. 1.
38. "Family Regulations," *Zhangshi zongpu*, vol. 2.
39. "Family Instruments," *Jingjiang Wangshi zupu*.
40. "Family Instructions," *Xuxiu Xushi jiapu*, vol. 1.
41. *Qufu Kongshi dangan shiliao xuanbian*, 3rd edition, 4993.
42. *Zhuxi Shenshi jiacheng*, vol. 1.
43. "Family Regulations," *Chenshi zongpu*, vol. 1.
44. Ancestral Temples," *Huangchao jingxi wenbian*, vol. 66.
45. Wu Rongguang, "Country Customs," *Foshan Zhongyi xiangzhi*, vol. 5.
46. "Ancestral Tablets," *Yunyang Tushi zupu*, vol. 12.
47. "Rules of Ancestral Temples," *Yunyang Tushi zupu*, vol. 12.
48. "Agreements of Sacrifice," *Jingjiang Wangshi zupu*.
49. "Ancestral Tablets," *Yunyang Tushi zupu*, vol. 12.
50. "Family Models," *Yunyang Tushi zupu*, vol. 11.
51. "Regulations of the Clan," *Yanshi zupu*, vol. 12.
52. "Regulations of the Clan," *Zhuxi Shenshi jiacheng*, vol. 7.
53. "Regulations of the Clan," *Chenshi zongpu*, vol. 2.
54. "Regulations of the Clan," *Zhuxi Shenshi jiacheng*, vol. 7.
55. Zhang Yongquan, "Ancestral Temple," *Huangchao jingxi wenbian*, vol. 66.
56. "Clan Fields of the Gui Family," *Jingzhao Guishi shipu*, no. 4.
57. Li Zhaoluo, *Zhaoyi Guishi jitian shutian ji*.
58. *Yanshi zupu*, vol. 12.
59. "Report on the Peasant Movement in Hunan," *Selected Works of Mao Zedong*, vol. 1, 31.
60. Sun Yuanxiang, "Clan Fields of the Gui Family," *Guishi shipu*, vol. 4.
61. Jiang Xiongchang, "Piling Chenshi xuxiu zongpu xu," *Chenshi zongpu*, vol. 1.
62. "Events," *(Guangdong) Zhaoqing fuzhi*, vol. 22.
63. Chen Hongmou, "Agreement on Electing the Head of Clan," *Huangchao jingxi wenbian*, vol. 58.
64. "Clan Village of the Lujiang Zhang Family," *Wei Yuan ji*, vol. 2, 503.
65. "Family Instructions," *Zhangshi zongpu*, vol. 2.
66. Li Shixiong, "Koubian ji," see *Data of History of the Qing Dynasty*, series 1, 46.
67. Ibid., 55.
68. Ibid., 57.
69. Zhang Haishan, "On Gathering People," *Huangchao jingxi wenbian*, vol. 58.
70. *Qing Shenzu shilu*, vol. 86 (the 12th month of the 18th year).

71. *Qing Shenzu shilu*, vol. 93 (the 11th month of the 19th year).
72. *Dayi juemi lu*.
73. "The Inadequacy of Philosophy," *Selected Works of Marx and Engels*, vol. 1, 145.
74. "Letter to Zhangyihou," *Yi wen zhi, Tongzhi Ruijin xianzhi*, vol. 11.
75. Defu, "Customs," *Minzheng lingyao*, vol. 2.
76. "Family Instructions," *Hanyang Longni Zaishi zongpu*, vol. 2.
77. *Qing Gaozong shilu*, vol. 245 (the 7th month of the 10th year).
78. "Miscellanies 2," *Guangxu Baling xian zhi*, vol. 52.
79. "Official Achievements," *Guangxu Chaozhou fu zhi*, vol. 33.
80. "Miscellanies 2," *Qianlong Guangzhou fu zhi*, vol. 60.
81. Ibid.
82. Sun Jiagan, "Public Products of the Eight Banners," *Sun Wending gong zoushu*, vol. 4.
83. *Qing Gaozong shilu*, vol. 1169.
84. File "Neiwufu laiwen" (the 2nd day of the 10th month of the 20th year of the Qianlong period).
85. Dong Han, *Sangang shilüe*, vol. 10.
86. "Qianlong period," *Donghua lu*, vol. 24 (the 8th month of the 11th year).
87. Ibid.
88. *Yongzheng zhupi yuzhi*, letter no. 18, vol. 6, presented by Yin Jishan on the 3rd day of the 6th month of the 8th year of the Yongzheng period.
89. Wang Jianan, "Remarks on Correcting Dou Presented by Guo Dongwu and Other Persons from Shanghang County," *Linting kaoyan*, vol. 18.
90. Dai Zhaojia, "Persuading the Rich to Collect Rents and Debts in a Good Manner to Alleviate the Poor Situation of the People and Protect Heaven and Things," *Tiantai zhilüe*, vol. 6.
91. "Political Achievements 2," *Tongzhi Changsha xian zhi*, vol. 20.
92. Dai Zhaojia, "Persuading the Rich to Collect Rents and Debts in a Good Manner to Alleviate the Poor Situation of the People and Protect Heaven and Things," *Tiantai zhilüe*, vol. 6.
93. Huang Zhongjian, "On Levy Taxation," *Xuzhai ji*.
94. *Qing Gaozong shilu*, vol. 329 (the 11th month of the 13th year).
95. "Warning of Bandit," *Guangxu Zhaowu xianzhi*, vol. 13.
96. "Miscellanea," *Tongzhi Xingguo xian zhi*, vol. 46.
97. "Art," *Tongzhi Yuedu xian zhi*, vol. 13.
98. "Changes of Bandit," *Tongzhi chongkan Kangxi Ninghua xian zhi*, vol. 7.
99. Ibid.
100. Yang Zhanian, "Presenting Process of Land Bandits to the Governor," *Soldier Bandit, Tongzhi Ruijin xian zhi*, vol. 16.
101. "Soldier Bandit," *Qianlong Shicheng xian zhi*, vol. 7.
102. "Annal of Military Events," *Daoguang Ningdu Zhili zhou zhi*, vol. 14.
103. "Magazine," *Jiaqing Ruian xian zhi*, vol. 10.
104. Yu Qian, *Yu Jingjie gong yishu*, vol. 4.
105. "Miscellanies," *Daoguang Yuanhe Weiting zhi*, vol. 20.
106. *Jiangsu sheng Mingqing yilai beike ziliao xuanji*, 437.

Notes

107. Wang Xianqian, "Qianlong period," *Donghua xulu*, vol. 24 (the 8th month of the 11th year).
108. *Qing Gaozong shilu*, vol. 274, the 9th month of the 11th year.
109. *Yongzheng zhupi yuzhi*, vol. 42, presented by Li Wei, etc. in the 7th month of the 8th year.
110. "Inscription of Appraising and Deciding the Wage of Chuai Jiang under Order of the Viceroy and Inspector General," *Jiangsu sheng Mingqing yilai beike ziliao xuanji*, 33.
111. "Suzhou Government Disposes the Case of Ganging, Acting Violently and Levy of Chuai Jiang Luo Gui etc., and Stipulates the Wage of Chuai Jiang in the Future," *Jiangsu sheng Mingqing yilai beike ziliao xuanji*, 34.
112. Ibid.
113. "Permanent Ban Tablet of Forgiving Observing the Ordinances of the Governor," *Jiangsu sheng Mingqing yilai beike ziliao xuanji*, 39.
114. Ibid.
115. "Chuai Jiang Agreement Kept in Changzhou and Wu County," *Jiangsu sheng Mingqing yilai beike ziliao xuanji*, 43.
116. "Household Service 6," *Huangchao zhengdian leizuan*, vol. 35.
117. "Inscription that the Suzhou Government Stipulated a Chuai Jiang's Wage for A Piece of Cloth including Timber, Vegetables, Rice is One Li Three Fen Silver," *Jiangsu sheng Mingqing yilai beike ziliao xuanji*, 49
118. "Inscription of Forever Banning Ji Jiang to ask for Breaks under the Order of Law," *Jiangsu sheng Mingqing yilai beike ziliao xuanji*, 6.
119. "Inscription of Yuanhe County for Ji Jiang Wang Nanguan and other People Gathering People to Cause Trouble in the Ji Gong Village on the Excuse of Reducing Foreign Prices," *Jiangsu sheng Mingqing yilai beike ziliao xuanji*, 13.
120. "Inscription of Yuanhe County for Wusan County of Forever Banning Candle Makers to Stop Working, Gathering People, Levying Money, Acting Violently and Causing Trouble," *Jiangsu sheng Mingqing yilai beike ziliao xuanji*, 218.
121. "Two Bureaus Discretionarily Draw up Articles of Association on Wooden Tablet," *Tongzheng bianlan*, vol. 4.
122. *Qianlong zhupi zouzhe* (the 22nd day of the 8th month of the 6th year).
123. *Qing Renzong shilu*, vol. 319 (the 27th day of the 6th month of the 21st year of the Jiaqing period).
124. Ling Tao, "Education Article," *Chronicle of the West River Inspection*, vol. 4.
125. Ibid.
126. "Inscription of Strictly Prohibiting Craftsmen in Paper-making Workshops from Controlling to Increase Wage," *Jiangsu sheng Mingqing yilai beike ziliao xuanji*, 67.
127. "Inscription of Forever Prohibiting Candle Workers from Collectively Stopping Work and Gathering to Act Violently and Make Trouble," *Jiangsu sheng Mingqing yilai beike ziliao xuanji*, 218.
128. Bao Shichen, *Anwu Sizhong*, vol. 6.
129. "Inscription of Driving out Chuai and Dye Rogues upon the Order of the Governor-General and Provincial Governor of the Imperial Envoy Department," *Jiangsu sheng Mingqing yilai beike ziliao xuanji*, 41.
130. Zhi Chaozi, *Jiujing suoji*, vol. 9.
131. "Inscriptions of Changzhou County on Abolishing the Xiaojia of Wooden Rafts," *Jiangsu sheng Mingqing yilai beike ziliao xuanji*, 100.
132. Gong Chai, "Taiwan xiaoji," see *Xiao Fang Hu Zhai Yu Di Chong Chao*, 9.

133. Lan Dingyuan, *Pingtai jilüe*.
134. Ibid.
135. Gong Chai, "*Taiwan xiaoji*."
136. Lian Heng, *Taiwan tongshi*, vol. 30.
137. Lan Dingyuan, *Pingtai jilüe*.
138. Ibid.
139. Ibid.
140. Wang Jingqi, *Dushutang xizheng suibi*.
141. *Yongzheng zhupi zouzhe* (the 3rd day of the 8th month of the 4th year).
142. *Junji chu lufu zouzhe*, presented by Yang Xiba etc. on the 18th day of the 7th month of the 6th year of the Qianlong period.
143. *Qing Gaozong shilu*, vol. 187 (the 29th day of the 3rd month of the 8th year).
144. Huang Yin, *Xijin shi xiaolu*, vol. 4 (the 3rd of the 8th month of the 4th year).
145. "Yongzheng period," *Donghua lu*, vol. 6 (the 7th month of the 3rd year).
146. Ibid., vol. 7 (the 8th month of the 3rd year).
147. Ibid., vol. 14(the 6th month of the 7th year).
148. Ibi d., vol. 15 (the 12th month of the 7th year).
149. *Yongzheng zhupi zouzhe*, presented by Hubei Judicial Commissioner Wang Su on the 8th day of the 9th month of the 6th year.
150. Ibid., presented by Jiangxi Lieutenant-Governor Song Jun on the 25th day of the 10th month of the 11th year.
151. "Yongzheng period," *Donghua lu*, vol. 13 (the 2nd month of the 4th year).
152. Ibid., vol. 8 (the 2 nd month of the 4th year).
153. Ibid., vol. 9 (the 8th month of the 4th year).
154. *Qianlong zhupi zouzhe*, presented by Judicial Commissioner Li Rulan on the 19th day of the 9th month of the 7th year.
155. *Chinese Historical Materials in the Real Record of the Li Dynasty of Korea*, vol. 10, 4518.
156. *Qianlong zhupi zouzhe*, presented by the Governor-General of Jiangsu and Jiangxi Yin Jishan on the 4th day of the 8th month of the 8th year.
157. *Qing Gaozong shilu*, vol. 230 (the 15th day of the 12th month of the 9th year).
158. *Qianlong zhupi zouzhe*, presented by Fujian Governor Wu Jinsheng on the 26th day of the 5th month of the 8th year.
159. *Qing Gaozong shilu*, vol. 159 (the 5th day of the 1st month of the 7th year of the Qianlong period).
160. *Qianlong zhupi zouzhe*, presented by Governor-General De Pei on the 26th day of the 1st month of the 8th year.
161. Ibid., presented by Military Governor of Hunan and Hubei Wang Tianjue on the 27th day of the 2st month of the 8th year.
162. *Qing Gaozong shilu*, vol. 197 (the 30th day of the 7th month of the 8th year).
163. Ibid., vol. 203 (the 30th day of the 10th month of the 8th year).
164. "Qianlong Section (c)," *Letters of Jesuits In China* (Japanese translation version), 210. Ma Chaozhu claimed that his base was in the "Western Village", and Jesuit missionaries were implicated in the search of Ma Chaozhu.

165. *Qianlong zhupi zouzhe*, presented by Henan Governor Yaertu on the 17th day of the 1st month of the 5th year.
166. Engels, "On the History of Early Christians," *Complete Works of Marx and Engels*, vol. 12, 142.
167. "Biography of Lu Kun," *Mingshi*, vol. 226.
168. *Mingqing shiliao*, section 3, no. 5.
169. "Minister of the Ministery of War, Report on Continuously Capturing Falsely Surrendered Enemies and Impeaching Negligent Officials," Memorial of Gushan'ezhengahongda.
170. Huang Yupian, *Xu poxie xiangqing*.
171. *Qing Shizu shilu*, vol. 26 (the 11th day of the 6th month of the 3rd year).
172. Na Yancheng, *Na Wenyi gong zouyi*, vol. 32.
173. Huang Yupian, *Xu poxie xiangqing*.
174. Ibid.
175. Ibid.
176. Zhou Kai, "Turmoil of Heresy Bandit Qier Widow," *Neizi Songzhai wenji*, vol. 1.
177. Na Yancheng, *Na Wenyi gong zouyi*, vol. 41.
178. Na Yancheng, *Na Wenyi gong zougao*, vol. 42.
179. *Qinding pingding jiaofei fanglüe*, vol. 1.
180. Na Yancheng, *Na Wenyi gong zougao*, vol. 42.
181. Xiangheng, *Chongke poxie xiangbian xu*.
182. "Events," *Tongzhi Fang xianzhi*, vol. 6.
183. Yan Ruyu, *Sansheng bianfang bilan*, vol. 17.
184. Ibid., vol. 12.
185. Zhou Kai, "Turmoil of Evil Bandit Qier Widow," *Neizi Songzhai wenji*, vol. 1.
186. *Jiuku Zhongxiao Yaoxuw Baojuan*.
187. *Gufo Tianzhen Kaozheng Longhua Baojuan*.
188. Huang Yupian, *Poxie xiangqing*, vol. 1.
189. *Tian di hui*, vol. 1, 33.
190. Luo Ergang, *Tian di hui wen xian lu*.
191. Dutch Schlegel and Xiao Yishan support this view.
192. Mr. Cai Shaoqing holds this opinion, see "On the Origin of the Heaven and Earth Society," *Peking University Journal*, 1 (1964).
193. "Junji chu lufu zouzhe," reported by Wang Zhiyi, approved on the 29th day of the 10th month of the 4th year of the Jiaqing period, quoted from *Tian di hui*, vol. 1, 141.
194. Wang Zhiyi, "Memorial of Administering and Educating Zhangzhou and Quanzhou Customs," *Huangchao jingxi wenbian*, 23.
195. "Confession of Xu Axie etc.," quoted from *Tian di hui*, vol. 1, 7.
196. "The Preface of Xilu" is one chapter of the documents of the Heaven and Earth Society. It states the origin of this Society as follows: in the Kangxi period, monks of the Shaolin Temple assisted the Qing court to conquer Xilufan. After winning they returned to the Temple to live and were slandered by bad people. The Qing court dispatched troops to attack and burn the Shaolin Temple. Most of monks were killed. Only 5 monks escaped from the temple and formed an alliance with Wan Yunlong to support Zhu Hongying, crown prince of Emperor Chongzhen, to ascend to the throne.

They initiated an uprising but were defeated by the Qing troops and Wan Yunlong was killed. The five monks fled to various provinces and swore to overthrow the Qing and restore the Ming. They were the "5 Founders" and became founders of branches of the Heaven and Earth Society in various provinces. This tragic story contains goodness, revenge, superstitious miracles, martial arts and overthrowing Qing and restoring Ming. It was an agitprop article with a devious plot. "The Preface of Xilu" has various versions. The earliest version that we can see today is the story recorded in the hand-written notebook hidden by Yao Dagao, leader of the Guangxi Donglangzhou Heaven and Earth Society, and confiscated in the 16th year of the Jiaqing period. Comparing with later versions, the story in the earlier version is brief and rough. Then later it was written more carefully and movingly, and the story was more detailed and rigorous.

197. *Qinding pingding Taiwan jilüe*, vol. 58, Report by Fukangan on the 14th day of the 4th month of the 53rd year of the Qianlong period.
198. Reported by Na Yancheng on the 16th day of the 12th month of the 7th year of the Jiaqing period.
199. See *Lishi dangan*, 1 (1981):113.
200. "Yanyan gongci bilu," see *Tian di hui*, vol. 1, 111.
201. See Secret Association Section, China No. 1 Historical Archives Collection.
202. Joachim Bouvet, "Biography of Emperor Kangxi," *Materials of History of the Qing Dynasty*, series 1, 242–243.
203. "Mingzhu," *Qing shigao*, vol. 269.
204. *Qing Shengzu shilu*, vol. 147 (the 7th month of the 29th year).
205. "Kangxi period," *Donghua lu*, vol. 71 (the 5th month of the 42nd year).
206. Ibid., vol. 91 (the 2nd month of the 52nd year).
207. Ibid., vol. 81 (the 8th month of the 47th year).
208. Joachim Bouvet, "Biography of Emperor Kangxi," *Materials of History of the Qing Dynasty*, series 1, 241.
209. "Kangxi period," *Donghua lu*, vol. 81 (the 9th month of the 47th year).
210. "Yongzheng period," *Donghua lu*, vol. 5 (the 8th month of the 2nd year).
211. *Chaoxian Lichao shilu zhongdi Zhongguo shiliao*, vol. 10, 4254, 4281.
212. Ibid., 4281, 4311, 4322.
213. "Kangxi period," *Donghua lu*, vol. 90 (the 9th and 10th months of the 51st year).
214. Matteo Ripa, *Thirteen Years in Beijing*, chap. 15.
215. *Chaoxian Lichao shilu zhongdi Zhongguo shiliao*, vol. 10, 4322.
216. "Kangxi period," *Donghua lu*, vol. 94 (the 11th month of the 53rd year).
217. *Funyuan Daizhangjun zuoyi.*
218. "Wenxian congbian," *Case of Yisi and Yitang*, confession of Qin Daoran.
219. Ibid.
220. *Shangyu neige*, instruction on the 22nd day of the 8th month of the 2nd year of the Yongzheng period.
221. "Yongzheng period," *Donghua lu*, vol. 3 (the 8th month of the 1st year).
222. Ibid.
223. *Dayi juemi lu.*
224. *Qing Shizong shilu*, vol. 45 (the 6th month of the 4th year).
225. *Shangyu baqi* (the 9th day of the 5th month of the 8th year of the Yongzheng period).

226. "Yongzheng period," *Donghua lu*, vol. 11 (the 10th month of the 5th year).
227. Matteo Ripa, *Thirteen Years in Beijing*, chap. 22.
228. "Yongzheng period," *Yinghua lu*, vol. 15 (the 10th month of the 7th year).
229. "Yunzhi," *Qing shigao*, vol. 22.
230. Quoted from Meng Sen, *Collected Papers of Works on History of the Ming and Qing Dynasties*, vol. 2, 549–554.
231. "Yunsi," *Qing shigao*, vol. 220.
232. "Yongzheng period," *Donghua lu*, vol. 5 (the 8th month of the 2nd year).
233. "Yongzheng period," *Donghua lu*, vol. 24 (the 1st month of the 2nd year).

Chapter 9

1. Pankratova, *General History of the Soviet Union*, vol. 1 (Moscow, 1955), 253.
2. Ravenstein, *Russians at the Heilong River*, English version (London, 1861), 11.
3. *Collection of Russian Historical Data*, vol. 1, ed. Fonadesiji (Yale University, 1972), 269.
4. Gort, *Russia's Expansion in the Pacific Region (1641-1850)*, English version (Cleveland, 1914), 38, 40.
5. Vasilyev, *History of Outer Baikal Cossacks*, vol. 1, Russian version (Chita, 1916), 65.
6. Ibid.
7. *Sino-Russian Relations in the 17th Century*, vol. 1, no. 56, ed. Tikhvinski (Moscow, 1969).
8. Gort, *Russia's Expansion in the Pacific Region (1641–1850)*, 59.
9. Vladimir, *Russia on the Pacific and the Syberian Railway*, English version (London, 1899), 105.
10. Vasilyev, *History of the Outer Baikal Cossacks*, vol. 1, 76.
11. "Factum of Khabarovsk (August 1652)," in *Selected Works of Soviet History*, vol. 1, ed. Lebegiv.
12. *Collection of Russian Historical Data*, vol. 1, ed. Fonadesiji (Yale University, 1972), 272.
13. "Report of Stepanov to Yakutsk Governor," in *Sino-Russian Relations in the 17th Century*, ed. Tikhvinski, vol. 1, no. 75.
14. *Qing Shizu shilu*, vol. 119, 4.
15. *Strategy of Putting down Russians*, vol. 1.
16. Vasilyev, *History of the Outer Baikal Cossacks*, vol. 1, 101.
17. *Qing Shizu shilu*, vol. 119, 41.
18. Baddeley, *Russia, Mongolia and China*, vol. 2, 339.
19. *Russian Historical Materials in the Palace Museum (Original File of Russian Documents in the Kangxi and Qianlong Periods)* (The Palace Museum, 1936), 267.
20. "Official Communication on the Ministry of Tribal Affairs Presenting Credentials for Nicholas and the Meeting Process and Situation Sent to the Cabinet for Copying and Presenting to the Throne" (the 1st day of the 7th month of the 15th year of the Kangxi period), collected in the Ming and Qing Archives Department of the Palace Museum.
21. Baddeley, *Russia, Mongolia and China*, vol. 2, 296.
22. "Official Communication on the Ministry of Tribal Affairs Presenting Credentials for Nicholas and the Meeting Process and Situation Sent to the Cabinet for Copying and Presenting to the Throne" (the 1st day of the 7th month of the 15th year of the Kangxi period), collected in the Ming and Qing Archives Department of the Palace Museum.

23. Tulishen, *Record of Foreign Countries*.
24. Baddeley, *Russia, Mongolia and China*, vol. 2, 257.
25. Ibid., 420.
26. Vasilyev, *History of the Outer Baikal Cossacks*, vol. 1, 146.
27. Parson, *Travel Diary of the Outer Baikal Border*, vol. 2 (Moscow, 1844), chap. 4.
28. *Strategy of Putting Down Russians*, vol. 1–2.
29. Liu Xianting, *Guangyang zeji*, vol. 2.
30. "Order and Send Minister to Announce Order to Russians to Require them to Return Invaded Land and to Spy out their Situation" (the 11th day of the 5th month of the 20th year of the Kangxi period), collected in the Ming and Qing Archives Department of the Palace Museum.
31. *Qing Shengzu shilu*, vol. 121, 11.
32. Mancol, *Russia and China* (U.S.: Harvard University, 1971), 156.
33. *Qing Shengzu shilu*, vol. 106, 23.
34. "land tax," *Shengjing tongzhi*, vol. 24.
35. Xiqing, *Heilongjiang waiji*.
36. *Strategy of Putting Down Russians*, vol. 1.
37. *Qing Shengzu shilu*, vol. 111, 7.
38. Ibid., vol. 112, 5.
39. Ibid., vol. 119, 6–8.
40. "Imperial Letter of Emperor Kangxi to Tsar for the Purpose of Making Russia Quickly Withdraw the Russians and Stop Making Troubles" (the 17th day of the 3rd month of the 24th year of the Kangxi period), collected in the Ming and Qing Archives Department of the Palace Museum.
41. "Biography of Langtan," *Baqi tongzhi chuji*, vol. 153.
42. *Qing Shengzu shilu*, vol. 124, 16.
43. *Sino-Russian Relations in the 17th Century*, ed. Tikhvinski, vol. 2, 769.
44. "Official Communication of the Ministry of War to the Tsar on Informing Russia of demarcating in Yaku" (the 30th day of the 7th month of the 25th year of the Kangxi period), collected in the Ming and Qing Archives Department of the Palace Museum.
45. Gann, *Early History of Sino-Russian Relations*, trans. Jiang Zaihua (The Commercial Press, 1961), 8.
46. *Qing Shengzu shilu*, vol. 127, 24.
47. Gann, *Early History of Sino-Russian Relations*, Appendix, 153–155.
48. *Sino-Russian Relations in the 17th Century*, ed. Tikhvinski, vol. 2, 178.
49. Shasijina, *Envoy Exchange Relations between Russia and Mongolia in the 17th Century*, 118.
50. *Sino-Russian Relations in the 17th Century*, ed. Tikhvinski, vol. 2, 223, 217, 222.
51. Ibid., 383–386.
52. Ibid., vol. 2, 413, 419.
53. *Qing Shengzu shilu*, vol. 135.
54. Ibid., vol. 140.
55. Pavlovsky, *Sino-Russian Relations* (New York, 1949), 124.
56. Mancol, *Russia and China* (U.S.: Harvard University, 1971), 156.
57. *Sino-Russian Relations in the 17th Century*, ed. Tikhvinski, vol. 2, 462.

58. "Diary of J. F. Gerbillon" (August 2, 1689).
59. *Sino-Russian Relations in the 17th Century*, ed. Tikhvinski, vol. 2, 462.
60. "Memorial of Suoetu etc. on Determining the Boundary with the Russian Envoy" (the 27th day of the 7th month of the 28th year of the Kangxi period), collected in the Ming and Qing Archives Department of the Palace Museum.
61. *Sino-Russian Relations in the 17th Century*, ed. Tikhvinski, vol. 2, 493.
62. See note 60 above.
63. *Sino-Russian Relations in the 17th Century*, ed. Tikhvinski, vol. 2, 461.
64. See note 60 above.
65. *Sino-Russian Relations in the 17th Century*, ed. Tikhvinski, vol. 2, 506–513.
66. Ibid.
67. "Memorial of Suoetu etc. on Determining the Boundary with the Russian Envoy" (the 27th day of the 7th month of the 28th year of the Kangxi period), collected in the Ming and Qing Archives Department of the Palace Museum.
68. *Strategy of Putting Down Russians*, vol. 4.
69. *Sino-Russian Relations in the 17th Century*, ed. Tikhvinski, vol. 2, 506–513.
70. "Memorial of Suoetu etc. on Determining the Boundary with the Russian Envoy" (the 27th day of the 7th month of the 28th year of the Kangxi period), collected in the Ming and Qing Archives Department of the Palace Museum.
71. "Diary of Jesuit Missionary Thomas Pereira on the Sino-Russian Nerchinsk Negotiation," section 31.
72. "Diary of J. F. Gerbillon" (August 24, 1689).
73. "Manchu Response of Our Minister to the Russia Envoy on the Russia Envoy's Official Communication of Informing that Dwellings along the Argun River have not been Moved for the Reason of Winter and Other Issues" (the 22nd day of the 5th month of the 29th year of the Kangxi period), collected in the Ming and Qing Archives Department of the Palace Museum.
74. *Sino-Russian Relations in the 17th Century*, ed. Tikhvinski, vol. 2, 567.
75. "Diary of Jesuit Missionary Thomas Pereira on the Sino-Russian Nerchinsk Negotiation," section 42.
76. Gann, *Early History of Sino-Russian Relations*, 9.
77. Baojuemujin, *Diplomatic History of the World*, vol. 1, 215.
78. *Dictionary of Diplomacy*, ed. Gromyko and others, 403–404.
79. Zhang Mu, Nomadic History of the Mongolians, vol. 7: "In the third year of the Chongde period, the three Khans sent envoys to the imperial court to settle issues concerning tributes". Footnote: "The three Khans each agreed to sent eight white horses and one white camel, namely the nine whites, as an annual tribute".
80. Vasilyev, *History of Outer Baikal Cossacks*, vol. 2, 5.
81. *Qing Zhengzu shilu*, vol. 273, 6.
82. *Russian Historical Materials in the Imperial Palace*, trans. and eds. Wang Zhixiang and Liu Zerong, 10.
83. Gann, *Early History of Sino-Russian Relations*, 111.
84. Ibid., 114.
85. Gann, *Early History of Sino-Russian Relations*, 116.
86. Ibid., 197.
87. "Yongzheng period," *Donghua lu*, vol. 8.

88. Gann, *Early History of Sino-Russian Relations*, 118.
89. *Qing Shizong shilu*, vol. 58.
90. Gann, *Early History of Sino-Russian Relations*, 122.
91. Bandishen-kamenchomsky, *Compilation of Information on Russian-Sino Diplomacy from 1619 to 1792*, 344.
92. Marx, "Greek Riot," in *Complete Works of Marx and Engels*, vol. 10, 142.
93. Joseph Serbis, "Diary of Jesuit Missionary Thomas Pereira on the Sino-Russian Nerchinsk Negotiation," 30.
94. Tu Lishen, *Record of Foreign Countries*.
95. Bartold, *Oriental Study History of Europe and Russia*, 271.
96. Bunakov, "Sino-Russian Relations in the early 19th Century," in *History of Russia's Aggression against China*, vol. 1, 267.
97. Glebov, "Diplomatic Functions of the Eastern Orthodox Missionary Group in Beijing," in *History of Russia's Aggression against China*, vol. 1, 269.
98. Ibid., 273.
99. Babkov, *Memories of My Service in West Siberia*, Russian version (Petersburg, 1912), 127.
100. Bernard R. P. Henri, *Annals of Missionary Work of Catholicism in China in the 16th Century*, trans. Xiao Linghua (The Commercial Press, 1936), 156.
101. De Mulron, *Meritorious Deeds of French Jesuits in China*, French version (Paris, 1928), 15.
102. Bernard R. P. Henri, *Annals of Missionary Work of Catholicism in China in the 16th Century*, 320.
103. Gresynge, *Society of Jesus, English version* (London, 1930), 77.
104. Ibid., 91.
105. Louis Pfister, *Biographies of the Jesuits in China*, trans. Feng Chengjun, 198.
106. Witt, *Biography of Adam Schall von Bell*, trans. Yang Bingchen (The Commercial Press, 1949), 299.
107. *Yang Guangxian*, Bu de yi, 4.
108. *Zheng jiao feng bao*, 59.
109. Yang Guangxian, *Qing zhu xiejiao shu*.
110. Louis Pfister, *Biographies of the Jesuits in China*, trans. Feng Chengjun.
111. "Yang Guangxian," in "Collected Biographies," *Qing shigao*, 59.
112. *Zheng jiao feng bao*, 47.
113. Ibid., 48.
114. Gann, *Early History of Sino-Russian Relations*, 194.
115. *Enlightenment and Marvelous Letters*, vol. 3, French version (Paris, 1877), 470.
116. Li Ming, *Xin huiyi lu*, vol. 1, French version (Paris, 1696), 75.
117. Baddeley, *Russia, Mongolia and China*, vol. 2, English version (London, 1919), 337, 368, 411.
118. Edmund Backhouse and Derek Sandhaus, *Chronology of the Chinese Imperial Palace*, English version (New York, 1914), 240.
119. "Yongzheng period," *Donghua lu*, vol. 38.
120. Thomas, *History of the Beijing Church*, French version (Paris, 1923), 361.
121. Luo Boshan, *Chuan jiaoshi he guanli*, English version (California, 1942), 154.
122. Ibid.

123. *Wenxian congbian*, vol. 12, 37.
124. *Chinese Sage Confucius* (Paris, 1687), 110.
125. "Documents of the Relationship between Emperor Kangxi and Roman Envoys" (the Palace Museum, 1932).
126. Ibid.
127. "Kangxi period," *Donghua lu*, vol. 24.
128. Ibid., vol. 99.
129. "Yongzheng period," *Donghua lu*, vol. 3.
130. *Enlightenment and Marvelous Letters*, vol. 3, French version (Paris, 1877), 364.
131. Xiao Ruose, *Missionary Work of Catholicism in China* (Hebei Xian County Catholic Church, 1931), 37.
132. *Qing Renzong shilu*, vol. 243.

Chapter 10

1. *Selected Works of Mao Zedong*, vol. 2 (1991), 622.
2. Zhang Mu, "Overview of the Four Khalkha Branches of Outer Mongolia," in *Menggu youmu ji*, vol. 7.
3. Ibid.
4. *Huangchao kaigao fanglüe*, vol. 22.
5. Qi Yunshi, "Overview of the Khalkha in Outer Mongolia, 1," in *Huangchao fanbu yaolüe*, vol. 3.
6. He Qiutao, "Overview of the Internal Affairs of Khalkha," in *Shuofang bicheng*, vol. 3.
7. Qi Yunshi, "Overview of the Elute, 1," in *Huangchao fanbu yaolüe*, vol. 9.
8. Hong Jun, *Yuanshi yiwen jibu*; Ke Shaomin, *The Xin Yuanshi*; and Zhang Mu, *Menggu youmu ji*.
9. Yano Renyi, *Jindai Menggu shi yanjiu*, 17.
10. Huo Wosi, *Menggu shi*, vol. 1, 497–498; and Baddeley, *Russia, Mongolia and China*, vol. 2, 16.
11. See details in Qi Yunshi, "Overview of the Elute, 1," in *Huangchao fanbu yaolüe*, vol. 9; and Zhang Mu, *Menggu youmu ji*, vol. 13.
12. *Ming Yongle shilu*, vol. 63.
13. "The History of Wala," *Mingshi*, vol. 38.
14. Baddeley, *Russia, Mongolia and China*, vol. 2, 44.
15. Ibid., 39.
16. Deng Tingzhen, *Menggu zhubu shulüe*.
17. Qi Yunshi, "Overview of the Elute, 1," in *Huangchao fanbu yaolüe*, vol. 9.
18. "Full Map of Western Region," "Maps, 1," *Xiyu tuzhi*, vol. 1.
19. As per *About Zanyabandida*; however, some records say that Batuer Huitaiji died in 1665.
20. Qi Yunshi, "Overview of the Elute, 1," in *Huangchao fanbu yaolüe*, vol. 9.
21. Wei Yuan said, "The Tribe Hui was residing in Southern Tianshan. Tianshan Mountains are the stem of the Congling Mountains, stretching thousands of li to Hami. The Junggar and Hui tribes were residing on its left and right." See Wei Yuan, "A History of Emperor Qianlong Suppressing the Hui Jiang," in *Shengwu ji*, vol. 4.
22. Qi Yunshi, *Huangchao fanbu yaolüe*, vol. 15.
23. Yu Siming, "Eastern Turkestan in the Late Ming and Early Qing Dynasties—A Study of Its Islamic

History," The Journal of Oriental Researches, 7, no. 5: 140.

24. Que Ming, "Huibu zhengxu lun," in *Monograph Series on Land Compiled in the Small and Square Pot Room*, book 2, 2.
25. Wei Yuan, "A History of Emperor Qianlong Suppressing the Hui Jiang," in *Shengwu ji*, vol. 4.
26. *Complete Works of Marx and Engels*, vol. 9, 18.
27. Joseph Serbis, "Introduction of Father Xu Risheng's Journal," Diary of Jesuit Missionary Thomas Pereira on the Sino-Russian Nerchinsk Negotiation.
28. Zlatkin, *The History of the Junggar Khanate*, 126.
29. Baddeley, *Russia, Mongolia and China*, vol. 2, 37.
30. Altai Khan, also known as Aritan Khan, lived in the vicinity of Uus Lake in the northwest of Mongolia. At the beginning of the 17th century the Altai Khanate represented a strong Mongolian branch with its power and reputation in Siberia and central Asia. The first Altai Khan was Shuolei Wubashi who was the uncle of Subadi the Zhasaketu Khan. Thereafter, Emubu (the son of Shuolei Wubashi) and Elinqin the Luobuzangtaiji (the grandson of Shuolei Wubashi) proclaimed themselves Khan in progression. In 1637, the Altai Khan together with the Khalkha paid the "tribute of nine whites" to the Qing Dynasty. In 1655 (the 12th year of the Shunzhi period), the Qing government made the eight most powerful leaders of Khalkha Mongolia the Zhasake. Elinqin was one of the eight most powerful leaders.
31. Zlatkin, *Overview of the Modern and Contemporary History of Mongolia*, 44.
32. Sharstina, *Diplomatic Relations between Russia and Mongolia in the 17th Century*, 110, 112.
33. *The Treaty of Nerchinsk Signed in 1689*, 112.
34. Sharstina, *Diplomatic Relations between Russia and Mongolia in the 17th Century*, 118.
35. *Sino-Russian Relations in the 17th Century*, ed. Tikhvinski, vol. 2, 217, 222.
36. The Emperor Led His Army to Fight against Galdan, handwritten copy, trans. Ao Fu.
37. He Qiutao, *Shuofang bicheng*.
38. Cheng Muheng, *Junggar kao*, vol. 1.
39. *Qing Shengzu shilu*, vol. 135 (the 2nd day of the 5th month of the 27th year of the Kangxi period).
40. Zhang Penghe, *Fengshi Eluosi riji*.
41. Qian Liangze, *Chusai jilüe*.
42. Song Yun, "Pacification Record Map Annotated by Poems," quoted from Zhang Mu, *Menggu youmu ji*, vol. 7.
43. *Sino-Russian Relations in the 17th Century*, ed. Tikhvinski, vol. 2, 18.
44. Gahan, *The History of Early Sino-Russian Relations*, 250
45. Sharstina, *Diplomatic Relations between Russia and Mongolia in the 17th Century*, 162.
46. Gahan, *The History of Early Sino-Russian Relations*, 73.
47. *Sino-Russian Relations in the 17th Century*, ed. Tikhvinski, vol. 2, 360.
48. Ibid., 623.
49. Ibid.
50. Ibid., 30.
51. Zlatkin, *The History of the Junggar Khanate*, 281.
52. *Pingding sanni fanglüe*, vol. 36.
53. *Qing Shengzu shilu*, vol. 110 (the 29th day of the 7th month of the 22nd year of the Kangxi period), 16.

54. Afterwards, the Qing government allowed only two hundred of Galdan's tribute bearers into Beijing since Galdan sent too many of them. See *Qing Shengzu shilu*, vol. 116 (the 12th day of the 9th month of the 23rd year of the Kangxi period).
55. *Qing Shengzu shilu*, vol. 137 (the 11th month of the 27th year of the Kangxi period).
56. Wenda, *Qinzheng pingding suomo fanglüe*, vol. 7.
57. *Qing Shengzu shilu*, vol. 136 (the 8th month of the 27th year of the Kangxi period).
58. From USSR Central and National Archival Repository for Ancient Documentations, no. 1221, quoted from Zlatkin, *The History of Junggar Khanate*, 286.
59. Liu Xianting, *Guangyang zeji*, vol. 1.
60. Ma Siha, *Chuzai jicheng*.
61. Wei Yuan, "Kangxi Led His Army Personally to Put Down the Junggar Rebellions," *Shengwu ji*, vol. 3.
62. Zhang Cheng, *Zhangcheng riji*.
63. Ma Siha, *Zaibei zhengcheng*.
64. "The Vassal Tribes 4," "The Biographies," in *Qing shigao*.
65. It is recorded that Dolon-nuur was also known as the Pond of Seven Stars. "The aborigines called it Dolon-nuur; Dolon means 'seven' in Chinese, and nuur means 'lake' in Chinese." See Zhang Mu, Overview of Four Khalkha Branches of Outer Mongolia," *Menggu youmu ji*, vol. 7.
66. Kangxi, *Huizong si beiji*.
67. Wei Yuan, "The Qing Government Pacified Mongolia," *Shengwu ji*, vol. 3.
68. Zhang Mu, "Overview of Four Khalkha Branches of Outer Mongolia," *Menggu youmu ji*, vol. 7.
69. *Qing Shengzu shilu*, vol. 152 (the 6th month of the 30th year of the Kangxi period).
70. Ibid., vol. 142 (the 10th month of the 28th year of the Kangxi period).
71. Kangxi, *Huizong si beiwen*.
72. Qianlong, *Puning si beiwen*.
73. *Qing Shengzu shilu*, vol. 151 (the 5th month of the 30th year of the Kangxi period).
74. Zlatkin, *Overview of the Modern and Contemporary History of Mongolia*, 55.
75. *Qinzheng pingding suomo fanglüe*, vol. 24.
76. Wei Yuan, "Kangxi Led His Army Personally to Put Down the Junggar Rebellions," *Shengwu ji*, vol. 3.
77. "Kangxi period," *Donghua lu*, vol. 59 (the 2nd month of the 36th year of the Kangxi period).
78. Ibid. (the 5th month of the 36th year of the Kangxi period).
79. *Qinzheng pingding suomo fanglüe*, vol. 22.
80. Wei Yuan, "Kangxi Led His Army Personally to Put Down the Junggar Rebellions," *Shengwu ji*, vol. 3.
81. Zlatkin, *The History of the Junggar Khanate*, 311.
82. *Qinzheng pingding suomo fanglüe*, vol. 47.
83. Ibid., vol. 35.
84. *Qing Shngzu shilu*, vol. 183.
85. "Yongzheng period," *Donghua lu*, vol.14 (the 2nd month of the 7th year of Yongzheng period).
86. "Summary of the Whole Junggar," *Xiyu tuzhi*, vol. 1.
87. *Qing Shengzu shilu*, vol. 128.
88. *Qing Gaozong shilu*, vol. 612.
89. "Initial Stability of Ili," *Xichui zongtong shilüe*, vol. 1.

90. *Qing Gaozong shilu* (the 9th month of the 20th year).
91. Qi Yunshi, "Overview of Oirat, 2," *Huangchao fanbu yaolüe*, vol. 10.
92. Wei Yuan, "The Qing Government's Pacification of Tibet," *Shengwu ji*, vol. 5.
93. *Qing Shengzu shilu*, vol. 174.
94. "Tibet," "Tribe 8," "Biographies No. 312," in *Qing shigao*.
95. There are different versions of the death and whereabouts of Tsangyang Gyatso. Wei Yuan believed that "Tsangyang Gyatso died of illness in Qinghai on his journey to Beijing". (Wei Yuan, "The Qing Government's Pacification of Tibet, 1," *Shengwu ji*, vol. 5); Desdely believed that he was murdered by the personnel of Langzang Khan on the journey (*Annals of Tibet*, chap. 10); but Fazun said in *The Political and Religious History of Tibet* that Tsangyang Gyatso abandoned his fame and position and decided to visit India, Nepal, Xikang-Tibet, Gansu, Qinghai and Mongolia etc. when he arrived in the Qinghai Region." (Vol. 6, 1).
96. Luciano Petech, *The Central Plains of China and Tibet in the Early 18th Century* (Laydon, 1972), 33.
97. Wei Yuan, "The Qing Government's Pacification of Tibet, 1," *Shengwu ji*, vol. 5 .
98. Ibid.
99. Desdely, *Annals of Tibet*, chap. 10.
100. Wei Yuan, "The Qing Government's Pacification of Tibet, 1," *Shengwu ji*, vol. 5.
101. "Jilüe, 1," *Weizang tongzhi*, vol. 13a.
102. Ibid.
103. "Border Pacification General-in-chief Yin Zhen's Memorial to the Throne that Reports on Dalai's Enthronement in Tibet Escorted by Yan Xin" (the 20th day of the 10th month of the 59th year of the Kangxi period), *Selected Historical Data of Tibet*, 93.
104. When the assistant minister Heshou was asked to enter into Tibet in the 48th year of the Kangxi period, the Qing government had already appointed Yixi Gyatso who was supported by Lha-bzang Khan as the 6th Dalai Lama; therefore, Kelzang Gyatso was called the 7th Dalai Lama by later generations.
105. *Complete Works of Marx and Engels*, vol. 12, 637.
106. Barthold, *Research History of the East*, trans. the Japanese Foreign Ministry Survey Departments (Life Publishing Company, 1942), 338.
107. Howorth, *The History of Mongolia*, vol. 2, 96.
108. Gahan, *The History of Early Sino-Russian Relations*, 77.
109. Zuokoutou, *Russia and the Asian Steppe* (Jichuan Hongwenguan, 1953), 94.
110. Gahan, *The History of Early Sino-Russian Relations*, 77.
111. Zlatkin, *The History of the Junggar Khanate*, 344.
112. Howorth, *The History of Mongolia*, vol. 1, 647.
113. Zlatkin, *The History of the Junggar Khanate*, 354.
114. Gahan, *The History of Early Sino-Russian Relations*, 80.
115. Zlatkin, *The History of the Junggar Khanate*, 354.
116. Gahan, *The History of Early Sino-Russian Relations*, 81.
117. See also "Total Biography of Qinghai Oirat," in *Biographies of the Princes of Waifan Mongolia Hui Tribe*, vol. 81 (See *Qixian Leizheng*, 1st edition, vol. 193).
118. "Total Biography of Qinghai Oirat," in *Biographies of the Princes of Waifan Mongolia Hui Tribe*, vol. 81.
119. "Tibet," "Tribe 8," "Biographies No. 312," in *Qing shigao*.

120. Wei Yuan, "Yongzheng' Two Campaigns of Suppressing the Oirat," *Shengwu ji*, vol. 3.
121. Nian Gengyao, "Memorial to the Throne that Reports on the Military Affairs in Places such as Xi Hai" (the 18th day of the 4th month of the 1st year of the Yongzheng period), *Nian Gengyao's Memorials to the Throne*, part 1, 3.
122. *Qing Shizong shilu*, vol. 10.
123. *Pingding Junggar fanglüe*, part 1, vol. 11.
124. Ibid.
125. Armament," *Xining fu xinzhi*, vol. 20.
126. Nian Gengyao, "Memorial to the Throne that Surveys the Public Feelings in Xining" (unknown date), *Nian Gengyao's Memorials to the Throne*, part 1, 49.
127. Ibid., 46.
128. Wei Yuan, "Yongzheng' Two Campaigns of Suppressing the Oirat," *Shengwu ji*, vol. 3.
129. Guonong Temple, situated at 130 *li* northeast of Xining, "was burned down by officers and soldiers in 1723 when rebellion occurred in Qinghai; and it was rebuilt at the request of Emperor Yongzheng and renamed Youning Temple in the spring of the 33rd year of the Yongzheng period." Guomang Temple, 70 *li* east of Datong city, was renamed Guanghui Temple. See "Religious Ritual in Monasteries," *New Survey of the Xining Prefecture*, vol. 15.
130. Wei Yuan, "Yongzheng' Two Campaigns of Suppressing the Oirat," *Shengwu ji*, vol. 3.
131. *Yue Zhongqi xinglüe*.
132. *Pingding Junggar fanglüe*, part 1, vol. 12.
133. Nian Gengyao, "Memorial to the Throne that Surveys the Public Feelings in Xining" (unknown date), *Nian Gengyao's Memorials to the Throne*, part 1, 52 with comments of Emperor Yongzheng.
134. *Qing Shizong shilu*, vol. 20.
135. "Art and Literature," *Xining fu xinzhi*, vol. 24.
136. *Qing Shizong shilu*, vol. 20.
137. Ibid.
138. Baddeley, *Russia, Mongolia and China*, vol. 2, 189.
139. Quote from Zlatkin, *The History of the Junggar Khanate*, 362.
140. Ibid., 383.
141. Ibid., 384.
142. "Yongzheng period," *Donghua lu*, vol. 16.
143. Zhao Lian, "Failure of the Soldiers in the 1911 Revolution," *Xiaoting zalu*, vol. 3.
144. Hetongbo was situated at 200 *li* from Hovd.
145. Wei Yuan, "Yongzheng's Two Campaigns of Suppressing the Oirat," *Shengwu ji*, vol. 3.
146. Ibid.
147. Ibid.
148. Zhang Mu, "The Place of Khalkha Outer Mongolia Where the Nomadic Qiqilikemeng Stayed," *Menggu youmu ji*, vol. 8.
149. Ibid.
150. Zhao Yi, "Outline of the Pacification of the Junggar," *Huangchao wugong jisheng*, vol. 2.
151. He Qiutao, "Overview of Internal Affairs of Khalkha," *Shuofang bicheng*, vol. 3.
152. Wei Yuan, "Emperor Qianlong's Pacification of the Junggar," *Shengwu ji*, vol. 4.

153. Qi Yunshi, "Overview of the Oirat, 4," *Huangchao fanbu yaolüe*, vol. 12.
154. Gulang, *Central Asia in 17th and 18th Century—Kalmyk Empire or Manchu Empire?* (Lyons, 1912), 98.
155. Qi Yunshi, "Overview of the Oirat, 4," *Huangchao fanbu yaolüe*, vol. 12.
156. Amursanaa was the posthumous child of Danzhong, the eldest son of Lha-bzang Khan from Khoshut. His mother Futuoluok, the daughter of Tsewang Rabtan, was married to Danzhong and first gave birth to Banzhuer and then was expecting Amursanaa. After Danzhong died, Futuoluok remarried Taij Weizheng Heshuoqi of the Huite tribe and then gave birth to Amursanaa.
157. Zlatkin, "Russian Profiles of Amursanaa," *Language and History of Mongolia* (Moscow, 1985), 293.
158. Zhao Lian, "The Whole Story of Military Forces in the Western Regions," *Xiaoting zalu*, vol. 3.
159. Zlatkin, "Russian Profiles of Amursanaa," *Language and History of Mongolia* (Moscow, 1985), 295.
160. *Qing Gaozong shilu*, vol. 489.
161. Zhang Mu, *Menggu youmu ji*, vol. 13.
162. *Qing Gaozong shilu*, vol. 465.
163. Quote from *Xinjiang jianshi*, 299.
164. Zhao Lian, "The Whole Story of Military Forces in the Western Regions," *Xiaoting zalu*, vol. 3.
165. Wei Yuan, "Emperor Qianlong's Pacification of the Junggar," *Shengwu ji*, vol. 4.
166. Ibid.
167. Ibid.
168. *Pingding Junggar fanglüe*, zhengbian, vol. 30.
169. As recorded in *Authorized Biographies of Princes in Waifan Mongolian Huibu*: "Elinqin Duoerji was the grand-son of Chahui Duoerji, the Khan of the Khalkha Tuxietu tribe. In the 8th year of the Qianlong period he inherited the title of jasak Hesuo Prince, but 20 years later he was executed and his peerage was cancelled." ("Khalkha Tuxietu Tribe," vol. 7, table 7).
170. See note 168 above.
171. Wei Yuan, "Emperor Qianlong's Pacification of the Junggar," *Shengwu ji*, vol. 4.
172. Zhao Lian, "The Whole Story of Military Forces in the Western Regions," *Xiaoting zalu*, vol. 3.
173. *Qing Gaozong shilu*, vol. 547.
174. Ibid.
175. Ibid., vol. 555.
176. Zlatkin, "Russian Profiles of Amursanaa," *Language and History of Mongolia*, 31.
177. Chun Yuan, *Xiyu wenjian lu*, vol. 6.
178. *Pingding Junggar fanglüe*, zhengbian, vol. 14.
179. *Huijiang tongzhi*, vol. 12.
180. Ibid. Zhao Lian, "The Whole Course of the Pacification of the Hui Tribe," *Xiaoting zalu*, vol. 6.
181. Zhao Yi, "Outline of the Pacification of the Junggar," *Huangchao wugong jisheng*, vol. 2.
182. As recorded in Gulang's *Central Asia in 17th and 18th Century—Kalmyk Empire or Manchu Empire?*: "Hojajahan built strong defenses in Yerqiang and he had 4000 cavalrymen and 6000 infantrymen, plus 3,000 cavalrymen dispatched by Burhanidin from Kashigaer." (See chap. 9, 117).
183. Zhao Yi, "Outline of the Pacification of the Junggar," *Huangchao wugong jisheng*, vol. 2.
184. *Pingding Junggar fanglüe*, xubian, vol. 19.
185. Parimov, A Survey of Kalmyks in Russia, Astrakhan edition (1922), 6.

Notes

186. Chun Yuan, "The Brief Record of the Torghuts' Submission," *Xiyu zongzhi*, vol. 2.
187. Qi Yunshi, "The Origin of Torghut," *Xichui yaolüe*, vol. 4.
188. See also Pankratova, *The History of Russia in Ancient and Mediaeval Times*, 268.
189. Ibid., 262.
190. He Qiutao, "The Whole Course of the Torghut's Submission," *Shuofang bicheng*, vol. 38.
191. Qi Yunshi, "Overview of Oirat, part 2," *Huangchao fanbu yaolüe*, vol. 10.
192. Ibid.
193. Qi Yunshi, "Overview of Oirat, part 5," *Huangchao fanbu yaolüe*, vol. 13.
194. See also Noveretov, *Kalmyks* (Petersburg, 1884), 17.
195. De Quincey, *The Rebellion of the Tatars* (Boston, 1898), 7.
196. *Outline of History of Kalmyk Soviet Socialist Republics*, 181.
197. Dun Dukov Family refers to the Torghut nobles which had converted to the Orthodox Christian Church. The main members were Dun Duk Aomuba (called Dun Luobu Wangbu in Chinese historical records, who was the chief of the Torghut from 1735 to 1741), his wife Jia En and his sons Daodibi and Ashalai. After Dun Duk Aomuba died, his wife and sons lived in Petersburg where they received baptism into the Orthodox Church and therefore changed their family name as Dun Dukov (See Noveretov, *Kalmyks*, 26.)
198. Beckman, "A Note on the Torghut's Migration from Russia to Manchu State," *Oriental Culture*, vol. 2, 95.
199. He Qiutao, "The Whole Course of the Torghut's Submission," *Shuofang bicheng*, vol. 38.
200. Chun Yuan, "The Brief Record of the Torghuts' Submission," *Xiyu zongzhi*, vol. 2.
201. "Kang Gertula was the Caren (post) on the Russian frontier. The Chinese border lay to the south of it." (See Chun Yuan, "The Brief Record of the Torghuts' Submission," *Xiyu zongzhi*, vol. 2). It is now called Wusijika Miannuogersik in Russia.
202. Chun Yuan, "The Brief Record of the Torghuts' Submission," *Xiyu zongzhi*, vol. 2.
203. *Preferential Treatment for the Torghuts*.
204. *Qing Gaozong shilu*, vol. 914.
205. Ibid.
206. *Preferential Treatment for the Torghuts*.
207. *Qing Shizong shilu*, vol. 20 (the 5th day of the 2nd year of the Yongzheng period).
208. "E'ertai," "Biographies, vol. 75," *Qing shigao*.
209. Ibid.
210. Wei Yuan, "Emperor Yongzheng's Political Reform of Southwestern Minority Groups," *Shengwu ji*, vol. 7.
211. "Yongzheng period," *Donghua lu*, vol. 17 (the 10th monthof the 8th year).
212. "E'ertai," "Biographies, vol. 75," *Qing shigao*.
213. Li Yuandu, "E'ertai," *Guochao xianzheng shilüe*, vol. 13.
214. "Tusi, 3," "Biographies, vol. 301," *Qing shigao*.
215. "E'ertai," "Biographies, vol. 75," *Qing shigao*.
216. "Zhang Guangsi," "Biographies, vol. 84," *Qing shigao*.
217. "Tusi, 4," "Biographies, vol. 302," *Qing shigao*.
218. Ibid.

219. Ibid.
220. Wei Yuan, "Emperor Yongzheng's Political Reform of Southwestern Minority Groups, 1," *Shngwu ji*, vol. 7.
221. Wei Yuan, "A Note of Emperor Qianlong's First Pacification of Tusi in Jinchuan," *Shengwu ji*, vol. 7.
222. Ibid.
223. Zhao Lian, "The Killing of Minister Naqin," *Xiaoting zalu*, vol. 1.
224. Zhao Lian, "The Battle of Jinchuan," *Xiaoting zalu*, vol. 4.
225. Ibid.
226. Quote from Xiao Yishan, *Qingdai tongshi*, article 1, 72.
227. Zhao Lian, "The Battle of Jinchuan," *Xiaoting zalu*, vol. 4.
228. "Yue Zhongqi," "Biographies vol. 83," *Qing shigao*.
229. Wei Yuan, "A Note of Emperor Qianlong's Second Pacification of Tusi in Jinchuan," *Shengwu ji*, vol. 7.
230. As recorded in Zhao Yi's *Huangchao wugong jisheng*, vol. 4, "'the Major Nine Tusis' were Zuosijiabu, Gebushiza, Bawang, Bulakedi, Dankan, Ekeshi, Gongga, Suomo and Zhuokecai".
231. Li Xinheng, "Jinchuan suoji," *Collected Notes of Small Square Teapot Zhai Yu Place*, chap. 8, vol. 1.
232. "Tusi, 2," "Biographies vol. 300," *Qing shigao*.
233. Ibid.
234. Zhao Lian, "The Failure of Muguomu," *Xiaoting zalu*, vol. 7.
235. Ibid.
236. Quote from Xiao Yishan, *Qingdai tongshi*, article 1, 102.
237. *Qing Gaozong shilu*, vol. 286 (the 3rd month of the 12th year).
238. Fu Kangan, *Shuongzhong cibei ji*.
239. Ibid.
240. Qi Yunshi, "Overview of the Oirat, 2," *Huangchao fanbu yaolüe*, vol. 18.
241. *Cangshi jiyao*, compiled by Zhang Qiqing, vol. 6.
242. Ibid.
243. Ibid.
244. Ibid.
245. *Qing Gaozong shilu*, vol. 535.
246. "Qianlong period," *Donghua lu*, vol. 116.
247. *Xicang tonglan*, vol. 2.
248. "A Memorial to the Throne on the Minister of Tibet Meeting Dalai and Panchen" (the 15th day of the leap 4th month of the 57th year of Qianlong period), quoted from *Collection of Tibetan Historical Materials*, 115.
249. Deboins was a military officer in charge of 500 soldiers.
250. Shang Zhuo Bate was the monk official in charge of the warehouse of the Grand Living Buddas.
251. According to the so-called "Xubilgan system" of Gelugpa, Dalai, Panchen and other Khutukhtus are all the incarnation of Buddha. Since Buddha is immortal, only his body will die and his soul will be reincarnated. Gelugpa stipulates that Dalai and Panchen are not allowed to marry, thus their position is not hereditary. In order to keep the continuity of the "religious authority", the special way of reincarnation is adopted. When Dalai, Panchen and other Khutukhtus (Living Buddhas) pass away they will be reincarnated in someone else within one year. This "reincarnated" "soul boy" is

called Xubilgan (which means "incarnation" in the Tibetan language).

252. *Weizang tongzhi*, vol. 5.
253. Qianlong, "Yuzhi lama shuo," *Weizang tongzhi*, vol. 1.
254. *Qinding kuoerka jilüe*, vol. 47.
255. Zhou Enlai, "Several Issues about China's Nationality Policy," *People's Daily* (December 31st, 1979).
256. Mamiya Rinzō, *Record of the Trip to Eastern Tartary*, appendix.
257. Qianlong, "Beyong Gubeikou," *Rihe zhi*, vol. 20.
258. Qianlong, "Lama shuo".
259. Chen Kangqi, *Lanqian jiwen*, vol. 1.
260. Ma Ke, *Heilongjiang youji*, chap. 2, 98.
261. Ibid, 101.
262. *Shengjing tongzhi*, vol. 16.
263. Ibid., vol. 52.
264. Xi Qing, *Heilongjiang waiji*.
265. *Qing Gaozong shilu*, vol. 743.
266. *Fengtian tongzhi*, vol. 78.
267. Yang Bin, *Liubian jilüe*, vol. 3.
268. *Qing Xuanzong shilu*, vol. 250.
269. Liu Jinzao, "Registered Residence, part 1," *Qingchao xu wenxian tongkao*, vol. 25.
270. *Aihui xuanzhi*.
271. *Trip to the Amur River, China and Japan*, 151.
272. Gao Shiqi, *Hucong dongxun rilu*.
273. Yang Bin, *Liubian jilüe*.
274. Wu Zhenchen, *Ningguta jilüe*.
275. Fang Shiji, *Longsha jilüe*.
276. *Heilongjiang zhigao*, vol. 49.
277. *Qing Gaozong shilu*, vol. 1487.
278. "Kangxi period," *Donghua lu* (the 7th month of the 46th year).
279. Qin Wuyu, *Wenjian banxiang lu*, vol. 1.
280. See Zeng Wenwu, *Zhongguo jingying xiyu shi*, 276.
281. Ibid., 275.
282. Xu Song, *Xiyu shuidao ji*, vol. 4.
283. Chun Yuan, *Xiyu wenjian lu*, vol. 2.
284. Fu Heng et al., *Xiyu tuzhi*, vol. 9.
285. Ibid., vol. 12.
286. Chun Yuan, *Xiyu wenjian lu*, vol. 2.
287. Ibid.
288. Fu Heng et al., *Pingding Junggar fanglüe*, xubian, vol. 16.
289. Zhao Yi, *Huangchao wugong jisheng*, vol. 2.
290. Chun Yuan, *Xiyu wenjian lu*, vol. 1.

291. Ibid. Bazaar was the traditional market of the Uyghur nationality in southern Xinjiang.
292. Ibid. Bazaar was the traditional market of the Uyghur nationality in southern Xinjiang.
293. Xu Ke, "Agri-business Category," *Qingbei leichao*, vol. 17.
294. *Qing Xizong shilu*, vol. 117 (the 4th month of the 10th year).
295. *Guangnan fu zhi* (Daoguang period).
296. "Preface by Liang Xingyuan," *Pu'er fuzhi* (Daoguang period).
297. Wei Yuan, "Record of Land Reform in the Southwest in Yongzheng Period, 1," *Shengwu ji*, vol. 7.
298. "Customs and Products," *Zhijiang xuanzhi*, vol. 5 (Qianlong period).
299. Lin Xinheng, *Jinchuan suoji*.
300. Tan Cui, *Dianhai yuhengzhi*, vol. 11.
301. Jiang Junyuan, "A Memorial to the Throne on Issues of Investigated Minority Nationality Areas," *Lin'an fuzhi*.
302. Xu Ke, "Agri-business Category," *Qingbei leichao*, vol. 17.
303. Wei Yuan, "Record of Land Reform in the Southwest in Yongzheng Period, 1," *Shengwu ji*, vol. 7.
304. Yang Ying, *Congzheng shilu*.
305. Shi Lang, "A Memorial to the Throne on Staying at Taiwan," *Taiwan fuzhi*, vol. 15 (Kangxi period).
306. "A Brief History of Transporting Rice to Taiwan," *Xiamen zhi*, vol. 6.
307. Lian Heng, "Record of Reclamation," *Taiwan tongshi*.
308. "Customs," *Zhuluo xuanzhi*, vol, 8.
309. Lian Heng, "Record of Agriculture," *Taiwan tongshi*, quoted from "the memorial to the throne by Gao Qizhuo, Governor-General of Fujian and Zhejiang".
310. *Taiwan jingjishi chuji*.
311. Liushiqi, *Fanshe caifeng tukao*.
312. "Customs in the Aboriginal Community," *Taiwan fuzhi*, vol. 14.
313. Lian Heng, "Record of Commerce," *Taiwan tongshi*.

Chapter 11

1. Shou Yi, "School," *Guangxu huolu xuanzhi*, vol. 8.
2. "Kangxi period," *Donghua lu* (the 2nd month of the 51st year).
3. *Yuzuan Zhuzi quanshu*, preface.
4. Li Guangdi, "The Preface of Reading Notes and Essays," *Rongcun quanshu*, vol. 10.
5. Zhang Qin, "Applying Talented People, 2," *Kangxi zhengyao*, vol. 4.
6. "Yongzheng period," *Donghua lu* (the 7th month of the 5th year).
7. The copy of *Siku Quanshu* in The Old Summer Palace Wenyuan Pavilion was damaged in the battle with the British and French expeditionary forces; the copy in the Hanlin Academy was damaged in the battle with the Eight-Nation Alliance; the copies in Yangzhou Wenhui Pavilion and Zhenjiang Wenzong Pavilion were damaged in the period of the Taiping Rebellion.
8. Ruan Yuan, "The Preface of the Ji Wenda Collection," *Yanjing shi sanji*, vol. 5.
9. "Qianlong period," *Donghua lu* (the 8th month of the 39th year).
10. Zhang Taiyan, "Ai fen shu, 58th," *Qiushu*.
11. *Qingdai jinshu zhijian lu*, complied by Sun Dianqi, perface.

12. Chen Kangqi, *Lanqian jiwen*, vol. 11.
13. "Yongzheng period," *Donghua lu* (the 3rd month of the third year).
14. *Dayi juemi lu*.
15. "The Case of Hu Zhongzao Jianmosheng Poem Collection," in *Qingdai wenzi yu dang*, 1, compiled by the document libraries in the Palace Museum.
16. Ibid., 8, "The Case of Zhu Sizao's Sympathy in the Current Time".
17. Ibid., 4, "The Case of Zhu Tingzheng's Sequel of the Three-Character Classic".
18. Ibid., 3, "The Case of Wang Eryang who Called Li Fan Huang Kao in his Epigraph".
19. Ibid., 7, "The Case of Wei Yuzheng Inscribing a Brief Biography for his Father".
20. Ibid., 1, "The Case of Liu Zhenyu's The New Policy of Zhiping".
21. Ibid.
22. *Zhanggu congbian*, sent on the 27th day of the 8th month of the 43rd year of Qianlong period.
23. *Zhanggu lingshi*, vol. 2, 8.
24. Li Zutao, "Letters to the Magistrate of a Prefecture Yang Rong," *Maitang wenlüe*, vol. 2.
25. "The Case of the Huis Hai Furun Bringing Five Kinds of Hui Classic and Books of Chinese Characters," *Qingdai wenji yu dang*, 7, compiled by the document libraries in the Palace Museum.
26. Ibid., "The Case of The Record of Cang Lang County handled by Gao Zhiqing".
27. Zhang Taiyan, "Confucianism in the Qing Dynasty, 12th," *Qiushu*.
28. Jiang Fan, *Hanxue shicheng ji*, vol. 1.
29. Qian Daxin, "The Biography of Wan Sitong," *Qianyan tang wenji*, vol. 38.
30. Yao Jiheng, *Gujin weishu kaozi xu*.
31. Mao Qiling, *Sishu gaicuo*, vol. 1.
32. Poems, Classics," *Siku quanshu congmu tiyao*, vol. 16.
33. Jiang Fan, *Hanxue shicheng ji*, vol. 1.
34. Liang Qichao, *Qingdai xueshu gailun*.
35. "Books, Classics," *Siku Quanshu congmu tiyao*, vol. 12.
36. Zhang Taiyan, "Confucianism in the Qing Dynasty, 12th," *Qiushu*.
37. Pi Xirui, "The Revival of the Confucian Classics," *Jingxue lishi*, 10.
38. Jiang Fan, *Hanxue shicheng ji*, vol. 2.
39. "The Picture of Teacher Hui Dingyu's Teaching of Classics," *Dai Dongyuan ji*, vol. 11.
40. Wang Mingsheng, *Shiqi shi shangque xu*.
41. Qian Daxin, "The Miscellany of the Classics of Zang Yulin," *Qianyan tang wenji*, vol. 24.
42. Fang Dongshu, *Hanxue shangdui*, vol. 2, 2.
43. Tao Shu, "The Legacy of Shu Sishi Confucian Classics," "Confucian Classics 7," *Guochao qi xian lei zheng chubian*, vol. 417.
44. Jiang Fan, *Hanxue shicheng ji*, vol. 2.
45. Jiao Xun, "The Discussion of the Scholars' Circle in this Dynasty," *Diaogu lou ji*, vol. 12.
46. Qian Daxin, "The Biography of Hui Dong," *Qianyan tang wenji*, Vol. 39.
47. Hui Dong, *Jiujing guyi shoushuo*.
48. Qian Daxin, "The Biography of Hui Dong," *Qianyan tang wenji*, vol. 39.
49. "The Spring and Autumn Annals, Classics," *Siku Quanshu congmu tiyao*, vol. 29.

50. Wang Yinzhi, "A Letter to Jiao Litang," *Wang Wenjian gong wenji*, vol. 4.
51. Zhang Taiyan, "Confucianism in the Qing Dynasty, 12th," *Qiushu*.
52. Hui Dong, "Comments on Yi", *Zhouyi shu*, vol. 2.
53. "The Picture of Teacher Hui Dingyu Teaching the Classics," *Dai Dongyuan ji*, vol. 11.
54. Hui Dong, "The Epitaph of Shen Juntong," *Songya wenchao*, vol. 2.
55. Wang Mingsheng, "Collecting Books and Citing Ancient Characters," quoted from *Qingru xue'an*, vol. 77.
56. Jiang Fan, *Hanxue shicheng ji*, vol. 2.
57. Jiang Sheng, *Shangshu ji zhuyin xushu*.
58. Jiang Fan, *Hanxue shicheng ji*, vol. 2.
59. Wang Mingsheng, *Shangshu hou'an*, preface.
60. Hang Shijun, "The Preface of Postcase of Shangshu," *Daogu tang wenji*, vol. 4.
61. Wang Mingsheng, *Shiqi shi shangque lun*.
62. Jiang Fan, *Hanxue shicheng ji*, vol. 3.
63. Ibid.
64. Qian Daxin, "Answer to Wangxi Zhuang," *Qianyang tang wenji*, vol. 35.
65. Ibid., vol. 24, "The Preface of the Differences between Twenty-two Histories".
66. Ibid., vol. 7, "Answer the Question, 4".
67. Ibid., vol. 8, "Answer the Question, 5".
68. Ibid., vol. 33, "Letters to Dai Dongyuan".
69. Ibid., vol. 15, "Answer the Question, 12".
70. Jiang Fan, *Hanxue shicheng ji*, vol. 3.
71. Quoted from Hong Bang, "Brief Biographical Sketch of Mr. Dai," *Chutang yigao*, vol. 1.
72. Zhang Taiyan, "Confucianism in the Qing Dynasty, 12th," *Qiushu*.
73. Ibid.
74. Zhao Lian, *Xiaoting zalu,* vol. 8.
75. Ruan Yuan, "The Preface of the Scholars' Circle in this Dynasty," *Yanjing shi yiji*, vol. 2.
76. Liang Qichao, *Qingdai xueshu gailun*.
77. Duan Yucai, *Dai Dongyuan nianpu*.
78. "The Biographical Sketch of Jiang Shenxiu," *Dai Dongyuan ji,* vol. 12.
79. Ibid.
80. Qian Daxin, "The Biography of Dai Zhen," *Qianyan tang wenji*, vol. 39.
81. Duan Yucai, *Dai dongyuan nianpu*.
82. Wang Chang, "The Epitaph of Dai Dongyuan," *Chunrong tangji*, vol. 55.
83. Jiang Fan, *Hanxue shicheng ji*, vol. 7.
84. "Using Meanings in Books of Rhythm to Answer Shangshu Qin Huitian," *Dai Dongyuan ji*, vol. 3.
85. Chen Huan, *Shuowen duanzhu*, ba.
86. "Book of Discussing Study with Zhongming," *Dai Dongyuan ji*, vol. 9.
87. Ji Yun, "Pictures of the Kaogong Record," *Jiwen Dagong yiji*, vol. 8.
88. "A Letter to Han Fengjie," *Dai Dongyuan ji*, vol. 3.
89. Ibid., vol. 6, "The Preface of Water Classic Li Daoyuan's Commentary".

90. Quan Zuwang and Zhao Yiqing who had sorted out the Water Classic and Commentary before Dai Zhen obtained similar results to Dai Zhen. Therefore there were two opinions in academic circles: one school thought that Dai Zhen copied Zhao Yiqing's research results. Wei Yuan, Yang Shoujing and Wang Guowei held this opinion. The other school thought that Quan, Zhao and Dai researched this separately and got similar results. Duan Yucai, Hu Shi and Xiong Huizhen held this opinion.
91. "The Supplementary Preface of Erya's Exegesis," *Dai Donyuan ji*, vol. 3.
92. Duan Yucai, *Dai Dongyuan jixu*.
93. "Da Zheng Zhang yong mu shu," *Dai Dongyuan ji*, vol. 9.
94. Duan Yucai, *Dai Dongyuan jixu*.
95. Ibid.
96. Dai Zhen, *Mengzi ziyi xuzheng*.
97. Dai Zhen, *Yuanshan*.
98. *Mengzi ziyi xuzheng*.
99. Ibid.
100. Ibid.
101. Ibid.
102. Ibid.
103. Ibid.
104. Dai Zhen, *Yuanshan*.
105. *Mengzi ziyi xuzheng*.
106. Ibid.
107. "A Letter to Someone," *Dai Dongyuan ji*, vol. 9.
108. Zhang Taiyan, *Daohan weiyan*.
109. *Mengzi ziyi xuzheng*.
110. Ibid.
111. Weng Fanggang, "Argument," *Fuchu zhai wenji*, vol. 7.
112. Yao Nai, *Xibao Xuan wenji*, vols. 5–6.
113. Ibid.
114. Ibid., vol. 6, "Letter of Answer to Jianzhai".
115. Jiang Fan, "Hong Bang," *Hanxue shicheng ji*, vol. 6.
116. Zhang Xuecheng, "The Posthumous Papers of Zhangshi," *Zhu Lu bian shuhou*.
117. Lu Wenchao, "The Preface of Duan Ruoying's Annotation of the Origin of Chinese Characters," *Baojing tang wenji*, vol. 3.
118. Wang Niansun, "The Preface of Duan Ruoying's Annotation of the Origin of Chinese Characters," *Wang Shiqu xiansheng yiwen*, vol. 2.
119. Wang Guowei, "A Narration on Seal Characters and Zouwen," *Guangtang jilin*, vol. 7.
120. Ruan Yuan, "The Epitaph of Wang Shiqu," *Yanjing shi xuji*, vol. 2, 2.
121. Xiao Yishan, *Qingdai tongshi*, vol. 2, 640.
122. Ruan Yuan, "The Epitaph of Wang Shiqu," *Yanjing shi xuji*, vol. 2, 2.
123. Ibid.
124. Zhang Taiyan, "Zhengming Zayi," "Dingwen, 25th," *Qiushu*.

125. Fang Dongshu, *Hanxue shangdui*, vol. 2, 2.
126. Wang Zhong, "A Letter to Grand Coordinator Bi Shilang," *Shuxue, Bielu*.
127. Wang Zhong, "The Discussion on Great Learning," *Shuxue, Buyi*.
128. Lu Wenchao, "Essay to Memorialize Wang Rongfu," *Baojing tang wenji*, vol. 34.
129. Lin Tingkan, *Jiao Litang shiji*, vol. 14.
130. Lin Tingkai, "Reply to Rites, 1," *Jiao Litang wenji*, vol. 4.
131. Ibid., "Reply to Rites, 2".
132. Lin Tingkan, *Lijing shili*, preface by the author.
133. Jiao Xun, "A Letter to Scholar Zhu Xiucheng," *Diaogu lou ji*, vol. 13.
134. Ibid., vol. 13, "Yu tu lüe zixu".
135. Wang Yinzhi, "A Letter to Jiao Litang," *Wang Wenjian gong wenji*, vol. 4.
136. Jiao Xun, "The Nature of Willow," *Mengzi zhengyi*.
137. Jiao Xun, "Shuo ding," *Diaogu lou ji*, vol. 10.
138. Jiao Xun, "The Explanation of Knowledge," *Lunyu tongshi*.
139. Ibid, "The Explanation of Heretic".
140. Ibid, "Evidence".
141. Jiao Xun, "Banxue," *Diaogu lou ji*, vol. 8.
142. Ruan Yuan, "Record of Xihu Exegesis and Classics," *Yanjing shi erji*, vol. 7.
143. Ruan Yuan, "The Preface of the Scholars' Circle of History," *Yanjing shi yiji*, vol. 2.
144. Ibid., vol. 8, "The Discussion on Benevolence in the Analects of Confucius".
145. Ibid., vol. 10, "Xingming guxun".
146. Ibid.

Glossary

Agreement on Electing the Head of Clan《選舉族正族約檄》
The Analects《論語》
The Ancient Chinese Prose of the Explanation of Shangshu《古文尚書疏證》
The Ancient Meaning of the Nine Classics《九經古義》
The Annotation of the Book of Changes《周易述義》
The Annotation of the Book of Rites《禮記義疏》
The Annotation of the Chinese Classic of Family Reverence《孝經集注》
The Annotation of the Etiquette《儀禮義疏》
The Annotation of the Origin of Chinese Characters《說文解字注》
The Annotation of the Phonetic Notation to Shangshu《尚書集注音疏》
The Annotation of the Rites Classic《禮經釋例》
The Annotation of the Spring and Autumn Annals《春秋直解》
The Annotation of Zhouguan《周官義疏》
bandang 伴當
banghang 幫行
Beizi 貝子
Biographical Sketch《行狀》
The Biography of Collections《詩集傳》
The Biography of Kong Anguo《孔安國傳》
Book of Ceremonial《禮記》
The Book of Changes《易經》
The Book of Songs《詩經》
Boxue Hongci Ke 博學鴻詞科
The Brief Drawing of Yi《易圖略》
Chanting the Poetry of Zhengdebei《詠正德盃詩》
The Chapters of Yi《易章句》
The Chinese Classic of Family Reverence《孝經》
chi 尺
Chronicle of Xilu《西魯敘事》
chuai jiang 踹匠
Code of Oirat-Mongol in 1640《一六四零年蒙古厄魯特法典》
The Collection of Jianmosheng Poems《堅磨生詩鈔》
The Collection of Li Qiufeng《李虬蜂集》
Comments on Yi《易微言》
Contrary Opinion of the Five Classics《五經異義》

The Correct and Sensible View of Hongfan《洪範正論》
Correcting Mistakes of the Four Books《四書改錯》
Dachengzhisheng Wenxuan Great Teacher 大成至聖文宣先師
Daily Discussion on the Explanation of the Four Books《日講四書解義》
dan 擔
danhu 戶
The Desultory Essay of Going on a Campaign to the West《西征隨筆》
Diba 第巴
The Differences between Twenty-two Histories《二十二史考異》
The Discrimination of Yitu《易圖明辨》
Discussion and Consideration of Sinology《漢學商兑》
The Discussion of Nature《論性》
The Discussion of Seventeen Histories《十七史商榷》
dongjiahang 東家行
dou 斗
A Dream of Red Chamber《紅樓夢》
duomin 惰民
The Encyclopedia of Five Rites《五禮通考》
Establishing the Tablet for Putting an End to Stealing Money from Ancestral Temples《杜盜祭款立碣記》
The Example of Yi《易例》
The Explanation of Function Words《經傳釋詞》
The Explanation of the Song Collections《詩集傳通釋》
Eyra《爾雅》
Famous Mountain Cang《名山藏》
fen 分
The Foreword of Mao Shi《毛詩序》
The Four Books Explaining the Earth《四書釋地》
gaihu 丐戶
The General Explanation of Yi《易通釋》
The General Summary of the Siku Quanshu《四庫全書總目題要》
The General Summary of the Siku Quanshu《四庫全書總目提要》
Gongyang《公羊》
The Great Learning《大學》
Han Feizi, Jie Lao《韓非子•解老》
hangtou 行頭
Hetu Luoshu《河圖洛書》
Historical Materials of Modern Secret Society《近代秘密社會史料》
The History of the Ming Dynasty《明史》

Huainanzi《淮南子》
huibu 回部
huiguan 會館
Imperial Map of China《皇輿全覽圖》
The Integration of Ancient and Modern Books《古今圖書集成》
Interpretation of Gangya《廣雅疏正》
Interpretation of Mencius Concepts《孟子字義疏證》
The Investigation of Ancient Chinese Shangshu《古文尚書考》
The Investigation on the Explanation of Ancient Classics《古經解鉤沉》
The Investigation on Yan Music《燕樂考原》
ji jiang 機匠
jianding 箭丁
jiebian 劫變
juren 舉人
Justice《正義》
The Lament《離騷》
lehu 樂戶
A Letter to Answer Peng Yunchu《答彭進士初書》
li 里
liang 兩
mang 氓
The Medical Certificate of the World's Countries《天下郡國利病書》
The Memorial to the Emperor of Longgangmo《瀧岡阡表》
Memorials of the Criminal Department《刑科題本》
The Mencius《孟子》
Mencius, Devotion《孟子 • 盡心》
mu 畝
mu li dou shi zhi tian xia 木立斗世知天下
The Narration of Zhou Yi《周易述》
The New Policy of Zhiping《治平新策》
The Notes of Mei Village《梅莊雜著》
The Notes of Shiyi《詩義折中》
The Notes on the Books of Changes《周易折中》
The Origin of Chinese Characters《說文解字》
Origin of the Church《教會源流考》
Outline of General Annals of the Imperial Family of Qing《皇清通志綱要》
The Outline of Rites《禮經綱日》
The Pandects of the Book of History《書經傳說匯纂》
The Pandects of the Book of Songs《欽定 詩經傳說匯纂》

The Pandects of the Spring and Autumn Annals《春秋傳說匯纂》
Perpetual Calendar《萬年曆》
The Picture of Shengxue《聖學圖》
The Picture of Yiguan《一貫圖》
Pictures of the Kaogong Record《考工記圖》
The Piece of Mao Poems and Researching Ancient Affairs《毛詩稽古篇》
The Plan of Da Yu《大禹謨》
Poem of a Child's Question《詩童子問》
Poetry Anthology of Biluo Houren《碧落後人詩》
The Poetry Anthology of Taohuan Pavilion《濤院亭詩集》
Poetry Anthology of Yi Zhu Lou《一柱樓詩集》
Poetry Anthology Recalling the Song《憶鳴詩集》
Postcase of Shangshu《尚書後案》
Preface of Xilu《西魯序》
Preferential Treatment for the Torghuts《優恤土爾扈特部眾記》
qi 氣/旗
qian 錢
qing 頃
Real Record《實錄》
The Record of Canglang County《滄浪鄉志》
The Record of Dian Qian《滇黔紀聞》
Record of Exotic Place《異域錄》
The Record of Kaogong《考工記》
Record of Ming Tang and Correct Reasons《明堂大道錄》
The Record of Reading《讀書雜志》
The Record of the Emperors' Taboo《聖譯實錄》
The Record of Tongjian《通鑒論》
The Regulations for the Better Governing of Tibet《西藏善後章程》
Reply to Rites《覆禮》
The Research on the Ancient and Modern Fake Books《古今偽書考》
Rites of Zhou《周禮》
Ritual《儀禮》
The Sacred Edicts《聖諭廣訓》
The Sequel of the Three-Character Classic《續三字經》
shang 晌/垧
Shangshu《尚書》
Shangshu, Yao Standard《尚書堯典》
sheng 升
shichen 時辰

Shiji《史記》
shipu 世僕
Shouwen《說文》
Siku Quanshu《四庫全書》
The Song Collections《詩集傳》
South Mountain Collection《南山集》
Spring and Autumn《春秋》
A Statement on Study《述學》
The Study on Zhou Officials' Farmland《周官祿田考》
Study on Classics《經義述聞》
suiding 隨丁
The Summary of Reading History and Areas《讀史方輿紀要》
suo 所
Sympathy in the Current Time《吊時文》
Taishi《泰誓》
Three Books of Yi《易學三書》
Tibet Regulation Made by Imperial Order《欽定西藏章程女》
Torghuts' Complete Submission to the Qing Dynasty《土爾扈特全部歸順記》
Water Classic and Commentary《水經注》
wei 衛
wen 文
xiaojia 小甲
xijiahang 西家行
ximin 細民
xiucai 秀才
xun 汛
Yi 易學
Yi Benyi《易本義》
Yi Sinology《易漢學》
Yongle Encyclopedia《永樂大典》
Yuanshan《原善》
Yugong Zhuizhi《禹項錐指》
zhang 丈
Zhaogao《召誥》
Zhisheng Great Teacher 至聖先師

References

Documentary Sources

Aihui xian zhi 璦琿縣志 (Annals of Aihui County).

Baqi tongzhi chuji 八旗通志初集 (First Collection of Annals of the Eight Banners).

Chaoxian Lichao shilu zhongdi Zhongguo shiliao 朝鮮李朝實錄中的中國史料 (Chinese Historical Materials in the Real Record of the Li Dynasty of Korea).

Chenshi zongpu 陳氏宗譜 (Genealogy of the Chen Family).

Dai Dongyuan ji 戴東原集 (The Collection of Dai Dongyuan).

Daiqing lüli tongkao 大清律例通考 (A General Study of the Great Qing Legal Code).

Daoguang Ningdu Zhili zhou zhi 道光寧都直隸州志 (Annals of Zhili Prefecture in Ningdu in the Daoguang Period).

Daoguang Yuanhe Weiting zhi 道光元和唯亭志 (Annals of Yuanhe Wei Ting in the Daoguang Period).

Dayi juemi lu 大義覺迷錄 (The Record of an Awoken Scholar).

Diary of Jesuit Missionary Thomas Pereira on the Sino-Russian Nerchinsk Negotiation.

Donghua lu 東華錄 (The History of the Qing Dynasty Written at Donghua).

Fengtian tongzhi 奉天通志 (Annals of Fengtian).

Funyuan Daizhangjun zuoyi 撫遠大將軍奏議 (Memorial of the Fuyuan General to the Throne).

Guangdong Zhaoqing fuzhi 廣東肇慶府志 (Annals of Zhaoqing in Guangdong).

Guangnan fu zhi 廣南府志 (Annals of Guangnan Prefecture).

Guangxu Baling xian zhi 光緒巴陵縣志 (Annals of Baling County in the Guangxu Period).

Guangxu Chaozhou fu zhi 光緒潮州府志 (Annals of Chaozhou in the Guangxu Period).

Guangxu Shitai Dushi zongpu 光緒石埭杜氏宗譜 (Genealogy of the Du Family in Shitai in the Guangxu Period).

Guishi shipu 歸氏世譜 (Genealogy of the Gui Family).

Hanyang Longni Zaishi zongpu 漢陽龍霓載氏宗譜 (Genealogy of the Zai Family in Longni in Hanyang).

Heilongjiang zhigao 黑龍江志稿 (Annals of Heilongjiang).

Huangchao jingxi wenbian 皇朝經世文編 (Anthology of Articles on Administering Affairs of the Dynasty).

References

Huangchao kaigao fanglüe 皇朝開國方略 (Overview of the Founding of the Dynasty).

Huangchao zhengdian leizuan 皇朝政典類纂 (Analects of Political Code of the Dynasty).

Jiangsu sheng Mingqing yilai beike ziliao xuanji 江蘇省明清以來碑刻資料選集 (Selected Collection of Inscription Information in Jiangsu Province since the Ming and Qing Dynasties).

Jiaqing Rui'an xian zhi 嘉慶瑞安縣志 (Annals of Rui'an County in the Jiaqing Period).

Jingjiang Wangshi zupu 京江王氏族譜 (Genealogy of the Wang Family in Jingjiang).

Jingzhao Guishi shipu 京兆歸氏世譜 (Genealogy of the Gui Family in Jingzhao).

Junji chu lufu zouzhe 軍機處錄副奏折 (Memorials Duplicate Copied by the Council of State).

Lin'an fu zhi 臨安府志 (Annals of Lin'an Prefecutre).

Lishi dangan 歷史檔案 (Historical Files).

Manzu jianshi 滿族簡史 (A Brief History of Manchu).

Ming Yongle shilu 明永樂實錄 (Memoir of Emperor Yongle).

Mingqing shiliao 明清史料 (Historical Data of the Ming and Qing Dynasties).

Mingshi 明史 (The History of the Ming Dynasty).

Neige daku dangan 內閣大庫檔案 (Files in the Big Storehouse of the Cabinet).

Neiwufu laiwen 內務府來文 (Official Documents from the Imperial Household Ministry).

Pingding sanni fanglüe 平定三逆方略 (General Plan for the Suppression of the Three Rebellions).

Pingding Zhunga'er fanglüe 平定準噶爾方略 (General Plan for the Suppression of Junggar).

Pu'er fu zhi 普洱府志 (Annals of Pu'er Prefecture).

Qianlong Guangshan xian zhi 乾隆光山縣志 (Annals of Guangshan County in the Qianlong Period).

Qianlong Guangzhou fu zhi 乾隆廣州府志 (Annals of Guangzhou in the Qianlong Period).

Qianlong Shicheng xian zhi 乾隆石城縣志 (Annals of Shicheng County in the Qianlong Period).

Qianlong Xupu xian zhi 乾隆溆浦縣志 (Annals of Xupu County in the Qianlong Period).

Qianlong zhupi zouzhe 乾隆朱批奏折 (Memorials Approved by Qianlong in Red with a Brush).

Qinding kuo'erka jilüe 欽定廓爾喀紀略 (The History of the Gurkha by Imperial Order) .

Qinding pingding Taiwan jilüe 欽定平定台灣紀略 (Strategy of Putting Down Taiwan Compiled and Published by Imperial Order).
Qing Gaozong shilu 清高宗實錄 (Real Record of Emperor Gaozong of the Qing Dynasty).
Qing Renzong shilu 清仁宗實錄 (Real Record of Emperor Renzong of the Qing Dynasty).
Qing Shengzu shilu 清聖祖實錄 (Real Record of Emperor Shengzu of the Qing Dynasty).
Qing shi gao 清史稿 (Manuscript of the History of the Qing Dynasty).
Qing Shizong shilu 清世宗實錄 (Real Record of Emperor Shizong of the Qing Dynasty).
Qing Shizu shilu 清世祖實錄 (Real Record of Emperor Shizu of the Qing Dynasty).
Qing Xuanzong shilu 清宣宗實錄 (Record of Emperor Xuanzong of the Qing Dynasty).
Qingchao wenxian tongkao 清朝文獻通考 (General Study of Literature of the Qing Dynasty).
Qingdai wenzi yu dang 清代文字獄檔 (The Files of the Literary Inquisition in the Qing Dynasty).
Qufu Kongfu dangan shiliao xuanbian 曲阜孔府檔案史料選編 (Selected Historical Data of Confucian Mansion in Qufu).
Rihe zhi 熱河志 (Annuals of Jehol).
Shangyu baqi 上諭八旗 (Imperial Edict on Eight Banners).
Shangyu neige 上諭內閣 (Imperial Edict on the Cabinet).
Shengjing tongzhi 盛京通志 (General Annals of Shengjing).
Siku quanshu congmu tiyao 四庫全書總目提要 (The General Summary of the Siku Quanshu).
Taiwan fu zhi 台灣府志 (Annals of Taiwan Prefecture).
Taiwan jingjishi chuji 台灣經濟史初集 (Anthology of Taiwan's Economic History).
Tian di hui 天地會 (The Heaven and Earth Society).
Tongzheng bianlan 銅政便覽 (Copper Policy Overview).
Tongzhi Changsha xian zhi 同治長沙縣志 (Annals of Changsha County in the Tongzhi Period).
Tongzhi chongkan Kangxi Ninghua xian zhi 同治重刊康熙寧化縣志 (Annals of Ninghua in the Kangxi Period Re-published in the Tongzhi Period).
Tongzhi Fang xian zhi 同治房縣志 (Annals of Fang County in the Tongzhi Period).
Tongzhi Ruijin xian zhi 同治瑞金縣志 (Annual of Ruijin County in the Tongzhi Period).

Tongzhi Suzhou fu zhi 同治蘇州府志 (Annals of Suzhou in the Tongzhi Period).
Tongzhi Xingguo xianzhi 同治興國縣志 (Annuals of Xingguo County in the Tongzhi Period).
Tongzhi Yuedu xian zhi 同治雩都縣志 (Annals of Yuedu County in the Tongzhi Period).
Wei Yuan ji 魏源集 (Collection of Wei Yuan).
Weizang tongzhi 衛藏通志 (General Annals of Central Tibet).
Wenxian congbian 文獻叢編 (Document Compendium Series).
Xiamen zhi 廈門志 (Annals of Amoy).
Xichui zongtong shilue 西陲總統事略 (Biographical Sketch of General Governance of Western Border Areas).
Xining fu xinzhi 西寧府新志 (New Annals of the Xining Prefecture).
Xinjiang jianshi 新疆簡史 (A Brief History of Xinjiang).
Xiyu tuzhi 西域圖志 (Records and Maps of the West Region).
Xizang tonglan 西藏通覽 (A Look Through Tibet).
Xuxiu Xushi jiaopu 續修徐氏家譜 (Continuous Compilation of Genealogy of the Xu Family).
Yanshi zupu 嚴氏族譜 (Genealogy of the Yan Family).
Yanyan gongci bilu 嚴煙供詞筆錄 (Yan Yan's Confession Record).
Yongzheng zhupi yuzhi 雍正朱批諭旨(Memorials Approved by Yongzheng in Red with a Brush).
Yue Zhongqi xinglüe 岳鐘琪行略 (Life Story of Yue Zhongqi).
Yuhua tang liangjiang shigao 玉華堂兩江示稿 (Brief of Jiangnan and Jiangxi Provinces of Yuhua Tang).
Yunyang Tushi zupu 雲陽塗氏族譜 (Genealogy of Tu Family in Yunyang).
Yuzhi lama shuo 御制喇嘛說 (On Lama by Imperial Order).
Yuzuan Zhuzi quanshu 御纂朱子全書 (The Book of Zhu Xi compiled by the Emperor).
Zhanggu congbian 掌故叢編 (Collected Writings of Anecdotes).
Zhangshi zongpu 張氏宗譜 (Genealogy of the Zhang Family).
Zhijiang xian zhi 芷江縣志 (Annals of Zhijiang County).
Zhuluo xianzhi 諸羅縣志 (Annals of Zhuluo County).
Zhuxi Shenshi jiacheng 竹溪沈氏家乘 (Genealogy of the Shen Family in Zhuxi).

Personal Works

Babkov. Memories of My Service in West Siberia.
Baddeley. *Russia, Mongolia and China.*

Bandishen-kamenchomsky. *Compilation of Information on Russian-Sino Diplomacy from 1619 to 1792.*

Bartold. *Oriental Study History of Europe and Russia.*

Bunakov. *Sino-Russian Relations in the early 19th Century.*

Chen Kangqi 陳康祺. *Lanqian jiwen* 朗潛紀聞 (Record of Lanqian).

Cheng Muheng 程穆衡. *Zhunga'er kao* 準噶爾考 (A History of Junggar).

Chun Yuan 椿園. *Xiyu wenjian lu* 西域聞見錄 (Chronicles of the Western Region).

Dai Zhaojia 戴兆佳. *Tiantai zhilüe* 天台治略 (Strategies of Tiantai).

Dai Zhen 戴震. *Mengzi ziyi xuzheng* 孟子字義疏證 (Interpretation of Mencius Concepts).

Defu 德福. *Minzheng lingyao* 閩政領要 (Outline of Fujian Administration).

Deng Tingzhen 鄧廷楨. *Menggu zhubu shulüe* 蒙古諸部述略 (Overview of Mongolian Tribes).

Dong Han 董含. *Sangang shilüe* 三綱識略 (Brief Knowledge of Sangang).

Duan Yucai 段玉裁. *Dai Dongyuan nianpu* 戴東原年譜 (A Chronicle of Dai Dongyuan).

Fang Dongshu 方東樹. *Hanxue shangdui* 漢學商兑 (The Discussion of Sinology).

Fang Shiji 方式濟. *Longsha jilüe* 龍沙紀略 (A Brief History of Longsha).

Fu Heng, et al. 傅恆等. *Pingding zhunga'er fanglüe* 平定準噶爾方略 (Sequel to the Strategic Plan for Suppressing the Junggar).

———. *Xiyu tuzhi* 西域圖志 (Records and Maps of the West Region).

Fu Kangan 福康安. *Shuongzhong cibei ji* 雙忠祠碑記 (Inscription Biography of Double Allegiance Temple).

Gann. *Early History of Sino-Russian Relations.*

Gao Shiqi 高士奇. *Hucong dongxun rilu* 扈從東巡日錄 (Log of Trip to the East).

Gong Chai 龔柴. *Taiwan xiaoji* 台灣小記 (Taiwan Record).

Gort. *Russia's Expansion in the Pacific Region (1641–1850).*

Hang Shijun 杭世駿. *Daogu tang wenji* 道古堂文集 (The Collection of Daogu Tang).

He Qiutao 何秋濤. *Shuofang bicheng* 朔方備乘 (Overview of Northern China).

Hong Bang 洪榜. *Chutang yigao* 初堂遺稿 (Posthumous Manuscript of Chu Tang).

Hong Jun 洪均. *Yuanshi yiwen jibu* 元史譯文記補 (Afterthought of Translation of History of the Yuan Dynasty).

Huang Yupian黄育楩. *Xu poxie xiangqing* 續破邪詳情 (Detailed Debate on Breaking the Heresy).

Huang Zhongjian 黄中堅. *Xuzhai ji* 蓄齋集 (Collection of Xuzhai).

Hui Dong 惠棟. *Jiujing guyi shoushuo* 九經古義首說 (The First Explanation of

the Ancient Meanings of the Nine Classics).
———. *Songya wenchao* 松崖文鈔 (The Copy of Song Ya).
———. *Zhouyi shu* 周易述 (The Narration of Zhou Yi).
Huo Wosi 霍渥斯. *Menggu shi* 蒙古史 (The History of Mongolia).
Ji Yun 紀昀. *Jiwen Dagong yiji* 紀文達公遺集 (The Remaining Collection of Jiwen Dagong).
Jiang Fan 江藩. *Hanxue shicheng ji* 漢學師承記 (The Record of Sinology Apprentice Learning).
Jiang Sheng 江聲. *Shangshu ji zhuyin xushu* 尚書集注音疏述 (The Narration of the Annotation of the Phonetic Notation to Shangshu).
Jiao Xun 焦循. *Diaogu lou ji* 雕菰樓集 (The Collection of Diao Gu Lou).
———. *Lunyu tongshi* 論語通釋 (The Explanation of the Analects of Confucius).
Kangxi 康熙. *Huizong si beiji* 匯宗寺碑記 (A Record in the Huizong Temple).
Ke Shaomin 柯劭忞. *Xin Yuan shi* 新元史 (The New History of the Yuan Dynasty).
Lan Dingyuan 藍鼎元. *Pingtai jilüe* 平台紀略 (Memorandum of Putting down Taiwan).
Li Guangdi 李光地. *Rongcun quanshu* 榕村全書 (The Collected Works of Rong Village).
Li Shixiong 李世熊. *Koubian ji* 寇變記 (Mutiny of the Enemy).
Li Xinheng 李心衡. *Jinchuan suoji* 金川瑣記 (Notes of Jinchuan).
Li Yuandu 李元度. *Guochao xianzheng shilüe* 國朝先正事略 (Biographical Sketch of People in the Qing Dynasty).
Li Zhaoluo 李兆洛. *Zhaoyi Guishi jitian shutian ji* 昭義歸氏祭田書田記 (Ancestral Temple's Fields of the Gui Family in Zhaoyi).
Li Zutao 李祖陶. *Maitang wenlüe* 邁堂文略 (The Summary of Mai Tang).
Lian Heng 連横. *Taiwan tongshi* 台灣通史 (General History of Taiwan).
Liang Qichao 梁啟超. *Qingdai xueshu gailun* 清代學術概論 (The Academic Conspectus in the Qing Dynasty).
Lin Tingkai 凌廷堪. *Jiao Litang wenji* 校禮堂文集 (Collection of Essays of Xiaoli Tang).
———. *Jiao Litang shiji* 校禮堂詩集 (Collection of Poetry of Xiaoli Tang).
———. *Lijing shili* 禮經堂釋例 (The Annotation of the Lijing Tang).
Liu Xianting 劉獻廷. *Guangyang zeji* 廣陽雜記 (Miscellanies of Guangyang).
Lu Wenchao 盧文弨. *Baojing tang wenji* 抱經堂文集 (The Collection of Baojing Tang).
Luo Ergang 羅爾綱. *Tian di hui wen xian lu* 天地會文獻錄 (Document Record of the Heaven and Earth Society).
Ma Ke. *Heilongjiang youji* 黑龍江外紀 (Trip to Heilongjiang).

Ma Siha 馬思哈. *Chuzai jicheng* 出塞紀程 (A Voyage of Diplomatic Mission).
———. *Zaibei zhengcheng* 塞北征程 (A Journey to the North to the Great Wall).
Mancol. Russia and China.
Mao Qiling 毛奇齡. *Sishu gaicuo* 四書改錯 (Correcting Mistakes of the Four Books).
Na Yancheng 那彥成. *Na Wenyi gong zouyi* 那文毅公奏議 (Memorials of Na Wenyi).
Pankratova. *General History of the Soviet Union.*
Parson. *Travel Diary of the Outer Baikal Border.*
Pavlovsky. *Sino-Russian Relations.*
Pi Xirui 皮錫瑞. *Jingxue lishi* 經學歷史 (The History of Confucian Classics Study).
Qi Yunshi 祁韻士. *Huangchao fanbu yaolüe* 皇朝藩部要略 (Overview of the Ethnic Groups of the Qing Dynasty).
———. *Xichui yaolüe* 西陲要略 (Outline of the Western Frontier).
Qian Daxin 錢大昕. *Qianyan tang wenji* 潛研堂文集 (The Collections of the Qianyan Tang).
Qian Liangze 錢良擇. *Chusai jilüe* 出塞紀略 (A Record on the Journey outside the Boundary).
Qianlong乾隆. *Puning Si bei wen* 普寧寺碑文 (Epitaph in Puning Temple).
Qin Wuyu 秦武域. *Wenjian banxiang lu* 聞見瓣香錄 (Record of Smelling Fragrance).
Que Ming闕名. *Huibu zhengxu lun* 回部政俗論 (Politics and Custom in Huibu).
Ravenstein. *Russians at the Heilong River.*
Ruan Yuan阮元. *Yan Jingshi erji* 揅經室二集 (The Second Collection of Yanjingshi).
———. *Yan Jingshi sanji* 揅經室三集 (The Third Collection of Yaniingshi).
———. *Yan Jingshi yiji* 揅經室一集 (The First Collection of Yanjingshi).
Shasijina. *Envoy Exchange Relations between Russia and Mongolia in the 17th Century.*
Shou Yi 壽頤. *Guangxu huolu xian zhi* 光緒獲鹿縣志 (Annals of Huolu County in the Guangxu Period).
Sun Dianqi 孫殿起. *Qingdai jinshu zhijian lu* 清代禁書知見錄 (Some Comments on the Banned Books of the Qing Dynasty).
Sun Jiagan 孫嘉淦. *Sun Wending gong zoushu* 孫文定公奏疏 (Memorial of Sun Wending).
Tan Cui 檀萃. *Dianhai yuhengzhi* 滇海虞衡志 (Record of Yunnan).
Tikhvinski. *Sino-Russian Relations in the early 17th Century.*
Tulishen. *Record of Foreign Countries.*

Vasilyev. *History of Outer Baikal Cossacks.*
Vladimir. *Russia on the Pacific and the Syberian Railway.*
Wang Chang王昶. *Chunrong tangji* 春融堂集 (The Collection of Chunrong Tang).
Wang Guowei 王國維. *Guangtang jilin* 觀堂集林 (The Collection of Guang Tang).
Wang Jianan 王簡庵. *Linting Kaoyan* 臨汀考言 (Remarks of Linting).
Wang Jingqi 汪景祺. *Dushutang xizheng suibi* 讀書堂西征隨筆 (Jottings of Dushu Tang on the Western Expedition).
Wang Mingsheng 王鳴盛. *Shiqi shi shangque xu* 十七史商榷序 (The Preface of Seventeen History Discussions).
Wang Niansun 王念孫. *Wang Shiqu xiansheng yiwen* 王石臞先生遺文 (Posthumous work of Wang Shiqu).
Wang Yinzhi 王引之. *Wang Wenjian gong wenji* 王文簡公文集 (The Collection of Wang Wenjian).
Wang Zhong 汪中. *Shuxue* 述學 (Study Record).
Wei Yuan 魏源. *Shengwu ji* 聖武記 (The History of Suppression).
Wen Da 溫達. *Qinzheng pingding suomo fanglüe* 親征平定朔漠方略 (General Plan for Suppressing the Northern Desert Rebellion against which the Emperor Led the Army Personally).
Weng Fanggang 翁方綱. *Fuchu zhai wenji* 復初齋文集 (The Collections of Fuchu Room).
Wu Rongguang 吳榮光. *Foshan Zhongyi xiang zhi* 佛山忠義鄉志 (Annals of Zhongyi Village in Foshan).
Wu Zhenchen 吳振臣. *Ningguta jilüe* 寧古塔紀略 (A Brief History of Ningguta).
Xi Qing 西清. *Heilongjiang waiji* 黑龍江外紀 (Record of Heilongjiang).
Xiangheng 祥亨. *Chongke poxie xiangbian xu* 重刻破邪詳辨序 (Preface for Re-Publishing Detailed Debate of Breaking the Heresy).
Xiao Yishan 蕭一山. *Qingdai tongshi* 清代通史 (General History of the Qing Dynasty).
Xiqing 西清. *Heilongjiang waiji* 黑龍江外紀 (Chronicles of Heilongjiang).
Xu Song 徐松. *Xiyu shuidao ji* 西域水道紀 (The Records of Streams in the Western Region).
Yan Ruyu 嚴如熤. *Sansheng bianfang bilan* 三省邊防備覽 (Overview of Frontier Defense of Three Provinces).
Yang Bin 楊賓. *Liubian jilüe* 柳邊紀略 (A Brief History of Liubian).
Yang Ying 楊英. *Congzheng shilu* 從征實錄 (Record of Expedition).
Yao Jiheng 姚際恆. *Gujin weishu kao zixu* 古今偽書考自敘 (The Discussion on the Fake Books in Ancient and Modern Times).
Yao Nai 姚鼐. *Xibao Xuan wenji* 惜抱軒文集 (Epistle of Xibao Xuan).

Yu Qian 裕謙. *Yu Jingjie gong yishu* 裕靖節公遺書 (Posthumous Works of Yu Jingjie).

Zeng Wenwu 曾問吾. *Zhongguo jingying xiyu shi* 中國經營西域史 (The History of China's Trade in the Western Region).

Zhang Cheng 張誠. *Zhangcheng riji* 張誠日記 (A Journal of Zhang Cheng).

Zhang Mu 張穆. *Menggu youmu ji* 蒙古游牧記 (Nomadic History of the Mongolians).

Zhang Penghe 張鵬翮. *Fengshi Eluosi riji* 奉使俄羅斯日記 (A Journal about Diplomatic Missions to Russia).

Zhang Qin 章梫. *Kangxi zhengyao* 康熙政要 (Kangxi's Government Affairs).

Zhang Qiqing 張其勤. *Cangshi jiyao* 藏事輯要 (Outline of Tibetan Affairs).

Zhang Taiyan 章太炎. *Daohan weiyan* 菿漢微言 (Daohan Sublime Words).

Zhang Xintai 張心泰. *Yueyao xiaoshi* 粵游小識 (Knowledge of Guangdong Travel).

Zhang Xuecheng 章學誠. *Zhu Lu bian shuhou* 朱陸篇書後 (The Postscript of Zhu and Lu).

Zhao Lian 昭槤. *Xiaoting zalu* 嘯亭雜錄 (Miscellanea of Xiaoting).

Zhao Yi 趙翼. *Huangchao wugong jisheng* 皇朝武功紀盛 (Martial Arts in Feudal Dynasties).

Zhi Chaozi 枝巢子. *Jiujing suoji* 舊京瑣記 (Trivia of Old Beijing).

Zhou Kai 周凱. *Neizi Songzhai wenji* 內自訟齋文集 (Anthology of Neizisongzhai).

Index

Aihui 96-7, 101, 103, 107, 208, 212-13, 215-16
Aksu 180, 182, 219-20
Altai Mountains 138-9, 157, 172, 175
Amursanaa 173, 175-9
ancestral temple 15, 19-21, 23-4
Anhui 12, 48, 257
anti-Qing struggles 45, 50, 142, 193
anti-rent struggles 28-32, 34-6
Argun River 94, 101, 108-9, 112, 114, 116, 120
aristocrats 3-4, 6, 10-11, 102, 105, 173, 207, 259
artisans 2, 6, 36, 40-2, 61-2

Baibagasi 140-1
Balikun 160, 169, 175, 181-2, 209
Bandang 12-13
Baojia 23, 38
Batuer Huitaiji 141-2
Beijing 26, 41, 44, 66-8, 72, 74, 79, 81, 92-3, 96-7, 102-3, 106, 111, 117-18, 120, 122-5, 128, 130-2, 134-6, 149-51, 163-4, 184-5, 210, 217-18, 258-9
Book of Changes 229, 246-7, 250
Book of Songs 229, 245-6, 256
Boshuoketu Khan 142, 149-50
boundary line 96, 100, 102, 107, 110-12, 114, 117, 213
Boyakefu 86, 109
Buddhism 55, 57, 127, 133, 147, 256, 263, 267, 272, 276
Burhanidin 179-80

Catholic Churches 121, 124, 132, 135
Catholicism 127, 133, 135
Celing 119, 171
Chahandanjin 164-5
Changchun Garden 72, 74-6, 78, 80-1
Chechen Khan 138-9, 144-5
Chen Qiyuan 243, 245-6
Cheng-Zhu Neo-Confucianism 227, 247, 251, 258, 264, 266-7
Chinese mission 107-12
Chongde period 85-6
Chongzhen Reign 138, 141, 144, 233, 246-7
Chuai Jiang 36-9, 41
civilians 6, 89-90, 96, 116, 121, 132, 145-7, 162
clan 15-23, 25, 87, 208
class Struggle 2-3, 5, 7, 9, 11, 13, 15, 17, 19, 21, 23-9, 31, 33, 35, 37, 39, 41, 43, 45, 47, 49, 51, 53, 55, 57
Confucian classics 226, 228, 248, 250-2, 255, 266
Confucianism 127, 133, 226, 228, 247, 272
Confucians 226, 248, 251, 256, 258, 263-5, 271
Confucius 16, 30, 57, 125, 133, 226-8, 246-7, 250, 272
Cossacks 87-92, 94, 117, 121, 145
cultural Policy 225-7, 229, 231, 233, 235, 237, 239, 241, 243, 245, 247, 249, 251, 253, 255, 257-9, 261, 263, 265, 267, 269, 271, 273, 275

Dai Mingshi 231-3
Dai Zhen 230, 249-50, 253-4, 257-69, 271-2, 274
Dalai Lama 147, 149, 157-61, 199-200, 202, 204-5, 209, 211
Danhu 12-14
Daur 86-9, 97, 170, 208
Dawaachi 173-4, 176, 179
Dayi juemi lu 75-7, 235
descendants 4, 8, 10, 15-21, 23, 27, 48, 110, 138, 226, 234, 250, 267
Directorate of Astronomy 126-30, 136

Index

Du Junying 43-4
Duan Yucai 268-9
Duolun 138, 148, 152-3, 218
Duolunchan 88-9, 95

Early aggression 85, 87, 89, 91, 93, 95, 97, 99, 101, 103, 105, 107, 109, 111, 113, 115, 117, 119, 121, 123, 125, 127, 129, 131, 133
Eastern Orthodox 118, 120-2
Eertai 190-3
eight character real words 54
Elute 139-41, 144
Emperor Chongzhen 26-7
Emperor Kangxi 3, 27, 66-78, 81-2, 92-3, 95-6, 99-103, 106-7, 111-12, 117-18, 129, 131, 134-5, 146, 156, 158-60, 163-4, 233, 242
reign of 232-3, 258
Emperor Qianlong 3, 25, 29, 34, 39, 81, 173-6, 186-7, 196-7, 199-200, 203, 230-1, 237
Emperor Shengzu 46, 75-6, 78
Emperor Shunzhi 126-8, 158, 232
Emperor Yongzheng 7, 10, 13-14, 27, 44, 69, 73, 76, 81-2, 119, 132, 135-6, 156, 166, 169, 199, 228, 236
reign of 44, 75, 227, 233
Empress Xiaocheng 65-6
envoys 92-3, 99-100, 104, 109, 118, 131-2, 140, 142, 144-9, 153, 155-7, 169
Eternal Mother 53-6
ethnic groups 14-15, 98, 102, 188, 190, 207
ethnic minorities 138, 188-9

families, imperial 3, 27, 48, 82, 135
Far East 103-4, 125, 133-4
farmers 15, 21-2, 24, 28-31, 33-4, 36, 42, 51, 54, 57, 60-2, 156, 218, 221-2
farming 24, 29, 33, 49, 97, 167, 216, 219, 222, 226
Feiyaka 94, 98
feudal government 24-5, 41-2, 62
feudal lords 14, 138, 146-7, 177
feudal rule 23, 42, 46, 52, 54
feudal society 2-3, 16, 22, 36, 43, 51, 57, 64, 231-2, 256
fight 24-5, 32-3, 40, 43, 49, 56, 86-8, 90-1, 97-8, 100, 104, 106-8, 117, 124, 141, 146, 150-1, 162-3, 170, 172-3, 176, 182-3, 191, 197, 204
filial piety 19, 22-3, 64, 226
Five Classics 134, 228, 251, 254
food 6, 10, 20, 31, 40, 56, 60, 86, 91, 98, 101-3, 107, 155, 162, 173, 187, 217, 223, 226, 259
foreign affairs 122-3, 126, 131, 148, 206
Frontier 137, 139, 141, 143, 145, 147, 149, 151, 153, 155, 157, 159, 161, 163, 165, 167, 169, 171, 173, 175, 177-9, 181, 183, 187, 213
Fu Qing 200
Fujian 15, 24, 28-30, 32-3, 43, 47, 49-50, 62-4, 135, 222-3

Galdan 106-7, 142-3, 146-51, 153-6, 159, 179
Galdan Rebellion 148-9, 151, 153, 156
Galdan Tseren 168-70, 172, 174, 179
Galoins 201-2, 204-6
Golovin 85, 103-6, 108-12, 146, 148
Golovin Mission 103, 105, 109
government, central 105-6, 139-40, 146, 149, 153-7, 164-5, 168, 179, 182, 184, 188-90, 192, 194-5, 197, 199, 201-2, 204, 206, 211, 214, 216
Governor-General of Sichuan 160, 195, 197, 200
Grand Minister Consultants 178, 182, 209
Great Wall 43, 153, 210
Gu Yanwu 231, 244, 249-50, 260
Guangdong 12-15, 23, 25, 28, 43, 45, 48-9, 58, 62, 128, 135-6, 192-3, 222-3
Guangxi 28, 45, 58, 60, 63, 136, 188, 190-1, 194
Guizhou 45, 48-9, 63, 82, 188, 190-2, 194, 221

Gurkha 203-6
Gushi Khan 141, 158, 163-4

Han 28, 63, 65, 142, 188-9, 194, 209, 215, 217, 220-3, 226, 235, 243, 254, 257, 265
Han Confucianism 250-3, 259-61
Han Dynasty 250-1, 270
Han nationality 210, 214, 223, 235
Hangtou 41-2
Heaven and Earth Society 45, 50-1, 57-64
Heilong River 84-6, 88-95, 97-8, 100, 102, 104, 107, 109-12, 114, 116, 121, 208, 212, 215-16
Heilongjiang 95-9, 110, 146, 213, 215
Heishui River 181
Henan 7, 44-5, 48-9, 97, 167, 238
Heshuote 140-2
Hetongbo battle 170, 174
Hojajahan 179-80
Hovd 153, 170-1, 213
Hu Wei 243-4, 246-7, 260
Hubei 9, 28, 45-50, 63, 190, 221, 235, 238
Hui Dong 248-54, 257, 260
Hui Shiqi 249-50
Huibu 142-3, 180-1
Huiguan 41-2
Huite tribe 173
Hulun Buir 208-9, 212-13
Hunan 15, 28, 31, 44-9, 63-4, 188, 190, 193-4, 221-2, 234-5

Ili General 178, 181-2, 187, 209
imperial edict 3, 7, 22, 27, 46, 75-9, 132, 200, 216, 219, 230
Imperial Household Department 10-11, 66
imperial order 112, 203-4, 244
Inner Mongolia 138, 150-2, 209, 218
invasion 90, 110, 116, 144-5, 147, 153, 160-1, 205
Irtysh River 140, 156, 161-2, 168, 173, 175

jasak 152, 167, 171, 187, 209
Jesuit missionaries 125-6, 130-1
Jesuits 125-7, 132-5
Ji Jiang 36, 38-9
Ji Yun 230, 259, 261
Jiang Sheng 253-4
Jiang Yong 256-7, 259-60
Jiangxi 15, 23, 28, 32-3, 45-9, 63, 136, 221, 260
Jiao Xun 250, 273-4
Jiaqing period 39, 58-60, 63-4, 123, 136
Jilin 97, 208, 213, 215-16
Jingqili River 86, 94, 98, 104, 212
Johann Adam Schall von Bell 125-8, 133
Junggar 73, 117, 140-4, 146-9, 156-7, 160-3, 166, 168-75, 177-8, 180-1, 184, 200, 217-18
jurisdiction 10, 15, 86-7, 111, 116, 122, 124, 140, 182, 189, 195-6

Kangxi 27-8, 58-9, 65-72, 75-82, 99, 105, 147, 149-55, 157-8, 160, 167, 174, 184, 212, 226-9, 233, 236, 244, 249
Kangxi period 9, 26-7, 29, 31-3, 36-7, 41-3, 46, 58-9, 65-9, 71-5, 79, 92-9, 101, 104, 106-7, 112, 116-17, 119, 121-2, 128-9, 132, 134-5
Kangxi reign 142-3, 145, 148-51, 153-61, 163-4, 167, 184, 189, 195, 212, 216, 246-7
Kangxi's reign 213, 215-16
Karuns 212-14
Kashigaer 143, 179-81
Khabarovsk 87-90, 109
Khalkha 105-6, 112, 116-17, 138-9, 145, 147-8, 150, 152-3, 155-6, 169-70, 172, 177-8, 205, 213
Khalkha Mongolia 82, 100, 105, 116, 119, 144-5, 148-9
Khalkha Mongolians 105-7, 139-40, 146, 148, 151
Khalkha tribes 146, 151-3
Khan King 158-9, 185
Khans 143, 158, 172-3, 176-7, 183
Khoshut 157-9, 163
Kiakhta 119-20

Index

Lake Baikal 93, 109-10, 114, 116, 146
east bank of 104-5, 107
Lamaism 152, 167, 211, 226
Lamdarjaa 172-3
land reform 221-2
land rent 7-8, 203
landowners 2, 4-8, 20, 24-5, 28-35, 44, 47
Lhabzang Khan 159-60
Lhasa 160, 199-201
Li Guangdi 66, 228
Li Shijie 241-2
Lin Tingkan 272-3
literary inquisitions 231-3, 236, 238-9, 241-2, 258, 266
Lobsang Danjin 163-6, 169
Longkeduo 74-8, 80-1, 119
loom owners 38-9, 42
Lu Liuliang 231, 234-6

Ma Qi 70-1, 131
Macau 127, 134-6
magistrate 44, 208
Manchu 28-9, 84, 88, 95, 160-1, 181, 205, 207, 210, 226, 235, 243
Mao Qiling 243-4
mathematics 256, 259, 273
Mencius 125, 133, 227-8, 247, 266, 272-3, 276
merchants 143, 216, 218-20
Miao 188, 192-3, 195, 235
military 96, 98, 106-7, 131-2, 181-2, 197, 204, 208-9, 215, 265
military power 79-80, 193
Ming Dynasty 5, 24, 26-7, 52, 54, 57, 84-6, 94, 116, 125, 138, 140, 144, 188-9, 195, 214, 229-33, 235, 237, 243-4, 246-7
Ming Government 125, 139-40
Mingzhu 66, 70
ministers 43, 66-8, 70-2, 75, 77, 80, 95, 97, 106, 118, 120, 122, 132, 139, 150, 159, 168, 182, 185, 228, 231, 235, 238, 243
Ministry of Personnel 7, 118
Ministry of Rites 20, 67, 135, 240
mission, diplomatic 46, 92, 94, 122, 145-6, 148
missionaries 79, 111-12, 124-8, 130-2, 134-6, 143
missionary activities 124-5, 133, 136
missionary work 122, 126, 132-3, 135, 143
monasteries 158-9, 165, 167-8
Mongolia 14, 105-6, 117, 139, 141, 146, 149, 151, 159, 208-10, 212-14, 216-18
Mongolian tribes 106-7, 116, 141, 145, 211
Mongolians 105-6, 145-6, 149, 154, 167, 207, 210-11, 216-17, 220
Moscow 90, 102, 104, 114, 116, 144-5, 153

nationalities 22, 84, 90, 183, 190, 207-8, 210, 214-16, 220-3, 226, 235-6
Native Chieftain System 188-90, 194
negotiations 93, 96, 102-5, 108-9, 111-12, 114, 118-20, 131, 145, 149, 179
Neo-Confucianism 130, 228, 242, 245, 247-8, 251, 258, 265
Nerchinsk 90, 92, 94, 100-2, 106-12, 114, 116, 118, 120, 148
Nian Gengyao 80-1, 160, 165-7, 234
Ningguta 89, 101, 208, 216
Ninghua 24, 32-3
Northeast China 84, 108, 116, 154, 213

Oirat 157-8, 176, 182
Outer Mongolia 209, 212, 214, 217

pacification 174, 192, 194, 197-8
Panchen 203-6
Panchen Lama 157-8, 203-4
peace 22, 26, 82, 90, 93, 96, 98-100, 103, 107-8, 110, 117, 119, 147, 151, 157, 160, 162, 165, 171-2, 174, 188, 203, 208, 214, 226
peasant uprisings 5, 24, 36, 50, 52
peasants 2, 5-6, 8, 24, 35, 54, 167, 183
political power 4, 8, 12, 22-3, 25, 71, 205, 242
population 16, 94, 117, 140, 186, 188, 192, 214, 217-18

Portugal 84, 125, 133

Qian Daxin 249, 255-6, 259
Qianlong 28, 45, 82, 136, 152, 175, 178, 185, 193, 203, 215, 218-19, 229-30, 236, 238-42, 258-9, 266, 269-74
Qianlong period 10, 12, 16, 29-30, 32, 38-41, 45-50, 58-9, 61-4, 122, 136, 218, 220
Qianlong reign 172-5, 177-8, 180-1, 185-6, 195, 197-8, 201-4, 213, 217, 219, 229, 249
Qianlong's reign 200-1, 213, 215-16, 218
Qileer 94, 98-9
Qing army 45, 89-90, 100, 102, 122, 139, 156, 160, 162, 164, 166, 169-70, 175-6, 178-81, 192, 197-8
Qing court 10, 31, 48, 59, 72, 126-8, 130, 135-6, 155, 157-9, 164, 169, 174, 177-8
Qing Dynasty 2-3, 5-9, 11-13, 15, 21-9, 33-7, 41-7, 49-55, 57-65, 83-8, 95, 116, 127-8, 138-9, 184-91, 207-8, 210-11, 214, 225-9, 231-3, 235-9, 241-7, 249-51, 255-61, 265-7
Qing Government 4-6, 14, 20-3, 36-9, 41, 43-5, 48-50, 58-9, 63, 91-3, 95-103, 105-7, 116-19, 122, 130-3, 135, 138-9, 142, 146-60, 163-82, 187-8, 192-220, 222, 233-4, 241
Qing rulers 23, 26, 51-2, 63, 65, 125
Qing troops 43-4, 48-50, 52, 89, 91-2, 97-8, 100-3, 105, 150-1, 153-5, 170, 177, 181, 203-4, 213
Qinghai 73, 82, 141-2, 146, 156-7, 159-60, 163-9, 174, 208-9, 220
Qiqihar 95, 212-13, 216

Rakog 174-5, 177
rebellion 4, 22, 26-7, 34, 38, 43, 45, 49-50, 63, 93, 95-6, 106, 139, 149, 152-5, 160, 165-6, 168, 177-9, 181, 183, 191-2, 194-5, 199-202, 239-41
rebels 25, 43-4, 69, 72, 149, 165-6, 168, 177, 180-1, 191, 195, 199-201, 240
regulations 17-21, 25, 34, 37, 40-1, 185, 201-2, 204, 227, 241, 251, 269
religion 14, 49-54, 56-7, 116, 120, 124, 133, 135, 140, 185, 205-7, 209, 241
rent 7, 11, 28-34, 45-7, 50, 132, 217, 223
revolt 54, 116, 164-6, 179-80, 183, 188, 234, 238
rites 17, 20, 65, 67, 73, 103, 128-9, 135, 229, 240, 250, 257, 259, 272-3
Rites of Zhou 253-4
River, Lena 84-5, 110
Ruan Yuan 230, 258, 270-1, 274-6
Russia 83-9, 91-123, 125, 127, 129, 131, 133, 135, 137-8, 143-5, 147-50, 155, 161-3, 168-9, 172, 178-9, 182, 185-6, 213
Russian aggressors 86, 88-92, 96, 98, 145, 147, 162
Russian army 84, 98, 106, 112, 145
Russian government 92-4, 100, 102-4, 107, 111, 117, 119, 122, 145-6, 148, 155, 162-3, 178-9, 182-3
Russian mission 93, 103, 111, 120
Russian troops 90-5, 98-106, 116-17, 146, 148-9, 169
Russians 84, 86, 88, 91, 94-7, 99-103, 108, 110-12, 114, 119-20, 122-3, 131, 139, 145-8, 162, 168-9, 178, 212-13, 215
Russia's invasion 95, 117, 143, 161-2, 189

Sabusu 97-9, 101, 103, 107-9
Sangy Gyatso 158-9
Sanxing 208, 213, 216
Savoie 118-20
scholars 117, 226-7, 229, 235, 242, 248-50, 253-60, 262, 265, 268, 271
Sengge 141-2, 144
separatist forces 157, 165, 177-9, 194
Shaluoben 195-7
shamanism 133, 157-8, 186, 201
Shangshu 246-8, 254, 259, 261, 270
Shanhaiguan 138, 142, 157, 214-16, 220, 226
Sharhuda 90-2
Shen Tong 253-4

Shipu 12-14
Shixian Calendar 127-8
Shunzhi period 24, 26, 33, 52, 58, 87-92, 126-7, 184
Shunzhi Reign 138-9, 141-2, 144-5, 158, 164, 184, 195, 214, 222, 228
Shuolei 138-9, 145
Sichuan 9, 15-16, 19, 27, 45-9, 82, 160, 166, 169, 188, 190-1, 194-5, 197, 220-1, 234
Siku Quanshu 229-31, 246-7, 252, 258-60
Siku Quanshu Hall 229-31
Sino-Russian Treaty of Kiakhta 116, 119-20, 131
Sino-Russian Treaty of Kyakhta 120, 122
Sino-Russian Treaty of Nerchinsk 95, 112-15, 117
Sinologists 249, 255, 258, 260, 262, 267
Sinology 225, 227, 229, 231, 233, 235, 237, 239, 241-3, 245-53, 255, 257-9, 261, 263, 265-9, 271, 273, 275
slavery 8, 12, 14-15, 116
slaves 2-5, 7-12, 15, 31, 79, 87, 89, 236, 240
Smaller Jinchuan 194-8
social order 161, 164, 207, 223
Song 229, 237, 242, 245-6, 248, 251-2, 256
Song Confucianism 251-3, 258, 274-5
Song Confucians 251, 258, 263-4
Song School 247-9
Songhua River 89-91, 96, 216
Stepanov 90-1
Sun Shiyi 58-9
Suoetu 66-8, 106, 108-11
Suolun 94, 97-8, 181
Suonuomu 197-8
suppression 39, 149, 154, 174, 176-7, 185
surrender 98, 100-1, 144, 147-8, 158, 163, 170, 173-5, 191, 193, 196, 198
Suzhou 15, 32, 34, 36, 38-41, 142, 257-8
systems, administrative 152, 181-2, 189, 198, 202

Taiji 55, 106, 144, 151-2
Taijs 163-5, 167, 170, 173, 176, 186-7, 217
Taiwan 43-4, 47, 50, 58, 63-4, 222-3
Tar Lamasery 166, 168
taxes 4-5, 12, 14, 23-4, 29, 86-7, 94, 99, 140, 167, 191, 210-11, 227
temples 38, 152, 160, 187, 202, 211, 218
tenants 5-8, 18, 28-34, 46-7, 165, 222-3
territory 86, 91, 106, 114, 120, 130, 144-6, 162, 164, 169, 181, 190, 192, 209, 235
textual research 244-8, 250, 256, 258, 261-3, 267-71, 273
throne 26, 32, 38, 54, 58, 65, 69-70, 72-82, 95, 118, 127, 131-2, 135, 161, 172-3, 193, 234
Tianshan Mountains 139, 142, 177, 179-81, 184, 208-9, 214, 218-19
Tibet 14, 73, 82, 140, 142, 146, 156-62, 164-6, 174, 188, 196, 199-200, 202-10, 220-1
Tibetan government 201-2, 204
Tibetans 138, 159-60, 164, 198-9, 201-2, 204, 209-10, 220
Tiechi Society 32
Tobolsk 100, 144-5, 148, 153, 162, 179
Tolbuzin 100-2
Torghuts 140-1, 182-8
tribes 15, 87, 110, 140-1, 147, 149, 156, 159, 165, 172, 174, 176-8, 184-6, 205
tribute 92, 116, 138-40, 142, 149, 156, 167, 184, 200, 216, 220
troops 33, 39, 43-4, 49, 73, 87, 89-91, 100-4, 108, 119, 124, 142-4, 146-7, 149-51, 154-7, 159-64, 166, 169-71, 174, 177-8, 180-1, 191-8, 203-4, 208-9, 212
Tsar 87-8, 90, 92-3, 99-100, 102, 104-6, 109, 112, 116-17, 131, 144-5, 148-9, 169
Tsarist government 84, 104, 112, 118, 120, 123, 131, 144
Tsarist Russia 142-9, 153-5, 182-3, 185-8, 208-9, 212-13, 215
Tsarist Russian 144-6, 148, 185-6, 188
Tsering Dondup 160, 162, 170
Tsewang Dash 172-3
Tsewang Rabtan 156-7, 159, 162-3, 166, 168, 173-4

Tulishen 118-19, 122
Tuoyinqi 88-9
Turhute tribe 182, 186-8
Tusis 190-2, 195-7
Tuxietu Khan 116, 138-9, 145-7, 150, 152, 171
Tuxietuhan 105-6, 116

Ubasi 185-8
Ulanbutong 148, 150-1
Unification 14, 153-5, 164, 189, 199, 201, 209-10, 273
uprising 24, 26, 44-5, 50-2, 61, 165-6, 241
Ural Mountains 84-5, 143
Urumchi 177, 181-2
Urumqi 170, 209, 214, 218, 220, 238

Verbiest, Ferdinand 129-31
Villa, Summer 174-5, 177, 210
villages 4, 13-15, 19, 25, 28-9, 33, 43-4, 57, 86-9, 191-2, 222, 242
Volga River 84, 182-4, 186

Wan School 257-9
Wang Mingsheng 249, 253-5, 257, 259
Wang Niansun 257, 260, 268-70
Wang Zhiyi 58-9
Wang Zhong 257, 260, 271-2
Wanli period 84, 144
wasteland 96-7, 170, 215-16, 221-2
weapons 25, 33, 45, 50, 86, 88-91, 98, 100-1, 109, 151, 160, 162, 168, 173, 193, 233
White Lotus Society 45, 50-7, 59, 62
Wu Mingxuan 127, 129
Wu School 248-53, 255, 257-8
Wula 97, 101, 215-16
Wushi 176, 180-2

Xiaojia 41-2
Xining 79, 159-60, 165-7
Xiucai 4-5, 227, 238-9

Yakesa 87, 92, 94, 96-108, 110-12, 114
Yaku 99-100, 102
Yakutsk 85-7
Yamen 27, 39, 200
Yan Ruoqu 243-4, 247-8, 260
Yangtze River 36, 38, 47-8, 63
Yangzhou 258-60
Yerqiang 143, 179-82
Yili 155, 181, 213-14, 218-20, 240
Yinreng 65-6, 68-71, 132
Yinsi 69-70, 72-3, 76-81
Yintang 73, 76-7, 79-81, 132
Yinti 73, 79-80, 135
Yinzhen 70, 73, 75, 79, 244
Yinzhi 75-7, 80
Yongzheng 28, 46, 59, 69-70, 74-82, 118, 135, 213, 227, 229, 233-6, 259, 266
Yongzheng period 7, 12-14, 32, 34, 38, 41, 44-6, 49, 58, 77-8, 80-1, 118-20, 135, 194
Yongzheng reign 156, 163, 165-72, 188, 190-5, 199, 234, 269
Yu Xiaoke 253-4
Yuan Dynasty 116, 138-9
Yue Zhongqi 160, 169, 195-6, 234
Yunnan 15, 45, 49, 82, 160, 190-2, 194, 197, 220-2

Zaergu 172, 185
Zhang Guangsi 193, 195-7
Zhang Taiyan 242, 244, 248, 257, 266, 271
Zhaohui 178, 180-1
Zhebuzundanba 105-6
Zheng Chenggong 57-8, 222
Zhili 26, 29, 45-6, 49, 52, 167, 216, 260
Zhou Yi 250-2
Zhu 26-7, 227-8, 233, 245-6, 264, 272
prince of 26-8
Zhu Jun 259, 267-8
Zhu Yigui 43-4
Zhuer Mote 199-200, 202